Jung on War, Politics and Nazi Germany

Exploring the Theory of Archetypes and the Collective Unconscious

Nicholas Adam Lewin
BSc (Econ), MA, PhD

First published 2009
by Karnac Books Ltd.
118 Finchley Road
London NW3 5HT

© Nicholas Adam Lewin
The moral right of the author has been asserted.

All rights reserved. No part of this book may be reproduced or utilised in any form or by any means, electronic or mechanical, without permission in writing from the publisher.

Excerpts and diagrams from the following works are reproduced by permission of Taylor & Francis Books UK: *The Organism of the Mind* by Gustav Heyer © 1933 Kegan Paul, Trench, Trubner & Co., Ltd.; *The Psychology of C.G. Jung* by Jolande Jacobi © 1950 Routledge & Kegan Paul; *ABC of Jung's Psychology* by J. Corrie © 1927 Kegan Paul; *The Seminars - Volume 3: Analytical Psychology* by C.G. Jung, ed. W. McGuire © 1990 Routledge; Nietzsche's Zarathustra *Notes of the Seminar* (in two volumes) by C.G. Jung, ed. J. Jarrett © 1989 Routledge & Kegan Paul; *Visions: Notes of the Seminar Given in 1930-1934* by C.G. Jung, ed. Claire Douglas © 1998 Routledge; *Collected Works*, vols. 4, 5, 7, 9i, 10, 11, 15, 17, 18 by C.G. Jung, trans. R.F.C. Hull © 1953-1978 Routledge & Kegan Paul. Excerpts from *Jung, My Mother and I* by J. Cabot Reid © 2001 are reproduced by permission of Daimon Verlag, Einsiedeln.

British Library Cataloguing in Publication Data
A C.I.P. is available for this book from the British Library.

ISBN-13: 978-1-85575-457-7

www.karnacbooks.com

Contents

Acknowledgements..5
Introduction..9
1. Concerning Freud and Jung on International Politics and War..19
2. Jung and His Politics..30
3. Jung on International Politics and the Causes of War................72
4. From the Individual to 'The Collective':
Examining Jung's Progression from Clinician to Grand Theorist..99
5. The Layered Model of the Collective Unconscious...................110
6. Archetypes:
'Towards the Distant Goal of a Genetic Psychology'..................161
7. The Effect of the Archetypes in the Political Arena...................196
8. The Test Case: Wotan and Nazi Germany................................211
9. Jung on Hitler:
A Case Study for Archetypal or Typology Theory?....................288
10. Post-Jungian Archetypal Theory and International Politics....306

Appendix A
The Question of Anti-Semitism in the Zofingia Lectures...............324

Appendix B
The Freudians and Collective Theory..326

Appendix C
Jung's Perspective on International Politics After 1945................329

Appendix D
Adolf Bastian and *Elementargedanken*......................................338

Appendix E
Key Dates For Jung During the Nazi Seizure of Power.................340

Notes..342
Bibliography..376
Index..405

Acknowledgements

Writing a book is in many ways a journey of discovery on which one learns both something of a subject and maybe more than one had bargained for about oneself! Many people have helped me along the way and it is a pleasure to remember all those who have contributed.

Firstly I would like to thank my parents for without their support this book would not have been possible. Not only have they provided endless practical assistance but also they have been brave enough to read the manuscript and my father has provided invaluable IT support. For this I also have to thank my late aunt, Gill Rickayzen, for her gift of a scanner and Mr and Mrs Benson who very generously provided my present PC.

At the beginning of these acknowledgements I must express deep gratitude to the late Venerable Myokyo-ni Sama who started my interest in Jungian psychology and over the years laboured to develop my education.

Among the staff at Essex University I gratefully recall how my supervisor, Professor Renos Papadopoulos showed great humour and hospitality and continually strove to broaden my focus and improve my writing style. From the other staff I must also thank Professors Robert Hinshelwood and Joan Raphael-Leff for excellent fortnightly doctoral seminars in my first year and the suggestions provided at the annual supervision board by Professors Karl Figlio, Renos Papadopoulos, Andrew Samuels and the late Ian Craib. I would also like to express my gratitude to the departmental secretary Mrs Marilyn Ward, whose patience, humour and help were invaluable during my time at Essex.

In the course of the work many people have been exceptionally kind in the help that they have given. I cannot give too many thanks to Andrew Burniston, a scholar and teacher of rare quality who was always willing to give advice, help with queries and offer suggestions. I also derived much benefit from his reading groups at the C.G. Jung Analytical Psychology Club. From the Club I must also express my thanks to Ann Colcord for her willingness to let me use the library at inconvenient times and for her unfailing hospitality to our reading group.

Friends and scholars have been very generous with their time and help so it is a great pleasure to thank Andrea Cone-Farran, Dr Gottfried Hauer and Harriet Cookson for reading through the manuscript and offering comments. I would also like to thank Professor Paul Bishop for his encouragement, Dr Sonu Shamdasani for his help and advice and Professor Sir Bernard Crick who was kind enough to make time and shared his thoughts on an early draft. Nor can I forget the late Nicholas Battye for all his help on tracing sources.

For the undercurrents of war that run through the book I remain deeply grateful to all my teachers at Aberystwyth Department of International Politics and Kings College Department of War Studies. From the former, I would especially like to thank Professor Booth who began my interest in the psychological dimension of strategy and, from the latter, Professor Bond who was a great role-model for me of methodical scholarship and encouraged my wider reading on the German Resistance that provided a basis for the part of the book on Nazi Germany.

While working on the book it was necessary to undertake as much study as possible to broaden my psychological understanding. In my first year some tutorials with Peter Berry provided an eloquent guide to Klein and Freud. I was also lucky enough to benefit from Dr Desmond Biddulph's Jung course at Birkbeck University; various reading groups of Molly Tuby; the IAAP conference at Cambridge in 2002 and Dr Martin Liebscher's courses at the German Institute on Jung and Nietzsche was useful background and he has continued to offer help and advice along the way.

Many people have helped and encouraged me with the book. While it is not possible individually to thank thank them all, I must express my great debt to Dr Fritz Böbel and his wife Eva for their continued hospitality, Wagnerian encouragement, and invaluable advice, and to this add equal thanks to Dr Fredrick Böbel and his wife Heike for the time I stayed with them and all their help. In England I would especially like to thank again my fellow students Dr Gottfried Heuer and Dr Mary Addenbrooke for their advice and support and it is with pleasure that I recall my stays with Mr and Mrs Tokeley in Wivenhoe and Mr and Mrs Hadley in Cambridge. I must also thank the late Sylvia Swain for her encouragement, and remember Colonel Sylvia Quayle who gave me invaluable support at a difficult time.

Lastly may I add my thanks to Mrs Marie Salter for her IT support and conclude with a pleasant duty of acknowledgement of the vital role librarians play in any research project. I would like to extend especial thanks to the library and interlibrary desk of Essex University, the library at The Goethe Institute and the Libraries at the Wellcome Institute and the Analytical Psychology Club London.

Many people have helped me along the way with advice and information that I have tried to learn from, but any errors that may have occurred are my own and I beg the reader's indulgence.

Introduction

Many people know that C.G. Jung was one of the key psychoanalytic innovators in the twentieth century, but what has often been underestimated is how international politics impacted on his life and how he came to devote a significant part of his work trying to understand wider events. In old age, Jung recalled in his biography how before the outbreak of the First World War he had suffered from apocalyptic dreams that showed Europe almost submerged in a sea of blood (Jung, 1963 [1961], p169). As events unfolded, Switzerland was spared the horrors of war, though Jung found himself directly involved on the sidelines as a commandant of an internment camp for enemy soldiers. Once the dust of battle settled Jung began to look for ways he could use his clinical work and theories to explore how irrational emotions had driven the conflict. Later, in the thirties, Jung was to make increasing use of these theories to try to explain what was happening in Europe and Nazi Germany as the continent drifted again towards war. This evolution of Jung's ideas came to fruition in the 1936 essay on 'Wotan' where he used his theory and eloquence to try to convey to the reader the danger of the times.

How to Get The Most From This Book.

This book covers a range of topics to appeal to different audiences. Some readers will be drawn to look at how Jung applied his theory to Nazi Germany. Others are interested in the issue of war and what Jung had to say about the subject. Another group may be more clinically or philosophically concerned with how Jung formulated his theory and how this heritage shapes the clinical practice of today's Jungians and their ability to respond to clinical innovation. Given these divergent groups and the possibility of different levels of knowledge of Jung's theory, readers may wish to read the book selectively to best suit their needs. To help those who want to read more tactically I would like to offer an overview of the book so that they can use the text as a resource to pursue their own interests. As a further aid, at the end of this introduction I have included a précis of each chapter that I hope will convey the shape of the argument for those who do not want to go into too much detail on a first reading.

The book is written in three phases. The first phase is a historical examination of Jung and his politics. First there is an introductory chapter to offer the psychotherapist a brief synopsis of the strategist's perspective so that later in phase three we have a framework by which to gauge Jung's political and strategic literacy and to assess the utility of his observations when he tried to use his theory to explain international events.

With this preliminary preparation out of the way we can look in detail at Jung's politics and his understanding of international events. For those readers with some knowledge of the secondary literature on his relationship with the political world, this part of the book offers a historical re-examination of his political perspective that will challenge those who have portrayed Jung as an unworldly scholar or a reactionary mystic. On close inspection Jung's writings have many political observations scattered through them and so we can revisit the question of how well-informed he was about the wider world. Having undertaken this re-evaluation we are in a better position to judge the application of his theories to world politics.

The second phase of the book changes style and content and begins to go deeply into the evolution of his theory. This phase is written for those concerned with the history of his ideas. This examination will look at the rise of two key strands of Jung's thinking: the theories of the collective unconscious and of the archetypes. Meanwhile, in the background, there looms the issue of race and we consider the role that this topic (race) played in his theory and the impact it had on his reception in the academic world.

Our theoretical exploration of Jung's work looks at how he constructed his ideas at the turn of the century and asks: How well was Jung able to formulate his ideas? And: How would the strengths and weaknesses of the theories' affect his ability to explain the wider political world? This reappraisal is one of the first attempts to assess critically Jung's theory in terms of his own premises. From this re-working of the theory the hope is to create the possibility for new theoretical formulations that can be applied to collective events. This will be taken up in the last chapter.

The third phase of the book returns to the historical story and looks at how Jung attempted to apply his theories to Nazi Germany. Here all the themes of the book come together. Part of this phase involves a critique of his major essay on 'Wotan' written in 1936, so in discussing this I will refer back to the previous exploration of the theory to show how these issues affected his interpretation of Hitler's Reich.

This essay was highly significant as it showed Jung trying to illustrate and justify his hypothesis with evidence drawn from immediate events. In retrospect, the essay represented a unique presentation of a piece of contemporary 'field work' on a national scale that would serve as a test case for much of his theory. Unfortunately due to the controversies that surrounded Jung at the time, the essay and its implications have been relatively neglected in later Jungian writings. This has been a serious omission for our understanding of Jung's work. This is because the problems he experienced at the time were to affect his own attitude to the theory and the work he put into them, which has contributed to a lack of definition in this part of his paradigm as his interests then moved back to questions about spiritual welfare that lie outside this book and much of the theory discussed here.

Having dealt with the theory, this phase of the book then involves a detailed examination of how well Jung was able to describe and account for events. Our discussion entails a close look at such topics as the nature of Nazi Germany's relationship with pagan ideas, as well as considering Jung's assessment of Hitler and the question of his portrayal of Hitler's psychology as an example of a charismatic messiah that led his country to ruin. We also look at the intriguing issue of Jung's failure to deploy his insights into Hitler's gift of intuition as a way to understand this enemy of democracy. We will consider whether Jung's theory gave a good explanation for what he saw, or whether other commentators provide more tenable accounts of events. Entwined with this date we also return to consider what insights Jung provides for those seeking to understand the causes of War.

The last part of the book leaves the history of Jung and his ideas, but takes up the issues he raised. In the last chapter I seek to offer a reformulation of parts of his hypothesis using some of the innovations discussed or developed in the book. This is a contribution to the move to extend Jungian theory and become more in-tune with modern psychological developments. There are different motives for this exercise. For the political scientist there is the hope that the ideas set out here will offer another tool with which we can approach political problems.

For my colleagues in the Jungian community it is hoped that these ideas will provide some tools with which we can understand, apply and improve on Jung's work. This will further debate and aid Jungian therapists in their dialogue with their co-workers in other parts of the mental health field. The facilitation of change is far from an obscure academic diversion. If Jungian psychotherapists do not keep pace with the collective processes of clinical and theoretical innovation we risk becoming isolated as an anachronistic school of pastoral care. Theory is part of our professional life and like all living things our work must change, adapt and grow, but to do this we need to refine our understanding of our theoretical roots in a continual process as more of Jung's texts come into the public domain.

All of this presents the reader with an unusual journey as we move from the consulting room, to the books where theories are forged, and then on to the clash of world events where ideas meet the acid-test of reality. On this path I will look at Jung's work through the eyes of a military historian and a Jungian clinician and I hope that this combination will offer fresh insights as we continue to work on our understanding of Jung and his world.

Chapter Summaries

Chapter One offers a discussion of the discipline of International Politics and the concept of political realism that will be used to assess Jung's political literacy throughout the book. The chapter also offers a summary and contrast between Jung and Freud's positions for those who want to put Jung in a psychoanalytic context.

Chapter Two starts and ends with the problems a reader faces when trying to interpret Jung and account for his different styles of communication or the way his ideas change over time. The chapter then goes on to consider Jung's perception of the Nazis and his view of the dictators and the totalitarian states as well as the accusation by some writers that Jung was ideologically or unconsciously anti-Semitic. This issue we return to when we reassess Jung's conflict with Freud in terms of Jung's perception that Freudian ideas would lead to a growth in materialism that would accelerate the soulless drift towards the dictators. As well as this debate we look at Jung's domestic political values and his anxiety about the threat the state poses to individual liberties.

Chapter Three explores Jung's understanding of the political situation and his grasp of strategic concepts. It also looks at Jung's more conventional insights into the psychological causes of war. These discussions draw on the introduction to strategic thought in Chapter One and also look forward to the way he would use his archetypal theory to explain other psychological factors, discussed in Chapters Seven and Eight. Another feature of this chapter is its examination of the role 'race' played in Jung's theory and there is a digression to discuss suggestions that his main concern was to present himself as a 'psychologist of nations'.

Chapter Four looks at some of the background factors that shaped Jung's theory and how his work with individuals prompted him to formulate a collective theory. The chapter also serves to alert the reader to Jung's problematic use of historical sources and his inconsistent attitude to social issues. Together with the next chapter we also consider the problem that a lot of the evidence Jung cites for his genetically collective theory is due to cultural and social factors rather than the inherited processes that his original thinking about a collective unconscious suggested.

Chapter Five looks at how the idea of the collective unconscious evolved and presents a detailed discussion of how Jung's work drew on Environmental Determinism and *Völkisch* roots. The theory of the collective unconscious would allow for the possibility of a racial and a national unconscious which have obvious political implications. After a digression on the issue of anti-Semitism, we come back to conclude our discussion on Jung's ideas on national psychology. Next we consider whether this distinction had any real significance in his ideas at this time. We then examine Jung's concern at how successfully all cultures (irrespective of their stage of development) were able to foster the process of moral and psychological maturity.

Chapter Six is concerned with Jung's theory of the archetypes and how the theory depended on Lamarckian roots and tried to weld together a number of incompatible mental phenomena. Later the theory evolved and drew closer to ideas about instincts. This material becomes relevant in the next chapter when we look at the varied ways Jung used the idea of Wotan and how the disparate ideas about archetypes affected his writing. After this review there is a synopsis of the defining qualities of an archetype. The chapter also introduces the idea of 'immanent archetypes' which are not true archetypes but ideas that are latent in the nature of the external world or the human condition. These are not an intrinsic part of our inherited mental make-up in the way that instincts and the true archetypes are.

Chapter Seven brings our study of archetypes into the political arena and looks at the impact of the emotional energy that archetypes can unleash in the psychological processes that affect politics. We introduce here the archetypes of the hero and the messiah that will be discussed more fully in Chapters Eight and Nine.

In *Chapter Eight* we come to our discussion of Jung's 'Wotan' essay and consider the implications of the confusions that result in Jung's style of explanation (see Chapter Two), his use of history (see Chapter Four) and the incompatible parts of his theory (See Chapters Five and Six). We also examine the political influence of archetypes that was outlined in Chapter Eight. We consider Jung's understanding of the history of Germany, his hopes for archetypally-driven progress and the courses of the changes in Jung's attitude to the Nazis. In looking at Jung's views we consider how pagan the Nazis were: from Hitler and his evocation of Wagner to the mythic phantasmagoria of Himmler and at a less powerful level what influence Professor Hauer and Walter Darré had in their attempts to re-launch paganism and how successful the German Christians' attempts were to produce a Christianity stripped of its Jewish roots. Lastly we look at Jung's attempt to act as a political prophet and this brings us back to the utility of his archetypal theory to explain or predict events.

Chapter Nine deals specifically with the task of explaining Hitler's character and compares contemporary commentators and some historians with Jung's assessment of the Fuhrer. In this chapter we refer back to the discussion of the emotional power of the archetypes and the religious processes that were explained in the previous chapter. By way of contrast we also consider the role intuition played in Hitler's personality. The chapter ends by revisiting the question of how Jungian psychology may be of help to political analysis.

Chapter Ten builds on the theoretical work in the second phase of the book and the critique of Jung's attempts to implement his theory in the political world in the two previous chapters. Having suggested that our use of the term 'archetype' needs to be much more disciplined than in Jung's early writings, and that much of his discussion involved evidence about cultural factors, we rework some of Jung's observations using post-Jungian innovations and meme theory to provide a new theoretical tool for Jungian thought. This can also be used in political science. The chapter concludes by briefly applying these ideas when looking at some aspects of Nazi history that were mentioned in the previous two chapters.

Phase One: The Political Jung

It is always dangerous to speak of one's own times because what is at stake is too vast to be comprehended. (Jung, 1986 [1930]/1950, §154). [Written in 1929.]

1. Concerning Freud and Jung on International Politics and War

Let us begin with a swift overview of how war will be discussed in this book. Our point of departure is that Jung's ideas must be judged within the context of his political era. As far as his political observations go, writing in the thirties, Jung was principally concerned with war and the political interaction between nation states and this was understandable at a time when war within Europe was an ever-present possibility as the World Wars and the Cold War were to show. In such dangerous times, how was war studied by those concerned with security issues?

For most of the twentieth century the core attitude to war for the discipline of International Politics and Strategic Studies could be summed up by the classic nineteenth century study of von Clausewitz's *On War*, in which he stated that 'War is the continuation of state policy by other means' (1962, p4). For nation states struggling to survive, war remained the ultimate reality test. In this light, in the discipline of International Politics, the understanding of the practical imperatives of force became known as the 'realist' approach as this is what could be tried and tested in the brutal reality of 'blood and iron'. This 'reality' means that International Politics has had a very 'rough and ready' approach to morality and philosophy. This seemingly crude philosophy needs to be acknowledged if the perspective is to be understood. It is above all else a way of making provisional classifications about international situations involving many states, actors, cultures and varied histories.

Under such conditions either a 'fine' understanding of events or ideological dogma is impossible or illusion and so the discipline instead requires the ability to sustain a workable picture of complex inter-woven imponderables based on frequently insufficient information.

With the collapse of the Cold War, the international stage has become more complex and our understanding more differentiated than in Jung's time. In his day the focus of power politics between nation states rested on an understanding of the balance of power, escalation, alliances and varied war-fighting strategies. So it is in this context that we should judge Jung's political statements.

When Jung looked at political events he saw nation-states as the main actors. Like the International Politics theorists of the twentieth century, he was concerned at how states attempt to pursue their diplomatic and strategic policies while constrained by a part-formedly, partly-articulated international system. This interconnection of inter-woven factors has meant that International Politics, as a discipline, has a systemic outlook that can look at the causes of war from different levels, and some International Politics theorists, like Kenneth Waltz (1965), have refined their analysis of events so as to see it in terms of three different levels of interacting events. Briefly stated, these are:

- the level of the individual where national leaders or key figures precipitate actions and have a major role in the conduct of war.
- the social level where inter-communal tension generates civil war or inter-state friction.
- the level of international system where states are locked in treaty systems, economic spheres or balance of power-chains, and go to war to protect their perceived key interests.

The significance of these different levels will vary depending on the historical case in question. A brief example of the use of these different layers of analysis can be taken from a summary of Germany in the First World War. There, one individual, the Kaiser, to compensate for numerous neuroses, drove the foreign policy of Germany in an increasingly unstable manner. At the social level

German society was profoundly tainted with feelings of inferiority towards Britain and so became increasingly hungry for her 'place in the sun'. European societies at the turn of the century took a romantic view of military service and gave it unparalleled support. In Germany this trend towards militarism was accelerated by an increasingly unstable social situation. Her democratic institutions were still very immature and could no longer guide or restrain the Kaiser as previously Bismarck had tried to do. Unquestioning loyalty to the Kaiser was enhanced by the tradition of Lutheran state control, while the nationalism which he sought to sponsor drew strength from recent unification, the successes of the Franco-Prussian war, and growing industrial success. The passions of people and Kaiser made a fertile bed for war fever.

At the international level, Germany felt she had just cause to compete internationally with what she saw as decadent and greedy French and British Empires. In addition, on her borders she was increasingly aware of the deadly threat posed by the hectic pace of Czarist Russia's industrialisation and railway modernisation which would give new strategic significance to Russia's two-million-strong army. Germany felt there was much it was her right to win, and much she had increasingly to fear (Bond, 1983; Howard, 1983; Ritter, 1972).

In summing up the perspective of International Politics theorists there is some truth in the generalisation that while they may be concerned with all levels of political activity, their priority is with the state and the International System. Overall, International Politics is systemic and hierarchical in its perspective and 'realist' in its approach to the philosophy of power and morality.

But inter-state politics is not the whole picture. What of the politicians and their psychological dimension? How can one achieve a 'sophisticated realism' that takes into account psychological factors that would be the concern of writers like Jung? If psychology can be said to have a major contribution to our understanding of wider politics then it comes from considering the impact of emotions on political life. For example, one of the major problems when trying to understand other politicians' political actions comes when trying to assess the role emotion plays in others' decision-making. Fear can obviously play a major role. But such is the compelling nature of many 'life and death issues' that strategists are at risk of over-estimating the utility of force in the strategic realm or under-estimating the complexities of a given situation and neglecting outside factors. There are great pressures on strategic thinkers to impose certainty on the chaos and uncertainty of war. Decision-makers may seek to suppress the uncertainty, ambiguity and fear of the unavoidable complexities of strategic situations with crude simplicities and impatient reductionism. There are tremendous pressures to adopt a 'worst case' realist perspective. Under such pressures it becomes increasingly difficult to delineate between different levels of crisis and adopt a proportional response. In international politics one is often faced with moral and pragmatic problems with no cost-free options. In a world of moral uncertainty, pessimism all too often urges the unrestrained use of force to overcompensate for the unpredictable (Walzer, 1984). All these emotional pressures create areas of ambiguity inherent in the seeming pragmatism and rationality of the realist perspective.

Given these pressures, not surprisingly the issue of rationality is a major debating point in International Politics. To put this in context, International Politics' concern with history and current affairs is divided between the diplomatic world where policies are furthered in peaceful ways and the military world were policies are pursued by force. Because the discipline overlaps the worlds of scholarship and policy, the most controversial area in the discipline surrounds the balance a writer puts on the conflict between the 'rationality of ends' and the 'rationality of means'. Both these equations are heavily influenced by the individual's culture and epoch, and in no case is this more clearly seen than in the way a political actor attempts to reconcile the clash between the ends of policy and the means used to achieve them (Booth, 1979). This issue is problematic for both the politician and the academic.

This debate about rationality also brings into focus the question of time-scale. Policy makers often have acute difficulty in sustaining a simultaneous awareness of the immediate, medium term and long term goals and consequences of their policies. This may be even more acute in a democracy where imminent elections focus attention on the short-term policies at the expense of strategic issues which fatally undermines a country's political stamina, as happened during America's Vietnam war with the clash between domestic politics and strategic imperatives.

These debates became more problematic in Jung's lifetime with the use of chemical and nuclear weapons. The debate over the rationality of ends and means has proved profoundly problematic and is probably philosophically and psychologically unanswerable. In some cases strategic theorists have simply avoided the moral realm and the irresolvable arguments about rational action. But when the majority of theorists do enter into a discussion they limit themselves to the question of the rationality of means, as it is less contentious.

Let us return to the question of Jung and political realism. The first phase of the book will consider Jung's understanding of international events outside of Switzerland and whether he was reasonably well-informed. We will examine whether his political perspective was compatible with political realism, and if so how well did he apply it? Could he identify key events and were his comments applicable to questions about the practicality of action or the rationality of objectives? The rest of the book will explore how coherent was his theoretical model in understanding the interaction of psychology and politics, and how successful Jung's attempts were at explaining events with it.

An Overview of Freud and Jung on Politics and War

The second part of this introductory chapter is to provide an overview of Freud's idea on international politics and war and compare and contrast the two men's views.

There was little peace in the twentieth century. The complacent sense of progress of the industrial nineteenth century and the gentility of turn-of-the-century Europe had been brought into question by the blood-letting of the Great War. The carnage smashed the illusion of civilised integrity among the European ruling class and prompted both psycho-analytic pioneers to consider the psychological causes of war.

Initially Freud's reaction had been patriotic support for the Central Powers, but pessimism soon took over and he wearily declared: 'war is not to be abolished, so long as the conditions of existence among the nations are so varied, and the repulsions between peoples so intense, there will be, must be, wars' (1915, p316).

After the war Freud continued in this vein, but the pessimistic strain in his thinking led him to argue that war had become too damaging to be considered a continuation of politics. In the 1932 article 'Why War?' Freud noted that 'in its present day form war is no longer an opportunity for achieving the old ideals of heroism' (1933 [1932], p213). Possibly drawing on his knowledge of past disasters in Austro-Hungarian history, Freud warned of the transience of military territorial gain: 'conquests are as a rule short-lived: the newly created units fall apart once again, usually owing to a lack of cohesion between the portions that have been united by violence' (1933 [1932], p278). This insight almost anticipated the disintegration of Europe's colonial empires. Freud also warned of the potential for instability in a country where a constitutional ruler only had limited power. Stability could be compromised by a tension between the desire of the rulers to set themselves above the law and the desire of the oppressed peoples to seek further equality before the law (1933 [1932], p277).

In 'Why War' Freud identified three causes of war at the social level. The first was, as he saw it, the inevitable instability of a democracy, the second the potentially fratricidal impact of competing pressure groups all contending to be rulers, while the third was the instability caused by material insecurity. Freud acknowledged prosperity was a key factor in maintaining stability, yet even he could not believe prosperity would be enough to maintain peace as, 'there is no use in trying to get rid of men's aggressive inclinations. We are told that in certain happy regions of the earth, where nature provides in abundance everything that man requires, there are races whose life is passed in tranquillity and who know neither coercion nor aggression. I can scarcely believe it and I should be glad to hear more of these fortunate beings' (1933 [1932], p211).

Where Freud had been less astute was in failing to recognise how some types of conflicts have their causes in the strategic pressures on nation states. In terms of inter-state politics, Freud was too optimistic when he assumed that democracies were necessarily more peaceful than dictatorships. This was an argument put forward by libertarian philosophers, such as John Stuart Mill. Freud admired Mill and translated the final volume of the German twelve volumes translation of his collected works (Kaufmann, 1980, p47). But if Freud had reflected more he might have noticed that imperial democracies could be highly combative.

Freud neglected to look at the wider strategic picture that was unfolding in Europe. If little of his great output was on international politics maybe he was restricted by persecution, old-age, ill-health and exile, but one must acknowledge that he was primarily concerned with ideas about the individual and the family situation, so while he considered wider issues in *Civilisation and its Discontents* (1930 [1929]), his primary concern was always the individual and the family. This weighting is admirably demonstrated with Freud's other major foray into thinking about contemporary events when he co-authored with William Bullitt *Thomas Woodrow Wilson: A Psychological Study* (1967). This little-known joint biography came about when the two friends met in Berlin where Freud was due for an operation. Ambassador Bullitt who had served with Wilson in Paris in 1919 told Freud that he was writing a biography of Wilson and Freud begged to join him as a co-author. The book was completed in manuscript by the spring of 1932, but after some disagreements it was only in 1939 in London that they agreed it was ready for publication although it was not published for years or included in the Standard Edition. Despite its subject matter the book is bare of any reflections on inter-state politics and confines itself to exploring how Wilson's childhood relations with his parents affected the way he related to his American colleagues. As such the psycho-biography is an interesting Freudian exercise but its domestic focus sets it outside the realm of our discussion.

When it came to war, his theoretical contribution was on the psychology of aggression, which again centred on the individual and the crowd and most of Freud's writing on aggression occurred after the split with Jung.

Freud's writings on hate and aggression focused on:

- The potential for social instability caused by the repression of the instincts.
- The emotions involved with aggression and death.

- The psychology of hate.
- The suggestibility of crowds and their need for leaders.

In contrast to Jung, Freud devoted relatively little attention to commentating on the international politics that occurred around him. Primarily Freud looked at the psychology of aggression in the individual's psychology, but as society and institutions had to find ways to deal with individual desires and frustrations and aggression his ideas gave an insight into aggression and conflict at a wider social level. With all the stresses involved between the rivalry of love and hate and the conflict between the sensual desires of the id and society's restrictions, the individual psyche is rarely able to achieve stability for long. Freud saw society resting on very unstable foundations as it imposed restrictive moral standards on the individual who is 'compelled to act continually in the sense of precepts which are not the expression of instinctual inclinations'. This meant that the individual is 'living psychologically... beyond his means.' He continued, 'we are certainly misled by our optimism into grossly exaggerating the number of human beings who have been transformed in a civilised sense' (1915, p299). A quarter of a century later, when the world was once again in the throes of war, Freud was to make the same points when he returned to the issue in 'An Outline of Psycho-Analysis', published in 1940: 'We must therefore not forget to include the influence of civilization among the determinants of neurosis. It is easy, as we can see, for a barbarian to be healthy; for a civilized man the task is hard' (Freud, 1940 [1938], p185).

Indirectly this point is echoed by Hitler whose avowed aim was to rid his vibrant re-emergent neo-pagan Germany of the curse of 'conscience' which he denounced as a Jewish invention. Obviously if one is conscience-less it is much easier to commit war crimes or participate in the SS-sponsored *Lebensborn* free-love program for proven warriors to impregnate racially pure young women and breed a new generation of war heroes!

For Freud the clash between the instinctual drives and the restraints of society set in motion tensions that caused wars. These observations were to find an echo in Jung's ideas on the problems caused when too great a gulf exists between a highly civilised, conscious culture and an emotionally primitive unconscious. Jung speculated that one of the reasons for the Germans' plummet into the Nazi abyss was the wide gulf between the ultra-civilised world that produced Goethe and the primitive hinterland which had not been socialised sufficiently.

Freud's ideas about the clash between libido and the death-wish have found contemporary advocates. Broyles writes from a classical Freudian perspective: 'The love of war stems from the union, deep in the core of your being, between sex and destruction, beauty and horror, love and death. War may be the only way in which most men touch the mystic domains of our soul. It is for men, at some terrible level, the closest thing to what childbirth is for women: the initiation into the power of life and death'(1984, p61). These ideas had some impact in modern Jungian thought when a contemporary Jungian took a neo-Freudian position and argued that there was a death-wish evident in nuclear strategy where the most dangerous emotion driving towards war was: 'the conflict between the rational mania for control and the longing for the great ecstasy of destruction' (Langendorf, 1986, p32).

This heady lure of the exhilaration of destruction is very seductive and Dudley comments that: 'Like no other experience, war creates what Jung termed a *participation mystique*, [an unconscious identity with something] in which the energy of myth flows irresistibly through the force-fields of the nation's psyche' (1992, p87). With this power, war develops a fascination akin to the numinous. This power Campbell (1988) labelled as 'sublime', describing the apocalyptic awe induced by the strategic bombing in World War Two. We will return to Jung's concern with the intoxicating dangers of certain psychological processes in the chapters on archetypal theory.

At this point it again needs stressing that Freud, and later Klein, were principally concerned with aggression. In contrast, Jung had relatively little to say about aggression and power. It may be that Jung, who had a considerable temper (Jung, 1963 [1961], p54), may have been inhibited from pondering such a problematic area. Another possibility was that he was not interested in theoretical introspection because he felt he had a working relationship with his temper and was happy to endure his quick-to-anger, quick-toquieten, outbursts. This may have been a reasonable strategy, but as we shall see in the next chapter when we come to look at his relationship with Freud and his followers, he was probably not conscious of how angry he could become.

Jung's lack of attention to aggression causes a problem when one tries to compare Freud's ideas on individual aggression with Jung's ideas on national and racial issues in international politics. While they were both writing about the psychological, their level of analysis was different.

Jung's ideas were an attempt to account for an underlying dimension of the historical processes and if one is to understand his ideas then they must be judged in their theoretical context. Jung was positing a deeper collective and instinctive basis for emotions. He was not trying to give a complete picture. Maybe if he had intended to produce such a picture he would have begun by looking at Freud and the other psychoanalysts' contributions. But after the schism both men were prone to ignore the other's ideas, and in Jung's case his perspective was focused beyond the personal and biographical influences on the individual. He wanted to look at collective historical factors beyond the time-span and scope of the sociologist and below the focus of the historian concentrating on documents and conscious motives. Jung meant for this approach to be an additional perspective; maybe it was to be the fundamental one, but he did not say it was the *only* perspective.

In clinical cases Jung was sometimes willing to defer to Freud's model, even if he did not ascribe the same importance to childhood developmental issues. Both men were concerned with the resolution of problems posed by the emotional demands of instinctual drives, but their conception of the problem was rather different. Freud tended to posit a clash between the instinctive drives of the primitive psyche and the norms of society. This clash was an insoluble feature of the need of civilisation to contain and direct primitive sexual urges to socially acceptable ends. Jung's perspective was of an ever-changing shift of balance; an emotional see-saw between competing norms and a more varied range of instinctive drives. This provided a more moderate perspective on the clash between the instincts and civilisation.

To greatly simplify complex positions, if Freud's concern was with the healthy reinforcement of civilisation against the eternal challenge of the barbaric instincts, Jung's concern was of the potential for civilised individuals to transform such clashes and so make their small but invaluable contribution to humanity's collective progress. But he feared that too many champions of social change were prisoners of their own unresolved complexes rather than the selfless philanthropists they believed themselves to be. When this was not recognised and corrected, their solutions to problems became distorted and reflected the biases of their own reformist complexes. This perpetuated the problem, or the remedy brought a new cycle of problems. If this were not dangerous enough, this idealism lent itself to ideological utopian dreams which the demagogue could easily exploit (Jung, 1991 [1957], §558). Alschuler may suggest that Jung was too pessimistic about the progressive potential of politics (1997, p282), but the all-too-frequent failure of short-term solutions in political history rather puts the burden of explanation on those like Alschuler to account for the failure of revolutionaries and reformers to achieve sustainable reform without negative side effects. This in a way brings us back to Jung's own brand of 'realist perspective' and the question of what really works as opposed to what we wish would work!

2. Jung and His Politics

It was usually safer to follow Jung's considered opinion than remarks he sometimes let fall at the moment. As he once said in a seminar: 'in the course of a long day, I drop a good many unripe cherries. And it is very annoying when people pick these up and treasure them!' (Hannah, 1976, p260).

On Jung's Personality and the Problems of Interpretation

When studying the ideas of a historical figure, it is useful to look at the contexts in which the thinker's ideas evolved and consider whether the individual's personality and life experience affected the sort of theories they generated. For this background material one could borrow Jung's term the 'personal equation'[1], so in this chapter we will be looking at how Jung's background, environment and personality, his 'personal equation' moulded and contributed to his theoretical work. This overview is especially important before trying to establish what Jung's political perspective was. His main focus was not politics, indeed his major concerns as a psychotherapist and critic of Freud were with morality, the problems of modernity and his interest in reinterpreting Christianity (Stevens, 1990, p274).

Jung was at pains to point out that his personal equation included the fact that he was a European, Swiss, scholar, scientist and psychiatrist, and he was saying all this because he was keenly aware of the impact of socialisation and environment in moulding unconscious perceptions. In studying this nineteenth century gentleman-scholar, one is not dealing with a naïve observer of either the external world or the internal world. But it is as well to be wary because one cannot assume he was always keeping his potential biases in mind or that he always tried, or was successful, in keeping his writings free of personal idiosyncrasies or deliberate image-building to raise his scientific or scholarly profile.

Many people have the impression that Jung was unconcerned with political events. This tendency to underestimate his political awareness is increased by the small number of political statements he made in proportion to his huge output, and means that piecing together a picture of his political profile is something of a detective story. Only some of Jung's political statements are contained in Volume Ten of the Collected Works and the rest are scattered through the Collected Works or more frequently found in small references in the letters or remarks in the Seminars.

Caution is also needed when one is trying to deduce and reconstruct his ideas from diverse sources written over a long period. Not everything he said can be treated as scientific or academically considered offerings. It is useful to make a distinction between what Jung said privately and what he said publicly as well as what he said spontaneously when being interviewed, so that one is confronted with statements ranging from Jung's taste for generalisations and being provocative to shrewd observation and intelligent commentary.

In this chapter, most of Jung's comments are taken from his interviews or essays on immediate events, so most of the material is not the product of lengthy reflection or an attempt at theoretical formulation. When reading Jung, one can see that as a commentator on political events he showed an increasingly sophisticated level of political realism. But the reader is often struck by his ill-considered *off the cuff remarks*, so special care is needed. The mismatch between the two types of statement is always a fertile basis for controversy. There is a common prejudice that what is said in private is necessarily the true opinion, and this supposes that everything that is said in such situations is deeply considered and is long held as a *genuine* opinion. This is questionable. People frequently give expression to an emotion, be it with humour or anger, but such statements do not necessarily reflect their considered opinions. To give an extreme example, while in one of his rages, de Gaulle in London in 1943 exclaimed to an aide that now was a time to make an alliance with the Germans against the Anglo-Saxons. This is a very clear case of a seemingly radical political outburst having no grounding in policy, but if it were taken at face value it would give an alarmingly false impression of de Gaulle as a potential collaborator. Jung too was capable of volcanic outbursts but what he said when angry is not always a sure guide to his considered views.

As will be shown in the course of the chapter, Jung was a staunch democrat, but some have argued that he had an unconscious predilection for reactionary politics. Indeed, McLynn declared: 'Jung was a man of extreme right-wing political views... he combined ferociously reactionary and Social Darwinist views' (1996, p344). Others have added varied accusations of authoritarianism, pro-fascism, militarist tendencies, anti-communism and anti-Semitism so these assertions need to be re-examined if we are to form a clear picture of Jung's thought.

THE QUESTION OF ANTI-SEMITISM

Maybe the most inflammatory issue to confront us in an examination of Jung's political beliefs is the allegation that Jung was anti-Semitic. These allegations are important in three ways.

On a practical level his writings about the Jews complicated his political interaction with Nazi Germany and this may affect our assessment of his political judgement.

On a theoretical level, as Jung was thinking about race, it is of some significance whether or not he was an anti-Semite as this could have a racial component and so affect the racial component of his theory of the collective unconscious.

On a wider level, the fallout from the controversy has affected the reception of Jung's ideas and this has had a number of implications. One of the most serious is that the issue deepened the split in the psycho-analytic world and this has probably increased the theoretical introversion of the Freudian and Jungian schools so that not only have they missed the opportunity to cross-fertilise and learn from their different bodies of clinical experience, but even more perniciously the culture of isolation has numbed their receptivity to outside influences. Clearly the significance of the controversy and its possible impact on his wider theory cannot be overlooked!

Given the stakes involved, the debate on Jung's attitude to the Jews continues to excite controversy and there is a huge amount of material written on this issue so that to deal with it in its entirety would require another book. Unfortunately while there is a wealth of comments, there is insufficient evidence to make a definitive case one way or the other and this needs to be acknowledged, given the passions that this area can arouse, but all one can do is consider the balance of the available evidence. We must limit ourselves to a synopsis of the current literature so that the balance of the evidence can be considered.

The literature can be divided into four perspectives. The first perspective is uncritically hostile and assumes that Jung was anti-Semitic, and for the most part was produced by Jung's contemporaries including insinuations by Ernest Jones and Karl Abraham (Kerr, 1993, p134, 181). The second perspective is made up of critics of the subsequent generations such as Andrew Samuels, who argue that Jung was anti-Semitic to a degree (1993). Unlike many representatives of the first perspective, some of these critics have read widely on the issue and constructed a plausible academic argument that may be true. This perspective at present is probably the most commonly held, but because it is so widespread and often repeated it is rarely critically examined. This is problematic, as the accusations that Jung was anti-Semitic suffer from a lack of evidence and an over-dependence on misrepresentation of much of what Jung said and wrote. Maybe it is indicative that a critic of Jung as enthusiastic as Richard Noll is unable to produce any telling instances of anti-Semitism. Indeed Noll shrewdly observed that much of the controversy surrounding the supposed anti-Semitism of Jung stems from the lack of evidence, which has allowed free reign for projection and emotion (1974, p103).

The third position is more subtle and argues that Jung was either unconsciously biased against the Jews or unconsciously anti-Semitic for a time in the thirties. Zabriskie suggests that 'some of his statements (until the middle thirties) also suggested unconscious prejudice, ignorance, condescension, and a sense of superiority, especially in relation to creativity or originality' (1989, p308). The validity of Zabriskie's suggestion depends on the reader's interpretation of what Jung said, and this must be done with care as Jung's statements usually contained positive statements for both parties. Even if one interprets in a negative fashion Jung's suggestions that the Jews as a more sophisticated culture have less unexploited potential (Jung, 1991 [1918], §18), this remark amounts to something that in everyday terms is more akin to bias than anti-Semitism, and even the charge of bias is difficult to sustain when Jung's comments are read in context.

A similar possibility is that Jung had elements of unconscious hostility that had either not shown up until the mid-thirties, or had grown up following the break with Freud. Kirsch, commenting on Jung's relations with the Jews, says that Jung tried consciously to help the Jews but that unconsciously a Jewish complex persisted. He suggests that it was activated by his relationship with Freud, but was transferred to Jews in general, and only resolved late in life when working through much personal and archetypal material in the writing of *Answer to Job* (1982, p86). Kirsch later added: 'Consciously, Jung could not have been an anti-Semite. He certainly did not hate the Jews as a people, and he never rejected any individual being on account of race, culture or religion' (1983, p15). In summing up all the evidence for Jung's aid to various Jews and positive statements about them Kirsch argues that: 'To my mind, Jung is the only man who, though he gave in to feelings and opinions of anti-Semitism for a short period, solved the problem of his unconscious anti-Semitism' (1983, p18-19).

The possibility of unconscious hostility is of course a difficult phenomenon to assess. One could argue that Jung had just enough unconscious hostility to inhibit his criticism of the Nazis in public. The argument here is that silence costs less emotional effort than overt action. One could also argue that this bias was not strong enough to stop him from helping individual cases that were known to him, or assisting fellow colleagues who fitted into a special category in his evaluation. This is conceivable, but it is a weak explanation given the lack of evidence.

Another view comes in two parts. The first suggestion is that Jung was not anti-Semitic, as looking at Jung's early life there is a lack of evidence for Jung having a latent Jewish complex prior to his meeting with Freud (Lewin, 2006, p17-20). Consequently, for reasons of space, I will discuss in the appendix Brockway's suggestion that Jung was anti-Semitic.

The second suggestion is that he *was* hostile to Freud. As McLynn observed: 'Jung was not really an anti-Semite but he allowed his hatred for Freud to poison his mind and invade his thoughts; it is almost always the case that when Jung says 'Jew' he means Freud and when he says 'Jewish' he means Freudian' (1996, p362; see also Gallard, 1994, p218). This perspective follows from a close inspection of Jung's so-called 'critical' remarks about the Jews and suggests that they were actually directed at Freud and his immediate following.

Having read all the material that is currently available and reviewed the different perspectives, I find that the balance of the evidence suggests that in all likelihood Jung was not even unconsciously anti-Semitic, but that he did make generalisations, and, more importantly, he became explicitly hostile to the circle of mainly Jewish psychoanalysts around Freud in Vienna who assumed that Jung was anti-Semitic and spread such accusations in an anti-Jung 'campaign'.[2] This partisan 'campaign' later became more dispersed as its members travelled and their assertions about Jung spread. The attacks continued to provoke and draw Jung's hostility and he expressed himself in terms that have been misinterpreted as general anti-Semitism, a misperception that has not been helped by his being too angry to systematically defend himself. Another twist to the story could be that Jung's anger may also have blinded him to the implications or consequences of some of his words and actions when he interacted with the Third Reich in the thirties, but that is a different issue!

These actions by Jung provoked a counter reaction in Freud, as Freud had come to assume that Jung was anti-Semitic and this impression was probably reinforced by misunderstanding Jung's actions in the thirties, which prevented any possibility of a reconciliation. From Jung's side, the ideological rift was sustained or increased, as will be explained, because he believed that Freud's ideas actually fertilised the climate in which extremism and Nazi ideologies could grow. In these ways political events and perceptions of political actions added a further tragic twist to the Freud-Jung rift.

To illustrate how Jung's anger affected his behaviour, let us look at what Jung wrote about his new book, *Wirklichkeit der Seele* on the 26th May 1934, which was the first published after the Nazi seizure of power. What is of interest to us is that an eighth of this book was a study by one of Jung's Jewish pupils, Hugo Rosenthal, on 'The Typological Opposites in the History of the Jewish Religion'. Jung explained to James Kirsch about his views on Jewish culture: 'I have included in it an essay by a Jewish author on the psychology of the Old Testament, *just to annoy the Nazis and all those who have decried me as an anti-Semite.* The next thing that will be invented about me is that I suffer from a complete absence of convictions and am neither an anti-Semite nor a Nazi. We happen to live in a time which overflows with lunacy' (Jung, 1973 [1906-1950], p162, my bold). As Harms points out this was hardly the sort of action of an anti-Semite or one going out of his way to cultivate the Nazis (1946, p43). But it shows very clearly the tension in Jung between his widening hostility to the Nazis and his enmity to the 'campaign'. Significantly in this letter the two were given equal weighting. Furthermore in doing this he is implicitly dividing the Jews into two groups, those that were hostile to him, and all the rest. This reinforces the argument that Jung was specifically hostile to those he perceived as belonging to the 'campaign'.

In May 1934, the Bad Nauheim meeting of the IAP took place. Here Jung began publicly to provoke the Nazis and defend Freud. Harms recorded:

> We have already reported Jung's fine and gallant attitude during the first meeting of the international association of the national group of psychotherapists in Bad Nauheim in central Germany in 1934, when he chose as the topic of his address the 'Theory of Complexes', in which he paid homage to Freud, who was then the target of Nazi hatred. I recall how, on the following day, the Berlin press raged against Jung and

carefully registered the number of times on which Jung had pronounced the hated name Freud. There would certainly have been no reason to expose himself in this manner during these weeks of the most fanatical outburst of anti-Semitism if one had wished to ingratiate himself with the National Socialist regime and its leaders. (1946, p41)

At first sight this seems to contradict the hypothesis about Jung's hostility to the 'campaign'. Jung remained hostile and continued to have unconscious emotional reactions that, when triggered, would lead to ill-considered outbursts. Under such circumstances he could refer to either Freud or the Jews. The book would argue that this contradiction was confined to the declaratory level. In practice, by this time Jung was becoming increasingly even-handed in his statements on Freud, which suggests he had digested much of his personal pain. He was also heavily engaged in struggling with the Nazis over their treatment of the Jews. What was happening, then, was that Jung was attempting to help the Jews by defending Freud, but as the letter to Kirsch makes plain this did not cause him to desist from his conflict with the 'campaign'.

In summary I agree with McLynn and Gallard that Jung was not anti-Semitic and here we must leave the issue for now, but we will return to it shortly at the end of this chapter.

The issue of Jung's response to the plight of the Jews is too complex to be looked at in any more detail here, but it is useful to conclude with Meier's argument that Jung: 'hated international politics or anything of the sort. I would say [however] he could indeed have said something but he thought it was of no use anyhow. These things took place anyhow and nobody could interfere at all. Nobody could. Not even somebody like Jung. Nobody could. It was a mass movement that there were no brakes to' (Maidenbaum, 2002, p206-207). This is perhaps an uncomfortably depressing historical assessment, but given what Jung saw then and what we know now, it is hard to challenge Jung's realism as a political observer.

Whether we like it or not, Jung was a prisoner of the political times in which he lived. He had to act and behave within his possibilities. If he was not overtly vocal on the Jewish crisis it was because his struggle was circumscribed by his work within the IGMSP (International General Medical Society for Psychotherapy) where explicit comments were inappropriate, but it is clear where his sympathies and concerns lay (as we will see in chapters eight and nine).

JUNG'S PRE-WAR THOUGHTS ON MATERIAL AND SPIRITUAL WELFARE

The next question to consider is how much Jung's socio-economic position influenced his political perspective. Certainly Jung was unashamedly middle-class in his own profession and scholarly lifestyle and had two properties, a large town house as befitted his academic standing and an idyllic lake-side retreat where he could exist free of electricity and visitors. Brockway suggests that Jung was a nineteenth century 'traditional conservative' who admired the aristocracy, and was nostalgic for the medieval, the romantic and the pastoral. He was 'the classical liberal of the nineteenth century' and as such he was 'devoted to individualism, *laissez faire*, and the sanctity of private property'(1996, p150).

Despite his early relative poverty as the son of a local parish priest who died while Jung was at University, Jung did not come from an impoverished class, or a marginal ethnic group like Freud, so he lacked immediate grounds for being class-conscious or politically sensitive.

The earliest extant writings by Jung are the Zofingia student association lectures written between 1896 and 1899. In these lectures embryonic themes that run through Jung's life can be found. Jung in his first Zofingia lecture demonstrated a degree of student radicalism with a scathing attack on people's mercenary tendencies and their pursuit of 'careers' (Jung, 1896, §23, 29). Although such a radical perspective did not continue, his critique of materialism did. In a later lecture Jung argued that in the Middle Ages men's main concern was with their 'inner life' and that they were in 'much closer touch [with] nature' (Jung, 1983 [1898], §168,170) whereas now people were 'intoxicated by the pleasures of material success' to the extent that they were neither idealist nor spiritually inclined (Jung, 1983 [1898], §166).

In part, these ideas in Jung may have had early biographical roots and Brockway suggests that Jung may have been influenced by *Völkisch* hostility to industrial progress and urbanism. This feeling could have started in his school days when he saw the expansion of the chemical industry across his beloved Klein-Basel countryside (1996, p45). But we also have to consider the wider historical dimension. To understand Jung here we have to be aware of Paul Bishop's warning to place Jung's ideas in the development of European thought and be aware of the long running debate, as encapsulated by Kant, who had warned of the dangers of *'seelenloser Materialism'* [soulless materialism] and *'grundloser Spiritualism'* [groundless spiritualism] (1995, p187).[3] Jung with his religious agenda was always to be aware of the dangers of *seelenloser Materialism*. In another lecture Jung complained that this secularisation had even begun to influence philosophers like von Hartmann and Wundt (Jung, 1983 [1898], §167). The most eloquent example of his argument comes with a succinct synopsis of Schopenhauer's critique of material acquisitions leading to endless desire and dissatisfaction that could not be externally satisfied (Jung, 1983 [1898], §170). It is noticeable that as Jung developed his argument he gave what could later be understood as a telling affirmation of how introvert's security is derived from their inner world, while the extravert's comfort depends on transient external riches (Jung, 1983 [1898], §173).

From his autobiography one can deduce that his early poverty at university made him money-conscious. Once he was well married and professionally established he enjoyed living well and may have been too insulated in his middle-class niche, with enough rich American clients, to be naturally concerned about class. As Jung confided in 1954, 'I am, you know, a conservative' (McGuire and Hull, 1980, p235).

But is this the whole picture? There is a discussion between Kirsch and Haymond centred on this controversy. Haymond argued that Jung was politically very sheltered (1982), but Kirsch modified this suggestion. He conceded that Jung had limited horizons prior to his break with Freud, but suggested that after the break Jung's perspective became more politically differentiated (1982, p71). Furthermore Kirsch argues that Haymond is wrong to assert that Jung had no deep concern and did not comment on the two World Wars and the Depression in his writings (Haymond, 1982, p86, p88). Kirsch, who knew Jung, discusses the suggestion that Jung was uninterested in economic issues:

> Jung showed deep interest and concern about the incredible economic depression... I remember his anger and upset especially when Switzerland devalued the Franc in 1935. But he did not write about it because it was not his business as a psychiatrist. He suffered psychically very much during both world wars... His profound interest in the collective unconscious implies that 'he ascribes significance to the social and economic context.' But... he always paid attention to the aspect sociologists tend to neglect, the psychological one. (1982, p71)

This is a revealing summary, both through what it tells directly and through what it implies. Kirsch states that Jung was aware of economic issues, yet did not feel it was his place to write on such things. Jung *did* however comment on such things in seminars, for example on 13th February 1935: 'International commerce, for instance, and all the laws to provide decent international dealings have now gone to the wind. Of course, you can explain the German inflation through the extreme misery of those people after the war, but you cannot explain why America has gone off the gold standard; that was a crime, highway robbery, just as black as the swastika' (Jung, 1989 [1934-1939], p376-377). But even if Jung was deeply concerned, this does not tell one what lay at the root of his concern. Talking in the 1936 seminars Jung expressly condemned the decline in the economic and diplomatic trustworthiness of modern states. But it is not clear whether his outrage was based on his personal concern for his middle-class security or a wider concern about the political ramifications of economic instability. If the latter, it implies he was not as economically ignorant or selfish as some have suggested.

Against Kirsch's defence of Jung one can observe that although Jung may have had a 'profound interest in the collective unconscious', this does not mean that Jung ascribed a great deal of 'significance to the social and economic context', or as Burniston suggests, maybe Jung did see the significance but did not make the connection between his theory and his concerns (Burniston, 2007). In any event, for us the connection is more directly met by an interest in the collective conscious, which is the business of the sociologist and will be discussed in chapter four!

It is hard to form a clear picture of Jung's thoughts on property. Probably he was concerned in a material sense. He certainly was very interested in his material comfort, but the following quotation from 1936 seems to suggest that he was more aware of economic factors and of the devastating affects of the Depression on Germany. He wrote: 'She saw her money becoming elastic and expanding to astronomical proportions and then evaporating altogether... The whole educated middle-class was utterly ruined, but the State was on top, putting on more and more of the "-istic" rouge as war-paint. The country was in a condition of extreme misery and insecurity, and waves of panic swept over the population' (Jung, 1986 [1936a], §1323). This suggestion would imply an increasingly sophisticated political appreciation of world events by Jung as he took into account the internal state of the dictatorships and their external relationship with the democracies in Europe.

In contrast with some of his brutally pragmatic pronouncements on foreign policy, which will be examined later, Jung could be very egalitarian and humane. In 'Analytical Psychology and Weltanschauung' he advocated the need to be exposed to human suffering and included in his examples mental hospitals, prisons and the slums of London (Jung, 1991 [1928-1931b], §706).[4] To give another example, during the Second World War he was concerned at the plight of Switzerland's conscripts and advocated a universal wage level which was distinctly socialistic (Brome, 1980, p235), while in his 1941 essay 'Return to the Simple Life'' Jung condemned what could loosely be termed 'American' progress and 'materialism'. After the war Jung became more radical in his attitude to property and the need for all the population to have a sufficiently independent nurturing home environment.

In 1951 Jung repeated his concern with the merits of owning land and a private house, rather than a collective farm. He criticised the life of the industrial working class in large cities in ways similar to Marx's idea of 'alienation' and eulogised the Utopian workers' society. He also stressed that community was important, 'A community is based on personal relationships... Life in a small city is better than life in a large one, politically, socially and in terms of community relations. Big cities are responsible for our uprootedness' (McGuire and Hull, 1980, p201).

JUNG'S PERSPECTIVE ON THE FREUDIAN THREAT TO SPIRITUAL WELFARE AND THE RESILIENCE OF DEMOCRACY

A significant aspect of his thinking in the thirties was that he increasingly began to see a link between healthy spiritual values and the preservation of democracy. Jung was increasingly concerned that what he perceived as the Freudian stress on sexuality and antipathy to religion would accelerate the drift to secular materialism and that world without religion and faith would be more vulnerable to the demagogues.

The following two passages from the thirties make the connection between what Jung saw as a dangerous myopia in the Freudian concern with superficial 'childish tunes' while below this surface lurked the terrible pressures of archetypal history.

> All those personal things like incestuous tendencies and other childish tunes are mere surface; what the unconscious really contains are the great collective events of the time. In the collective unconscious of the individual, history prepares itself; and when the archetypes are activated in a number of individuals and come to the surface, we are in the midst of history... and everybody is seized by it. (Jung, 1986 [1935a], §371)

> ...a purely personalistic psychology, by reducing everything to personal causes, tries its level best to deny the existence of archetypal motifs... Today you can judge better than you could twenty years ago the

nature of the forces involved. Can we not see how a whole nation is reviving an archaic symbol, yes, even archaic religious forms, and how this mass emotion is influencing and revolutionizing the life of the individual in a catastrophic manner? The man of the past is alive in us today to a degree undreamed of before the war, and in the last analysis what is the fate of great nations but a summation of the psychic changes in individuals? (Jung, 1969 [1936], §97)

The following passage, which comes from the revised edition of 1952,[5] shows how Jung consciously or unconsciously continued to juxtapose his concern about reductive intellectualism (Freudian ideas) against his fear of political fanatics and his anxiety that if the emotional roots of religion were naively decoupled from their containing institutions, the resulting freely ranging devotional fervour would be at the mercy of hijacking by political demagogues.

What the 'blind faith' so long preached from the pulpit was able to do in Germany, when that country finally turned its back on Christian dogma, has been bloodily demonstrated before our eyes by contemporary history. *The really dangerous people are not the great heretics and unbelievers, but the swarm of petty thinkers, the rationalizing intellectuals, who suddenly discover how irrational all religious dogmas are.* Anything not understood is given short shrift, and the highest values of symbolic truth are irretrievably lost. What can a rationalist do with the dogma of the virgin birth, or with Christ's sacrificial death, or the Trinity? (Jung, 1911-12 / 52, §339, my italics)

The passage is significant as it gives an insight into Jung's emotional state with the extraordinary insensitivity of his linking the Freudian 'rationalizing intellectuals' and the Nazis. This eloquently suggests how Jung's anger at the 'campaign' could affect his words and thoughts, and this entrenched the tragic cycle of mutual anger and misunderstanding. From all this we see how

Jung's argument that 'religious' health was vital for democracy was imprisoned within the theoretical conflict with Freud and, while he was later able to make some attempt to heal the personal breach, he continued to hold to this part of his thinking.

JUNG'S ATTITUDE TO SWISS DEMOCRACY

In reviewing Jung's general political beliefs, the most conspicuous factor was his conscientious support of Swiss democracy. According to von Franz, Jung remained a 'liberal' in a non-political sense from his early views in the Zofingia club to his later electoral politics and seldom voted for the conservative party in Zurich (Jung, 1983, p.xv, xix). However, this does not mean he was very political. Given the monumental workload he carried through his life, it would be surprising if he were able to devote much time to politics. On a related point, about his political sophistication and his involvement in the politics of early psychoanalysis, Samuels points out that the correspondence between Freud and Jung shows Jung to have been more interested in organisational politics than he has been credited with, or sought to portray himself (1985, p2). Here it might be useful to make a distinction between having an interest in politics and the active involvement in organisational issues which was always a concern to Freud.

When trying to assess Jung's level of political activity it is also important to consider which period of Jung's life one is studying. In the case of the early psychoanalytic years, Jung was a relatively young man with a vested interest in building up a field and his place in it. Later he could afford to be more institutionally anarchic, and it is his image from this time that has remained with many people.

Jung's student association had a long tradition of liberal ideals combined with a Swiss nationalist support for the army and state (Jung, 1983, p.xv). He showed a great love of his native Switzerland (Hannah, 1976, p.13) and while he was conscious of being part of the German-speaking world, he did not confuse his German culture with his Swiss identity.[6] Ellenberger noted that it is part of the Swiss culture to be interested in the past and have loyalty to its memory and one's ancestors (1970, p650). This aspect of Swiss life could have reinforced Jung's conservative disposition, as

Jung was mindful of the past with his ideas on the psychological effects of past generations.

Jung was proud of his military service which was a mandatory part of his Swiss civic duty (von Franz, 1975, p65). As a young man Jung enjoyed military parades (Donn, 1976, p73). In 1895 he began his service with the infantry, and in 1901 he became an officer in the medical corps where he was promoted to captain in 1908. In 1914 he became a commander of a unit, until his retirement in 1930 (Jung, 1974 [1906-1914], p74, fn8). If at first he had hated his military service, once he got his commission he confided to a friend: 'The military arts have their satisfactions—I let loose a lot of aggression in them. But the only satisfactory role is that of General' (Brome, 1980, p63, p74). During the First World War, he served as the commandant of a Swiss POW camp and eventually held the rank of *Sanitatshauptmann* (a Medical Corps Colonel [Kirsch, 1982, p74]). The later periods of reserve duty afforded him a break from his clinical practice and gave him time and space to review his ideas. This was especially important during his psychological crisis following his break with Freud where the external order of service life helped provide him with stability to support his embattled sanity. All these factors gave him a positive attitude to his military service but there is no evidence that Jung's military involvement affected his political or psychological views significantly.[7]

JUNG'S PERSPECTIVE ON THE STATE AND THE INDIVIDUAL: ORDER AND DEMOCRACY

For historians it is often difficult to attempt to reconstruct someone's position from infrequent and scattered evidence. But as Jung made a number of statements about the political structure of society it may be possible to identify certain themes.

In his Zofingia lectures, despite his early radical critique of materialism, Jung was willing to credit the benefits of industrial progress and 'the modern nation state'. He uncritically acknowledged the 'well ordered states... social development... the smooth fitting structure of the modern nation-state' (Jung, 1983 [1898], §166) and the way the state 'redistributes [material success] in a diluted form, to all the members of the confederation' (Jung, 1983 [1898], §174).

However, he began to see that the development of the modern state and nationalism posed a threat to the individual. He warned, 'Modern man is characterised by an immanent egotism... Modern man knows nothing of the individual. The individuals he knows are cantons and nation states. As a rule he has already lost his consciousness of himself as an individual. He feels that he is an atom, a mere link in the endless chain that makes up the state. Modern man shifts responsibility for the creation of individual happiness from himself to the state' (Jung, 1983 [1898], §168). Jung then added that: 'modern man seeks to level, that is, to wipe out, individuality by educating everyone, as much as possible, to be exactly the same' (Jung, 1983 [1898], §168).

Jung briefly linked together 'nationalism, the total devotion to the state [and] social democracy' (Jung, 1983 [1898], §166). But his sympathies were more with Nietzsche who he quoted when he denounced the idea that 'man has no higher duty than to serve the state... as... stupidity'[8] (Jung, 1983 [1898], §166). In this context he was witheringly critical of the inter-penetration of church and state (Jung, 1983 [1898], §166), which was even more evident in Protestant Lutheranism.

As an adult Jung may have become even more scathing in his attitude to politics. For example, in 1928 he stated: 'For society as an abstract thing I don't care a hang, but I am connected with society through the representatives of society, those nearest to me, beginning with my own wife, children, relatives, and friends, the bridges that connect me with society' (Jung, 1991 [1928]-30, p27). This was Jung at his most individualistic, and statements of this timbre have led numerous commentators to question Jung's perspective on social issues. For example, Haymond criticised Jung's indiscriminate lumping of three European revolutions together, in *Mysterium Coniunctionis*, written between 1941 and 1954, as an act of 'glib' sociological analysis (1982, p87). Alschuler went even further when he thought that Jung displayed a negative attitude to mass movements by condemning in general terms such widely different revolutions as those of the American, the French, and Russian revolutions (1997, p282). He went on to suggest that Jung was pathologising politics (1997, p282). He suggests that in *The Undiscovered Self* (1957) Jung argued that political mass movements were made up of numbers of individuals who suffered from a pathological split between the conscious and the unconscious. This had come about through the need for consciousness to suppress the instincts and the irrational. Alschuler's concern is that Jung concentrated on the role of the individual, be it as a leader or as one of the led, but ignored how the system generates and manages trouble. He concludes that Jung's thought is one-sided, emphasising the pathological more than the normal, and the individual more than systemic political behaviour (1997, p282).

How valid is Alschuler's critique? Clearly Jung's appreciation of an aristocratic or oligarchic political order was very much in the tradition of Burkhardian Swiss Republicanism and its suspicion of mass rule (Pietikäinen, 1999, p297) but in considering Jung's views it is all too easy to get a strong impression from some statements and neglect others. Instead more care is often needed to explore his thoughts more fully.

In a modification of his largely optimistic attitude in the Zofingia lectures, by the thirties Jung had begun to show a more pessimistic view of society. This is hardly surprising as the Depression and the thirties profoundly shook the confidence of the democratic states. As Michael Burleigh reminds us, in today's world where capitalist democracy is in the ascendant, it takes 'an effort of the imagination' to recall that the democracies of France and Britain struggled with internal divisions and responded with appeasement to the expansionist challenge from the fascist 'states of the future'. Indeed, 'by 1939 undemocratic regimes already outnumbered constitutional democracies by sixteen to twelve' (2000, p61). The democracies of Western Europe were fighting a cold war and their survival was by no means assured.

In looking at Jung's views at this time a number of themes become apparent.

Democracy Needs Sufficient Internal Order if it is to Survive under Threat.

Jung's poor opinion of massed people and his subsequent concern for basic order gave him an increasingly ambivalent view of the State. Jung extended Le Bon's and Durkheim's pessimism about crowds and saw the State as an equally crude counter-force. As he said on 26th June 1935, 'against the monster of the people you have the monster of the state, and that is simply a necessary evil; there are no other means. You cannot rule a people by decent means... you cannot keep it in order by good intentions and pious words and nice deeds because they won't be appreciated. The people only appreciate it when they beat or when they are beaten. That is a fact, and it is perfectly ridiculous to think of ruling people by kindness and wisdom: that is just air' (Jung, 1989 [1934-1939], p585). This was brutally authoritarian, but it was a private statement where Jung was prone to speak with exaggerated élan, which was raised even higher as Jung was 'speaking with Nietzsche's voices and his own which added to the drama of the occasion' (Burniston, 2007).

In the inter-war period, as turbulence swept Europe, Jung became increasingly pessimistic about democracy's chances of survival. His concern was sharpened by the awareness of the brutality and anarchy in many states. He began to realise the urgent need for some sort of order in many of these countries. Jung's evolving perspective, and his concern for order in the thirties shows how one needs to take care when examining Jung's relationship to contemporary politics. Jung's weakness for expressing himself crudely, especially when he was being interviewed or writing in private letters did not mean he held such crude opinions when he had the leisure to express himself more exactly. In the confusion of national identities and economic uncertainty of the times, Jung spoke on 30th October 1935 in praise of a strong national consciousness, a need for some consensus of ideology and firm leadership (1934-1939, p647). Such views cannot simply be dismissed as a reflex apology for authoritarian government; in those times confusion and anarchy were real threats to society and the rule of law. The fact that later horrors have overshadowed the excesses after World War One should not blind one to the thousands killed by Lenin's consolidation of power after the civil war or the brutality of the revolution in Hungary and the murders on both sides as the communist revolt was put down in Bavaria.

In 1936 Jung again spoke out against left-wing unrest: 'Communistic or Socialistic democracy is an upheaval of the unfit against attempts at order. Consider the stay-in strikes in France, the former socialistic upheavals in Germany and Italy. This state of disorder called democratic freedom or liberalism brings its own reactions—enforced order... The dictatorships of Germany, Russia, and Italy may not be the best form of government, but they are the only possible form of government at the moment' (Jung, 1937 [1936], p341). In this statement he was ignoring debates about the moral situation or local politics, which left him open to charges of crudity, but in terms of his pessimistic pragmatism, he proved to be correct. The demagogues were exploiting anarchy and winning from Portugal to Moscow.

Despite this pragmatism Jung was capable of considering the political evolution of the dictatorships. The problem for the reader is that his thoughts were spontaneous and scattered. That same year when he was asked what he thought would happen after the dictators, he replied:

> After the dictators? Oligarchy in some form. A decent oligarchy—call it aristocracy if you like—is the most ideal form of government. It depends on the quality of a nation whether they evolve a decent oligarchy or not. I am not sure that Russia will, but Germany and Italy have a chance.
>
> Without the aristocratic ideal there is no stability. You in England owe it to the 'gentleman' that you possess the world. (McGuire and Hull, 1980, p104)

The statement's plausibility is compromised because, by not fully acknowledging all the healthy democracies of the Anglo-Saxon world, Jung was giving an unbalanced picture of European civilisation and was getting carried away by his own oratory. But one should not make the mistake of assuming he was commenting on the viability of democracy as such. Nor should one give too much weight to the comment about England, as it was a comment on her imperial past, not her egalitarian present.

This statement was not just a eulogy for a platonic elite. But read in context, one realises that Jung was talking about those European states where democracy was too young and had failed. Jung recognised that democracy presupposes stability and the rule of law. As he said elsewhere 'Compulsory order seems to be preferable to the terrors of chaos, at all events the lesser of two great evils. Orders, I am afraid have to be heard in silence' (Jung, 1986 [1936a], §1342). It is important to stress that for him dictatorship was not the ideal. Dictatorship would 'not be the best form of government', but any country first had to be given 'a chance' to establish a minimum of order. Here Jung was being pragmatic. In a similar vein he showed no sympathy with those democratic citizens who complained without recognising the reality of how badly much of Europe was regressing and democracy was in danger of becoming 'a bad comedy' (Jung, 1986 [1936a], §1342).

On another occasion in 1935, while discussing the idea of leadership, Jung explained that a disintegrating society would be only too vulnerable to an outside aggressor (Jung, 1989 [1934-1939], p-646). To illustrate this vividly one can contrast the relatively successful defiance of Soviet Russia by tiny Finland during the winter war, with the unprecedented collapse of France against the more equally matched Germany in 1940. While Finland was united under Marshal Mannerheim, France was undermined by internal divisions and rapidly collapsed.[9]

THE STATE CAN BE A THREAT TO DEMOCRACY

Some of Jung's statements were derived from the way Jung psychologised the State and then drew conclusions from this diagnosis. Jung suggested that the State exhibited a psychological process that mirrored that of the individual: 'The State is the psychological mirror-image of the democracy monster. As the nation always rises as one man, the State is just as good as one man. As a matter of fact it is quite a person, of unlimited means, more exacting than any tyrant ever was, greedy to the limit and biologically dangerous' (Jung, 1986 [1936a], §1318-1320). This psychologising occurred continually in Jung's thought, indeed his penchant for transposing psychological processes onto social or historical entities or ideas was a fundamental characteristic of his collective theories.

In 1936, although Jung referred to 'the democracy monster', he was not undertaking a wholesale condemnation of democracy, but rather developing some of his Nietzschian pessimism which dated back to his Zofingia lecture on how the growing infrastructure of the State undermined democracy. He went on to suggest that the ideology embodied in the slogan 'for the good of the state' had swallowed the democratic reality. He further suggested that the developed large modern State was abrogating to itself so much power at the cost of individual participation that the forms of government were evolving into Socialism and Communism and away from participatory democracy. People were thus controlled by an impersonal bureaucratic State, indeed Democracy had been swallowed by the ghost called 'the State'. He also suggested that over-taxation stifled initiative. Taken together, these arguments show an ultra-liberal attitude akin to contemporary American libertarianism which could not be further away from the anti-democratic leanings Jung has been accused of!

Jung's Ambivalent Attitude to Party Politics

The last area to be looked at concerns Jung's relationship to party politics. This comes from a comment from September 1936 when Jung travelled to America to give a lecture at the Harvard Tercentenary Celebrations. When his boat arrived in New York harbour he prepared a statement[10] to give to waiting journalists to disarm the expected controversy following various accusations suggesting that Jung held Nazi sympathies. When the communiqué is studied with care a number of things become apparent.

Jung starts paragraph 1301 and ends paragraph 1303 by using charm on his American audience, which was good political salesmanship. He then went on to explain his position and the terms in which he did this shows he was aware of the controversies that had dogged him.

> As a psychologist I am deeply interested in mental disturbances, particularly when they infect whole nations. I want to emphasize that I despise politics wholeheartedly: thus I am neither a Bolshevik, nor a National Socialist, nor an anti-Semite.

He then went on to try to explain his position as not being one of crude hostility to politics but an attempt to look even deeper into the causes of events.

> I am a neutral Swiss and even in my own country I am uninterested in politics, because I am convinced that 99 per cent of politics are mere symptoms and anything but a cure for social evils. About 50 per cent of politics is definitely obnoxious inasmuch as it poisons the utterly incompetent mind of the masses. We are on our guard against contagious diseases of the body, but we are exasperatingly careless when it comes to the even more dangerous collective diseases of the mind.

He exaggerated his lack of interest in Swiss domestic politics to try and reinforce his antipathy to political ideology and this line of argument then ran into a general 'pathologisation' of politics which his critics have so taken against. This was unfortunately part of Jung's style as he was just talking about the wider issues that he was anxious about (*'I am neither a Bolshevik, nor a National Socialist, nor an anti-Semite'*). In this way he exaggerated and then inadvertently admitted his position: 'I make this statement in order to disillusion any attempt to claim me for any particular political party.' Jung then continued for almost half the article by giving his ideas about the interrelation of the 'differences in national and racial psychology' but shorn of the detail of the German-Jewish situation and Jung's entanglement in that area.

> I have some reason for it, since my name has been repeatedly drawn into the political discussion, which is, as you best know, in a feverish condition actually. It happened chiefly on account of the fact that I am interested in the undeniable differences in national and racial psychology, which chiefly account for a series of most fatal misunderstandings and practical mistakes in international dealings as well as in internal social frictions. In a politically poisoned and overheated atmosphere the sane and dispassionate scientific discussion of such delicate, yet most important problems has become well-nigh impossible. To discuss such matters in public would be about as successful as if the direct-

or of a lunatic asylum were to set out to discuss the particular delusions of his patients in the midst of them. You know, the tragicomical thing is that they are all convinced of their normality as much as the doctor himself of his own mental balance. (1936g, §1302)

There 'the political discussion' and 'politically poisoned and overheated atmosphere' that he referred to was probably the politicised debates in the psycho-analytic world and his conflict with the 'campaign'? In summing up this article which superficially could be taken as a rejection of democratic politics, one instead finds that it contains:

- Some mild political flattery.
- A defence of Jung's antipathy to party ideology.
- An exaggerated apolitical rhetoric driven by anxiety.
- A cloaked continuation of his struggle with the 'campaign'.

Another aspect of Jung's awareness of political dynamics was his warning about the seductive power of abstract ideas in ideology. Jung came to this while discussing the decline of the West's cultural identity on 12th November 1930 in the Visions seminars. There he began to discuss the 'guiding ideas' that shape one's *Weltanschauung*, and he borrowed the word 'mantra', 'the word of power'. To explain how this worked he mentioned Carl Spitteler (1845-1924), a Swiss poet who referred to the 'invisible whale on a pole.' Jung explained Spittler's idea:

> Whenever anybody wants to say something very convincing, to express his point of view which is really not convincing at all, he points to that invisible whale on the pole, and then everybody believes him. All our abstract German nouns end with 'heit' or 'keit,' and therefore so do all our general concepts: for instance, if you say something is done for the liberty of the country, 'Freiheit,' everybody believes it; that is Spitteler's invisible whale. In America 'social service' is

> the mantra that is believed in. Every country has such a whale, sometimes several. In France, *'pour la gloire de notre patrie'* carries. In Italy, under Mussolini, it is 'Italy is at work.' The most formidable nonsense goes under the cover of 'heit' and 'keit'; that is a mantra, a sort of slogan. (Jung, 1998 [1930-1934], p75)

This critique of rhetoric is applicable to both the democratic politician's lofty 'Education, Education, Education' or the dictator's lauding 'the people's will'. They are all whales and Jung was shrewd to warn of the danger they represented.

For all these criticisms of democratic states, one should not be in any doubt about Jung's commitment to democracy or his critique of the dictators. He could not have been clearer than when he declared:

> Now we behold the amazing spectacle of states taking over the age-old totalitarian claims of theocracy, which are inevitably accompanied by suppression of free opinion. Once more we see people cutting each other's throats in support of childish theories of how to create paradise on earth. [They] are now creating, or trying to create, a State slavery and a State prison devoid of any mental or spiritual charm. (Jung, 1938-40, §83)

Jung grimly saw events as a trial between the evils of chaos and dictatorship and he did not regard either of these regressions as progress. This is seen even more clearly in a letter from February 16th 1939, where Jung declared: 'There is no such thing as a liberal dictatorship, because a dictator just can't afford to be liberal' (Allan, 1992, p149-151). The letter also contains a plea for an understanding of the impact of the irrational: 'The goal of life is not and cannot be a continuous improvement of conditions because if conditions become better, the people become worse. The only sensible goal can be the increase of understanding and wisdom. Everything else is bunk!' (Allan, 1992, p150). Yet in the letter he was scathing about political 'humbug' in America, he urged the end of American isolationism, showed a level of pessimism that is understandable given the approaching war, and finished with a ringing endorsement of political realism:

> The world is not ideal, as man is not ideal. If one slips through with one's existence, if nations just can manage to live in relative safety having a reasonable amount of food, it is all they can ever wish for. We all ought to be happy if we just happen to have no revolution, no war and no epidemics. Existence has always been a fight and will ever be one. (Allan, 1992, p149-151)

Summing up this period, Jung continued to show a fear of large states, or the ability of democracy to thrive in them. As he declared in 1938, 'a nation is a monster. Everybody ought to fear a nation. It is a horrible thing. How can such a thing have honour or a word? That's why I am for small nations. Small nations mean small catastrophes. Big nations mean big catastrophes' (McGuire and Hull, 1980, p140). But if one considers this passage, one sees that Jung's contempt was aimed at mass democracy in huge states, not the local affairs of a smaller country like Switzerland.

When it came to democracy and Switzerland, Jung was quite clear where his sympathies lay and was prepared to act on them. With the outbreak of war, an independent political coalition called *Landesring der Unabhängigen* asked Jung to stand for the National Council. Jung proposed that all Swiss males should be mobilized for the duration and that all earnings above the military pay level should go to the public purse so that the country was unified and soldiers not disadvantaged (Pietikäinen, 1999, p, 259). Much to his relief he was not elected, but clearly Jung was prepared to advocate measures that would have severely disadvantaged a wealthy man such as himself, that is no small indication of his commitment to democracy!

Looking at the evolution of Jung's views, one can see that over time he came to see how fragile democracy was amid the horrors of war and how brutal the alternatives were in the revolutionary politics of left and right. As with so many issues Jung was able to change others' ideas creatively. After carefully reviewing Jung's politics, Pietikäinen acknowledges that Jung was heavily identified with the culture of the German scholarly elite and their suspicion of modernity and materialist science, which could have anti-Semitic overtones given the equation of Jews and materialism; but this trend must be qualified by acknowledging that Jung displayed many key differences; as a Swiss he was firmly identified with the moderate liberal conservative spirit of the Swiss middle classes. Unlike his German peers he was an independent doctor not a state employee and his own psychological school was highly innovative of both secular medicine and the psycho-analytic dogma. Furthermore Jung was hostile to state control and condemned all extreme ideologies. He was very open to other cultural ideas that ran parallel with his ideas on individuation and so, for the times in which he lived, was remarkably free of Eurocentrism (1999, p251-2).

Jung's Perspective on Realism and the Individual's Effective Political Action

In the *Visions* seminars Jung, while discussing how the Great War had swept away the naïve optimism of the nineteenth century, considered the looming crisis in Europe. He argued that the only solution, the only 'magic', was for individuals to acknowledge the shadow side of the psyche and balance their awareness of the higher and lower psychological states in themselves, then maybe if enough people did this, disarmament could happen. But, he added, the illusion that good aspirations alone would constellate progress he regarded as a delusion and 'black magic'.

> So we have attained a higher consciousness, we have scored one point; we are no longer so certain in our convictions, we now allow the deep shadow of humanity to exist, and that means a certain progress; we have at least got our heads above the mist. That suggests that we should not only manipulate the powers of good as we said before, but we might also manipulate the powers of evil by a superior consciousness, and thereby work some magic. *I do not believe in magic made by man, magic as made in Germany or in Great Bri-*

> tain or in America; it does not work. But I firmly believe in the natural magic of facts. I believe in the rain maker of *Kiao Tchou*—that one should do the right thing to oneself and by oneself, and wait until the rain falls. Perhaps when that process of doing the right thing in an individual case has been repeated often enough and by as many people as possible, the rain will actually fall, a result will be reached which could not be reached in any, other way. Then another miracle might happen, disarmament might become possible. But such a thing will never come to pass as long as one tries to work black magic, to pull the wool over one's eyes...*The mere thought that one could raise oneself above humanity and pull strings is a black-magic thought which I would utterly discourage.* Put yourself below humanity, and see whether you are just as wrong as mankind in general; do the right thing by yourself and then something can happen, then the rain can fall. That would be the right procedure according to my conviction. (Jung, 1998 [1930-1934], p1204-5, 29th November 1933, my italics)

I am aware that to offer this lengthy quotation of Jung on political action with a Taoist reference in the middle may once again evoke thoughts that Jung was a mystic. That seems unfair given Jung's requirement that there be enough people with enough internal and external realism to change the climate of events. That is demanding of Jung, but it is hardly mysticism for as he had warned on the 10th of May, 'One sees all over the world that the true argument is the cannon and the machine gun' (Jung, 1998 [1930-1934], p972).

Did Jung Favour Dictators?

As McLynn has suggested that Jung was the holder of 'extreme right-wing political views', and it has also been suggested that Jung had an unconscious predilection for autocrats or right wing dictators, the evidence must be considered again. This time we will look at things from a slightly different angle.

There is a suggestion that Jung had an overly positive attitude to powerful leaders which may have had its root in his difficult relationship with his father and with paternal authority figures. Indeed, Jung stated: 'I also admit my so-called "father complex": I do not want to knuckle under to any "fathers" and never shall' (Jung, 1991 [1934a], §1026).[11] This complex in part contributed to his schism with Freud and, so the argument could run, as a counter-reaction he may have had an element in his psyche with a predisposition to look favourably on strong leadership to make up for these failed fathers.

An early manifestation of this bias was identified by von Franz. She suggested in her introduction to *The Zofingia Lectures* that in Jung's third lecture (1897/98), there was a '"heroic" undertone' and an admiration for great political leaders (Jung, 1983, p.xix). She suggests that Jung later in December 1913 abandoned this 'heroic' perspective after a dream in which he shot down the hero-figure Siegfried, and interpreted this as an indication from the unconscious that he must outgrow his power drive.[12] From then on he gave up his hope in external cures for man's problems and instead sought answers in the 'primitive', in the unconscious.

Was von Franz correct and how successful was Jung in outgrowing his attraction to the heroic? This will be explored in this chapter by examining his obvious appreciation of Roosevelt and Mussolini; and the issue will be returned to later when trying to assess Jung's attitude to Hitler and his theorising about charismatic leadership.

To begin with, Jung voiced reservations about the power and personality of the American president. At Harvard in September 1936, Jung told how in Europe he had the impression that Roosevelt 'was an opportunist, perhaps even an erratic mind. Now that I have seen him and heard him... I am convinced that here is a strong man, a man who is really great. Perhaps that's why many people do not like him' (McGuire and Hull, 1980, p99). A month later, looking back on the American trip, he recalled his views about Roosevelt: 'Make no mistake, he is a force—a man of superior and impenetrable mind, but perfectly ruthless, a highly versatile mind which you cannot foresee. He has the most amazing power complex, the Mussolini substance, the stuff of a dictator absolutely'

(McGuire and Hull, 1980, p103). These are strong words, but if Jung approved of Roosevelt as a strong leader, this was not support for a dictator and one wonders if Jung felt it prudent to praise the American leader in the hope of winning support for his ideas in America.

Evidently Jung admired strong personalities. Between 1923 and 1939, there were a number of occasions when Jung described *Il Duce* in a positive light as a charismatic character. For example, in 1939 he stated: 'Mussolini has a certain vitality about him. He is a man—natural, warm, rough and ruthless. If he says 'no' he means no. He can speak as a real person' (McGuire and Hull, 1980, p143). But Jung was also highly critical. In 1936 Jung described Hitler and Mussolini as: 'more or less ordinary human beings... [who] assume that they themselves know what to do in a situation which practically nobody understands.' He went on to dismiss their claims of 'superhuman courage' as 'superhuman recklessness to shoulder a responsibility which apparently nobody else is willing or able to carry' (Jung, 1986 [1936a], §1333).

In the Knickerbocker interview which took place in October 1938 just after the demise of Czechoslovakia, and was published in January 1939, Jung described Mussolini as a 'man of physical strength. When you see him you are aware of it at once. His body suggests good muscles. He is the chief by reason of the fact that he is individually stronger than any of his competitors' (McGuire and Hull, 1980, p124). Later in the interview he stated: 'When the Fascists took power in Italy, Mussolini did not even remove the King. Mussolini worked not with ecstasy of Spirit, but with a hammer in his hand, beating Italy into the shape he wanted it.' Jung explained that he 'had discerned in Mussolini's conduct a certain style, a certain format of an original man with good taste in certain matters.' Jung cites as examples of Mussolini's style the choice of the title of *'Duce'*, leader, rather than anything more grandiose. Jung also approved of Mussolini's obvious enjoyment of a military parade 'with the zest of a small boy at a circus', which showed his feelings, unlike Hitler who seemed like an automaton. Jung unfavourably compared the two dictators: 'What an amazing difference there is between Hitler and Mussolini! I couldn't help liking Mussolini. His bodily energy and elasticity are warm, human, and contagious.

You have the homely feeling with Mussolini of being with a human being. With Hitler, you are scared. You know you would never be able to talk to that man: because there is nobody there' (McGuire and Hull, 1980, p132-134).

Later on January 22nd 1941 Jung commented in a similar way to Catharine Rush Cabot,

> [T]he first time Mussolini met Hitler, he exclaimed, *"Ma che è un Signorino!"* [Why, he is but a boy!] Mussolini is all that he is on the surface, whereas Hitler, on the surface, is all that he is not. Hitler is sinister—like the mild little schoolmaster who has lived and taught all his life in a quiet village, and whom everyone presumes to be harmless. Then, suddenly, this mild little man ups and murders his whole family. Mussolini's life is a reality, and everything that he is in the foreground: it is in his face and manner and in his every gesture. Hitler is just the contrary; he can only impress a German who is very intuitive and who 'smells' what is behind Hitler. Hitler is infected by the Unconscious and only a person who is 'infected' can 'infect'. (Cabot Reid, 2001, p322)

The Knickerbocker interview and this anecdote show the contrast in Jung's attitude to the two dictators. If one compares what he says about Mussolini to what he says about Hitler, one finds that his thoughts on the latter are more psychologically detailed, and almost all highly critical.[13] However, these thoughts on Hitler were sometimes expressed in a fashion that is double-edged and easy to misinterpret as will be discussed in chapter nine.

From all this one observes that Jung, like many, was taken in by Mussolini's public posture of dynamic efficiency, which was very different from the private reality. Jung was not the only one to misjudge *Il Duce*. For a time the British Foreign Office hoped to recruit him as an ally against Hitler, and he received praise from conservative British statesmen like Eden, Halifax, and Churchill, even after Italy invaded Abyssinia. His admirers even included Mahatma Gandhi who, accompanied by his goat, visited Mussolini

(Redlich, 1998, p138).[14] Freud too misjudged the character of Mussolini so badly that in the book written by Einstein and himself, 'Why War?', (1932), he wrote as the dedication: 'For Benito Mussolini with the humble greeting of an old man, who recognises the cultural hero in the ruler.—Vienna 26.4.33. Freud'[15] (Jaffé, 1989, p93). Freud also was naively impressed that Mussolini had 'educated' the Italians to run their trains on time (Rieff, 1990, p55-56).

But whatever Jung's naïve sympathy for Mussolini as a man, when it came to politics, Jung was capable of recognising the good and bad in Fascist Italy. On the 13th February 1935, he acknowledged the rise in living conditions: 'One cannot help admitting that Fascism has done any amount of good for Italy; it is a different country' (Jung, 1989 [1934-1939], p376-377). Yet when it came to Mussolini's grandiose foreign adventures he remarked very early on: 'And look at Italy! It is as if she had not lost half a million young men. They are propagating like rabbits down there in preparation. It is the psychology of despair. That is what Mussolini is doing. Everywhere it looks as if nothing had been learned' (Jung, 1998 [1930-1934], p76). One can also see continuity in Jung's perspective on Mussolini as he wrote to Hans Illing on the 26th January 1955: 'Socially good results have to be paid for too, usually later, but then with interest and compound interest (witness the Mussolini era in Italy and its catastrophic end)' (Jung, 1976 [1951-1961], p221).

Some have suggested that Jung's statements of approval for Mussolini stemmed from an admiration of strong leaders. Certainly Jung was no admirer of anarchy, but nor was he an admirer of dictatorship. Could it be that a more powerful motive to account for Jung's obvious warmth for Mussolini was a sense of fellow feeling? Maybe Jung was just sympathetic to someone he had some similarities with because, while their professions could not be more different, both men enjoyed parades, possessed rugged physical strength and projected energetic masculinity, as well as being keen family men and enjoying the company of women.[16] Overall, if one considers Jung's statements on the Fascist autocrats, Mussolini got rather benign treatment while his Fascist party and conditions in Italy got barely a mention. This may indicate how little information Jung had on Italy, or how little events there concerned him in contrast to Germany. Germany's centrality is also demonstrated by Jung's neglect of Franco, who one might suppose Jung would have approved of as he restored order after a civil war against anarchists and communists, yet he receives barely a mention in the Collected Works.

On Jung's general attitude, Andrew Samuels has suggested that the letter of February 16th 1939 (referred to previously on page), shows that Jung had rejected any positive ideas about dictatorship (Allan, 1992, p149-151). But this may not be so. Jung may have rejected the possibility of a 'liberal dictatorship', but he had not yet begun to see dictatorship as worse than his horror of absolute anarchy. Dictatorship was still seen as a provisional evil. Perhaps it was only when the world learnt of the horrors Hitler had unleashed that Jung finally rejected any positive ideas about dictatorship.

Jung's Post-War Thoughts on the Masses, the State and Democracy

How did Jung's post-war political views change? After the Second World War, he continued to be suspicious of large states and commented on 6th September 1947: 'mass man breeds mass catastrophe. The greatest dangers today are the huge mass States like Russia and America. However, history teaches that such monsters are usually short-lived' (Jung, 1973 [1906-1950], p476). He took a more balanced attitude when he showed a realistic appreciation of the terrible organisational burdens governments wrestle with in the complex modern State when he stated on 31st October 1946: 'Of course governments could do something, but nowadays when you want anything from any government you are referred to the world situation, which causes the governments enough headaches as it is and leaves them no time to think about how the death penalty could be abolished or human life made sacred' (Jung, 1973 [1906-1950], p446).

On 2nd July 1948, he looked back on the horrors of mass movements and drew the distinction between the freedom of a democratic peoples and their 'splendid team work', even in large democracies, and the 'helpless formidable masses' of the dictatorships. Thus Jung seemed to have re-evaluated his views on the viability of the large democracies. His recognition and fear of the compulsion of such large groups could not be more clearly seen than in his assertion that: 'Le Bon does not mean theories, he means the facts. It is difficult to get around them' (Jung, 1973 [1906-1950], p504).

If Jung had become more tolerant of large democracies, he was still highly suspicious of the state apparatus. Jung's last and longest analysis of the State came in *The Undiscovered Self* written in 1956. He reaffirmed his perspective of the State as a 'quasi-animate personality', but added an almost Marxian twist that: 'In reality it is only a camouflage for those individuals who know how to manipulate it' (Jung, 1991 [1957], §504). Indeed Jung showed a level of distaste for mass man that matched his 1909 interview. He argued that the greater the numbers of people, the greater the credulity, greed and childish unquestioning dependence on exploitative leaders. 'In the clamour of the many resides the power to snatch wish-fulfilment's by force; sweetest of all, however, is that gentle and painless slipping back into the kingdom of childhood... The infantile dream-state of the mass man is so unrealistic that he never thinks to ask who is paying for this paradise' (Jung, 1991 [1957], §538).

In direct contrast to this pessimism, in this late work Jung took care to explore his original, or continual interest with the religious dimension of political life. This was hardly surprising as the religious dimension had always been one of his primary concerns. In these thoughts Jung brought together his democratic values, his Swiss love of small democracies, his suspicion of large groups, and his concern for spiritual values. In doing this he unified various aspects and trends in his thinking that had a long evolution. With *The Undiscovered Self* Jung's perspective had escaped from his prewar polemic and broadened its perspective to look beyond his earlier plea for general religious values.

For democracy to survive he argued that fellow-feeling and charity were vital. Thus Jung brought into his equation the social health of society as indispensable to the wider democracy and the individual's spiritual health. Jung mixed his concern about the 'atomisation' of modern industrial society with the horrors of the dictator states where 'justice is uncertain and police spying and terror are at work, human beings fall into isolation, which, of course, is the aim and purpose of the dictator State'. He was also concerned about the ideological and emotional threat posed by the Soviet block and added: 'It would therefore be very much in the interest of the free society to give some thought to the question of human relationship... for in this resides its real cohesion and consequently its strength. Where love stops, power begins, and violence, and terror' (Jung, 1991 [1957], §580). Here Jung was fully acknowledging the social dimension and was also demonstrating a very realistic appreciation of Cold War politics, which was hardly psychologising and pathologising.

At the same time Jung gave thought to the neo-religious ideology of the dictator states. He returned to the argument about a non-religious society being more vulnerable to fanatical totalitarian ideologies, but in the post-war years he dropped the anti-Freudian component of this argument. He again argued that without an internal religious point of reference the individual was too vulnerable to the external pressures of mass society and the tyranny of the state (Jung, 1991 [1957], §511). Furthermore he thought that the 'dictator State' often 'takes the place of God; that is why, seen from this angle, the socialist dictatorships are religions and State slavery is a form of worship.' For Jung this was a falsification of the 'religious function' that was obscured by ruthless ideological fanaticism; but beneath this one can detect a range of religious phenomena, which included demigods, martyrs, apostles and heretics. In such a situation: 'Only the party boss, who holds the political power in his hands, can interpret the State doctrine authentically, and he does so just as suits him' (Jung, 1991 [1957], §511-512).

Explaining further, Jung argued that the 'religious function' was 'natural function'. However, it had two influences in a dictatorship. Firstly men need to have an outlet for the instinct, which could be exploited. In this way the religious function is 'evilly distorted—in the deification of the State and the dictator' who cynically hide their exploitation of religion with protestations of 'atheism' (Jung, 1991 [1957], §514).

JUNG' POST WAR THOUGHTS ON THE SOVIETS

While Jung's lifestyle was all that one might expect of a wealthy cosmopolitan academic, his politics were not simple or stereotypically reactionary. Given this flexibility it may not be surprising that in 1934 he could write: 'If the doctors of Petersburg [sic] or Moscow had sought my help I would have acceded without hesitation, because I am concerned with human beings and not with Bolsheviks —and if I was then inevitably branded a Bolshevik it would have bothered me just as little. Man after all still has a soul and is not just an ox fatted for political slaughter' (Jung, 1991 [1934a], §1022). Despite this positive note, in general Jung was less naïve about Soviet Russia than many Western intellectuals like the Webbs who were taken in by Soviet propaganda (Blainey, 1988), and even Freud was briefly optimistic.[17] Freud welcomed the Bolsheviks' eradication of the 'opium' of religion while they were 'wise enough to give them a reasonable amount of sexual liberty, however primitively cruel had been the coercion to freedom' (Freud, 1939, [1934-38], p54).

Compared to many of his contemporaries, Jung was less taken in and consequently—as an opponent of dictatorships—anti-Soviet. One may not be surprised that, in a letter to Baynes on 22nd January 1942, he referred to Socialism as *'political infantilism... which is always the first step towards Leviathan'* (Baynes Jansen, 2003, p320). He mentioned the Soviet massacre of the Kulaks: 'Russians killed a million bourgeois' (Jung, 1934-39, p812-814) and was realistic about Stalin's character, although he underestimated his charm. According to Catharine Rush Cabot, on November 14th 1939 Jung commented on Stalin's straightforward ruthlessness:

> Lady Astor[18] asked him how long he was going to keep on killing people, he answered her, 'As long as it is necessary!' Stalin feels that certain elements are unhealthy so he wipes them out. Stalin does not presume and invent such stories and such lies [as Hitler]. He is a straightforward brute, a cunning brute, while, on the other hand, Hitler is just a rotten devil, and an hysterical, neurotic individual, always excited and believing what he says. Stalin is just an 'Oriental'—cynical, matter-of-fact and brutal. (Cabot Reid, 2001, p230)

Jung's later comments show he gradually became even better informed. Talking on 31st October 1946 he noted the Soviets pursued indirect genocide by sticking their victims in labour camps in Siberia, 'where people are not exactly murdered but are housed and fed so that they can work, and where they then perish of various diseases' (Jung, 1973 [1906-1950], p447). In 1952 he wrote of 'the uncounted victims of the slave labour camps in Russia' (Jung, 1986 [1952], §1505). Later he increased his estimate of Soviet victims: 'You can carry through any social and economic reforms you please if, like Stalin, you let three million peasants starve to death and have a few million unpaid labourers at your disposal' (Jung, 1991 [1957], §517).[19]

POLITICAL POLICY: CONTRASTING THE PRIVATE AND THE PUBLIC JUNG

Thus far we have looked at how politically aware Jung was. Our next task is to consider the following question: if Jung was not naive or isolationist, why did he not communicate his ideas more effectively, because he has been heavily criticised for a lack of public feeling for the plight of the Jews and his contact with Hitler's Germany? Indeed, he was not as publicly outspoken as many might wish and this subject remains controversial as some modern political extraverts clearly have difficulty relating to and accounting for Jung's lack of public statements directed at the Third Reich.

Evidently he was very interested in events and was actively involved in resisting the Nazis, so what deterred him from making public statements? His low profile is all the more intriguing as during the thirties Jung was deeply concerned with helping many individuals, and during the war he was politically active in a private capacity and it is clear from Jung's contemporary accounts of his dreams and the letters he wrote that he was very strongly involved emotionally in the two World Wars as well as the threat of Nazism, which will be returned to in chapter eight. So what inhibited Jung from acting as a public advocate?

WAS JUNG AFFECTED BY SWITZERLAND'S ISOLATION?

It has been suggested that Jung was unduly influenced by his Swiss neutrality. This long tradition of isolation may have inhibited Jung's willingness to comment extensively on external political events. This can only have compounded Jung's self-confessed introversion and may have inhibited the degree to which he felt he could speak out publicly on external events.

How Did Jung's Perception of his Professional Role Affect His Public Stance?

Was Jung, working in academia and the consulting room, too isolated from political events and the political implications of his ideas and actions? (Ellenberger, 1970; Progoff, 1981; Haymond, 1982). Jung seems to have been inhibited by his perception of the range of action permitted to the psycho-analyst in the public sphere. He believed a psychiatrist could publicly comment on general situations in the broadest of terms, but that it was either not his role, or counter productive to comment on specific issues.

Prior to the war he felt limited by professional restraints and his place in the IGMSP In 1946 he explained how he felt limited in how outspoken he could be about Germany in the thirties.[20] He felt he was facing a psychic epidemic, and under such circumstances a doctor could not 'afford to let himself be too much impressed by the real or apparent hopelessness of a situation, even if this meant exposing himself to danger.' He argued that the correct 'medical attitude... allows no hasty judgements... and is willing to give things "a fair trial"'. He felt it was vital to strengthen consciousness and rationality 'so that the evil that is hidden in every archetype shall not seize hold of the individual and drag him to destruction. The therapist's aim is to bring the positive, valuable, and living quality of the archetype—which will sooner or later be integrated into consciousness in any case—into reality, and at the same time to obstruct as far as possible its damaging and pernicious tendencies' (Jung, 1991 [1946b], §474).

This passage contains many issues. It centres on Jung's perception of the role of archetypes (to be discussed later in the theoretical discussion and the assessment of the idea in 'Wotan'). At this point it is enough to register Jung's superimposition of a perspective developed from a clinical relationship with a patient onto a wider understanding of a political situation.[21] In doing this he was also carrying across his optimistic assumption that events 'will sooner or later' work out. If Jung was trying to sustain an attitude of professional optimism, it is possible that this inhibited his ability to see some of the complexities and emotional implications of a situation. It is also possible that on an unconscious level his sensitivity to the situation was diminished by the analyst's equivalent of the surgeon's ruthless clinical distance. Alternatively, he may have used up all his resources of empathy when dealing with individual patients, which would leave him less sensitive when dealing with political issues.

Despite suggestions of unconscious influences on Jung, one must allow that Jung became aware of the limitations of his position. Writing about the war years he commented that it was natural for a psychiatrist to offer a psychiatric opinion which could only be regarded as 'one contribution to the enormously complicated task of finding a comprehensive explanation' (1946b, §444). This may just reflect Jung's reappraisal of how his pre-war perspective had been inadequate, but it also points to the enduring problem that it is not easy to discuss psychopathology with an audience 'who know nothing of this specialised and difficult field.'

Was Jung too Esoteric and Prone to Quietism?

Jung's character was full of contradictions. As has been shown, while he was a political realist committed to democracy, he showed a paradoxically ambivalent attitude to politics. At times his distaste for ideologies and massed groups gave him an anti-political spirit, but this should not be taken as undemocratic. Jung was a quietist who had an introverted, contemplative element in his character. Jung at times behaved like a medieval sage. In this manner he occasionally used an intuitively archetypal approach to politics. He also behaved as a political luminary and enjoyed using his authority as a leading psychiatrist to comment on the wider political picture. All of these roles inhibited or limited the amount he wrote on politics. Together they formed a mind-set that was not compatible with the contemporary fashion of 'engaged' politics. This must be kept in mind when accounting for what, by today's standards, was a dearth of political pronouncements and political theorising.

In *Memories Dreams Reflections* Jung stated that the main focus of his life had been to find 'the myth of his life' (1963, p17). Some writers have accepted Jung's portrait of himself as an isolated shamanistic scholar pursuing dangerous knowledge of the unconscious to enrich Western man's soul (Bernstein, 1989, p24). Others have acknowledged his determination to pursue his introverted quest, but have queried his success (Winnicott, 1964, p327). Whether Jung was successful is not the issue in question as, for practical purposes, his spiritual and introverted search affected the time he had available and the way he regarded the outside world.

Jung testified to how his mythic concerns affected his political outlook. He was very aware of much that happened, but for him politics was not a priority. In 1934 he said,

> I am not concerned about the world. I am concerned about the people with whom I live. The other world is all in the newspapers. My family and my neighbours are my life—the only life that I can experience. What lies beyond is newspaper mythology. It is not of vast importance that I make a career or achieve great things for myself. What is important and meaningful to my life is that I shall live as fully as possible to fulfil the divine will within me... Let me point out that if we were all to live in that way we would need no armies, no police, no diplomacy, no politics, no banks. We would have a meaningful life and not what we have now—madness. (McGuire and Hull, 1980, p87)

Again, to Peter Baynes in May 1941, he said: 'Don't think, please, that I am callous in not mentioning the horrors of our time. I am confirmed in my fundamental disbelief in this world' (Hayman, 1999, p371[22]).

This contemplative side to Jung needs to be taken seriously and should not be mistaken as an excuse for indolence or naivety. Jung was widely informed, and seriously concerned with events; however, he also needed distance from the world and politics, just as the analyst needs to protect his privacy in the analytic work.

The quietist element may explain why Jung did not readily relate his ideas to social conditions. It may also have confused his pragmatic judgement. Patiently waiting for insight may have been appropriate in dealing with finely balanced clinical matters, but was this a valid approach to understand the grosser processes of the international system? In other words, was Jung invalidly applying attitudes which may be valid for one level of human interaction, but inappropriate at another level?

The conflict and demands on a political commentator, an institutional figure and a psychotherapist may not be reconcilable. Käthe Dräger was a Berlin-trained psychoanalyst who survived both the Nazi years and the Soviet occupation. Reflecting on those years, she commented: 'A thorough-going opponent of National Socialism was not necessarily a good analyst. However, one who was a good psychoanalyst often did not have sufficient interest in social and political evens. If someone combined both, and was engaged in the political resistance, he had to lead a double life' (1972, p221). This observation holds good for a Freudian or a Jungian, and Jung was stretched between more than two roles.

In tandem with his quietist leanings Jung also looked to advice from his unconscious. Aneila Jaffé recalled his advice on political issues was that of 'Don't interfere!' for as long as possible. This was not due to indolence on Jung's part, but a combination of curiosity and profound respect for the possibility that the unconscious or the wider situation, as he conceived of 'life' and the unity of things, may allow a more holistic evolution of a problem and its solution (1971, p102-103).[23]

This approach was not just confined to responding to the meaningful coincidences of synchronistic events in the consulting room. When asked why he never commented on the Chinese invasion and subsequent genocide in Tibet, Jung responded on the 28th April 1959: 'In such matters I usually wait for an order from within; I have heard nothing of the kind' (Hayman, 1999, p414).[24] This intuitive archetypal perception is directed at events with a close attention to almost imperceptible feelings and intuitions and this is radically at odds with the realist perspective. It also contrasts strongly with Jung's attempts to deploy his hypothesis in an intellectually accessible fashion. But this aspect of the theory cannot be ignored as it modified Jung's understanding of events and so is an indivisible part of his thinking.

Was Jung Too Introverted to Make Public Statements?

The last factor which I hesitatingly offer is to wonder whether Jung who regarded himself as very introverted was simply too inhibited from making public statements? This is very difficult to assess. Walter Kaufmann offers a very thought-provoking reading of Jung's character and suggests that Jung was more extroverted than he realised and cites Jung's fondness for press interviews (in contradistinction to Freud's introversion with the press) as part of his evidence (1980, p300). Without taking up Kaufmann's larger question I would suggest that Jung enjoyed interviews, but evidently never displayed just how much he knew. On many occasions it is clear from the context that Jung was well-informed, and once he even admitted it. In the Visions seminars on 10th of May 1933, when commenting on the plight of the Jews and the situation in Nazi Germany, Jung observed: 'it is exceedingly difficult to judge events that are happening right under our noses, one can easily go astray in one's judgement. *But I know a little about the situation naturally*, and there really are certain symptoms which one could emphasize' (Jung, 1998 [1930-1934], p971, my italics). He was clearly understating his knowledge. Maybe with regard to Jung's public stance we can conclude that he did not feel it was his place to go into detail and be drawn into debate, but as Kaufmann suggests, sometimes his extravert side and the joy of the raconteur prompted him to be more outspoken.

3. Jung on International Politics and the Causes of War

Jung presents us with an unusual phenomenon: he was a psychiatrist who was both interested in wider political events and became enmeshed in them. Indeed, right from his student days Jung took an interest in politics. In his Zofingia lectures Jung mentioned the Turkish persecution of Armenians and the Turkish suppression of the Cretans' attempt to join with Greece (Jung, 1896, §35). He expressed disgust at the cynical power politics of the European powers and heartily approved of Marshal Blucher's outburst: 'They are damned bastards, those diplomats!' (Jung, 1983 [1897]/1898, §152). Yet despite such striking comments, to understand Jung's thoughts and actions we have a problem: his ideas and observations are scattered throughout his writings, so once again we must reconstruct his position from many pieces.

To assess Jung's attitude to war and politics is not always as easy as it might seem. For those born after the World Wars, and living in prosperity after the Cold War, it is easy to forget how full of war Jung's lifetime was. Those events changed the way war was looked at by the public and political circles so it is appropriate to examine how Jung as a psychiatrist responded to the conflicts around him in European politics. However, when we consider Jung's perspective it is important to remember that he was not a strategist and was not concerned with the strategist's distinctions. He was writing before scholarship had generated many of the academic tools now common to strategic literature, so it is appropriate to look to Jung only for general points that can be applied to almost any level of political conflict.

As explained in chapter one, when trying to relate Jung's ideas on International Politics in the strategic literature, it is useful to do so in terms of Waltz's model. Waltz's perspective situates events at three levels in both the past and the present. Jung was not systematically attempting to account for all levels of political interaction. When he was referring to war or commenting about events at the personal, the social and the international level, he tended to interpret events psychologically, or refer to psychological aspects which can only manifest themselves in individuals or groups. Thus Jung generally deals with Waltz's *individual* or *social* levels of analysis. Consequently Jung only provided a partial examination of international politics, as most of what he wrote was an interpretation of the psychology of historic periods, groups, ideologies and the psychological mechanisms that affected people in political conflict. In writing in this way, Jung contributed to the understanding of the individual and social aspects of events by highlighting the psychological implications of factors operating in consciousness and the unconscious and the role rationality or irrationality plays in both. This attention to the conscious and unconscious is compatible with Waltz's framework; indeed it enriches one's understanding of the complexity of individual and social patterns of behaviour beyond the orbit of where Waltz, and the majority of historians concerned with armed states in international politics, are accustomed to operate.

Having decided how we can assess this part of Jung's thought, the first part of the chapter will look at what Jung wrote about the international scene before the end of the Second World War. In bringing together this material we can assess how well he was informed on military and wider political issues. This is important to consider when weighing up Jung's political credibility. Having made this assessment we can then go on to look at the specifically psychological ideas he used during the period that can contribute an understanding of International Politics. However, in this book we will only discuss in detail Jung's ideas prior to World War Two, when he was primarily concerned with understanding and explaining events in terms of his theories of the collective.

After the war he continued to show an awareness of the wider political situation but his theoretical perspective changed and he focused more on the individual and the contemporary culture. In these later writings he returned to stressing the impact of negative emotions ('the shadow') and reworking his concerns about the dangers of charismatic messianic leaders. This change reflects a significant downgrading of his original conception of the collective unconscious, which is a subject in its own right and has yet to be sufficiently addressed in the Jungian literature. For those who are interested, Jung's post-war observations are discussed in the appendix.

JUNG'S PRE-1945 PERSPECTIVE ON INTERNATIONAL POLITICS

As the inter-war period became increasingly unstable it became apparent that the League of Nations was failing. Jung grew more sceptical about international law and the international system. In 1928 he was remarkably accurate in predicting that peace would not be preserved by deterrence, idealism, economic self-interest, international communism or pacifism (Jung, 1991 [1928]-31, §155). In another comment from that year he suggested that war was caused by opinions and declared: 'The World War came about through mere opinions that war should be declared on Serbia, opinions based on fantasy, imagination. Fantasies are most dangerous' (Jung, 1984 [28-30], p52). In this case it was not clear what he meant by 'opinions', but he could have been referring to the mutual hysteria of the politicians and populace. Alternatively he may have been referring to the pre-war system of diplomacy that had failed to preserve peace in 1914.[25]

To those who suggested that Jung was unworldly (Bernstein, 1987, p12), his pronouncements on the need to preserve the democracies in the inter-war period showed a remarkable level of pragmatism. Commentating on the nascent Cold War in 1931, Jung shrewdly contrasted the quality of life within the emerging superpowers when he observed that America symbolised a 'standard of living' while Soviet Russia had achieved a 'standard of poverty'. He predicted that they would fight over their 'differences to the death' rather than merge (McGuire and Hull, 1980, p63). In making this 'realist' prediction about their continued confrontation and competition he proved correct. What Jung was not able to foresee was that the West's triumph would come indirectly through economic power rather than through direct conflict on a battlefield.[26]

By 1931 Jung was again warning of the instability of the armed balance of power, but he began to shift his focus from the systemic instability of the balance of power to look at the irrationality of decision makers. He worried that an 'unconscious wish for deserted places' might push man into another war which would devastate the cities with gas attacks (McGuire and Hull, 1980, p64). This echoed Freud's theories in *Beyond the Pleasure Principle* (1920), about a death wish and the 'Nirvana principle' that drove people to seek the endless quiet following mass destruction (1924, p159). By focusing on this irrational urge to destruction Jung was implicitly focusing on the impact of irrational instability in international politics which acted as an unconscious counterforce to balance-of-power processes, and here he was using his ideas about *enantiodromia* (which will be discussed later in the chapter), to see how events swung between irrational instability and systemic order.

He suggested that whereas medieval man had faith in 'metaphysical certainties', modern man unconsciously recognised the vulnerability of civilisation and this led to the dangerous desire to achieve deterrence: 'the great cities today are perfecting defence measures against gas attacks, and even practise them in dress rehearsals? It can only mean that these attacks have already been planned and provided for, again on the principle 'in time of peace prepare for war'. Let man but accumulate sufficient engines of destruction and the devil within him will soon be unable to resist putting them to their fated use.' Jung then went on to state that the clash between 'building and destroying' was a mirror of the 'chaos and a darkness' in everyone's psyche (Jung, 1991 [1928]-1931a, §163-5).

The international scene was darkening, as Jung noted in 1932, with the fighting in Shanghai and he recalled the destruction of Northern France (Jung, 1998 [1930-1934], p568-9). In April 1934, Jung returned to the theme of increasing instability.

> For a time, after we gave up that medieval God, we had gold for a deity. But now that, too, has been de-

clared incompetent. We trusted in armies, but the threat of poison gas defeated them. Already people talk about the next war. In Berlin they have built dugouts... If they go on talking in this way, thinking this way, the next war will explode of itself... 'But' I say, 'do high explosives make themselves? Do they declare war and march to war? Do they bring the men with them?' It is the psyche of man that makes wars. Not his consciousness. (McGuire and Hull, 1980, p85, 86).

Jung again mentioned the processes of deterrence and the balance of power on 20th June 1934 and made the interesting observation that increasingly complex systems heightened tension and raised the likely scale of destruction when they fail. Awareness of this insecurity unconsciously increased people's anxieties and further exacerbated any crisis.

We try to prevent wars, we make our situation as safe as possible, but of course we create by that the best chance for having a war. We gather a large army and enormous heaps of ammunition to prevent anybody from attacking us, but the other side is doing the same for their own defence, and finally everybody is defending themselves and this means a war with the most wholesale slaughter. Former wars were just Sunday evening rows in comparison with what we can do now with all our means of safety. Thus, our good intentions are always double-crossed by an unaccountable, unforeseen power which one calls chance or something like that. (Jung, 1989 [1934-1939], p126)

Not surprisingly he spoke witheringly of the League's well-intentioned efforts:

Before the Great War all intelligent people said: 'We shall not have any more war, we are far too reasonable to let it happen, and our commerce and finance are so interlaced internationally that war is absolutely out of the question.' And then we produced the most gorgeous war ever seen. And now they begin to talk that foolish kind of talk about reason and peace plans and such things; they blindfold themselves by clinging to a childish optimism—and now look at reality! Sure enough, the archetypal images decide the fate of man. Man's unconscious psychology decides, and not what we think and talk in the brain-chamber up in the attic. (Jung, 1986 [1935a], §371)

The League of Nations, which was supposed to possess supranational authority, is regarded by some as a child in need of care and protection, by others as an abortion. (Jung, 1991 [1936], §395)

These are good examples of Jung at his politically shrewdest. This was not evidence of occult prophecy, but Jung showing more of his political common sense at a time when Churchill was calling the Democracies to arms. At least Jung had enough grasp of political pressures to see further than many of the professional politicians in the democracies, and he also was able to reflect on the naive hope that many invested in the ideas of peace treaties. He warned that 'no treaty is made which people don't suppose to be forever; no state, no church, is founded which is not for eternity: everything should last forever. It is an apparently desirable condition which has been brought about and which should always last, in spite of the fact that we know very well how long treaties usually last' (Jung, 1989 [1934-1939], p78-79).

In 1935 Jung was concerned with over-population and talked of war as a means of keeping populations down (Jung, 1989 [1934-1939], p554). In a seminar on 26th June 1935, Jung talked in a crudely 'realist' manner. Jung was asked if he thought Italy's invasion of Abyssinia was a policy designed to absorb the unemployed. Jung answered with relish: 'Yes, malaria is an excellent means to get rid of the many-too-many. This is a bit of good statesmanship—if it succeeds!' He was then asked why if over-population was a problem did Mussolini give prizes to big families? Jung replied, 'If there are many human beings, he has a big army. Italy is then great and powerful and everybody is proud to have such a state; they believe in it, and so they can be kept in order. But if you have too many you must destroy them, must invent a colonial war in a particularly pestilential country where there is a reasonable chance that so many thousands will be wiped out.' War with France would be too close and too risky, so Mussolini 'can only risk a reasonable loss of blood, a war with a state like Abyssinia. These things are inevitable inasmuch as there is humanity and the state... Because they cannot help themselves in a reasonable way, it must be done in an unreasonable way' (Jung, 1934-49, p585-586). This concluding chilling statement is almost reminiscent of Machiavelli's *The Prince* and is very much at odds with suggestions that Jung was a politically isolated mystic. Its also noteworthy that while Jung was obviously enjoying holding forth in a blunt fashion he was not being laudatory of Mussolini and he anticipated the defeat the Italians would suffer at French hands when, in 1940, just weeks before the French surrender, Italy attacked the stricken France with over twenty divisions that were soundly defeated by seven French reserve divisions (Steeds, 1984).

Jung thought that whatever the immediate problems on the international stage, what was really significant occurred at a more fundamental level. He thought that the psychological underpinning of conscious and unconscious attitudes that upheld all these institutions had become dysfunctional. The symptoms of this malaise were the illusion of rationality and the intoxication of nationalism and artificial money. These pathological attitudes had their impact on all Waltz's levels of analysis. But by looking beneath the concrete institutions to the psychological *gestalt* that underpinned them, Jung was looking at a deeper more subtle level of influence on political events than was usual in political analysis.

In presenting a picture of social institutions that had been degraded by the onslaught of various irrational emotions, Jung was echoing Freud's concern with the viability of civilisation to withstand the assault of primitive emotions (1930a [1929]). Jung noted how the prosperous educated and scientific pre-war Europe had been secure in its rationalism and philosophical positivism. He recalled that everyone 'was thoroughly convinced that international, financial, commercial, and industrial relations were so tightly knit together as to exclude the mere possibility of a war. The Agadir incident and similar gestures seemed to be mere pranks of a psychopathic monarch, otherwise safely enmeshed in an international network of financial obligations, whose gigantic proportions were supposed to rule out any attempts of a serious military nature' (Jung, 1986 [1936a], §1305).

Then with the war the old securities were seen to be unfounded.

> The benevolent god of science... produced the most diabolical war machinery, including the abomination of poison gases, and human reason got more and more obscured by strange and absurd ideas. International relations turned into the most exaggerated nationalism, and the very God of the earth, the *ultima ratio* of all things worldly—money—developed a more and more fictitious character never dreamt of before. Not only the security of the gold standard but also that of treaties and other international arrangements, already badly shaken by the War, did not recover but became increasingly illusory. Nearly all major attempts at reduction of armaments and at stabilisation of international finances went wrong. Slowly it dawned upon mankind that it was caught in one of the worst moral crises the world had ever known. (Jung, 1986 [1936], §1306)

Later in 1937 Jung returned to the point that the greater the fear, the greater the potential instability.

> Since nobody is capable of recognising just where and how much he himself is possessed and unconscious, he simply projects his own condition upon his neighbour, and thus it becomes a sacred duty to have the biggest guns and the most poisonous gas. The worst of it is that he is quite right. All one's neighbours are

in the grip of some uncontrolled and uncontrollable fear, just like oneself. (Jung, 1991 [1937], §83)

Here Jung was able to identify the phenomenon of arms producers and the technicians of mass destruction.

Look at the devilish engines of destruction! They are invented by completely innocuous gentlemen, reasonable, respectable citizens who are everything we could wish. And when the whole thing blows up and an indescribable hell of destruction is let loose, nobody seems to be responsible. It simply happens, and yet it is all man-made. But since everybody is blindly convinced that he is nothing more than his own extremely unassuming and insignificant conscious self, which performs its duties decently and earns a moderate living. (Jung, 1991 [1938-1940], §85)

But Jung missed the opportunity to ponder their psychology, as others did after the holocaust (Lifton, 1986; Arendt, 1994; Sereny, 1994).

In the Knickerbocker interview of 1938, Jung diagnosed Hitler and said there was little he could recommend for treatment. When he talked about international politics he again talked of countries as if they were patients. Jung suggested that the West should divert Hitler's attention from planning to attack the democracies and instead attack Russia, who he doubted the Germans could defeat. Stalin was to deploy a similar logic in his 1939 pact with Germany. This pact left Hitler free to attack in the West in 1940 secure in the knowledge that Russia would not attack Germany's rear, and that the vital supplies of Soviet oil and minerals would continue to supply the German war machine (Carell, 1971). Fear of Russia was not confined to the German Nazis. For example, from the 'great and the good', Churchill had advocated British support of Finland against Russia in the winter war (Steeds, 1984), and in 1941, Bishop (later Cardinal) Galen praised Germany's attack of Russia in the same sermon that he denounced the Euthanasia Program (Lukacs, 1997, p217).

Jung also correctly predicted that France and Britain would not honour their pledge to Czechoslovakia. He urged America to: 'Keep your army and navy large, but save them. If war comes, wait. America must keep big armed forces to help keep the world at peace, or to decide the war if it comes. You are the last resort of Western democracy' (McGuire and Hull, 1980, p138).

At this time there are indications that he may have been remarkably well-informed about events. In January 1939 Jung wrote to Baynes:

> The general mood in Germany is not just brilliant. The great progrome [sic] has caused a terrific revulsion in all decent Germans. I have heard very interesting details concerning the attitude of the army during the Tcheque crisis. Below the surface there is a division in the German mind which goes very deep. I think we have to reckon with the possibility of internal trouble, particularly in case of war. (Baynes Jansen, 2003, p287-288)

This passage is of considerable interest. Firstly it is a critical pre-war reference by Jung to *Kristallnacht* in which hundreds of Jews died and which saw massive destruction of property. That is important for the controversy about Jung's attitude to the Jewish situation.

Secondly, there is his reference to the 'Tcheque crisis' and the 'very interesting details' he had heard. What these might have been may never become known, but as is now understood, Colonel General Ludwig Beck and other key figures in the German resistance had been desperately negotiating with the unsympathetic British Foreign Office to get British backing for a pre-emptive strike by German army units to seize Hitler before he dragged Germany into a European war (Meehan, 1992; von Klemperer, 1992).

We get another insight into Jung's ability to think strategically on reading an account of his description of events surrounding the Molotov Ribbentrop pact and the strategic situation Hitler had caught himself in. According to Catharine Rush Cabot's diary of October the 19th 1939, Jung explained that by his treatment of

Czechoslovakia during the Sudetenland crisis Hitler had shown his true colours to the Western powers:

> Hitler lost his reputation over Czechoslovakia. In order to get out of that disagreeable situation, he called the Russians, who then cut him off from Rumania and who now surround *Ostpreussen* [East Prussia], and who could easily control it if they wanted to. If the Russians take the Åland Islands, then they control the iron ore in Sweden; then it depends on Stalin whether or not the Germans get it. Stalin wants Hitler to weaken the French and English first; then, when Hitler has thoroughly weakened himself, Stalin will pounce on him. Hitler certainly handed himself over to the devil, *Er verkaufte sich dem Teufel mit Haut und Haar.* [He sold himself skin and hair to the devil.] (Cabot Reid, 2001, p215).

Jung went on to note that Hitler was now caught by his untrustworthy track record so that not only had his relations with Italy become increasingly strained, but he had become so untrustworthy that now he could not change track and re-align with the Western powers against Stalin. This was perceptive of Jung because Hitler was frustrated and increasingly fearful of Russia. He had never wanted war with Britain and once it had broken out, between 1939 and 1941 Nazi Germany made sixteen attempts through various channels to entice Britain into a negotiated peace (Allen, 2005, p55).

Once war broke out Jung continued to follow events in a shrewd and informed way. Another good insight into Jung's military knowledge and his ability to think about political events can be seen in a record of his conversation with Catharine Rush Cabot from November 14th 1939. Jung realised that the French and English were more casualty-conscious after the Great War than the Germans and would fight less aggressively (Cabot Reid, 2001, p229). Events bore this out when the Western allies made no attempt to attack Germany's thinly-defended Western border while her armies where deployed invading Poland. Jung expanded his thoughts on the reality of war and the cost of an attack on the Maginot line:

> If the Germans could make one hole somewhere [in the French defences] anything could be reached, for one can reach almost anything if one sacrifices the necessary amount of people. The terrible question is, could the French shoot fast enough to kill all? There would always be a few million who would get through. In 1917, the Germans forced regiment after regiment through in an endeavour to take a certain fort. They were mown down by British machine-gun fire. It was a horrible sight. (Cabot Reid, 2001, p229)

He also seemed to be remarkably informed about the German generals and noted that 'Keitel and Brauchitsch want to make their career' (Cabot Reid, 2001, p229), which was certainly true of Keitel who was a notoriously mediocre officer with a slavish admiration for Hitler. Jung showed he also knew that the German General Staff advised Hitler not to attack France, and as we know subsequently it was only the tactical genius of General von Manstein who supplied Hitler with the indirect option of a flanking attack through the supposedly impenetrable Maginot line.

Interestingly Jung thought the assassination attempt on Hitler on November 8th 1939 by a lone ex-communist carpenter Georg Elser in the *Bürgerbraukeller* in Munich was staged. He speculated that some Nazi agents were willing to see the deaths of many old *Parteigenossen* [party members] to generate war hysteria as the population was anxious and showed no enthusiasm for the coming war[27] (Cabot Reid, 2001, p229). While as yet there is no evidence for this suspicion, is it unreasonable to speculate about this remarkable attempt by a lone bomber who came closer to success than many other better resourced assassination attempts? It remains curious that after Elser's capture, Reinhard Heydrich, the second in command of the SS, kept him alive and incarcerated till the final stages of the war for no evident reason, and Heydrich was not known for his clemency! Jung was also shrewd in being suspicious of the ruthless steps the Nazis could take for propaganda purposes. The

Nazis had a long record of ruthless propaganda. For example on the 1st of September 1939, to provide an excuse for war the Nazis carried out a fake attack on their own radio station at Gleiwitz. The provocation included attackers in Polish uniforms and what appeared to be dead Polish soldiers. These unfortunates were in fact the corpses of freshly killed concentration camp inmates in Polish uniform to prove the 'provocation' (Witting, 1999, p13-19). One can only add that it was Heydrich who was in charge of this operation. So returning to Jung's speculations about the Munich bomb plot, one can see how well he judged characteristics of parts of the Nazi leadership and how closely he was following events.

Jung treated Catharine Cabot to another long strategic interlude on December 13th 1941. She recorded,

> we spoke of the War in Russia, and the arctic winter which the German High Command was not prepared for. Jung said that he had met some of the doctors who had come back from Smolensk. They said that they had spent their time amputating the frozen limbs of German soldiers. He said that the German soldiers did not want to go to Russia. German troops stationed in Lille [Northern France] had revolted because they had been ordered to Russia.
>
> Then he went back to the English and Americans and said that the stupidity, impotence and awful 'talk' of the British just made him sick. They come out with such stuff as, 'Now we are going to launch a big offensive in Africa!' It is ridiculous to talk and write as they do. The whole world is upset because of British stupidities. If only they would be modest and keep their mouth shut and act instead, and let people see what they can do. This eternal talk with nothing accomplished is just nonsense. They ought to be more modest when they are inefficient and unprepared. They take a few kilometres and then brag about it... He went on to say that the British had bluffed so often that one could not trust them any longer. (Cabot Reid, 2001, p387, 388)

Jung went on to criticise the Americans for not detecting the surprise attack on Pearl Harbour, but he also noted that 'now that Roosevelt can put through all the measures he wants' (Cabot Reid, 2001, p386, 387).

On January 22nd 1941 he was caustic about the British lack of weapons and their pre-war attitude of denial and appeasement:

> They simply ignored Hitler's strong position, and saw 'nothing'! Hore Belisha[28] saw the German threat, so he was kicked out! The British just put their heads in the sand—a damn foolish and dangerous thing to do, either politically or in one's personal life. It is typically English, even when they see a problem, to make believe that they have not seen it. (Cabot Reid, 2001, p320, 321)

> The British are just about to be overcome... yet if they do get through, it will be by the skin of their teeth and with terrific losses. (Cabot Reid, 2001, p323)

Jung as a Pre-War International Politics Theorist

As Jung clearly had an interest in the wider world it is interesting to consider the 'political tools' he used to interpret events that lay outside the repertoire of the conventional political commentator.

The Psychology of Nations

The first idea that we will consider, and one of the main features of the way Jung understood the world, can be seen in *The Psychology of the Unconscious* written in 1916. There he made the assumption that there was a 'psychology of the nation' and that this could be understood as an extension of multiple individuals' psychologies. Why did he make this assumption? Freud and Jung were aware, from reading Le Bon, that there is a psychological aspect of crowd behaviour. What Jung did was to extend this idea and assume that there was an unchallenged linkage from the psychological processes of the individual to that of the group and then to the nation.

In the following passages one can see how Jung assumed an equivalence between individual psychologies and 'national psychologies'.

> Nations being the largest organisation are from a psychological point of view clumsy, stupid, and immoral monsters... They are inaccessible to reasonable argument, they are suggestible like hysterical patients, they are childish and moody, helpless victims of their emotions... they are stupid to an amazing degree, they are greedy, reckless and blindly violent... and they get ensnared by the cheapest of all obvious tricks. Most of the time they live in dreams and primitive illusions usually rigged out as 'isms'. (Jung, 1986 [1936a], §1316)

> What is true of humanity in general is also true of each individual, for humanity consists only of individuals. And as it is the psychology of humanity so also is the psychology of the individual. The World War brought a terrible reckoning with the rational intentions of civilisation. What is called 'will' in the individual is called 'imperialism' in nations; for all will is a demonstration of power over fate... (Jung, 1990 [1917/1926/1943], §74)

In suggesting that one could talk in terms of 'national psychologies' Jung was advancing several ideas. He assumed that it would be possible to make a diagnosis of a 'national psychology' as one did with a patient. This is a highly tendentious idea. In a way he made some acknowledgement of the complexity that he was trying to interpret when in 'Wotan' he acknowledged that 'national fates' were more complex than individual psychologies, but Jung added a new twist to this complexity by suggesting the importance of archetypal factors. Jung also observed that the life of nations was more difficult to control: 'All human control comes to an end when the individual is caught in a mass movement. Then the archetypes begin to function, as happens also in the lives of individuals when they are confronted with situations that cannot be dealt with in any of the familiar ways' (Jung, 1991 [1936], §395).

Taking this further, he argued that as the deeper layers of the collective unconscious affect whole nations, when archetypal processes are triggered, the psychological situation is qualitatively changed for everyone. It follows from this that as only individuals can interact and transform archetypal symptoms in their psychology, only individual efforts can bring about changes in national psychology. This was a recurrent theme. In 1939 he added: 'the man at peace with himself, who accepts himself, contributes an infinitesimal amount to the good of the universe. Attend to your private and personal conflicts and you will be reducing by one millionth the world conflict' (McGuire and Hull, 1980, p145).[29] This link between the clinical and international politics remained in Jung's mind. After the Second World War he noted that the psychiatrist could successfully treat 'dangerous unconscious forces' in the individual. However: 'If it is a whole family, the chances are ten to one against, and only a miracle can provide the remedy. But when it is a whole nation the artillery speaks the final word' (Jung, 1986 [1945], §1377).[30]

Jung's most developed expression of his interest in the current psychological conditions and political events was made in his post-war writing to explain his pre-war assessment of Nazi Germany (Jung, 1991 [1946a], §466). There he showed an awareness of conventional historical and strategic factors and stated his interest in the possibility of national psychologies, but he was not able to show how an entity such as national psychology was somehow separate and additional to 'political, social, economic, and historical' factors. It was also characteristic of Jung that he reverted to using an analogy from individual psychology, in this case that of the criminal, to support his idea that one could extend his ideas to nations.

ENANTIODROMIA: THE PSYCHOLOGICAL ENGINE OF CHANGE

The second major feature that determined his understanding of events was his view of the psychological dynamics of change.

From his clinical work he found useful the ancient Greek idea of *enantiodromia*. He used this word to describe the way that emotional energy behaves as if it is caught between two poles. He came to believe that there is an unconscious process of self-correction built into the dynamics of emotional energy, a 'compensatory function', so that sooner or later an imbalance in one direction will provoke a counter reaction at the other end of the continuum. In this way the tension between the two poles will serve as a major source of psychological change and creativity (Jung, 1990 [1916-34], §237).

One of the major demonstrations of *enantiodromia* at work in the political world for Jung was provided by the 1914-1918 war. As noted in chapter one, during the Great War, both Freud and Jung had been struck by the ferocity of the propaganda, and the brutal scraping away of the veneer of civilisation to reveal the barbarism underneath. Jung interpreted the transition from society's peacetime attempts at building culture to its war-time destructive aggression as an example of *enantiodromia*[31]; the rigidity of the pre-war society had sown the seeds of war with its brittle inability to respond to change or the pressures of new irrational forces.

In the same way Jung believed that within the individual this process of enantiodromia meant that instability was ineradicable. No matter how conflicting behavioural patterns attempt to establish a shifting relationship of checks and balances to each other, but this can never guarantee stability. For Jung then, both for the individual and for the international system, conflict and instability were part of man's instinctive heritage. This view of emotional instability was not as pessimistic as Freud's (for Jung change prompted by instinct could have a progressive potential), but clearly neither thinker could conceive of psychological perpetual peace and this caution can be seen in their perception of world events. Indeed, after the Great War, Jung thought the shock to European man's self-image had been profound and in his October 1918 preface to *The Psychology of the Unconscious*, he argued that individual psychological and spiritual development would be needed for peace and healing to take place. But, instead, many had become pessimistic and reaffirmed traditional power politics, 'believing in the illusion of victory and of victorious power', or a naïve faith in treaties and laws. For others there was a belief in 'the overthrow of the existing order' or for many optimistic disarmers the retreat into 'the hypocritical cloak of Christian love or the sense of social responsibility or any of the other beautiful euphemisms for unconscious urges to personal power' (p5, CW7).

Psychological Insights into the Causes of War

Having looked at Jung's reflections on the international system, we will now consider what Jung saw as the principle causes of war. These reflections date mainly from the inter-war period. In following these statements a picture emerges of Jung moving from relatively superficial psychological explanations of events to hypotheses that were located much deeper in the psyche.

Jung had long argued that psychological factors were a major cause of war. In 1946 he recalled how in 1916, before the United States entered the First World War, he had written: 'Is the present war supposed to be a war of economics? That is a neutral American "business-like" standpoint, that does not take the blood, tears, unprecedented deeds of infamy and great distress into account, and which completely ignores the fact that this war is really an *epidemic of madness*' (Jung, 1991 [1946a], §467.[32] Following these observations in the inter-war years he had other thoughts on the psychological features of the international system. The instability of this period prompted new ideas for him and reinforced earlier observations so that he identified a number of psychological dangers that we can evaluate.

Idealism

In 1930, Jung wrote for a whole page on his views about how psychology caused the Great War and lengthened the fighting. He concluded: 'You see when you boil down the psychology of war and ask yourself what produced it and what psychological idea induced people to continue the war, you find that it was their idealism that extraordinary devotion to their own cause' (Jung, 1998 [1930-1934], p85).

If one reads the passage one finds a badly informed discussion on the conduct of the war, but it is important to acknowledge Jung's military ignorance as a corrective to an overly positive picture of his political awareness. Jung only referred to modern wars as a product of idealism. He noted that modern war was increasingly bloody due to the ferocity and inflexibility of mass ideas—an observation made by a number of strategic historians (Bond, 1983). But the strategic writers have argued that such ideas can also stem from the ancient plague of religious intolerance or from the more modern curses of nationalism (Howard, 1976). Jung was correct that the lowest levels of primitive war can leave very few dead, but to confuse such conflicts, which often have strong symbolic and taboo elements, with medieval warfare with its genocidal Albigensian crusade, or the Wars of Religion which wiped out more than half Europe's population, is folly. Equally, for Jung to confuse ideology and adherence to abstract thought with Christianity is simplistic and even a little absurd when the country under discussion is 'unchristian' Tsarist Russia, which had a strong religious tradition in the period Jung was describing. In World War One, Russia collapsed primarily due to poor political and military leadership, while in the next war she fought just as valiantly for abstract ideas of nationalism (see Howard, 1976, 1983, Ritter, 1972). Indeed, many would argue that she was able to fight for as long as she did in both World Wars due to the physical toughness of her troops whereas Jung had dismissed them as 'much closer to the animal than any of the other nations' and thus missed the military virtues of such stamina (Lucas, 1979; Rauss and Natzmer, 1994).

MATERIALISM AND THE LOSS OF COLLECTIVE NORMS

Jung wrote that the Great War had not only caused 'havoc economically and politically' but had swept away much of the social fabric of Western Society's common culture and values. This situation had left many bereft of social norms and the mental tools to define the meaning of their lives. He feared that this in turn had made them vulnerable to the lure of the demagogue's slogans and empty promises.

> On the surface it may look as if the war had had no effect at all as if it had taught man nothing. Governments go on playing the same tricks as before. The world is spending two and a half millions more in

preparation than before the war. Human psychology today is as if people had learned absolutely nothing. German psychology remains the same... Everywhere it looks as if nothing had been learned... The war accounts for the disorientation of the individual in our time. The religious and moral and philosophical confusion, even the confusion in our art, is due to the World War. (Jung, 1998 [1930-1934], p77)

Looking at what Jung said about the effects of the trauma of defeat, one sees him move from just recording the symptoms of stress, to advancing his ideas on the psychological processes involved. In doing this he also moved from a psychology of individuals to a psychology of nations.

Jung noted how the misery of the defeat made Russia, Germany, Austria and Italy prone to mass movements and emotions of 'depression, fear, despair, insecurity, unrest and resentments of every description.' He saw Germany's economic collapse and the ruin of the educated middle classes. This created panic and prompted an up-rush of 'archaic material, archetypes that join forces with the individual as well as the people.' Such emotional upheavals created strength and energy but eroded old values and the level of civilisation regressed (1936c, §1311-1323). He argued that misery could provoke a positive effort to overcome obstacles with greater will-power, but if this failed an emotional reaction took place which always: 'Denotes an inferior adjustment with more primitive and infantile reactions which may have the energy to carry the day.' If people then fail, further helplessness and panic sets in and people become even more dependent on the group (1936c, §1311-1312).

As part of this argument Jung returned to his habit of projecting patterns of individual psychology onto nations: 'Nations in a condition of collective misery behave like neurotic or even psychotic individuals.' He listed the symptoms of dissociation and disintegration, confusion and disorientation of the conscious and the subconscious layers of the psyche. At the same time the collective unconscious would generate a 'personality surrogate, an archaic personality equipped with superior instinctive forces' (1936c, §1330).

This unconscious ideal will be projected on to an external saviour who may be a doctor, priest or political demagogue.

Jung was so confident of these ideas that when he saw a new epidemic arising he was moved to predict that:

> The gigantic catastrophes that threaten us today are not elemental happenings of a physical or biological order, but psychic events. To a quite terrifying degree we are threatened by wars and revolutions which are nothing other than psychic epidemics. At any moment several million of human beings may be smitten with a new madness, and then we shall have another world war or devastating revolution. (Jung, 1981 [1934a], §302)

In 1939 Jung made passing references to the German feeling of inferiority to the other European powers and how this prompted jealousy for their 'place in the sun'. He also suggested that as Germany was very late in acquiring an overseas empire she lacked the experience of Imperial responsibilities, which he saw as having such a maturing effect on English culture (McGuire & Hull, 1980, p129).

Jung came to see the latent danger in groups and psychic epidemics as the most destructive threat facing man:

> Not by arming to the teeth, each for itself, can the nations defend themselves in the long run from the frightful catastrophes of modern war. The heaping up of arms is itself a call to war. Rather must they recognise those psychic conditions under which the unconscious bursts the dykes of consciousness and overwhelms it. (Jung, 1986 [1944], §1358)[33]

Jung also briefly mentioned as another cause of war the link between property, materialism and instability. Here again he gave a spiritual interpretation to what at first appeared to be a Marxist argument. Jung argued that a cycle of instability was created which made war more likely. On the international level the insecurity of the inter-war years increased the neurotic need of consumers to become dependent on the reassuring comfort of materialism. This reliance on material satisfaction created ever greater demands for more which, in turn, increased international instability as the competition for resources grew. If this reinforcing cycle was not dangerous enough, Jung argued that the ultimate emptiness of consumerism meant that war became an escape from the boring consumerism of peoples' lives. Thus war exerted a terrible lure because it was something greater and more terrible than the unfulfilling lives of many (Jung, 1986 [1939], §627). This observation goes some way to explaining the nostalgia many feel for the unity and sense of purpose felt in wartime.

Religious Fanaticism

Having suggested that materialism and idealism were causes of war, Jung went on to ponder what drove fanaticism. In following this line of enquiry Jung suggested that secular idealism had its roots in religious idealism. This part of Jung's thought will be looked at in detail in chapter eight on 'Wotan'.

The Shadow

Another major contributor to extremism noted by Freud and Jung was the ability of one side to demonise their enemy. This built on Jung's idea of the shadow. In 1931, Jung argued that there would be less demonisation if people and politicians were aware of their unconscious drives. They would be less likely to be 'led astray by [their] own bad motives' (Jung, 1991 [1928]-1931, §165). This topic received much more attention in his post-war writings. There Jung made references to man's capacity for war and destruction as part of a supra-individual capacity for aggression and evil (Jung, 1948 and 1957). However, where he discussed evil it was principally in the context of the process of individuation and theology, which are topics outside the remit of this book.

Discussion of Chapters Two and Three

These last two chapters have reviewed what Jung said and wrote about politics and war. Even though Jung had a taste for prophetic insights and sweeping historical generalisations his political observations are remarkably level-headed. This survey suggests that Jung was more informed and politically sophisticated than some have credited. Indeed he evidently was interested in events and was prepared to get involved in a way he thought was appropriate, but he was not intervening in the public eye or theorising explicitly as overt action in the political world was never his focus. This mismatch between Jung's actions and abilities and the image of him presented by his detractors alerts one to the need to proceed with care when assessing Jung's thought. It is too easy to be distracted by some of his questionable references to clinical parallels.

So how can we account for the clash between such diametrically opposed impressions? The answer it is to distinguish between what Jung understood when he commented on a political situation; what ideas he developed of his own about the situation; and what he permitted himself to say in public about the situation. The latter is significant when dealing with such a writer who was very capable of withholding theories or ideas until he believed the public were ready for them or it had become his duty to comment. The best example of this delay was his resistance to producing a generally accessible introduction to his psychology or an autobiography. This is especially significant when one includes his post-war writing in the assessment.

If one were to sum up Jung politically:

- He was unashamedly middle-class, but post-war he increasingly came to hold a number of beliefs that could be described as radical and libertarian.
- He was a convinced democrat, but favoured small states and was suspicious of large ones.
- He was pessimistic about the viability of the weak democracies in the thirties.
- He favoured what he took to be strong leaders like Mussolini or Roosevelt, but never spoke warmly of Stalin whom he saw as more dangerous.
- He was most critical of Hitler, but his psychological analysis was dispersed amongst a number of texts and shrouded

by his use of metaphors (as chapters eight and nine will show).

To sum him up politically from the strategist's perspective:

- He could be classed as being a 'realist' inasmuch as he took war and evil to be inevitable consequences of the human condition for the foreseeable future.
- In looking at international politics and the threat posed to the democracies by Nazi Germany and Soviet Russia, he took a realist perspective and favoured containment.
- Looking at what he said on the psychology of war he showed an overly psychological understanding of some of the principal features of military affairs.
- Considering what he said on the impact of enough individuals working on themselves, the peaceful overthrow of the Warsaw Pact and the subsequent Orange revolutions seem to support his view of the effectiveness of action by enough individuated people prepared to witness their freedom.

To sum Jung up as a 'psychologist of nations':

- During this period the basis of his ideas changed from his work with individuals in a clinical setting to a broader perspective, as he tried to apply his collective theory to a wider canvas and proposed ideas about national psychologies.
- He focused on the impact of irrationality on international politics.
- His concern was with instability both in the political system and in the responses of people to these realities.

Overall, Jung's concern was to draw attention to the psychological aspect of international politics. If this is a limitation, we should at least acknowledge that because political studies was neither his field nor an area of central concern to him we can hardly be surprised that, as a commentator on war and strategy, he had no major insights.

With this survey completed we finish phase one of the book on Jung's politics. The next phase will look at Jung's theory of the collective unconscious and archetypes. This will be in preparation for the third phase on Nazi Germany which begins with the chapter on 'Wotan'. There, all the issues raised so far will be revisited so that we can assess how Jung used his ideas to understand the political world.

Phase Two:
Exploring the Theory

One can study the symptomatology of such a public movement exactly as a doctor would study the symptomatology of a certain disease; one can make the assumption that the nation is something like a person, that the whole nation is one human being who is shaken by peculiar psychological spasms... for the ordinary layman, as well as the nonspecialists among the doctors, it is often exceedingly difficult, a most baffling task, to construct a true picture of the total symptomatology of a neurosis. It is the same in studying a nation. One doesn't know whether the traits one sees should be ascribed to the particular normal nature of that nation, or whether they are neurotic. Certain traits seem to be peculiarities of a more or less local nature, and one doesn't know how to value them. (Jung, 1998 [1930-1934], p970-971)[34]

4. From the Individual to 'The Collective': Examining Jung's Progression from Clinician to Grand Theorist

We now begin the second phase of the book which explores Jung's conception of the structure of the psyche. This was based on the existence of two psychological mechanisms, that of the collective unconscious and that of archetypes. Briefly put, the first idea postulated that mankind's psychology evolved in stages as different strata of experience that were set down like a 'geological' model with racial and national layers. With this perception Jung felt he made a unique contribution to psychology by adding a prehistoric time-scale and a perspective that included the psychological significance of whole societies whether they were isolated tribes or whole races. This perspective is unusual and provides us with a rare opportunity to study a thinker willing to consider the relationship between race, nationalism and psychology. The second idea—archetypes—suggests that there are within the unconscious universal psychic imperatives that are akin to the instincts of our species. With these two ideas, which for brevity's sake will sometimes be referred to as the 'theories of the collective', Jung supposed himself to be dealing with a level of psychic activity common to all, which operated at a deeper and wider level beyond the range of most historians or psychologists, and here we must pause for a brief aside on the sensitive subject of race.

This is not a new problem, for even in Jung's lifetime he was caught in political controversy that made the critical discussion of his work very problematic. This issue has not become any easier to discuss for, of late, concerns about issues of race have led some readers to overlook the historical context of Jung's ideas and so misinterpret and misjudge him. If we are to re-evaluate Jung's theory we need to suspend our contemporary perspective and endeavour to evaluate Jung and his ideas in their own time before we think of trying to apply these ideas to our own era. So, in re-examining Jung's work we face an exciting challenge and the reader may find that the image of Jung and his work is substantially different from the picture that has often been presented by those who portrayed Jung as a racist.

Jung's Progression from Clinician to Grand Theorist

At the start of chapter two it was explained that if we want to assess the viability of Jung's collective theory in the wider world we needed to take stock of his political acumen. In much the same way, before we can look in detail at his theories of the collective we must consider some of the theoretical landscape in which we find his ideas. To do this we need a short chapter to explore how Jung's professional orientation influenced the way he theorised, to help us understand some of the controversies that Jung's work has provoked. Jung formulated much of his theory in an unconventional manner. Many of his ideas were derived from his introspective work on himself which he formulated into hypotheses and then applied to others. In his writings he was drawing on his voyage of discovery and the colourful material he found in the unconscious. This material gives his work an impact that many readers are drawn to, but as we shall see in looking at his theory, this style of work did not help the theoretical distillation and scientific formulation of what goes on behind the emotional images.

The Clinical Influence on Jung's Collective Theories

Contemporary Jungians often forget that collective theories about the existence of a transpersonal unconscious were common currency in the nineteenth century, so the perception that the collective unconscious was unique to Jung is an unfortunate misperception. Indeed, as Shamdasani explains in some detail, when in 1916 Jung was formulating the idea of a phylogenetic unconscious he was continuing in the tradition of organic memory theorists like Hering, Butler, Ribot, Forel, Laycock and Hall. Of these maybe the most significant was Forel who retired from the Burghölzli in 1898 (2003, p184-189, 234) two years before Jung joined the staff in 1900. Though Jung drew on other collective theorists, here we are going to follow a different line of influence on Jung and look at how the sort of collective theory he would generate was shaped by working with individual patients.

At first sight it seems ironic that Jung was to produce a collective theory that would seek to include all people irrespective of their time, class or religion when his working life was spent treating individuals. This paradox is understandable when one recalls that both Freud and Jung, as psycho-analytic pioneers, used their clinical work to generate general theories that could explain the behaviour of all individuals and shed new light on the workings of society.

Jung started as a clinician treating the personal problems and complexes of individuals. He was confident he could extrapolate general principles from individual clinical cases and stated: 'the psyche of a people is only a somewhat more complex structure than the psyche of an individual' (Jung, 1991 [1928]-31, §175).

His early ideas owed much to the theories of the French psychologists Janet and Flournoy on individual psychopathology (Haule, 1984; Shamdasani, 1998) and later he attempted to integrate Freud's theoretical framework into this work. Freud's central concern had been with the outcome of 'the family romance', of how the child confronted its desire for the mother and its feeling of competition and threat from the father. This Freud termed 'the Oedipus complex', complex being a term for an unconscious knot of emotional themes that are entwined around a common source. Freud saw this complex as the definitive character-forming struggle and the universal experience of humanity. The other common shaper of consciousness was the individual's struggle between instinctive sexual desires and the inhibitions of society. Freud saw this common event as vital for the advance or inhibition of civilisation. In *Civilisation and its Discontents* (1930 [1929]) he suggested that the repression of the sexual urges was vital for humans, lest they be lost in sexual indolence and gratification. As society imposed some restraints on the instinctual drive, some of the frustrated energy was re-directed or sublimated into the evolution of culture and building the fabric of society. In summary, in Freud's conception humans as individuals faced common events that moulded consciousness. While these complexes were nearly universal, the presence of almost universal complexes did not imply common unconscious links across humanity (as did Jung's later ideas of the collective unconscious), so for a time Jung complied with Freud's perception. Indeed while still aligned with Freud he wrote the following passage, which as we shall see would be dramatically divergent from the sorts of things he would later write:

> [T]he cause of the pathogenic conflict lies mainly in the present moment. It is just as if a nation were to blame its miserable political conditions on the past; as if the Germany of the nineteenth century had attributed her political dismemberment and incapacity to her oppression by the Romans, instead of seeking the causes of her difficulties in the actual present. (Jung, 1912, §373)

Gradually Jung came to see some of the types of problems he encountered as afflicting large numbers of people. He began to suspect that these common problems had causes set in the historic past, or so far back in evolutionary time that they had become inborn characteristics of mankind that he would call 'archetypes'. He developed a perspective of the psyche that had two sources. There were the individual life experiences that had filtered down into the personal unconscious and those factors that were common to humanity as a whole, which he called the 'collective unconscious'.

As one follows the evolution of Jung's collective and archetypal theories one can see his ideas being transformed from their varied Romantic, French and Freudian origins into a new theoretical synthesis about the collective and instinctive aspects of the psyche.[35] After all this theoretical creativity, by the mid-thirties Jung was increasingly drawn to exploring the historical, metaphysical and wider implications of his theories, and his writings reflect a shift from to clinical material to his growing range of academic and scholarly questions (Bair, 2004, p395).

In positing a collective psyche he was advancing a biologically-based concept, which required some mechanism for the collective psyche to be inherited. He made little attempt to explain or account for possible ways that this might happen and implied that as the inheritance of physical characteristics was proved, so the inheritance of mental characteristics was at least equally probable. The idea that there was a mechanism of inheritance was vital for Jung's theory and the significance of his assumptions about this process are central to our discussion in the next chapter.

Jung's View of Historical Ages

Drawing on some of the German Romantics, Jung developed a concept of historical ages that mirrored developmental ideas of individual psychology. This idea was very vaguely articulated by Jung, but it was significant in as much as it added an element of teleology to his conception of the collective unconscious. This happened through his perception of the individual's drive towards consciousness and health. Jung in turn duplicated this in his perception of historical ages, which showed his tendency to build from a theory based on individual clinical work and then think in terms of collective trends affecting vast vistas of time and groups of people. Given this link it is unsurprising to find that Jung's view of historical periods, with their own characteristic level of psychological development, echoed his experience with individuals.

The connection in Jung's mind between the individual psyche and wider society and its history was so strong that he declared: 'My medical bias prevents me from seeing [historical coincidences involving whole cultures] simply as an accident. Everything happened in accordance with a psychological law which is unfailingly valid in personal affairs' (Jung, 1991 [1928]/1931, §175). On another occasion he wrote: 'Every period has its bias, its particular prejudice, and its psychic malaise. An epoch is like an individual, it has its own limitations of conscious outlook... this blind collective need results in good or evil, in the salvation of an epoch or its destruction' (Jung, 1986 [1930]/1950, §153).

Much later Jung revisited his interest in historical ages and the evolution of religious thought. One of the themes of his book *Aion* was to chart the link between individual mental development and the wider culture. He suggested that suitable mythological dreams and visions produced in the unconscious may be taken up and used in the conscious religious themes of an era that then affect the wider political culture. As an example he suggested that the age of cults in the late Roman Empire showed how individuals' 'religious inflation' affected the whole society in a way that was very different from the 'rationalistic and political psychosis that is the affliction of our day' (Jung, 1974 [1951], §139).

Jung was concerned with the psychological processes by which a society achieved change or continuity of its religion and culture (Jung, 1989 [1934-1939], p78-79). He fitted this thinking in terms of psychological ages into his ideas on how myths were formed. He argued that a culture's mythologies evolved from the sum of the emotional themes in its collective unconscious at a given time. These energies were then projected as myths that portrayed the problems and preoccupations of that level of development. In this way mythologies were like shared dreams that catch the popular imagination. Jung suggested that eventually when such ideas lost their compelling nature a society lost its unity and collapsed (von Franz, 1992, p124). With this fall, new tensions or new situations were created which would bring about a new unconscious response, and from this new symbols arose that released fresh psychic energy (Jung, 1991 [1957], §549). Given all this, for Jung myths, like dreams, may contain the seeds for the next stage of development (Jung, 1989 [1934-1939], p206) and this idea cast its shadow when he saw the Nazi revolution and came to write 'Wotan'.

JUNG AND THE SOCIOLOGICAL PERSPECTIVE

Thus far we have seen how his clinical work focused Jung on the individual, but what account did he take of social influences? One's first impressions can be striking and Jung repeatedly laid stress on the individual as the ultimate reality and had little interest in 'society as an abstract thing'. For example, in 1952 when questioned on this point Jung declared: 'You see, I am not a philosopher. I am not a sociologist—I am a medical man. I deal with facts. This cannot be emphasised too much' (McGuire and Hull, 1980, p203). Jung rarely wrote specifically on the social dimension or its impact on either the individual or wider historical events. He was not intellectually interested in this area. The causes of this lack of interest are difficult to determine, but given Jung's intensely introverted nature and his psychiatric profession it is understandable that his attention was concentrated towards the psychological and away from social institutions and sociological or economic assessments of an academic study of social phenomena. Instead he tried to look within the individual's psychology to ascertain what lay at the heart of human society beyond the reach of the sociologist (Progoff, 1981, p266-268).

One might assume that when Jung came to write group psychology he would include a discussion of socio-economic factors, but this is not the case as, like Freud, he drew heavily on the work of Le Bon, who had studied crowd psychology and the mechanisms of group cohesion. Freud developed these ideas in his thoughts on the cohesion of military and church institutions as well as considering group dependency and the lure of strong father figures as leaders (1924). Jung's ideas overlapped to a degree, and Odajnyk (1976) gives masterful coverage of how Jung's ideas about scapegoats, projection, and the psychology of messianic leaders can be used to help understand political history.

However, all three writers largely ignored the socio-economic dimension and, given this omission, many sociologically-minded thinkers writing on Jung's collective theories have been highly critical at his apparent lack of concern for social issues (McLynn, 1996, p348). Most of Jung's collective ideas do not discuss groupings within a society but are about larger bodies of people or whole societies on the scale of tribes, races, or nations. This is beyond the perspective that most sociologically minded writers operate within as they have tended to focus on contemporary issues and intra-societal groups. Their time-scale tends to be immediate and the size of the groups they are prepared to discuss reflects their school of sociological theory, although the largest groups tend to be defined by varied economic definitions of 'class'. But whilst conceding that Jung did not place so much emphasis on the sociological dimension, this need not be a damning critique, as one does not have to take the sociologist's perspective as sovereign. If Jung's approach highlighted the individual and the psychological this may not be academically fashionable, but that does not make it illegitimate, so one can take a postmodernist's position and argue that what is needed is a plurality of methods to enrich the debate.

However, sociologists do provide a powerful critique of Jung. Undoubtedly he gave relatively little thought to socio-economic and systemic factors and their impact on psychology. As Clarke comments: 'his concern for the autonomy of the individual led him to under-estimate the more devious ways in which the iron of political and social authority can enter the human soul' (1992, p182). Clarke argues that Jung devoted a lot of time to talking about his theory, but Jung provided little in the way of case-studies in sufficient depth to provide adequate proof of his ideas or show how these factors affected people in the day-to-day world.

In a similar vein, Haymond observed: 'His perception of the social unit was simply the addition of discrete individuals united by a common archetype but uninformed by the material conditions of life.' Haymond continued that Jung's collective ideas were too vague and neither explained the rise of past sociological movements nor could predict new ones. 'His sociological descriptions remain at the level of quasi-mystical psychological reductionism, brilliant in its analysis but of slight substantive value' (1982, p87). Criticisms have been so strong that Alschuler even suggested that Jung was pathologising politics (1997, p282).[36] His concern is that Jung concentrated on the role of the individual, be it as a leader or as one of the led, but ignored how the system generates and manages trouble. He concludes that Jung's thought is one-sided, emphasising the pathological more than the normal, and the individual more than systemic political behaviour (1997, p282).

These are weighty criticisms but how valid are they? Was Jung's position quite as simple as Jung would have us believe and his critics readily complain, or is it more complex?

In considering whether Jung was as implicitly blind to social factors one must acknowledge that Jung's position was more multi-dimensional than that of the sociologist. As chapter two on Jung's politics and chapter five's discussion of race and nationalism will show, Jung did acknowledge the full range of socio-historic and geo-strategic issues, but he did not give much space to these areas—and why should he? He was not seeking to forge tools for a sociological exercise any more than a sociologist claims his discipline is appropriate to fathom the complexities of each individual's psyche. Jung had some interest in society and societies but he lacked the time or vocabulary to pursue what for him was a marginal interest. It should be added that in Jung's time sociology was not so developed a discipline. As his perspective is not incompatible with sociological thought, this leaves others to build this aspect into a Jungian understanding of individual and social psychology (Papadopoulos, 2003).

So, what did Jung say on the social aspect of collective events? In one of his fullest discussions of the interplay between the current social reality and the collective unconscious Jung wrote: 'ego-consciousness seems to be dependent on two factors: firstly, on the conditions of the collective, i.e., the social consciousness; and secondly, on the archetypes, or dominants, of the collective unconscious' (Jung, 1991 [1947/54], §423).[37] By 'social consciousness' he was referring to social factors that impinge on consciousness. As is clear from the *Visions Seminars*, the collective unconscious has both an innate and an external aspect. He explained that the collective unconscious was not only 'a sort of psychological factor' but was 'in the outside world. Society, for instance, is just as dissolving in its effect; one can be dissolved in the collective conscious as well as in the collective unconscious... the collective unconscious is without as well as within' (Jung, 1998 [1930-1934], p318).

Jung explained his understanding of the nature of the interaction between consciousness and the individual's unconscious, and suggested that in general, the subjective conscious complies and conforms with the ideas and opinions of the mass society and the collective conscious. The price of this however is that mass society has no interest in looking at the emotional contents of the collective unconscious. Those issues and emotions that are denied can easily become primitive and negative, and so are suppressed in the individual or the collective mind into what Jung termed 'the shadow'. From this state unconscious emotions can suddenly erupt in the individual or the society in the form of a fanatical and often monocausal faith or 'ism' (Jung, 1991 [1947/54], §423-425). In his *Za-*

rathustra seminar in 1934, Jung explained how these 'isms' and fanatical ideas erupt out of the collective unconscious in such a way that they clothe the 'prophet' in borrowed glory and dazzle the masses with 'revealed' wisdom. This power is derived from the unconscious desires of the many which intoxicates their leaders with the force of the collective power (Jung, 1989 [1934-1939], p206).

For Jung the collective unconscious had a social dimension in contemporary life that included all those commonly held ideas and emotions that were formed in every individual's unconscious—the part of the psyche that was common to the current generation but had been absorbed at an unconscious level. This is clearly an example of 'nurture' as it is generally understood. It includes all the repressed desires and hopes of a population that are more or less collective and unconscious. However, he omitted to give this much attention in his concept of the collective unconscious, or provide a term for a sociological adjunct to his theory. In his writings he left a place for the collective conscious, which is rightly the province of the sociologist, but he contributed little to this area. He was aware of the interplay of internal psychological factors and the wider environment[38] but wrote mainly about internal factors. He was equally willing to acknowledge historical factors when he declared, 'No collective problems have arisen just today, our conditions are thoroughly historical... if a problem is collective, it is historical, and we can't explain it without explaining history; unavoidably we get into historical discussions' (Jung, 1984 [1928-1930], p64).

For Jung the collective unconscious had both an unconscious hereditary aspect and an unconscious contemporary collective aspect. In his writings Jung gave precedence to internalised psychological mechanisms rather than the external institutions. Rightly, Homans calls Jung's characteristic perspective 'a world within a world' that was clearly the work of an introvert (1979, p201). If this criticism is correct, was Jung offering an additional perspective or undervaluing the more conventional socio-economic perspectives, and so: how pragmatically sound was his perspective? If he underestimated the influence of external factors, can one question what he said about the impact of internal factors, or archetypes, or events at the social level? How valid is it to discuss any psychological dimension in isolation? To what degree has this lack weakened his thoughts about society and history?

In response one can say that while Jung may have over-stressed the psychological and disadvantaged his theory by not setting it squarely against its historical and sociological criticisms, it does not follow that he had no contribution to make. Jung's priority was to look at the internal world, and only then would he consider outer factors. In assessing Jung's minimal coverage of social issues it needs to be acknowledged that his perception of historical factors was more long-term and indeterminate than most other social theorists and this perspective helped to lead him away from considering contemporary issues. Having acknowledged his rationale, one is then in a position to assess Jung's use of his theory in 'Wotan' in chapter eight.

Conclusion

In this chapter we have seen how starting from a clinical base Jung tended to produce general trans-generational grand theory. However he was generating hypotheses about individuals and history without testing it with detailed social studies. This lack shaped his theory and, as we shall see, produced a number of problems for his work. It is important that we look closely at these difficulties for our examination of Jung's theory is not just a theoretical or historical exercise, but has important consequences for the clinician trying to work with and validate Jung's ideas. Jung clearly saw himself as a pathfinder; it was for later generations to refine the map, to test what he only claimed were hypotheses and develop his work as a psychotherapist struggling to heal the mind or develop the soul (Jung, 1986 [1948], §1234-1235). What are offered in this book are not new clinical tools, but some theoretical additions and the chance to take a fresh look at Jung's project. The task of unpacking core parts of Jung's theoretical paradigm is exciting work, for if we can identify any theoretical flaws and assess their implications this gives contemporary Jungians the chance to continue Jung's work and move theory and practice forward to be of more help to those in therapy.

5. THE LAYERED MODEL OF THE COLLECTIVE UNCONSCIOUS

The study of... folk-psychology... is far from being complete, but it is extremely probable that myths, for instance, are distorted vestiges of the wishful phantasies of whole nations,—the secular dreams of youthful humanity. (Freud, (1908 [1907]), p182)

For those concerned with the reception and survival of Jung's ideas in the wider clinical community the internal structure and coherence of his work merits close study. In the following two chapters we will look at how Jung constructed his ideas and how his knowledge and understanding of evolution was central to his interpretation of the evidence he cited and the way he came to use this data to formulate his distinctive theories.

Jung thought that different nations had unique psychological characteristics which could be identified. How did he think this was possible? From early in his writings he wrote that over a long enough expanse of time socially formed psychological characteristics became biologically transmitted racial differences. Fundamentally this part of his theory depended on a neo-Lamarckian concept of inheritance which will be discussed in more detail in the next chapter, but for now it is sufficient to understand that the theory suggested that physiological adaptations within a creature's lifetime, if sufficiently beneficial to the species, could be genetically passed on to the next generation. As we shall see, although Jung came to specifically deny that his ideas were Lamarckian (without specifically mentioning Lamarck) the whole idea of a racial unconscious demands such a mechanism because the different races of mankind evolved too recently to have brought forth genetic differences in behaviour patterns (Stevens, 1997, p684). Although Jung's understanding of genetics gradually became more sophisticated and he distanced himself from Lamarckian traditions (his later writings on archetypes place a much greater significance on instincts) he never made a complete break and went back to review his primary concepts. Because Jung failed to undertake this revision, his theory remains organically tied to its Lamarckian roots and this has profound implications.

For historians of Jungian theory the recognition of the role played by inheritance is a key component to understand the evolution of Jung's interpretation of his clinical work in the twenties and thirties. For other Jungians, their acknowledgement and response to this legacy has profound implications for the survival and development of Jung's work, if they are to reconcile his intuitions with scientific advances now, almost a hundred years later.

The Varied Roots of Jung's Layered Theory of the Collective Unconscious

Where did the theory of the collective unconscious begin? According to Jung's account the germination of the theory came with a crucial dream he had on the 1909 trip to Clark University in America with Freud. The timing of the dream is not without its pathos and drama. As Shamdasani observes, the trip came at the high-point of the two men's collaboration (2003, p137), but on the way back to Europe Jung had his fateful dream of the many-storeyed house that set him to build his theory of the collective unconscious, which precipitated his break with Freud.

> I was in a house I did not know, which had two storeys. It was 'my house.' I found myself in the upper storey, where there was a kind of salon furnished with fine old pieces in rococo style. On the walls hung a number of precious old paintings. I wondered that this should be my house, and thought, 'Not bad.' But then it occurred to me that I did not know what the

lower floor looked like. Descending the stairs, I reached the ground floor. There everything was much older, and I realised that this part of the house must date from about the fifteenth or sixteenth century. The furnishings were medieval; the floors were of red brick. Everywhere it was rather dark. I went from one room to another, thinking, 'Now I really must explore the whole house.' I came upon a heavy door, and opened it. Beyond it, I discovered a stone stairway that led down into the cellar. Descending again, I found myself in a beautifully vaulted room which looked exceedingly ancient. Examining the walls, I discovered layers of brick among the ordinary stone blocks, and chips of brick in the mortar. As soon as I saw this I knew that the walls dated from Roman times. My interest by now was intense. I looked more closely at the floor. It was of stone slabs, and in one of these I discovered a ring. When I pulled it, the stone slab lifted, and again I saw a stairway of narrow stone steps leading down into the depths. These, too, I descended, and entered a low cave cut into the rock. Thick dust lay on the floor, and in the dust were scattered bones and broken pottery, like remains of a primitive culture. I discovered two human skulls, obviously very old and half disintegrated. Then I awoke.
(Jung, 1963 [1961], p155)

The house with its medieval, classical and prehistoric storeys, Jung interpreted as representing the psyche with its relatively thin veneer of civilisation, which contrasted with the long pre-history of man as a hunter-gatherer. Jung went on to add further evolutionary layers that he presented using a geological metaphor that expressed how he thought these evolutionary strata were genetically transmitted and might be organically replicated in the structure of brain.

It is significant that in interpreting the dream Jung readily assumed that the seemingly historical layers of the dream referred to genetically inherited material and the existence of innate structured layers in the brain. What he did not do was pause to consider that the dream could refer to cultural layers that were the product of his European classical education. So, given this startling omission, what lay behind his ability to so rapidly generate a theory of a collective unconscious based on a hierarchical geological model?

There has been much recent research on the various ideas that Jung could have drawn on when formulating his idea of a collective unconscious. To add to this work we will focus on two themes. The first theme involves looking at the 'geological' model of the unconscious, because this allowed him to discuss questions of race and allows us to explore how important race was to Jung and his theory. The second area for discussion is to look at the influence on Jung of the theories of Environmental Determinism and *Völkisch* ideas in Geography and Biology that fed into his ideas about the unconscious and race at this time.

THE GEOLOGICAL COLLECTIVE UNCONSCIOUS: ITS NATIONAL AND RACIAL LAYERS

Ellenberger has written persuasively of the Romantic roots of many of Jung's ideas (1970, p201). One of the products of Romanticism was the precursor of modern biology, *Naturphilosophie*, which was very influential in German scientific circles between 1790 and 1830. This movement developed a number of ideas that served as roots for Jung's model of the collective unconscious and the one that concerns us here is their idea of the *scala naturae*—that it was possible to identify a rational and inherent hierarchical ordering of living species. This fascination with stratified orders was complemented by the concept of *Stufenfolge*—which was an idea that development came through a succession of stages (Noll, 1994, p272). These ideas were in currency in Jung's time and probably had an impact on him (Brockway, 1996, p45, p144)[39], and maybe even as one of the factors that fed into his crucial dream of the many floored house.

From his 1909 dream, Jung developed a model of a '"geology" of the personality' which he first expounded in 1925. This seminar saw the first use of the geological diagram.

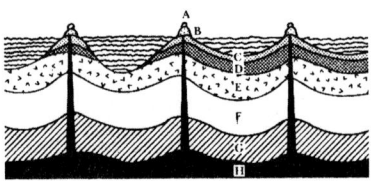

A = Individuals; B = Families; C = Clans; D = Nations; E = Large Group (European Man, for example); F = Primate Ancestors; G = Animal Ancestors in General; H = 'Central Fire'.

Here Jung gave the most detailed explanation of his ideas.[40]

> The first connection between certain individuals is that of the family, then comes the clan which unites a member of families, then the nation which unites a still bigger group. After that we could take a large group of connected nations such as would be included under the heading 'European man.' Going further down, we would come to what we could call the monkey group, or that of the primate ancestors, and after that would come the animal layer in general, and finally the central fire, with which as the diagram shows, we are still in connection. (Jung, 1990 [1925], p133)

The second use of the diagram comes from a little known book by Miss Joan Corrie, *ABC of Jung's Psychology*. She had attended the 1925 seminars (Jung, 1990 [1925], p.xvviii)[41] and in her introduction wrote that she was 'a pupil of Jung for some years' and that 'it was suggested to me that a short and simple outline of his principal theories might lead to a better understanding. I was glad to attempt to supply it', and she thanked Dr Jung for 'reading the work in manuscript' (1927, p.x).

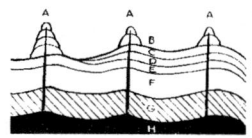

A = Individuals; B = Families; C = Clans; D = Nations; E = Large Group (European Man, for example); F = Primate Ancestors; G = Animal Ancestors in General; H = Life in General.

This diagram was the same as the 1925 diagram except 'H' was defined as 'Life in general' rather than 'Central Fire' (1927, p19-20). Was this slightly less *Völkisch* translation significant? Noll's asserts that Jung was pursuing a covert agenda of *Völkisch* mysticism, with his ideas of a 'Central Fire'. Was this omission due to Jung downplaying this 'secret teaching' outside of the select audience of the Zurich seminar? There are a number of reasons for discounting Noll's 'cultic' theory. Firstly, Noll is unable to substantiate his suggestion that there was a *Völkisch* root to Jung's 'Central Fire', so it seems more probable that Adrian Cunningham is correct when he suggests that Jung was referring here to Heraclitus's 'ever living fire' as he did repeatedly in the Collected Works[42] (Cunningham, 2003). If there was no cultic agenda, more mundane possibilities for the switch can be suggested. Perhaps this was merely a translation or editorial change by Miss Corrie that Jung overlooked as unimportant? This possibility is given added support because in the next use of the diagram by Heyer, which was for an audience in the land of the *Volk* where one might expect the *Völkisch* aspect to re-emerge, one finds only the prosaic 'Life in general'.

This third use of the diagram came in Gustav Heyer's *The Organism of the Mind* published in Germany in 1932. He referred to Miss Corrie's book as the source of his diagram, though he admitted: 'I have modified it a little' (1933, p135). This he did by adding a Vegetable and Mineral layer and dropping the layer of the Primate Ancestors. In making these changes he did not offer significant comments on Jung's model. However, the text warrants more curiosity as Jung not only read it, but fulsomely reviewed it: 'I know of no other book that grasps the essential problems of modern therapy and its conflicting views in just this knowledgeable, unprejudiced, and wholly impartial manner' (Jung, 1986 [1933], §1774).

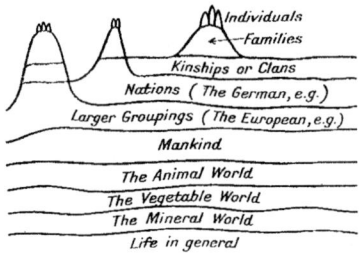

Was any of this material that Jung praised so generously relevant to our discussion about race? Heyer gives a long list of what Hellpach calls *geopsychic phenomena*, such as connections between the seasons and the body's growth-patterns or susceptibilities to various diseases. Heyer linked a range of springtime phenomena together and suggested that: 'what we call "spring" occurs in various ways at different phenomenal planes, and yet is the same springtime... simultaneously the ascending wave of universal nature produces this in the clinic, that in the political world, and the other in social or in erotic life' (1933, p132-133).

Heyer also quoted Hellpach's research on skull size, which echoed Boas's work that so interested Jung, which we will look at later. Heyer explained that Hellpach had found that 'Franconian children, when removed to Swabia soon after birth, undergo, in the latter region, a change in the shape of the skull' (1933, p133).

Heyer's observations on German-Jewish issues were potentially significant. In his discussion of the Germans and Jews in 1933, he talked in terms of a 'psychological ancestry as well as a physical one'. The latter he describes as genetic, while the former is described as made up of a conscious cultural heritage and an unconscious cultural heritage. He suggested that psychiatric health requires an equitable relationship between the two heritages. It is noteworthy that he was not making any mention of racial superiority, nor was he referring to the issue of there being problematic clashes between genetics and culture, he even observed that 'the blood['s]... importance has perhaps of late years been overestimated in this field' (Heyer, 1933, p134).

Another revealing aspect of Heyer's book was his eloquent Jungian critique of excessive individualism. He warned that it was only too easy to fall into the trap of egocentric rationalism or regress into collectivity, and that one could find 'large numbers of [such people]... in all the creeds, in all the nationalities, in all associations, and in all political parties' (1933, p137). This was unexceptionable, but, one can see that Heyer could have been getting dangerously close to the Nazi's attack on anti-Western individualism and the new German psychotherapy's stress on community and conformity (Goggin and Goggin, 2001, p45).

In reviewing the first three uses of the diagram between 1925 and 1933, one sees that Jung held to a stratified conception of evolution with national and racial collective layers. It may also be that his thinking had become less *Völkisch*.

The forth use of the diagram was in 1942 in Jolande Jacobi's *The Psychology of C. G. Jung*, which Jung had also read (1951, p50). This contained one further modification, which Samuels focused on in his critique of Jung's perspective on nationalism.

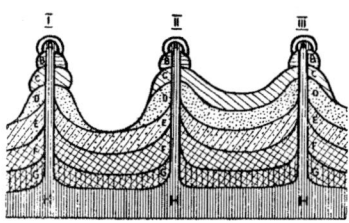

I = *Single Nations*; II *and* III = *Groups of Nations (e.g., Europe)*; A = *Individual*; B = *Family*; C = *Tribe*; D = *Nations*; E = *Groups of People*; F = *Primitive Human Ancestors*; G = *Animal Ancestors*; H = *Central Force.*

Samuels compared the 1925 and 1942 editions of the geological diagram and argued that they show that nationalism had become more important in Jung's thinking. He notes that the 1942 geological diagram contains a diagram modified by the addition of numbers, so that when talking about the same race a distinction can be drawn between isolated nations and culturally linked groups of nations. Samuels comments, 'Notice that at layer D, "nation", a quality change has come into the diagram. The introduction of the idea of the nation... involves an economic, social, political and historical construct of relatively modern origin: the nation... "race" is too general... When we look a little more closely at Jung's not-absolutely-collective layer of the collective unconscious, we find that it is not "race", not "tribe", and not "family" that engage Jung, but nation' (1993, p310).

When Samuels suggested that with the addition of the national layer to the diagram, Jung's ideas changed because Jung had now to account for the introduction of socio-political and historic factors, he made a useful observation, but the same argument can be deployed a stage further, back at level E, 'Groups of People', which is generally held to correspond to the word 'race,' as it is now used. Samuels' point is weakened because given the historical conditions in the ancient world that Jung was referring to, the same arguments about social-political factors can be applied with the advent of new races into a geographical area. To give an example, one interpretation of early European history is that the influx of proto-Celtic peoples eventually formed what has become classified as the cultural group of Halstatt Celts. This new cultural or racial group brought with them a host of socio-economic changes and this happened before the emergence of clearly defined nations.

A distinction is being made between 'Groups of Nations', which would be the Caucasian countries of Europe, and 'Groups of People', which is a larger entity and would be all the Caucasians of Europe, the Americas and the old Commonwealth, or to give another example: all the Negroes of Africa, the Americas and Europe.

In any event, within the diagrams themselves, there is no substantial indication that Jung had become more nation-centric in his thinking. Both the 1925 and 1942 diagrams made provision for the distinction between isolated nations and national groupings.

Nor is there any indication of a rise of nation-centric thinking in Jung's references to the geological model in his verbal and written explanations. In 1934 Jung explained his view of the significance of an individual's biologically inherited characteristics, which he called 'psychoid idiosyncrasies'.[43] He explained in 'A Rejoinder to Dr Bally', how the inherited characteristics influenced individuals' subjective perspectives. He argued that this 'subjective premise is identical with our psychoid idiosyncrasy' because both the social and the genetic, were conditioned by the individual, the family, and then 'the nation, race, climate, locality, and history' (Jung, 1991

[1934a], §1025). But Jung qualified the significance of the wider differences by stating: 'Psychological differences obtain between all nations and races... [but] all branches of mankind unite in one stem... but what is a stem without separate branches?' (Jung, 1991 [1934a], §1029). This was not an elegant explanation of his ideas on race and nations. It showed an intractable confusion of the physical and mental external influences, but, at least, he shared this combination of ideas with contemporaries like Boas, and if he failed to explain the distinction between nations and races, he did not take the step of making value judgements. As such the 'Rejoinder' was a typical representation of the various confused lines of Jung's thought, and in this late explanation of the geological unconscious Jung failed to establish the existence of significant psychological features that were a product of a supposed hierarchical evolution.

Environmental Determinism and Völkisch Ideas in Geography and Biology in the German-Speaking World.

We now come to look at Jung's thoughts on the interrelation between physiology and geography. This topic sounds very anachronistic to contemporary sensibilities, but once we have reviewed the background material we can then see how it affected his thinking about race and national psychologies and how he attempted to use the whole ensemble to understand historical events.

One of the academic controversies in late nineteenth century Germany was between indigenous Historicism, which explained human activities in terms of the way people's thinking and culture affected their interaction with the environment; and Environmental Determinism, which was derived from the European positivist perspective, and focused on the impact of external factors on the way people lived (Speth, 1978, p24). This was a wide-ranging debate across many different disciplines and Jung's writings on nature, biology and race all show Geographical and Biological Environmental Determinist elements.

At that time, academic Geography was split by a debate constellated around two theoretical schools. The Cultural Defusionists from the Historicist tradition argued that cultural variation was spread by migration. The positivist Environmental Determinists, who were also called Geographical Determinists, argued that different types of environment dictated the sorts of cultural patterns that were produced (Kuper, 1988, p126). In Germany, Geographical Determinism was known as *Bodenbeschaffenheit* (Brockway, 1996, p42). Jung was clearly influenced by the latter school and scholars on both sides of the Atlantic shared its pre-suppositions concerning the influence of physical geography on social conditions.[44]

However, Jung was not only exposed to pure Geographical Determinist ideas, because in Germany these ideas were influenced, or ran in parallel with, older Romantic *Völkisch*[45] ideas about the mystical relationship between a people and their cultural landscape (Mosse, 1964, p14). In this way *Bodenbeschaffenheit* was more influenced by Romanticism than its more prosaic Anglo-Saxon Geographical Determinism so it is understandable that Noll defines Germanic *Bodenbeschaffenheit* as 'landscape mysticism', about the 'formative forces of the soil' (1996, p272, p93).[46]

Beyond Geographical Determinism, Jung was also influenced by trends in academic Biology where the debate about Environmental Determinism led to questions about the impact of the living environment on biology. Was it possible that as physical environment was thought to affect biological development, the cultural environment might also affect biological development? This question stemmed from the Lamarckian theory concerning inheritance.

Darwin's ideas had not been readily accepted in German scientific circles. At the close of the nineteenth century they came under renewed attack from a revival of Lamarckism that supported Environmental Determinism and these arguments fed into Jung's theory from a number of possible sources that influenced the climate of ideas in which Jung worked.[47] The work of Theodor Waitz, a pioneer ethnologist, led the attack. He was resolutely critical of Darwin's work and asserted that a range of historical variation could be identified in the development of the biological forms (Kuper, 1988, p128-129). Waitz argued that man's intellectual capacity was common to all populations, but secondary cultural variations developed as a consequence of historical accidents.[48] Kuper explains that Waitz further suggested that while cultural variations were not of great importance, what was significant was that once a culture was established, it would mould fundamental mental capacities, even to the extent of modifying the shape of the head, which he believed shaped mental capacities. This process would then be replicated by a change in the genetic pattern of the germ plasm.[49] This suggestion of the possibility of a causal relationship between skull size and external factors was only possible if Lamarck's perception of evolution was correct. All of these ideas were of obvious interest to Jung and we get a clearer idea of the overlap between Jung and these ideas when we consider the work of Jung's contemporary, Franz Boas (1858-1942), who began his studies in Germany.

Boas was influenced by many of the leaders in the area of anthropology like Virchow and Waitz, and had worked with Bastian in Berlin, but spent most of his working life in America where he became Professor of Anthropology at Columbia University. His Jewish background spurred his desire to fight for racial equality against the increasing anti-Semitism in Europe and he insisted that race was not a significant issue in accounting for human differences (Blainey, 1988, p114). As a historicist Boas argued that culture was ultimately changeable and that geographical influences were not absolute. People were not prisoners of their environment and ultimately all races were equal (Blainey, 1988, p114-115). Boas attempted to balance the controversy between Cultural Defusionists and Environmental Determinists and he criticised mono-causal explanations of human development based on social phenomena like economics, race or environment[50] (Speth, 1978, p9).[51]

Boas and Jung came together when they attended the 1909 anniversary lectures at Clarke University. On 9th September, Freud was the first speaker (Ellenberger, 1970, p801) and later that day Dr Boas explored the idea of race and the notion of racial purity (Rosenzweig, 1994, p120). Unfortunately Freud and Jung who where present when he gave his paper 'Psychological Problems in Anthropology' did not heed his critique and this early omission left the psycho-analytic disciplines with the older, cruder anthropological perspective. As Shamdasani observes, this was to mar anthropologists' reactions to psychoanalysis and probably biased the psycho-therapists attempts at anthropological cross-cultural studies (2003, p277).

As far as Jung's theory went, whatever else he heard at Clarke, Jung only assimilated what he was already interested in from

Boas's work. These trends in Jung's thought were the ground on which he would have the fateful dream of the many floored house which furnished the theory of the collective unconscious and sealed the break from Freud.

THE INFLUENCE OF BODENBESCHAFFENHEIT AND VÖLKISCH IDEAS ABOUT THE LANDSCAPE

Having introduced a variety of *Völkisch* and Geographical Determinist ideas, one can now look at how they featured in Jung's writing. We get an insight into the complexity of different strands in Jung's thinking in the *'Visions'* seminars where he spoke of how many peoples' emotional values were often formulated a hundred or more years before they were born (Jung, 1998 [1930-1934], p60-61). Jung went on to give an account of an incredibly primitive family who lived in his locality. He seemed to be suggesting that what had occurred was some form of a genetic throwback to ancient human stock because he wrote about their skull type, rather than ascribing their primitivism to poverty. He described how one might meet:

> anthropological types of all these ages... there is a Neanderthal man sitting right opposite you, his psychological level of humanity... If you could have stuffed that family after their deaths, they would have made excellent specimens for an anthropological collection. Their skulls were quite primitive. So the lower forms of man are still living among us; they even have the psychology of the primitive man. (Jung, 1998 [1930-1934], p60)

In this instance Jung would appear not to be referring to Geographical Determinism, but to have advanced a crude nineteenth century Social Darwinist interest in skull types. However, as the idea was not taken up and developed, it would be unwise to take it as a serious piece of Jung's thinking. In all likelihood it is one of those numerous cases of Jung speculating in a colourful way as he waxed lyrical on an interesting hobby-horse, but it did not constitute part of his developed theory. The concern for the reader is that

Jung has muddled up the historical, the instinctive, and the possibility of genetic throwbacks in one passage about behaviour.

Jung also wrote as if the Land itself had an impact on the collective unconscious, so this also must be considered. Admittedly Jung never included the Land in his diagram of the collective unconscious, but Heyer did; and as Jung wrote a positive review of his book it is appropriate to look at the role the Land played in Jung's thoughts.

Jung thought about the landscape and its effect on psychology in a number of ways and in chapter two we referred to his ideas about land ownership and man's need for a living relationship with the Land. Jung wrote of the Land's impact on man's physiology and psychology, which showed Geographical Determinist influences. Jung's writings also seem to suggest the possibility of a psychological influence of the Land that goes beyond Geographical Determinism and echoes the mystical elements of the *Völkisch* influence on *Bodenbeschaffenheit*.

Given these influences, Noll suggests that Jung's 1918 essay 'The Role of the Unconscious' and the 1927 'Mind and Earth' clearly demonstrate how Jung was influenced by *Völkisch* mysticism, as he wrote about 'the mystery of earth' in almost occult terms (1974, p95-99). There is an element of overstatement here as Noll includes in this *Völkisch* material Jung's speculations about the effect of maritime influence on a culture. This was a reasonable hypothesis from a Geographical Determinist perspective, but when Jung wrote about 'the mystery of earth' Noll was surely correct that he was straying into *Völkisch* mysticism. If all this sounds fantastically occult, one must not forget that Jung had contact with people who lived very primitive lives. For example, Jung recounted in 1928 the case of a Swiss woman who cured herself by drinking blood on the advice of an old man. Jung concluded: 'There is still a lot of very buried and archaic earth mysticism in Switzerland' (Jung, 1984 [28-30], p36). Although this is not earth mysticism, it does indicate a level of pagan superstition that was not unlike the excesses of *Völkisch* Romanticism. While Jung did not acquire his mystical views from these superstitions, he did not allow for the possibility that these ancient superstitions were the product of a still extant culture; but instead he suggested that such recurrences were the result of an inherited deposit in the psyche. So, as in the case of his many-floored house, Jung was ignoring the simple interpretation that culture and environment were the cause of the dream and using the material as evidence for his theory of a collective unconscious.

Noll argues that in 'Mind and Earth' Jung was influenced by his long correspondence with the *Völkisch* German philosopher Keyserling, who believed in *Bodenbeschaffenheit*. Here, unfortunately, one returns to the problem of definitions. Sherry argues that Noll was mistaken in defining Keyserling as deeply *Völkisch* and suggests that he is better understood as one of the 'conservative avant-garde'.[52] In any event, during the inter-war period until 1934, Jung wrote three very positive reviews of Keyserling's work, and in 1927 contributed 'Mind and Earth' to a book by Keyserling on how the 'earthly environment' shapes the human soul (1996, p96). Consequently Noll argues that in this essay Jung was using *Bodenbeschaffenheit* ideas, but is this so?

Jung explained, 'Just as, in the process of evolution, the mind has been moulded by earthly conditions, so the same process repeats itself under our eyes today. Imagine a large section of some European nation transplanted to a strange soil and another climate. We can confidently expect this human group to undergo certain psychic and perhaps also physical changes in the course of a few generations, even without the admixture of foreign blood' (Jung, 1991 [1927/1931b], §93). As another example of this process Jung cited the 'marked differences' between Spanish, North African, German, and various Russian 'varieties of Jews'.[53] Jung also predicted the 'Indianisation of the American people' who were originally a 'predominantly Germanic people'. He based this 1912 prediction on seeing crowds of factory workers in 1912 in Buffalo and mistakenly assumed that they displayed a remarkably 'high percentage of Indian blood'.[54] When told that this was not the case, Jung attributed his observation to geography shaping their phenotypic expression rather than blood (i.e. genetic influences). Was this the 'earth mysticism' of parts of *Bodenbeschaffenheit* that Noll claims, or was it closer to Geographical Determinism, as when Jung cited the anthropometric work of Boas, whom he claimed had 'shown that anatomical changes begin already in the second generation of immigrants, chiefly in the measurements of the skull' (Jung, 1991 [1927-1931b], §94).[55] Noll seems to overplay his *Völkisch* argument.

Jung is vulnerable to those who would make *Völkisch* accusations, especially as this all sounds arcane and reactionary, but is it fair to imply that Jung was so out of place amongst his academic contemporaries? For a comparison, Boas with his anti-racist credentials provides an intriguing peer. As Pietikäinen notes from Barkan's study of racist ideas,[56] even Boas (as well as Russell and Huxley) expressed 'explicitly racist views' at the beginning of the twentieth century (1999, p160); so one cannot simply assume that even this German-Jewish emigrant's position is unproblematic to modern ears. Even if later Boas demonstrated impeccable anti-racist sentiments, in 1889 he wrote an article which was scrupulously non-aligned in favouring the influence of environment or culture, but still used terms which could be mistaken for nature mysticism, if one did not know his intellectual pedigree! When he wrote: '*A relation between soil and history cannot be denied, but we are not in a position to explain social and mental behaviour on this basis and anthropo-geographical "laws' are valid only as vague, empty generalities. Climate and soil exert an influence upon the body and its functions*, but it is not possible to prove that the character of the country finds immediate expression in that of its inhabitants' (Speth, 1978, p7, my italics).][57]—in both the turn of phrase and the ideas that refer to 'the soil' he prefigured Jung's writing in 'Mind and Earth' (1927-1931b).

The second example of parallels in Boas's work comes from the aforementioned 1912 study of the head-shapes of immigrants, which concluded that the head-forms of American-born individuals changed 'almost immediately after the arrival of their parents in America'. Boas found that the younger the child arrived in America the narrower their face was in comparison to their older sibling. He believed this reflected their different mental upbringing affecting their skull physiology, although he also believed that 'the mental make-up of a certain type of man may be considerably influenced by his *social and geographical environment*' (Kuper, 1988, p129, my italics).[58]

The point to note is that in this period one can find Geographical Determinist ideas in use by many writers, but they may lack the Romantic mysticism and value judgements of *Völkisch* ideology. But even this distinction is not as clear as one might hope. For example, Boas's ideas also contained elements of a more *Völkisch Bodenbeschaffenheit* when he supported ideas from German scholarship that 'folktales offered a privileged point of access to the folk mentality, and that they even preserved layers of historical experience' (Kuper, 1988, p134). In this mixture of *Völkisch* traditions and Lamarckism, Boas, like Jung, mixed his ideas.

To return to 'Mind and Earth', Jung had been speculating about the influence of the geographical environment on physiology and psychology. He then began to compare the psychological influence of Negro cultural patterns and the 'physiognomical similarities' of the Red Indians to the Caucasian majority of the USA:

> The remarkable thing is that one notices little or nothing of the Indian influence. The above-mentioned physiognomical similarities do not point to Africa but are specifically American. Does the body react to America, and the psyche to Africa? I must answer this question by saying that only the outward behaviour is influenced by the Negro, but what goes on in the psyche must be the subject of further investigation. (Jung, 1991 [1927-1931b], §98-99)

In the article Jung went on to ponder why there were heroic representations of Red Indians in Caucasian Americans' culture and dreams, but in his discussion of why there was no Indian influence on physiology or culture he did not explore the obvious fact that most of the Indians had been killed! The dream hero images, he had noted in *Symbols of Transformation*, were better explained by Rousseau-esque Romanticism than his explanations of deep archetypal images buried in the American Miss Millar's psyche by some geological Lamarckian imprinting. These two examples of his startling neglect of the sociological dimension give an indication of how much influence Geographical Determinism had on him at this time.

This is also seen in his 1928 article, 'The Swiss Line in the European Spectrum'. Jung waxed lyrical on his beloved Switzerland. He made a historical observation that Switzerland was: 'surrounded by more powerful nations that are linked with the wide world, that expand into colonies or can grow rich on the treasures of their soil. The Swiss cling to what they have, for the others, the more powerful ones, have grabbed everything else. Under no circumstances will the Swiss be robbed of their own. Their country is small, their possessions limited. If they lose what they have, what is going to replace it?' (Jung, 1991 [1928], §914). This was not *Völkisch* thinking, but was it Geographical Determinism or just common sense, or did Jung combine elements of all three?

The next paragraph provides a good example of why care is needed when reading Jung:

> From this comes their [Swiss] national resentment, which, as Keyserling rightly remarks, is not unlike that of the Jews. This is understandable enough, since the Jews as a people are in the same precarious situation and are forced to develop the same defence-mechanisms. Resentment is a defence reaction against the threat of interference. (Jung, 1991 [1928], §915)

If one reads this last sentence out of context it appears that Jung is being anti-Semitic in as much as he is coupling Jews and 'resentment', which is hardly a noble emotion. But in context Jung is talking directly about his beloved Swiss. Clearly his style of writing was unhelpful because he then lapsed into *Völkisch* ideas: 'The national character is imprinted on a man as a fate he has not chosen— like a beautiful or an ugly body. It is not the will of individuals that moulds the destinies of nations, but supra-personal factors, the spirit and the earth, which work in mysterious ways and in unfathomable darkness' (Jung, 1991 [1928], §915).

In the same period, he talked of Europeans that had lived for long periods in India, Africa, or Latin America. Jung suggested that the unconscious more readily picked up the influences of the local 'the chthonic factor, the earth upon which one lives' (Jung, 1998 [1930-1934], p617). Here he seemed to be giving primacy to the influence of the 'earth', which shows he was still thinking, or at least expressing himself, in Romantic terms. He recalled on 15th September 1943, how he had linked landscape to psychology in his article on Paracelsus:

> and also dropped similar hints in my answer to Keyserling's expose of Switzerland. I am deeply convinced of the fortunately still very mysterious relation between man and landscape, but hesitate to say anything about it because I could not substantiate it rationally. But I am fully persuaded that if you settled a Siberian tribe for a few hundred years in Switzerland, regular *Appenzellers* would come out in the end. It is probably a matter of something like psychic mimicry. (Jung, 1973 [1906-1950], p338)

Yet it is not possible to say definitely that Jung had dropped all traces of these ideas. In 1955 Jung again mentioned his ideas about the geographical effects on national character and accounted for the independent attitude of the Swiss by referring to the geo-political situation of Switzerland (McGuire and Hull, 1980, p250). Here Jung observed that the Swiss were a small people surrounded by three of Europe's great powers for much of their history, and the land is vital as mountains are cruel masters that breed rugged independence, and make for good defences. This was the pragmatism of Geographical Determinism, not the romanticism of *Völkisch* ideas.

A Provisional Review of Jung's Ideas on 'the Land'

At the beginning of this chapter it was explained that various lines of thought provided the background for the geological collective unconscious. Of these ideas, the most significant were the geological metaphor, the stratified psyche and the Lamarckian conception of the evolutionary acquisition of psychic traits.

In Jung's theoretical amalgam one is struck by contradictory trends. One can see that Jung's interests were little affected by the Historicist tradition and more aligned with the Biological and Geographical Determinists. This is unsurprising considering his medical background and his lack of exposure to the disciplines of academic history or the infant sociology. This trend is also reflected in his references to scientific methods and proofs. But the trend contrasts with some of his thinking on the land that showed he continued to be influenced by *Naturphilosophie*. This was a triumph of Romanticism in the face of the more positive aspects of Geographical Determinism and modern science in general.

While it was not possible to define clearly, or assess the relative impact of many of the ideas that influenced Jung, awareness of the differences may help one to understand incompatible styles of ideas and arguments in Jung's work. *Bodenbeschaffenheit* was more intuitive, emotive and Romantic than the more prosaic Anglo-Saxon Geographical Determinism. Given this, it may be that the German perspective was more influential on Jung at the intuitive and Romantic end of his speculations about the collective unconscious, while the more mundane aspects of Geographical Determinism were more influential on his model-building. His ideas about genetics fit uneasily between the two. As the influence of Lamarck waned he moved from the Romantic to the Determinist perspective, as is explored in the next chapter.

THE RACIAL LAYER OF THE UNCONSCIOUS

As has been explained, Jung's 'geological' collective unconscious included all levels of the psyche from the pre-mammalian universal depths, through the pre-historic racial layer to national groups in historic times and then the modern world with its family histories and personal experience. In covering such a span of time the theory was combining innate biological factors with external historic and sociological factors, but Jung was not always clear about the distinction between innate characteristics of behaviour and social factors. This unstable combination makes the collective unconscious a very problematic idea to assess because its different levels can only be accounted for by a range of explanations that have varied levels of credibility.

As our concern is with the theoretical cohesion of his ideas and their significance for Jung's understanding of wider political events, the next section begins to examine Jung's thoughts about the racial layer of the collective unconscious. For reasons of space, and due to the political focus of this book, it will be necessary to omit an examination of the family and animal layers of the collective unconscious that received relatively little attention in his writing.

The Problematic Concepts of 'The Primitive' and 'Race'

Much of the following discussion will involve Jung's use of the emotive terms 'primitive' and 'race'. There seem to be two areas of interlocking concern. Anthropologists have raised questions about the scholarly rigour of Jung's attempt at field studies and his armchair comparative anthropology, while Marxist-orientated academics have voiced concern that Jung was imposing a European class-based value system on other cultures. Unfortunately there has also been a tendency for some writers to make unsubstantiated, or poorly supported accusations of racism and cultural projection, and to take on trust others' accusations against Jung. For this reason the issue needs close attention.[59] I will borrow Andrew Samuels' working definition of racism: he usefully identifies the core racist idea that races are inherently (genetically) hierachically gradable. We shall see if Jung makes this genetic or judgmental assumption.

> According to most modern definitions, racism divides humankind into distinct and hierarchically gradable groups on the basis of biological or quasi-biological characteristics. A racist is therefore someone who believes that people of a particular race, colour, or origin are inherently inferior, so that their identity, culture, self-esteem, views, and feelings are of less value and may be treated as less important than those of the groups believed to be superior. (Samuels 1989, p184-5)

When considering the status of Jung's anthropological work a number of issues have to be raised. From the beginning we need to be clear that our task is not to criticise Jung's early attempts at cross-cultural studies and his ideas about race by the standards of modern anthropological scholarship; to do so would be anachronistic. Jung's thinking should be judged by the standards of his time, but as we also want to discuss how applicable his ideas may be for today, modern criticism needs to be given due recognition, but caution must be taken not to get caught in 'politically correct' fixations. Vocabularies change, and when Jung used the term 'primitive cultures' he did not have available the phrase 'primary cultures'. Closely entangled with our modern sensitivities about the word 'primitive' is the issue of race. There remain concerns that when Jung was referring to the 'primitive' he was implying some form of racial slur. In view of this his use of 'primitive' and 'race' need close attention.

Jung had neither the scholarly tools nor academic resources of a modern anthropologist or sociologist. Anthropology was vital to Jung and his library contained the *Annual Report of the Bureau of Ethnology to the Secretary of the Smithsonian Institute* from 1879 to 1919. During this period the two disciplines were much less differentiated than they have since become (Shamdasani, 2003, p272). Furthermore, Anthropology was much less specialised so that, as Burleson argues, Jung could in good conscience make his attempts at African and Pueblo field studies despite not being trained to modern standards (2006). As Clarke observes, within his means he did use scientific tests, statistical studies and field-work to back up his hypothesis (1992, p22).

This is not to say that Jung's work is without problems. Pietikäinen notes how area specialists like Anna Rooth (an anthropologist), Tim Moore (a linguistic analyst), Richard Dorson (a folklorist), and the classicist Robert Eisner have been scathing of the depth psychologists' attempts to prove their theory with historical or cross-cultural material. As the classicist and historian of religion G.S. Kirk remarks, Jung and subsequent Jungians have made no attempt to statistically validate their universal claims through sufficiently wide anthropological studies (1999, p, 106-7).[60] This has meant that Jungian and Freudian theory tends to suffer from what Pietikäinen calls 'theory-ladenness' where all anthropological and historical evidence is used as a resource to find the evidence to substantiate a theory that is already taken as given (1999, p109). Jung's work must be treated with caution, but care is also needed when dealing with his critics, for anthropologists are also vulnerable to their own fashion agendas and many of the optimistic studies by anthropologists in the sixties have subsequently been shown to be flawed.[61]

THE LAYING DOWN OF THE RACIAL LAYER OF THE PSYCHE AND THE STRATA WITHIN THE PRIMITIVE

We will begin our exploration of Jung's ideas about 'race' by looking at his perception of 'the primitive' and how this perception encompassed a hierarchy of psychological cultural development.

Let us start with two early examples of Jung's description of the racial layer of the Collective Unconscious, and note how they show the gradual evolution of his thoughts as the impact of Lamarck waned.

In 'The Role of the Unconscious' Jung explained his ideas about the 'primitive psychology' and how layers were set down:

> As civilised human beings, we in Western Europe have a history reaching back perhaps 2,500 years. Before that there is a prehistoric period of considerably greater duration, during which man reached the cultural level of, say, the Sioux Indians. Then come the hundreds of thousands of years of Neolithic culture, and before that an unimaginably vast stretch of time during which man evolved from the animal. A mere fifty generations ago many of us in Europe were no better than primitives.[62] The layer of culture, this pleasing patina, must therefore be quite extraordinarily thin in comparison with the powerfully developed layers of the primitive psyche. But it is these layers that form the collective unconscious, together with the vestiges of animality that lose themselves in the nebulous abyss of time. (Jung, 1991 [1918], §16).[63]

When in 1930 he wrote for an American audience on Negroid and Indian behaviour, and its impact on the psychology of the white Americans, he explained:

> The *inferior man* [by which Jung in this context appears to mean 'the primitive'] has a tremendous pull

because he fascinates the *inferior layers* of our psyche [which in this context appears to mean the undeveloped aspect of the psyche, the shadow], which has lived through untold ages of similar conditions... He reminds us... not only of childhood but also of our prehistory, which would take us back not more than about twelve hundred years so far as the Germanic races are concerned. The barbarian in us is still wonderfully strong and he yields easily to the lure of his youthful memories... The Latin peoples being older don't need to be so much on their guard, hence their approach to the coloured man is different. (Jung, 1991 [1930b], §962, my italics)

In both passages Jung was referring to internalised, innate psychological characteristics of a time before high culture. This was a universal phase of human development, but as Jung understood it, the Germanic race had been in this naïve state until relatively recently. He then extended this idea with his comment about the Latin peoples. Here he suggested that the duration of the cultural phase was important in setting down the thickness of the cultural layer. This argument was the same one he used concerning the Jews and the Germans in the 1918 text 'The Role of the Unconscious'. There he suggested that the key issue was the antiquity of a group's culture; there was no suggestion of an idea about a race's supposed innate biological superiority. This needs to be stressed as Jung was not suggesting a biological model of superiority, as is generally implied in racist ideas. In both these quotes Jung talked about 'layers' of the primitive, so clearly 'the primitive' contains a hierarchy. Yet while making distinctions he was not making a value judgement about 'primary' cultures. He was always ready to give credit to any culture. For example in his criticism of Western prudery he contrasted the moral integrity of those many dismiss as 'primitives' with Western 'barbarism'. He stated: 'So often among so-called "primitives" one comes across spiritual personalities who immediately inspire respect, as though they were the fully matured products of an undisturbed fate. I speak here from personal experience. But where among present-day Europeans can one find people not deformed by acts of moral violence? We are still barbarous enough to believe both in asceticism and its opposite' (Jung, 1990 [1925], §336).

In Jung's conception the most basic level of human cognitive activity was 'the primitive', by which he meant:

> the layer of the man who did not yet possess his thought, to whom mind was something objective which appeared outside, like the primitive who has no psychology, or only traces of it, like little children. His psychology appears outside of himself. All the archetypal figures, inasmuch as they are constellated, appear in his surroundings, in animals, in men, in trees, in rocks and so on. *He* does not think, *it* thinks, *it* speaks; an animal or a bird tells it to him, or he hears the trees whisper together in the night, telling secrets...
>
> That is primitive mentality, the objectivation of the mental process, and it is amazingly frequent but naturally quite invisible to the people concerned. It happens all the time in ordinary practical life that people really behave like primitives. (Jung, 1998 [1930-1934], p94-95)

So for Jung the 'primitive' mentality was one which operated by 'the objectivation of the mental process', or at a level of *participation mystique*, to use Lévy-Bruhl's phrase.[64] This is the level of the collective unconscious as one sees from the next quotation from 11th February 1931: 'The very primitive man is still identical with the collective unconscious, he is just a piece of this world, a part of visible nature, and values himself as one among the other animals; so he is like an indistinguishable part of the collective unconscious and naturally there is no such dissociation as with us' (Jung, 1998 [1930-1934], p211). Thus far Jung was suggesting that the psyche had a universal layer at the bottom which operated by *participation mystique*.

In 1931, Jung went on to explain what operated above this primitive level. He wrote that:

as civilization begins, there is that differentiation from nature; then consciousness moves away from the unconscious and then mediation becomes necessary. Therefore you find in the very beginning of civilization certain people who realized the necessity of a mediating link. The sorcerer or medicine man is himself such a link he deals with ghosts and if anything difficult occurs, say a war or a pestilence, he has recourse to that method; that is, he tries to re-establish the lost connection with the collective unconscious. For it is supposed that if that connection is perfect, nothing can happen which is out of order, only regular things can happen. (Jung, 1998 [1930-1934], p211)

In this passage Jung was first talking of 'the very primitive man [who] is still identical with the collective unconscious'. He was not talking about generic 'primitive man' but about those individuals in a cultural group who are psychologically immature and lack this mediational layer. It is these individuals that Jung was referring to as 'primitive', who only (or mainly?) function through the symbolic capacity of *participation mystique,* which is derived from the symbolic layer of the psyche. After this base layer in primary culture he suggested there will be people with a mediational layer of the psyche who are the individuated shaman. Beyond this stage of development one gradually ascends into the 'modern' psyche that is neurotically divorced from its symbolic mediation with the instinctive.

This interpretation of Jung's implicit model is confirmed by a 1952 conversation between Ira Progoff and Jung. Progoff voiced doubts about whether a yogin or a shaman could be considered individuated as they either externally projected their unconscious processes or saw them as revealed as myth inside them. Jung replied that: 'They may not be conscious but they hear the inner voice, they *act* on it, they do not go against it—that is what counts. The primitive may not *formulate* it in the way you mean, but he has a pretty clear idea what goes on: I understand his language. When

I go to him, we speak the same language' (McGuire and Hull, 1980, p207).

The nature of this tiered form of distinction needs stressing. Jung was making no value judgement about the respective cultures outside of their potential for furthering individuation. These were not racial comments or suggestions of innate biological difference as for Jung this mediational layer was acquired by individual effort. That being so, the mediational layer represents a discrete part of Jung's hierarchy of the unconscious. This is important for us to register because a process dependent on individual effort clearly contradicts any suggestion of racial inheritance and invalidates the impression that the layers in the primitive are (racial) inherited layers.

Unfortunately for Jungian scholars, Jung was not clear on this in some of his writings in the thirties and this confusion increases the possibility of misunderstandings, especially where his arguments jar with modern preoccupations. However, once one has understood the significance of the mediational layer, one is able to account for some of Jung's seemingly most obscure discussions on race in the 1935 Tavistock lectures. There we find Lamarckian and Geographical Determinist traits that may be due to theoretical regressions or lapses of intellectual habit on Jung's part. For example, Jung said:

> Our unconscious mind, like our body, is a storehouse of relics and memories of the past. A study of the structure of the unconscious collective mind would reveal the same discoveries as you make in comparative anatomy... the collective unconscious... is just a new branch of science, and it is really common sense to admit the existence of unconscious collective processes. For, though a child is not born conscious, his mind is not a *tabula rasa*. (Jung, 1986 [1935a], §84)

Here Jung seemed to be deploying a Lamarckian idea about the genetic transmission of memories across generations. As he developed his argument he suggested that there was a substantial amount of psychological differences set down by Lamarckian cultural deposits:

> The child is born with a definite brain, and the brain of an English child will work not like that of an Australian black fellow but in the way of a modern English person. The brain is born with a finished structure, it will work in a modern way, but this brain has its history. It has been built up in the course of millions of years and represents a history of which it is the result. Naturally it carries with it the traces of that history, exactly like the body, and if you grope down into the basic structure of the mind you naturally find traces of the archaic mind. (Jung, 1986 [1935a], §84)

This passage has a lack of clarity. Was Jung comparing new, uneducated infants or culturally socialised children? If he was suggesting a comparison between infants exposed to different degrees of socialisation, this was clumsy sociological thinking. But beyond this confusion, Jung seemed to have reverted to Lamarckian and Geographical Determinist ideas by suggesting that a culture of sufficient age changes the structure of the brain in succeeding generations so that after a time there is a difference between the Aboriginal and the Caucasian brain. This hypothesis would posit major racial difference and the possibility of comparative anatomy and comparative psychology.

Thus far one is lost in a confusion of possibilities, so one needs to pause and consider the following paragraph:

> Then there is another class of contents... which cannot be ascribed to individual acquisition. These contents have one outstanding peculiarity, and that is their mythological character. It is as if they belong to a pattern not peculiar to any particular mind or person, but rather to a pattern peculiar *to mankind in general*. When I first came across such contents I wondered very much whether they might not be due to heredity, and I thought they might be explained by racial inher-

> itance. In order to settle that question I went to the United States and studied the dreams of pure-blooded Negroes, and *I was able to satisfy myself that these images have nothing to do with so-called blood or racial inheritance, nor are they personally acquired by the individual. They belong to mankind in general, and therefore they are of a collective nature.* (Jung, 1986 [1935a], §79, my italics)

The part of the quotation in italics highlights Jung's use of the 'collective' to refer to the species-wide common genetic inheritance of mankind. Jung even reinforces the importance of the universal by almost dismissing the 'so-called blood or racial inheritance'. As he goes on to explain:

> somewhere you are the same as the Negro or the Chinese or whoever you live with, you are all just human beings. In the collective unconscious you are the same as a man of another race, you have the same archetypes, just as you have, like him, eyes, a heart, a liver, and so on. It does not matter that his skin is black. It matters to a certain extent, sure enough—*he has probably a whole historical layer less than you.* The different strata of the mind correspond to the history of the races. (Jung, 1986 [1935a], §93, my italics)

By 'a whole historical layer' he was referring to a culturally socialised level of psychological development. Thus one sees that for Jung the key issue was still one of culture, it's just that in this case he had lapsed into his Lamarckian assumptions about the acquisition and retention of ideas and so in this statement confused culture and genetics.

Having reviewed the material about the layered unconscious covered so far in this chapter, one sees that Jung had a much more variegated model than his diagram of the geological strata suggests. This can be presented as a table:

Type of Layer	Characteristic Psychology of the Layer
Modern 'Psychological' Man	A sophisticated awareness of the unconscious.
Modern (Rational) Man	A naive ignorance of psychology or a pathological antipathy to the unconscious.
The shaman	The 'mediational' consciousness attained by individuals capable of withdrawing projections and sustaining the interaction between the symbolic unconscious and conscious thought.
The 'Primitive' Man	A state of naive *participation mystique*, which includes the external projection of mental processes and a tendency to unconscious group identification.

To sum up thus far, Jung's idea of the 'primitive' does not have a racial aspect, and it is beginning to look as if Jung was not making any racial distinctions. On consideration it becomes apparent that these layers are all the product of individual psychological maturity. This being the case, how then is one to understand the collective aspects of the collective unconscious layer? Part of the answer can be provided by the idea of the cultural unconscious, which we will consider next.

The Cultural Layer of the Collective Unconscious

There are a number of passages where at first sight Jung was talking specifically about racial differences and made a number of comments on the psychological relationship between Negroes and Whites. In examining the statements one gets a clearer idea of the significance of culture in Jung's ideas and so can determine what status, if any, 'race' actually had in his thinking.

In 'Mind and Earth' (1927-31), Jung attributed the open way the Americans laughed, their loose-jointed style of walking and their music and dance to Negro influence. He specified that the great influence of the Negro was psychological and 'not due to the mixing of blood.' By specifically rejecting any suggestion of 'racially' transmitted (Lamarckian) differences, one sees that, for Jung, cultural influences had become the significant idea.

Some of Jung's comments could be construed as being culturally critical. He compared the restraint of many Americans' 'Germanic forefathers' with modern chatter, which he likened to what he had heard in 'a Negro village' with its 'total lack of privacy and the all-devouring mass sociability... of primitive life in open huts, where there is complete identity with all members of the tribe.' He found the lack of privacy and outdoor life of Americans strange and wondered 'how much of all this is due to symbiosis with the Negro, and how much to the fact that America is still a pioneering nation on virgin soil' (Jung, 1991 [1927-1931b], §95-96). Here, then, Jung was making some assumptions about qualitative differences between cultures, which one can term 'culturist', to distinguish ideas of cultural superiority from ideologies of racial superiority.

In the same period Jung wrote: 'I am quite convinced that some American peculiarities can be traced back directly to the coloured man, while others result from a compensatory defence against his laxity' (Jung, 1991 [1930b], §967). In this article Jung's 'culturist' opinions can again be seen when he wrote of how Negro culture affected America and Europe.

When he spoke of his perception of the effects of Jazz or primitive art, he stated: 'we are just as much *infected* by that primitive mind; the primitive man is becoming almost a sort of ideal. Look at our dances!' Here it is clear that his use of 'the primitive' was to describe a developmental stage, not to make a racist comment. He was also expressing part of his critique of psychoanalysis, because he went on to criticise society's morbid interest in 'dirty crimes'. He thought European papers were 'not yet quite so *infected* in that way, but in other countries there are headlines of enormous size when anything horrible happens, and everybody swallows it greedily. Then the way psychoanalysis reduces everything to power or sex is still another manifestation of the primitive which shows its actual force' (Jung, 1998 [1930-1934], p374, my italics).

How easy is it to interpret Jung's use of the words 'infected' or 'primitive' as racist? In the passage Jung used the word 'infected' twice in the context of a cultural debate. The first use could be considered 'racist', and was certainly 'culturist'. The second use probably referred in part, or completely, to Western decadence. Was Jung being racist here? The use of public health imagery was part of the political vocabulary of the time and he was using it in a general discussion from his class perspective, but there is no suggestion of this being part of a racist presentation.

Jung's lack of negative intent is even more clearly seen when he discussed how the *infection* by the primitive could affect White minorities in Africa. This he contrasted with the impact of the Negro minority in America which he saw as 'not a degenerative influence, but rather one which, peculiar though it is, cannot be termed unfavourable—unless one happens to have a jazz phobia' (Jung, 1991 [1927-31b], §97). Clearly he was not being negative per se about Negro culture when he wrote so dismissively of those with 'a jazz phobia'. What Jung was criticising was the possible erosion of middle class European norms. This would suggest that even if the 'primitive' style he was criticising was 'African' in its origin, Jung would have had no difficulty in finding an individuated elder from the Mahgrib or Sudan to condemn the decadent Western follies. Jung was being snobbish in a psychological sense, and there was a suggestion of middle class culturism, but his pan-cultural use of individuation negates the implications of racism.[65]

In the Tavistock lecture, Jung also implicitly referred to cultural issues. He stated: 'If you study races as I have done you can make very interesting discoveries... The American, on account of the fact that he lives on virgin soil, has the Red Indian in him. The Red man, even if he has never seen one, and the Negro, though he may be cast out and the tram-cars reserved for white men only, have got into the American and you will realise that he belongs to a partly coloured nation. These things are wholly unconscious' (Jung, 1986 [1935a], §94). What was Jung suggesting?

By referring to a 'partly coloured nation' a modern reader can all too easily assume Jung was making a superficial observation about America being a 'melting pot' of mixed races but actually Jung was mixing a number of ideas. The references to 'virgin soil' and Red Indians were a product of Jung's taste for Romantic rhetoric, but may also have owed something to his exposure to *Bodenbeschaffenheit* and *Völkisch* ideas. Here Jung's main idea was that the American culture had assimilated a great deal of Black American psychology by unconscious cultural transmission. This reading of Jung's assessment of the importance of culture is supported by von Franz who recalled Jung specifying that this influence occurred with Whites who had 'no blood connection' with Blacks (1994, p8).

In the light of this awareness, one must understand Jung's seemingly 'racial' idea as an observation about the transmission of culture. He understood culture as a complicated psychological complex made up of both imitation and reaction, which evolved in response to the impact of the presence of other races. As an example of the latter, Jung observed that in America the shadow of Whites' often appeared in dreams as a Black man, whereas in Europe the shadow was more normally projected onto the image of a tramp or criminal (Jung, 1991 [1927-1931b], §99). This all suggests that the cultural layer of the collective psyche is a highly malleable mix of imitation, projection and reaction.

Jung could be culturist, but if one looks at his problematic statements in their context and allows for his occasional culturist observations, he makes so few racist statements that it becomes almost meaningless to argue that he was racist. However there are a few statements that do seem to be racist lapses, and these need to be acknowledged and set against his explicit anti-colonialism and his anti-racism after the Second World War. One pseudo-biological comment was made on the 30th October 1935:

> There is also that danger in the mixture of races, against which our instincts always set up a resistance. Sometimes one thinks it is snobbish prejudice, but it is an instinctive prejudice, and the fact is that if distant races are mixed, the fertility is very low, as one sees

with the white and the Negro; a Negro woman very rarely conceives from a white man. If she does, a mulatto is the result and he is apt to be a bad character. The Malays are a very distinct race, very remote from the white man, and the mixture of Malay and white is as a rule bad. (Jung, 1989 [1934-1939], p642-643)[66]

The other example is noted by Dalal in his regrettably anachronistic polemic against Jung (1988, p269). This was Jung's criticism of the modern Hindu man who 'is too fond of ease and coolness' (Jung, 1991 [1939], §995). Jung displayed a common European prejudice against the airy relaxed clothes of Southern Hindus that are a necessity in the humid South. Interestingly he seemed to have accepted the British pre-war Indian Army assumption of an infallible connection between martial bearing and military prowess (Slim, 1956,1970). Jung's comments are not of a very serious order, and considering he had just been highly critical of European females' clothes in the previous paragraph, this opinion is more an example of class and culturist prejudice than a racist comment. After the early thirties Jung became less concerned with his stratified hierarchy and made less references to race or 'the primitive'. One gets an early indication of this change in 1932 when he suggested: 'All human beings are much alike... and the psychic substratum upon which the individual consciousness is based is universally the same'. Jung concludes that the only differences to be found were in 'the individual nature of the personality' (Jung, 1981 [1934a], §307). This neglect of the national and the racial layer of the unconscious at this time should not be taken too far, given his other statements, but it was clearly an indication of how he was retreating from his earlier focus of interest.

In Jung's later writings on culture and race, his focus changed from the cultural categorisation that he indulged during the first decades of the century, to the level of the individuation and psychiatric health of individuals in their respective cultures. For example he declared: 'we have an extraordinary amount of unconsciousness in our civilisation, but if you go to other races, to India or to China, for example, you discover that these people are conscious of things for which the psychoanalyst in our country has to dig for months'

(1935, §91).⁶⁷ As always when dealing with Jung's comments on race, care is needed.⁶⁸

Significantly, despite being a lifelong Anglophile and travelling in the Empire in the first half of the century, Jung held strong anti-colonial views. After the Second World War he became increasingly critical of European materialism and the soullessness of the West (Jung, 1991 [1945] §431). It is hardly the remark of a racist to write, on 31st October 1946: 'The Americans are certainly a very humane nation, or at least imagine they are, but this does not prevent so-and-so many Negroes from being lynched every year' (Jung, 1973 [1906-1950], p447). Later he added: 'the European has also to answer for all the crimes he has committed against the coloured races during the process of colonisation' (Jung, 1991 [1957], §571).

In this late period the importance of the cultural layer was highlighted by a letter in July 1956 in which he stated that cultured 'Indians and Chinese have just as little relation to the collective unconscious as Europeans' (Jung, 1976 [1951-1961], p320⁶⁹) and that it was only the primitive who may have uncorrupted access to it. In other words, various races do not have different access to the collective unconscious, but the respective levels of culture do affect the access. This demonstrates that even when Jung used the term 'race', on examination he was referring to cultural variables, not biological differences. What were being discussed were layers of historical culture smothering the archetypal unconscious. What needs to be underlined here is that Jung's fundamental position had not changed. The hierarchy still remained; it just was no longer expressed in terms of 'race'.

Yet this does not mean that for Jung everything was finally decided. To the end, Jung still had the feeling that the racial issue was important but regretted he was unable to 'undertake very extensive researches'. As he wrote in the same letter: 'While the inference of a universal psychic disposition [archetypes] of this kind is sufficiently assured by experience, *I feel less certain when it comes to the question of hereditary 'ramifications,' i.e., specific differentiations conditioned by locality or race*. It seems to me altogether possible and even probable that such differentiations really do exist (like the wingless insects of the Galapagos Islands) regardless of theoretical prejudices. But as yet I have found no certain proofs' (Jung, 1976

[1951-1961], p320, my emphasis). In writing of 'differentiations conditioned by locality or race' one sees that Jung never entirely forsook his Geographical Determinist and Lamarckian roots.

JUNG'S VIEWS ON SPIRITUALISM, MATERIALISM AND POLITICS: EVIDENCE OF A RACIAL BIAS?

To conclude our review of Jung's ideas about race, let us revisit the Marxist thinkers who have challenged Jung's spiritual-material synthesis. Clarke demonstrates how a Marxist critique could borrow the idea of projection and suggest that the whole Jungian definition of spiritual health and individuation represents an unconscious projection of the Western bourgeois ideology, with its implicit idea of an elite hierarchy of self-knowledge. If this were so, the Jungian paradigm's claim to be universally valid could be seen as an example of cultural imperialism.

In his discussion of this issue, Dalal (1988, p274) recognises that Jung seemed to be judging each culture by its ability to produce individuated individuals. It follows from this that Jung was implicitly talking about a hierarchy of cultures based on the culture's ability to foster individuation. This Jungian judgement involves a combination of factors that include the internalisation of projections, integration of the shadow, a synthesis of freedom from collective norms as well as social and political maturity. One can argue from a Marxian perspective that this is implicitly an elite, culturally-bound class reference scale. That suggestion is a logically sound position, but one can just as easily say 'individuation' is an a-cultural and a-class feature, as it can be seen in the Chinese mandarin, the Eskimo shaman, or even the Swiss bourgeois! As Gallard realised, this part of Jung's thinking 'makes a reading of his work so difficult and even gives rise to distortions' (1994, p223). Jung can be both intensely nationalist and yet also identify with the best of Chinese culture as he salutes the universal potential of individuation.

The argument that Jung was being culturally elitist and imperialist is untenable given that his real concern was not the status of a culture, but its ability to produce individuated healthy adults. By that reasoning, Bushman culture would probably rate as superior to modern mass European culture if one accepts Julian David's estimate that maybe as many as forty percent of them were shamans (David, 1999).

The possibility of Jung's ideas being Euro-centric is another debate. A Marxist might claim that Jungian values had been used to judge other cultures. But Jung's advocacy of spiritual development meant he often favoured non-Western or even 'primitive' cultures over so-called 'Western Imperialist' ones. The Marxist claim of class bias can be out-flanked. A Jungian is just as entitled to suggest that the Marxist projects his ideological biases onto his claimed 'objective class consciousness'. Furthermore one can suggest that the Marxist's ideology was a delusional socio-political system which was not a 'necessary consequence of external conditions, but [was]... precipitated by the collective unconscious' (Jung, 1969 [1934/1954], §49).

This is a circular debate that cannot be resolved by logic; it cannot be solved by appeals to evidence; and it is of little intellectual or historical significance, given the demise of most of the Marxist political monolith. For those that still consider such issues worth debating, one can offer Clarke's acknowledgement that Jung in his work on archetypal theory 'adopted a far from blinkered methodology, drawing on evidence from a very wide range of divergent cultural and historical sources', thus he tried to maintain a critical stance on his own culture and beliefs. This is not to say that one should forget that Jung did neglect 'the link between belief systems and the institutions of political and social power' (1992, p139-140). However this neglect is better dealt with as part of a sociological critique of Jung rather than an ideological polemic.

In response to Jung's Marxist critics, it is over-simplistic to allege that Jung was just unconsciously projecting Western bourgeois values. On closer examination he was explicitly advocating his own anti-materialist spiritual perspective that condemned both Western materialism and imperialism.

SUMMARY OF THE RACIAL LAYER OF THE UNCONSCIOUS

The layered model of the unconscious is important because of the way it reflects Jung's conception of history as progressive and moving through stages. This conception of progress was given an unusual twist in some of his early writings about the layered psyche. He implied that progress for individuals or collectivities was potentially constrained by the level of cultural development achieved by their nation or race. Thus his understanding of the psyche implied that psychic development was either aided by genetic inheritance or hindered by the lack of a developmental layer. These ideas did not play a great role in Jung's writing as he was more interested in the possibility of categorising differences than exploring differences in a social context.

Jung's principle concern was with the individual's psychological development, regardless of culture or race. Jung was not writing about the sociology of complex African societies such as the Medieval trader kingdoms of Benin or Zimbabwe as Samuel's might have wished, (1993, p309), nor was he referring to late twentieth century Africa, which so exercises Dalal's anachronistic criticism (1988, p265). Instead, Jung had an equally legitimate concern with small primary cultures and their still extant shamanic practices. This puts Jung outside much of the biological and pejorative package of ideas that is generally understood to constitute racism. Harms argued that Jung's psychology tends to be labelled as racist because he talked about differences in an attempt to question the dynamics of race and nationality. Jung's psychology was concerned with comparisons and this inevitably meant the search for and creation of categories and then—logically—the need to account for these differences. Thus where Freud started from a perspective that sought to provide a universal theory, Jung worked towards looking for differences and accounting for them (1946, p32).

If Jung is read only superficially then modern hypersensitivity can lead one to misinterpret the very fact that Jung elected to refer to different races. One may need to recall that, at the time when Jung was writing, one could draw a crude correlation between different races and different levels of industrial development. At that time Jung was making generalisations that had some validity in an age free from the niceties of politically correct semantics. To criticise him for this is anachronistic, but this may not be easy, as Magilner warns: 'race' is now such a taboo area that even to talk about race is to plant in the mind of the audience the possibility that one is being pejorative or racist (2000).

In his earlier work Jung was interested in race, but race could only have the impact he envisaged in his original model of the collective unconscious if Lamarckian ideas about inheritance were correct. Modern biology has dismissed this possibility, and with it one must remove or redefine a stratum of Jung's model of the collective unconscious.

If one wanted to construct a critical case one could accuse Jung of inter-cultural elitism or culturism, but not racism with its biological perspective. The hierarchy that Jung implied was cultural not racial. Furthermore his idea is anthropologically vague and open to controversy. Given this, the interesting issue for the Jungian perspective is: *if individuation is a multi-dimensional continuum, then may one culture be more successful in fostering 'individuation' than another culture?* Sadly such a discussion about individuation and its definition in global or local terms lies outside the remit of this book.

THE NATIONAL LAYER OF THE UNCONSCIOUS : CONFUSIONS IN JUNG'S HISTORICAL PERSPECTIVE

How successful was Jung in trying to establishing a national layer of the collective unconscious? It may come as no surprise to learn that Jung's evidence is repeatedly compromised by his eccentric use of historical 'evidence'. For example in the *Visions* seminars, one reads how Jung thought he could perceive different evolutionary strata of thinking with parallels in different stages of historical development which would account for the inheritance of social perspectives that shape behaviour. Jung recalled how people retain customs such as putting up Christmas trees when they have long since forgotten, or never knew, the custom's 'exceedingly ancient' roots (Jung, 1998 [1930-1934], p60). He then argued that 'as long as we continue these practices, we are in a way like the people who first expressed themselves through such rites.' Though why this should be the case is not made clear. Jung made no attempt to show a direct connection between the purpose of the pagan rites and the nineteenth century revival of a possibly seventeenth century custom, other than that both represent an image of hope. There is no necessity to suggest a causal unconscious connection because the nineteenth century historical adaptation of this piece of symbolism is historically documented.

It is easy to see why he suggested that people inherited old values as he came from the very traditional hinterland of Switzerland; but today, with the increasing velocity of change, old emotional values are being eroded or forgotten as long term cultural norms are swamped by the cult of progress and the immediacy of television. Even if one allows that Jung's observation on the influence and retention of old ideas had some validity, as a phenomenon it is readily explainable by sociologists and historians. One does not need to suggest an innate aspect.

Our reservations concerning the collective unconscious may increase when we read that Jung tried to explain his idea by suggesting it is as if ideas generated by the intellect in the head were a hundred years behind the times; ideas of the heart three centuries old; and ideas of the stomach from the age of the cave man (Jung, 1998 [1930-1934], p59). It followed from this that going into the collective unconscious was akin to going back in time, in terms of the emotional provenance of the psyche's evolution. Should one take his idea as a colourful image? Or as the germ of an idea that different bio-organic systems (of head, heart and stomach) correspond to different instinctive response systems, with their own characteristic impact on emotional behaviour, as followed later by Campbell (1988, p51). Evidently Jung mixed poorly thought-through historical examples with his Environmental Determinist perspective.

In effect what Jung seems to be describing is *collective culture* rather than a genetically transmitted collective unconscious. Indeed, Andrew Samuels, with his abiding interest in political issues, has taken this idea up in a different context and suggested that such was Jung's interest in the psychology of nations that he should be understood as a 'psychologist of nations' (1997, p287); so it is useful to co-opt some of the issues Samuels raises as we look at Jung's psychology of nations.

Jung's 'Psychology of Nations'

How did Jung's historical perspective and his perception of national psychologies fit into his theory of the collective unconscious? Jung was convinced of the validity of national psychologies and argued that an understanding of them was vital for understanding of international politics. In a letter of March 2nd 1934, he eloquently explained what lay behind his thinking when he had written the much-misunderstood article 'The State of Psychotherapy Today'. He argued that, in looking at other nations, one should not label others with one's 'subjective assumptions' or be betrayed into assuming that just because nations have some ideas in common, that does not go for all ideas, and these 'differences' are 'a worthy subject of investigation' (Jung, 1973 [1906-1950], p147-148).

Jung returned to his defence of the utility of 'national psychologies' with his 1949 reply to criticism in the *Saturday Review of Literature*:

> Some people show a funny kind of resentment when one speaks of differences in psychology—but one must admit that different nationalities and different races have different outlooks and different psychologies. Take the difference between the French and the English, or for that matter, between the English and the Americans! There is a marked difference in psychology everywhere. Only an idiot cannot see it. It is too ridiculous to be so hypersensitive about such things. (McGuire and Hull, 1980, p194)

These are pragmatic considerations that echo Jung's political realism. But if the hypothesis might have some use, was its theory sound?

To start with, the national layer could not claim a biologically defined basis, as the racial layer might have been able to. Instead it was founded on a number of observations and ideas. One group of observations could be defined as observations about 'national complexes'—that is, specific events or ideas held by each individual culture. The other, wider idea is one of national typologies, which suggests that one can extend observations about national complexes to identify a series of linked characteristics that together give a general typology of a nation. This idea must be dealt with first, as it was more fundamental to Jung's theoretical paradigm.

NATIONAL TYPOLOGIES

How well did Jung identify and explore his hypothesis of national typologies? He argued: 'Nations have their own peculiar psychology, and their own particular kind of psychopathology' (Jung, 1991 [1946a], §466). He suggested that these differences were due to a range of factors and gave examples of the long-term impact of cultural history on contemporary political culture. Talking on the historical reasons for the difference between the French and the Anglo-Saxon viewpoints, Jung saw the key difference as the partial continuity between the Roman civilisation and its Frankish successors. He wrote of the survival of pagan attitudes in France as part of an antique civilisation that had enough continuity with the post-Roman world to influence the rise of early medieval Christianity (Jung, 1990 [1925], p154-55). This phenomenon of national heritage is by definition a long-term factor, but there was no indication of this cultural tradition being passed on biologically. So far in our examination of his evidence it seems that Jung's account of a national heritage may be due to an unconscious cultural tradition, but one does not need an innate mechanism and a collective unconscious to account for it.

Another variation of Jung's thoughts on national typologies came in the 1928 article on the Swiss with a comment on national character that had a *Völkisch* style and showed a Geographical Determinist perspective: 'The national character is imprinted on a man as a fate he has not chosen... It is not the will of individuals that moulds the destinies of nations, but supra-personal factors, the spirit and the earth, which work in mysterious ways and in unfathomable darkness... the 'nation' (like the 'state') is a personified concept that corresponds in reality only to a specific nuance of the individual psyche. The nation... is nothing but an inborn character' (Jung, 1991 [1928], §921).[70] Here again, although Jung used the words 'inborn character', he was referring to Geographical Determinist factors repeatedly affecting each generation.

These two examples both represent influences that are very long-term and refer to the way the culture responds to emotion. In these cases Jung offered some sort of explanation as to why a difference had initially occurred in the past, but he did not say if the difference was perpetuated by external social norms or by Lamarckian processes. Significantly, as he was locating his remarks in the historical past he was not offering a racial explanation, unless one understands him to be still strongly under the influences of Lamarckian ideas.

An important observation from all this is that, as was discussed earlier, most of Jung's ideas about individual character and national character were dependent on the culture and the processes of nurture, but this 'nurture' was seen as having a very long time scale and being largely unconscious. In this respect, the cultural patterns mimic the archetypal or instinctive behaviour patterns, but are still much too recent to be accounted for by that theory. Cultural forms and their allied emotional mannerisms can last for a long time. There is no need to posit the resurgence of hypothetical Lamarckian buried memories when legends or myths are explicitly referred to or aped by contemporaries.

Beyond Jung's idiosyncratic long-term historical explanations, one can also consider Jung's academic methods when he referred to more contemporary issues. Samuels suggests that Jung was reductive 'to the point at which the nation itself is regarded as a solely psychological entity and observed from a solely psychological point of view'. He suggests that Jung's 'ideas on national psychology degenerate into nothing more than typology. His method is to assemble lists of characteristics' and through all this categorising and list-making he was pursuing his 'ethos of complementarity' (1989, p190, 191). This produced a mass of generalisations whose crudity was masked by Jung's use of jargon and his own stature.

Samuels' reservations about some of Jung's observations are unexceptional, if maybe a little judgemental, given Jung's resources and his early attempts at field-work that we have discussed. Certainly some of Jung's writings warrant such criticism, but was Jung just airing generalities? An alternative perspective is that in his more considered formulations, Jung was making some interesting points that can be treated a different way if one is deploying a looser frame of analysis, and this ironically is what Samuels later did in *Politics on the Couch* (2001), to which we will return in chapter ten, but for now let us stick with his critique of Jung's methodology. What is the theoretical viability of the concept of national typologies? Samuels' general position is that Jung's 'emphasis is on classification by characteristics, emphasising differences, not on the living experience of difference' (1989, p190). In response to Samuels' critique of the use of generalisations, the counter argument is that generalisations can be looked at from a number of angles that include their utility and their legitimacy. In practice one often finds that the utility of generalisations depends on their pragmatic accuracy as general observations. If they are then abused, that is another issue. In any event, their legitimacy is often a matter of academic fashion. For example the economic generalisation of 'class' is still acceptable within the fashions of postwar European academia. This contrasts with generalisations about 'race' that have become almost taboo after the Nazis' politics of biological elitism (Lifton, 1986).

Was Jung's classification by 'characteristics of difference' as pernicious as Samuels implies? On this issue, Harms argued that Jung's ideas tend to be labelled as racist because he talked about differences in an attempt to question the dynamics of race and nationality. Jung's psychology was concerned with comparisons and this inevitably meant the search for and creation of categories and the need to account for these differences, in contrast with Freud, who sought to provide a universal theory (1946, p32). Might not such a classification, and one based on 'the living experience of difference', be equally valid tools for research? One cannot discount Samuels' post-modernist qualms concerning the inherent problems of external classifications; but as Clarke explains, using Dilthey's suggestion, the historian has to find analogies and distil data into categories 'because exact measurement and objective assessments are unattainable' (1992, p46).[71] In this way Jung is only offering historians another tool. It may be different from the more subtle sociology of Samuels's plea for a 'living experience of difference', but it is still a legitimate exercise. It is another issue whether Jung misused the tool, or the tool was found to be too crude; but at least from a pragmatic point of view, Jung's realist defence of national psychologies retains a telling utility, whatever the flaws in his idea of national psychologies as an academic category.

While aware of the dangers of using typologies, it is not so evident that cultures do not reinforce a psychological and emotional position so that for practical purposes there may be some validity in cultural typologies. Campbell, in many of his books on mythological systems, suggests that the unconscious gestalt a mythology fosters can affect subsequent political cultures (1985, p54). For example, he suggested that one factor in the acceptance of a Marxist dictatorship by the Chinese would be the long tradition of Imperial central control. In contrast, in the West, one can argue that an extrovert culture directs individuals' endeavours towards outward goals, rather than the introspection that historically has been more widespread in the East (de Castillejo, 1973, p48).[72]

The last issue to examine is Jung's discussion of National Psychology in his writings about Jews and Germans. I want to start by addressing Samuels' fear that Jung was using the 'scientific' theatre to pursue invidious polemical comparisons between Germans and Jews in pursuit of a nationalist agenda (1993, p314). Samuels interprets Jung as having made 'offensive generalisations about Jews' and assumes that Jung was anti-Semitic.

This is a serious accusation, but as the brief look at the issue of Jung's anti-Semitism in chapter two concluded, the anti-Semitic argument was insufficiently sustainable on present evidence. However, it is again useful to use some of Jung's arguments to revisit elements of his thinking on national groups, so let us take a case where Samuels has suggested that Jung was stressing the national dimension and demonstrating anti-Semitic overtones.

What we are now going to look at are Jung's ideas on race and 'the Land' in the context of his German-Jewish preoccupation in the 1918 essay 'The Role of the Unconscious'. This essay came two years after Jung first aired the idea of the collective unconscious and saw his use of many of the *Völkisch* and Geographical Determinist ideas.

Unfortunately, in this essay, part of Jung's discussion of his ideas on the importance of the Land took place within the late nineteenth century debate about the nature of Jewish nationalism. In view of what happened two decades later, this could lead the reader to dismiss Jung's theoretical ideas as obsolete and distasteful, but that reaction would be premature and simplistic. Unfortunate though his example was, Jung was raising valid issues. To disentangle these it is necessary to work carefully through what Jung said:

> The Jew... is domesticated to a higher degree than we are, but he is badly at a loss for that quality in man which roots him to the earth and draws new strength from below. This chthonic quality is found in dangerous concentration in the Germanic peoples... The Jew has too little of this quality—where has he his own earth underfoot? The mystery of earth is no joke and no paradox. One only needs to see how, in America, the skull and pelvis measurements of all the European races begin to Indianise themselves in the second generation of immigrants. That is the mystery of the American earth.
>
> The soil of every country holds some such mystery. We have an unconscious reflection of this in the psyche: just as there is a relationship of mind to body, so there is a relationship of body to earth... It is not easy to describe, definite though it is. There are people —quite a number of them—who live outside and above their bodies, who float like bodiless shadows above their earth, their earthy component, which is their body. Others live wholly in their bodies. As a rule, the Jew lives in amicable relationship with the earth, but without feeling the power of the chthonic. His receptivity to this seems to have weakened with time. This may explain the specific need of the Jew to reduce everything to its material beginnings; he needs these beginnings in order to counterbalance the dangerous ascendancy of his two cultures. A little bit of primitivity does not hurt him; on the contrary, I can understand very well that Freud's and Adler's reduction of everything psychic to primitive sexual wishes and power-drives has something about it that is beneficial and satisfying to the Jew, because it is a form of simplification. (Jung, 1991 [1918], §19)

To modern sensibilities this is an uncomfortable passage, so to prevent one getting lost in anachronistic discussions one needs to separate a number of issues.

Firstly, one needs to be clear about his purpose in referring to 'the Jews'. Jung was clearly still fascinated with the motif of German-Jewish parallels, but does it follow that this discussion of German-Jewish issues was what drove Jung? Samuels has suggested that Jung's fascination with this issue was based on his fixation with 'an ethos of complementarity', so that with many issues Jung tended to look for matched opposites which he could then combine to produce an absolutely wonderful-sounding 'wholeness' (1989, p191). This is a useful observation, and one of the best examples of Jung's fascination with this 'ethos' was his early relationship with Sabina Spielrein and their metaphor of a love child, the new Siegfried to symbolise the union of German and Jew, male and female (Kerr, 1994). So given that Jung thought in terms of such an ethos of complementarity and acknowledged the symbolic agenda in his relationship with Spielrein, is it quite so easy to interpret the 1918 essay as an exercise in anti-Semitic polemic?

Instead, if we return to the passage in the 1918 essay, another way to look at this is to understand that here Jung was using the words 'the Jew' and 'Freud' as synonymous, as if for him Freud represented all Jews, or that Freud represented the sorts of Jews he was concerned with. Why was Jung making this generalisation and what did he mean by it? When Jung was referring to 'the Jew' the only first-hand experience he had was his Jewish clientele and colleagues, of which Freud's Vienna circle probably represented the largest group. These Jews were largely products of the post-Napoleonic Jewish enlightenment, divorced for the most part from Talmudic culture, and steeped in the mores of the nineteenth century European commercial class or intelligentsia. The other possible source for generalisations could be European stereotypes of Jews, which broadly came in two categories: that of the mercantile intelligentsia (the group Jung had direct experience of) and the Jews from the *Stedtl*, the Jewish pale of settlement in Czarist Poland, who lived on the land. There is no evidence that Jung ever met any of the latter group. But Jung did think he knew about Jews, as he wrote to Neumann on December 22nd 1935: 'What the

European Jews do, I know already, but what the Jews do on archetypal soil, that interests me extraordinarily'(Neumann, 1989, p281). Given that prior to the end of World War Two Neumann charged Jung with being lamentably uninformed about Jewish matters, this implies that when Jung was referring to 'the Jew' he was referring to the urban intelligentsia or mercantile group. With this knowledge of Jung's limited experience one can say that the passage shows something of Jung's perception of what was 'a Jew', yet the topic's significance for Jung was not concerned with race, but again centred on Freud as the apostle of post-religious materialism as was explained in chapter two.

One gets another insight into this when one considers Jung's ideas about the significance of land ownership. Jung was correct that at his time the emotional nationalism of statehood was not available to Central Europe's Jews, until nationalism became an option with the advent of Hertzl's Zionism. But in terms of the line of his argument, he seems to be taking a view of mixed *Völkisch* and Geographical Determinist ideas. He was implying that not owning land was a disadvantage psychologically, but there was no moral condemnation to warrant Noll's argument that this essay was an anti-Semitic *Völkisch* discussion about German nationality in contradistinction to Europe's Jewish minority. Just because the text contained *Völkisch* elements like 'rooted',[73] does not mean that one can assume Jung was using a discussion about the land to conduct an anti-Semitic polemic. There is a fundamental distinction to be made between a discussion of 'disadvantage' and one of moral disapproval. The weight and concentration of Jung's argument suggest that he certainly thought in terms of the positive aspects of rootedness, but unlike the *Völkisch* writers he was not extending the lack of rootedness into a xenophobic polemic against Jews.[74]

The two themes of paragraphs 18 and 19 (Jung 1991 [1918]) were Jung's Romantic idea of the Land and his critique of modernism. This Romantic perspective was to stay with Jung throughout his life and provide the kernel of his personal micro-culture in Bollingen. This critique of materialism fitted in with his critique of Freud, whom he took to represent the modern milieu. It was only incidental to his thinking that he assumed that Freud was representative of modern Jewry.

How then should one understand the implication of this essay? Clearly race as a biological issue did not feature as a significant theme and so the concern that it might have a racist agenda does not seem to be substantiated. Rather Jung was making a generalised distinction between cultures that did, or did not, retain a connection to the land, which was vital for a primitive level of the psyche. This observation seems to accord with Heyer's explanation of the need for the integration of all levels of the psyche for mental health, as was mentioned previously.

NATIONAL COMPLEXES

Jung discussed a number of national complexes, and the ones that most engaged his attention were those involving the psychological consequences of cultural, political and economic inequalities. This aspect of his thinking was not dependent on his theories of different innate layers, although obviously it was a related idea. In two interviews about American culture that Jung gave in 1912, and 'in 1930 or thereabouts', he gave a view of problems caused by cultural inequality, and then explained his characteristic view of the potential inherent in undeveloped cultures.[75]

Jung wrote of complexes produced by colonial inequality. He suggested that in America and South Africa, the outnumbered colonial people were forced to be brutal to master the indigenous population and in this way the occupier regressed culturally and psychologically. Jung contrasted the lack of political power of the slave with the massive psychological impact the slave-master relationship had on the colonialist. He suggested that in America the Indians were too few to create this sort of dynamic, but in the South, the recently freed Negroes were still disadvantaged and had a very great influence. However, Jung weakened his case with hyperbole and confused psychological influence with political power when he declared: 'They are really in control. I notice that your Southerners speak with the Negro accent; your women are coming to walk more and more like the Negro. In the South I find what they call sentiment and chivalry and romance to be the covering of cruelty. Cruelty and chivalry are another pair of opposites' (McGuire and Hull, 1980, p36).

In this thirties interview, Jung defended his position of comparing different cultural levels. He argued that his 1918 discussion of a possible Jewish psychology using the contrasts presented in the German-Jewish context, was the same idea as he had used when contrasting Americans and Europeans. This demonstrates that his intention was to promote a general conception of national psychology, and weakens Samuels' interpretation that he was pursuing a pejorative German-Jewish agenda because a general conception is the antithesis of a divisive prejudice (1989, p90). Jung stated in October 1949: 'I can just as well speak of the primitive contents of the European unconscious. There is no critical slur in these things. Indeed, for a wide-awake person, the primitive contents may often prove to be a source of renewal' (McGuire and Hull, 1980, p195). Jung then made the same comparison of the benefits of the naïve potential of Americans in comparison to the Europeans that he had previously used when comparing Germans and Jews in 1918.

He mentioned other national complexes. One was the complex caused by Germany's long run of defeats and traumas, which had created a sense of 'psychopathic inferiority' that amounted to 'a mass psychosis' (Jung, 1991 [1946a], §466). Another late example of a national complex may be found in Harry Slochower's paraphrase of the 1955 letter to Hans Illing about the 'chosen people' complex of the Jews (1981, p5). Both these complexes may be unconsciously assimilated by individuals, or consciously exploited by politicians. Other psychoanalytic theorists have made similar observations. In particular, Erikson speculated on how the generally repeated authoritarian patriarchal pattern in pre-war German family life provided a fertile base for the Kaiser's and Hitler's militarism. He concluded that 'historical and geographic reality amplify familial patterns and to what extent, in turn, these patterns influence a people's interpretation of reality' (1982, p311).[76]

Both these theoretical formulations, in as much as they relate to national psychologies, can be fitted into the geological unconscious, but, of themselves, they can also be formulated and employed independently of that paradigm. Furthermore both formulations allow one to explore the sociological and psychological differences at a high level of generality. If one allows for this level of observation they may have some utility.

Clearly typologies and national complexes do have some utility for the discipline of International Politics as long as they are used with discretion. However, as Jung failed to establish a clear distinction between 'race' and 'nation', these insights have remained buried in the confusion of the inadequately formulated concept of the collective unconscious.

6. Archetypes: 'Towards the Distant Goal of a Genetic Psychology'[77]

The universal human tendency to keep making new prints of the clichés we bear within us. (Sigmund Freud, 1907)[78]

Jung argued that his theory of the archetypes offered significant insights into a dimension of political psychology (Jung, 1976 [1951-1961], p593). The purpose of this chapter is to assess the theory's coherence and explore the varied strands of Jung's theory to see how successful he was in reconciling the diverse elements of his theories. But in making this review we need to be warned that Jung never systematised his definition of archetypes, never established or applied set criteria for what constituted proof of an archetype, and his writings confuse the distinction between the archetypes and the symbolic image. If we are to understand his perception of political events and the arguments in 'Wotan', we first need to look at the theory he was trying to apply.

Historical Overview

Throughout his career, Jung's synthetic genius sought to combine ideas and evidence from a number of sources. In the autumn of 1913 Jung had written of his hopes that new insights into the psyche would be yielded by the study of both clinical material and the symbolism found in mythologies and religion. He thought that this 'collaboration' would lead to 'the distant goal of a genetic psychology' (Jung, 1973 [1906-1950], p30). However this collaboration engendered a certain amount of confusion as he tried to combine a number of separate phenomena under the same label.

Jung was intrigued by the creative fertility of the symbolic images that appeared in the fantasies of his psychiatric patients. He wrote about the symbols he found and speculated on their function.[79] This interest in images represented a significant part of his thinking and one finds examples and speculations scattered through his writings.

Almost parallel with this line of thought, he began to wonder how these symbols were established and began to construct his archetypal theory to account for how these psychic phenomena were transmitted. His ideas on the repetition of symbols followed two parallel tracks. One was to account for repeating patterns using Lamarckian assumptions that allowed for images being genetically transmitted. This avenue of thinking concentrated on the symbolic image, or what he later called the 'manifest image'[80], an example of which would be the symbolic picture that appears in material dreams.

The other line of thought was to try to look deeper at the origin of these symbols and was based on reflections about aspects of the way the mind developed. These theories sought to explain archetypes in terms of the evolved organic structure of the brain as discussed in the previous chapter on Geographical Determinism. This explanation was gradually replaced, or superseded, by evolutionary ideas about instincts and advances in the understanding of genetics that provided a more sophisticated mechanism to account for 'the layered structure' of the brain. Subsequently these ideas about evolution allowed Jung to draw together the two lines of his speculation, but he did not make a clean transition, and some of his statements about archetypes continued to be contaminated by Lamarckian ideas.

The argument here is that it is important for the modern reader to understand the genesis of the archetypal hypothesis, because Jung's attempt to combine a number of separate phenomena under the same label undermined his theory's overall coherence and this left significant ambiguities in the paradigm, weakening Jung's ability to articulate questions and offer answers to historical or clinical issues.

THE CHANGING IMPORTANCE OF SYMBOLS IN THE ARCHETYPAL HYPOTHESIS

From the beginning of his psychiatric practice in 1900 at the Burghölzli, Jung had been fascinated with the symbolic images that appeared in the fantasies of his patients. (Jung would later in 1918 refer to these images as the 'manifest' form of the archetype, as will be explained later in the chapter). Shamdasani explains that Jung was already predisposed to an interest in this area as, prior to reading Freud, he had already been exposed to the work of Flournoy, Janet and the German Romantics that acted as a basis of his essential attitude to dreams and their interpretation (2003, p132-3).[81] The interest in symbolic images grew after he met Freud who, at the third psychoanalytic Congress in Weimar in 1911, paid tribute to Jung and declared: 'Jung had excellent grounds for his assertion that the mythopoetic forces of mankind are not extinct.'[82]

The following year, Jung was writing about the significance of the symbol in *Symbols of Transformation*. This work gives an indication of how symbols were important in his early thinking, for it would be seven years before he introduced the term 'archetype' as a theory to account for the origin of the symbol (Nagy, 1991, p138). In this formative stage of his thinking Jung was interested in the immediate source of 'manifest images' and the process by which they were created. He offered different accounts of the origin of the manifest symbolic image: as products of the symbolic function; as Lamarckian inherited images; and as neurological echoes.

'THE SYMBOLIC FUNCTION' AND THE PRODUCTION OF THE 'MANIFEST IMAGE'

In the same year as the Weimar Conference (on the 17th October 1911) Jung wrote to Freud that: 'certain other observations... have forced me to conclude that the so-called 'early memories of childhood' are not individual memories at all but phylogenetic ones. I mean of course the very early memories like birth, sucking, etc. There are things whose only explanation is *intrauterine*: much of the water symbolism, then the enwrappings and encoilings which seem to be accompanied by strange skin sensations (umbilical cord and amnion)' (Jung, 1974 [1906-1914], 275J). Here Jung seems to be inferring that an as-yet unnamed process took early experiences and used them as images in later dreams.

Having become intrigued by dream images Jung tried to account for the process by which dream symbols were created. In 1916 in an early attempt to do this he referred to Nietzsche's[83] observation of the parallels between dream thinking and archaic myths, and suggested that dreams were a 'phylogenetically older mode of thought.' He added that 'the figurative language of dreams is a survival from an archaic mode of thought' (Jung, 1991 [1916/1948], §474-475).[84] Jung argued that mythological ways of thinking would produce similar analogies in different contexts so that the outer trappings of a myth, religion or piece of imagination may be different, but, as he expressed it in another seminar: 'our minds think in the same way and about the same things that man has thought in the past and will always think' (Jung, 1998 [1930-1934], p80). In this way a powerful image would get passed on to subsequent generations.[85]

From this premise Jung began to focus on how the manifest image was created. He asked himself: 'How does a symbol originate? This question brings one to the most important function of the unconscious: the *symbol-creating function*.[86] There is something very remarkable about this function, because it has only a relative existence' (Jung, 1991 [1918], §25, my italics). He suggested that there was a 'truly creative fantasy activity of the brain'. This was unconscious and was 'buried in the structure of the brain... *the medium of creative fantasy*, is the *suprapersonal unconscious*. It comes alive in the creative man, it reveals itself in the vision of the artist, in the inspiration of the thinker, in the inner experience of the mystic. The suprapersonal unconscious, being distributed throughout the brain-structure, is like an all-pervading, omnipresent, omniscient spirit' (Jung, 1991 [1918], §12-13, my emphasis). Here one sees that by 1918 Jung had made some effort to locate the symbolic function 'in the neurological structure of the brain'. But in the passage it is not clear whether Jung was referring to what we now might describe as 'neurological hard-wired structures' or Lamarckian mental deposits.[87]

These speculations of Jung's may be born out by modern neurological research with its increasing understanding of the role of neural pathways in the parts of the brain connected to memory. It suggests that memory works by an inconceivably complex ability to make cross-connections between themes that are not connected organically in terms of brain structure or externally in terms of their subject matter (Blackmore, 1999, p57). The nature of these neurological processes may also give a clue to the processes of intuition, as well as offering the psycho-analytic schools the possibility of an organic process to account for their observations of the symbolic linkage in dream material. This possibility would also accord with Jung's speculation on the vital role of intuition in archetypal and symbolic thinking. He even wrote of the archetypes 'of perception and apprehension' and stated: 'Just as his instincts compel man to a specifically human mode of existence, so the archetypes force his ways of perception and apprehension into specifically human patterns' (Jung, 1991 [1919], §270, 278). Jung described problem-solving as a process of 'perception and apprehension' to find possible solutions as a process of a-rational intuition and pattern recognition rather than a facet of rational thought. He suggested that intuition was 'a process analogous to instinct' inasmuch as it is unconscious and leads to action. However, it is also the reverse of instinct, inasmuch as the products of intuition are original creations (Jung, 1991 [1919], §269). Jung also speculated that these intuitively derived behaviour patterns could become established as new instincts through repetition (Jung, 1991 [1919], §268). This twist back to Lamarckian ideas in the very article where he began to make a break, once again demonstrates how deeply the old ideas were buried in his thinking.

THE LAMARCKIAN ACCOUNT OF THE SYMBOLIC 'MANIFEST IMAGE'

This Lamarckian train of thought can also be seen once he had begun to write about the archetype's manifest image. Jung repeatedly wrote that many archetypal images appear in dreams with the characteristics of the ancient world. He wondered whether this was because archetypal images were of such prehistoric age that they naturally align themselves with obsolete historical periods and less developed cultural levels. As an example of his perception of this process, he suggested that in dreams, the anima (the Jungian term for the personification of the feminine aspect of a man's unconscious) was likely to feature in the guise of the ancient classical world and in these representations the anima demonstrated the lack of moral differentiation between 'the good' and 'the beautiful' that characterised the classical world (Jung, 1969 [1934/1954], §59).

Many of these examples almost suggest that the images are inherited, a distinctly Lamarckian idea, and demonstrates Jung's desire to find a historical element in the unconscious. In such cases one sees that Jung neglected to allow that the classical influence could be a product of his contemporaries' classical education and fantasies, or that the anima as an aspect of human sexuality could naturally appear in relation to ideas of beauty. These more obvious explanations had nothing to do with the history of ancient civilisation.

It can also be noted at this point that Jung seemed much more likely to make such dramatic claims when he was referring to a general idea that he was tempted to amplify with a historical reference. This style contrasts with his more restrained observations when commenting on political events from a realist perspective.

THE PHYSIOLOGICALLY DERIVED ARCHETYPAL 'MANIFEST IMAGES'

Later in Jung's writings there were references to a different type of symbol that owes its origin to the body's operation. Here Jung provided an account of the origin of symbols that suggested a link between the symbolic function and the body's unconscious mechanisms so that one could say some archetypes are physiologically generated. This echoed his initial 1911 speculation on pre-natal water symbolism mentioned at the start of the chapter. Jung also had a number of ideas about the neurological origins of psychic processes at the interface between the organic and the cognitive, which he called, 'the psychoid'. Examples of these ideas come in Jung's diagnoses of dreams where the appearance of invertebrates was indicative of problems with the more primitive parts of the nervous system so that the serpent often represented the brain stem and spine (Jung, 1969 [1940], §282; 1950: §667; 1958d, §582).[88]

Taking these examples together, one notes that these 'symbolic patterns' convey information via the symbolic function. Although this process is unconscious, like instinctive action, its purpose is to provide a form of cognitive recognition, a very different activity from that of the instincts that initiate action. Furthermore, these physiologically generated archetypes may be worthy of further consideration by psychologists working outside of the Jungian paradigm, as they do not pose the methodological problems raised by archetypal symbols.

THE FATE OF THE THEORY OF THE SYMBOLIC FUNCTION

The idea of the workings and consequences of the symbolic function of the mythopoetic imagination was a unique contribution to the way psycho-analysts accounted for the 'manifest' forms of symbols. It offered an alternative to Freud's explanation for the creativity of the unconscious psyche, which had suggested that the creative confusion in dreams was the result of the psychic faculty called the censor, and its attempts to obscure unacceptable wish fulfilment. Clearly the symbolic function had enormous potential as an explanatory psycho-analytic entity. Unfortunately the significance of the creativity of the symbolic function would be undercut in two ways. Firstly, at this time Jung's thinking was also heavily involved with the theoretical implications of Lamarckian ideas on inheritance. These ideas shifted attention from the creativity of the symbolic function to the mechanism by which the psychic images were inherited. This shift saw Jung's interest pass from exploring the creativity of the psyche, to focus on what psychic processes caused the creation of the 'manifest' form of the archetypal image. This shift may have harmed the overall coherence and balance of his line of enquiry. In his writings, despite his protests, he continued to confuse the 'manifest' form and the underlying reality of the archetypes when he took an uncritical attitude to the 'manifest image'. This degraded his attempts to define and prove what archetypes were.

Secondly, his ideas about symbolic thinking and the origins of archetypes were methodologically problematic. When looking for mythological parallels, who decides where the parallel is? How does one validate what is a common type of image; decide how many repetitions are necessary for a significant case; or justify what is a parallel line of thought?[89] Jung admitted that much of his work was based on his own inner life[90], and this brought into question both his claim to objectivity and the universality of this ideas (Homans, 1979, p29; McGowan, 1994, p89). Furthermore, if Jung's inner life was a questionable source, looking at other cases was no less problematic. The 'phallic man'[91] episode was Jung's favourite example of what he took to be proof of a mythic product of the unconscious. Nagy has commented that while it may be impressive, if it was really spontaneous, and if there were such a image in the collective unconscious, then why are there not more examples of this case? (1991 p147-8).

More generally, his work was not helped by his 'off-the-cuff' speculations, which debased his argument by leaving him vulnerable to ridicule. It is hard to take him seriously when he declared on 6th May 1936: 'The dragon is an age-old archetype handed down I suppose from the age when man and dragons lived at the same time—when man lived with saurians and bad saurians at that' (Jung, 1989 [1934-1939], p900). Such over-zealous contributions considerably increase the difficulty in determining the development of his ideas and identifying the different strands of his thought.

GENESIS OF THE ARCHETYPES

As Jung's work began to diverge from Freud, Jung looked at the rich wealth of symbols and realised that they could be categorised into a number of universal themes in the same way that Darwin had found homologues in anatomy (Stevens, 1982, p23). As this conviction grew, it became important to determine if symbols could be genetically transmitted.

By 1916, he was sufficiently sure of this common inheritance to make the distinction between the personal and the collective unconscious for the first time. Gradually he came to see the innate psychic structures as more important, and by 1917 was talking about the 'dominants of the collective unconscious' around which imagery coalesced.[92] As he wrote the following year: 'Indubitably [mythological fantasies] come from the brain—indeed, precisely from the brain and not from personal memory-traces, but from the inherited brain-structure itself' (Jung, 1991 [1918], §12). The first use of the term 'archetype' occurred in 1919 in 'Instincts and the

Unconscious' where he wrote about archetypes as analogous to instincts in that they performed functions that influenced both psychology and biology. Later he was to write on the function of the archetypes as 'regulators of behaviour'. With all these ideas he was able to link instinct and archetypal images together as the foundation of the collective unconscious.

As Jung evolved his archetypal theory as an explanation of the source of symbolic images, his conception of the mythopoetic imagination received less attention. He was no longer attempting to account for why some symbolic images appeared to be repeated across generations and locations. He neglected to think further about the form an archetype took, and instead confined his efforts to explaining what lay behind the 'manifest image' and what an archetype's effects were. Jung was increasingly trying to give his archetypal theory a genetic base, and later trying to give archetypes a physiological location at an organic psychoid level to account for their origin, psychic location and the processes of their transmission.

The Lamarckian Inheritance and Its Confusions

To understand the evolution of the theories of both Freud and Jung it is important to understand that both men did much of their thinking when Lamarckian ideas were still in vogue (Stevens, 1997, p677). Jean-Baptiste Lamarck was a French zoologist working at the beginning of the nineteenth century who produced an early theory to account for the mechanism of the transmutation of species (Bowler, 1989, p 20). His ideas began to be questioned with the work of the Freiburg zoologist August Weismann in the 1880's. Further debate was delayed as Mendel's celebrated 1866 paper was almost entirely overlooked until 1900. With the 'rediscovery' of Mendel, Lamarckism could be more seriously challenged and consequently Lamarck was more or less discredited by the start of the Great War (Proctor, 1988, p31-32). But in the German speaking world, Lamarck's ideas survived for longer as part of the attack on Darwinism so these ideas had more impact on Freud and Jung.

George Hogenson has suggested that as Jung makes no reference to Lamarck one cannot assume he was as influenced as Stevens suggests. Hogenson argues that: 'there are some hints, at least by 1919, and perhaps earlier, that he was well aware of the inadequacy of Lamarckian thinking and in fact rejected it' and instead was much more indebted to the neo-Darwinian James Baldwin (Hogenson 2001, p593). My suggestion is that whatever Jung came to believe, the formative ground on which his pre-1919 thinking was done was Lamarckian and that he never worked through the implications of how this came to shape his initial ideas.

Although Lamarck had left no school of thought and died in obscurity (Bowler, 1989, p88), he influenced the next generation of biologists in the German-speaking world through Haeckel's theories, which depended on Lamarckian processes of inheritance (Sulloway, 1979, p274; Nagy, 1991, p132).[93]

From 1800 Lamarck had begun developing his ideas on evolution, which are usually referred to as the theory of 'inheritance of acquired characteristics' (Burkhardt, 1977, p145). In *Philosophie Zoologique* (1809), he proposed two essentially mechanistic laws to explain the processes of change and inheritance (Burkhardt, 1977, p167). The 'First Law' was that if a physical change was required to meet environmental change, then the animal would strive to develop that physical or behavioural faculty, and conversely if a faculty became obsolete that function would wither. The 'Second Law' was that over generations this change would become inherited and replicated.[94] In this way he suggested giraffes' necks became longer as they strained to reach higher branches and within a short space of time this became an inherited characteristic (Bowler, 1989, p86).

Lamarckian ideas were vital for Jung and Freud as the First Law suggested a process by which behaviour and ideas might be internalised and the Second Law allowed for the change to be inherited.[95] Looking at Lamarck's ideas in more detail, one gains an insight into why they were fruitful for the development of Freud and Jung's thinking. It is important to stress here that while Jung referred to Lamarck's ideas of change and inheritance, he did not go into further detail. When the ideas are examined in detail however, one can see the way Lamarck's ideas about the interaction of 'subtle fluids' and *sentiment intérieur* foreshadowed aspects of Jung's later ideas. There are similarities between *sentiment intérieur* and Jung's idea of psychic energy. Furthermore the operation of Lamarck's *sentiment intérieur* in man gave Jung a potential way for archetypal ideas to be transmitted.

To explain this, Lamarck believed that organic change came about as unconscious emotional pressure (*sentiment intérieur*) forced as yet scientifically undefined[96] 'subtle fluids' into developing new organs and laying down new behavioural patterns. Lamarck wrote that: 'These subtle fluids... according to the diversity of circumstances... open different routes for themselves in the interior of the animals in question; and, once traced by repeated passings, these routes become the immediate causes of a constant likeness in the actions and the nature of the movements of the individuals of each race' (Burkhardt, 1977, p168).[97] For Lamarck, instinct[98] was the result of two processes: 'the invasions and the dissipations of the subtle fluids from outside' and the 'particular sketch, in the organisation of each species, of the routes that the subtle fluids were first forced to take and which they then always follow necessarily' (Burkhardt, 1977, p168).[99] This echoes Jung's early metaphor of the river (Jung, 1974 [1913], §367) to explain the effect of psychic energy being like the course of a river cutting deep into the bank to establish an archetypal pattern.

These subtle fluids were driven by *sentiment intérieur*, which Lamarck admitted was hard to define, but it included a 'feeling of existence' which was a 'very obscure feeling possessed by all the animals having a nervous system sufficiently developed to give them the faculty to feel.'[100] An animal, he supposed, could have this 'feeling of existence' without being aware of it (Burkhardt, 1977, p167). [101] In 1815 he defined it as 'a power which, aroused by a felt need, causes the individual to act immediately, in other words, in the same instant [as] the emotion expressed. If the individual is endowed with the faculties of intelligence it nonetheless acts in this circumstance before any premeditation or operation could arouse its will.'[102] This *sentiment intérieur* he explained in the third volume of his *Histoire Naturelle*: 'is not a sensation, it is a very obscure feeling... which [once excited] then acts immediately, which has the power, in the same instant, to cause the individual to act as necessary' (Burkhardt, 1977, p170).[103]

Lamarck thought that in primitive invertebrates the primary cause of behaviour was instinct, which he recognised to be unconscious. But as Burkhardt explains, this action was nevertheless propelled by *'sentiment intérieur,* or inner feeling'. Lamarck went on to suggest that the higher vertebrates may also be motivated by ideas, but this tended to be limited to man and some of the higher mammals (1977, p167).[104]

This was a significant qualification, because this combination of thought and *sentiment intérieur* could allow one to theorise how mental images could be inherited and how 'subtle fluid' could carve new neural pathways to set down instincts, archetypes and archetypal images. For Freud, these ideas were necessary for the continuing trans-generational impact of the murder of the primal father and the psychology of the horde, which affects group psychology and the interaction between the leader and the led. Freud never attempted to make a break with Lamarckian ideas and as late as 1939, while working on *Moses and Monotheism*, Freud refused to retract a sentence that followed a Lamarckian line, despite Ernest Jones's plea (Brome, 1982, p197[105]). For Jung, in his early accounts of the origin of archetypes, Lamarckian ideas offered a way to account for the possibility that archetypal images were acquired by timeless repetition, and that these psychic stages where evident in dreams (Jung, 1990 [1917/1926/1943], §151). Jung even briefly attempted to account for a Lamarckian process by borrowing Semon's ideas about mnemic deposits called *engrams*,[106] which he used in Volume Six of the Collected Works, prepared between 1913 and 1918 and first published in 1923 (Shelburne, 1988, p52).[107] However, this was his last explicit attempt to use a Lamarckian form of ideas.

By 1918, Jung began to make a break with Lamarckian ideas and made the distinction between the symbol's 'manifest image' and its origin, which he would later clarify by calling the 'archetype *per se'*, which was the original source of the symbol:

> It should on no account be imagined that there are such things as *inherited ideas*...There are, however, innate possibilities of ideas, *a priori* conditions for fantasy-production, which are somewhat similar to the Kantian categories. Though these innate conditions do not produce any contents of themselves, they

give definite form to contents that have already been acquired. Being a part of the inherited structure of the brain, they are the reason for the identity of symbols and myth-motifs in all parts of the earth. (Jung, 1991 [1918], §14)

Having made this clarification, Jung subsequently used two different approaches in explaining his thoughts. When discussing symbols he tended to work phenomenologically,[108] and when discussing the archetype *per se* he attempted to refer to more scientific methods and research. However, the distinction that was meant to herald a break with Lamarckian ideas was not as clear as he implied in his explanations (Clarke, 1992, p124). His accounts of the inheritance of 'forms of ideas' still amounted to a pseudo-Lamarckian process. An example of this can be seen in his 1925 account of the impact of Christianity on the Western psyche. He suggested that the unconscious recorded the subjective reaction to events at the same time as the conscious recorded the material events. These subjective reactions could have 'repercussions' at different depths of the stratified mind, and these repercussions could reach 'the unconscious strata and persist in our minds as an archetype.' This process was greatly accelerated if the material that was to leave an impression was already of a mythological form that would have a stronger unconscious reaction (Jung, 1990 [1925], p136). This Lamarckian argument would seem to suggest that emotions were the medium by which impressions were forced into the collective psyche.[109]

To give a different example of this argument, Jung described the sun archetype as being implanted by a Lamarckian process of repetition, but he shied away from explaining how this happened, apart from observing that 'this idea has been stamped on the human brain for aeons. That is why it lies ready to hand in the unconscious of every man... their origin can only be explained by assuming them to be deposits of the constantly repeated experiences of humanity' (Jung, 1990 [1917/1926/1943], §109). He then suggested that what was set down was not a memory of celestial events but:

> the myth of the sun-hero in all its countless modifications. It is this myth, and not the physical process, that forms the sun archetype... [and] the same or similar *mythical ideas*. Hence it seems as though what is impressed upon the unconscious were exclusively the *subjective fantasy-ideas aroused by the physical process*. Therefore we may take it that archetypes are recurrent impressions made by subjective reactions. (Jung, 1990 [1917/1926/1943], §109, my italics)[110]

> There are present in every individual, besides his personal memories, the great 'primordial images', as Jacob Burckhardt once aptly called them, *the inherited powers of human imagination as it was from time immemorial*. The fact of this inheritance explains the truly amazing phenomenon that certain motifs from myths and legends repeat themselves the world over in identical forms. (Jung, 1990 [1917/1926/1943], §101, my italics)[111]

Jung again stressed that: 'I do not by any means assert the inheritance of ideas, but only of the possibility of such ideas, which is something very different' (Jung, 1990 [1917/1926/1943], §101). But was his argument clear? When he was talking about the inheritance of 'motifs', Jung had just moved the inheritance issue another step on its chain of cause and effect. The problem was how similar were these 'identical forms' to those 'exactly the same images'? Obviously the closer the exactitude of the image to be duplicated the more Jung's ideas would require a Lamarckian process to account for them.

Not surprisingly there is some disagreement about when Jung made his break with Lamarckian ideas.[112] Unfortunately there is no possibility of a clear and final definition of Jung's position. This is not to detract from the sincerity with which he advanced his 'forms of ideas' definition for some varieties of archetypes. But, even allowing for the re-use of old passages in later editions and accidental regressions in explanations, some of Jung's writings do give the impression that he was describing near reproductions of exact images, as is the case with his favourite example of the mental asylum patient and the solar phallus. One wonders whether Jung could have exaggerated the repetition of such amazing mythical images when he made his not infrequent generalisations. Jung magisterially dismissed explanations like cryptomnesia (Jung, 1956 [1911-12/1952], §474), but he never informed the reader what efforts he made to discount these possibilities, and where he did explore other possible explanations, like migration, he marginalised their impact (Jung, 1991 [1938-1940], §69).

Even more startling, in a letter of 14th June 1958, Jung asserted: 'For our purposes it is highly indifferent whether archetypes are handed down by tradition and migration or by inheritance' (Jung, 1976 [1951-1961], p450). He even suggested that archetypes were so close to animal instincts that they could be assumed to be the same. Perhaps the way to interpret this is to understand him as meaning the representational 'form' of the archetype was modified by tradition and migration, but the psychoid aspect was genetic.

Even in relatively late writings Jung was reluctant to give up the possibility of a Lamarckian process. For example, he stated that archetypes: 'are in a sense the deposits of all our ancestral experiences, but they are not the experiences themselves. So at least it seems to us, in the present limited state of our knowledge. (I must confess that I have never yet found infallible evidence for the inheritance of memory images, but I do not regard it as positively precluded that in addition to these collective deposits which contain nothing specifically individual, there may also be inherited memories that are individually determined)" (Jung, 1990 [1917/ 1926/1943], §300). Here Jung was distinguishing between the form, which he wished to account for without Lamarckian lapses, and some possibility of the inheritance of images, which presumably did require a Lamarckian process of sorts. Clearly Jung never entirely dismissed the idea as he stated on 14th June 1958: 'As a matter of fact we have practically no evidence for inherited representations (although even this statement is not quite safe), but we have plenty of proof that archetypal patterns exist in the human mind' (Jung, 1976 [1951-1961], p451).

In summary, Jung's thoughts on archetypes never entirely escaped from their Lamarckian roots, and the failure to work through this connection inhibited the critical development of part of his paradigm. The hypothesis of the archetype remained an over-extended concept that lacked resolution in its definition and led to confusions in its use. These problems will be important to recall in reading chapter eight, because Jung's attempts to define Wotan as an archetype in 1936 were heavily influenced by Lamarckian errors.

THE THEORETICAL OVERLAP OF INSTINCTS AND ARCHETYPES

The historical overview now moves on to consider the overlap between the ideas of instincts and archetypes that I will sometimes refer to together as 'psychic organs'. As it is not always easy to remain clear about the distinction between the two, it may help to be aware of von Franz's broad explanation: 'The difference between instinct and archetype is the following: instinct is represented by physical behaviour, similar in all human beings, while archetypes are represented by a mental form of realisation, similar in all human being' (1981, p148). This guide is useful, but one must also recall that as Shamdasani explains, in German biology and philosophy the word 'instinct' was used to describe animal behaviour while 'drive' was reserved for explaining human action (2003, p191).

As Jung began to distance himself from Lamarckian ideas, it became increasingly important for archetypal theory to have links to genetics and the study of instincts. As the theoretical overlap of instincts and archetypes grew, Jung offered a variety of speculations based on different types of evidence which attempted to tie archetypes to instincts and hence to genetics. In doing this he further consolidated his interest in the role and reproduction of archetypes but this took him further away from his early speculations about the symbolic function.

Jung's ideas on the relationship between instincts and archetypes changed over time and he could offer different formulations. In an early text he suggested that: 'the majority of symbols are more or less close analogies' to 'one of the strongest instincts, sexuality' (Jung, 1956 [1911-12/1952], §338).[113] Later he would refer to five instincts: 'hunger, sexuality, activity, reflection and creativity' (Jung, 1991 [1937], §246).

In Jung's later work he began to define archetypes in terms of their working relationship with the instincts. Jung formulated this in a number of ways that included suggesting that the archetype was 'the *instinct's perception of itself*' and added that the 'unconscious apprehension through the archetype determines the form and direction of instinct' (Jung, 1991 [1931a], §277). An alternative formulation was that archetypes 'are patterns of instinctual behaviour' (Jung, 1969 [1936], §91), which would suggest that archetypes *per se* are the patterns of instinctual behaviour.[114]

On another occasion archetypes were also defined as 'penchants'. This comes in a brief mention in a letter on 14th June 1958. Jung suggested that: 'archetypes are representations; but in reality they are preferences or "penchants," likes and dislikes' (Jung, 1976 [1951-1961], p451). The penchants lack specific representations as they were very close to descriptions of the very primitive, almost 'gut reaction' of positive or negative; advance or retreat, that are displayed by the most primitive organism (Ledoux, 1998, p17). These reactions work independently of the reasoning parts of the brain and are more akin to the unconscious instincts than the more symbolic way archetypes are manifest.

This focus on pre-conscious explanations for archetypal activity reached its most detailed expression with Jung's ideas on the interface between psychological and organic reactions at a cellular level, which he termed 'the psychoid', and which was his last addition to his archetypal theory in 1946 (Jaffé, 1984, p23).[115] Later Jung expanded the idea and suggested 'the postulate that the phenomenon of archetypal configurations—which are psychic events par excellence—may be founded upon a psychoid base, that is, upon an only partially psychic and possibly altogether different form of being' (Jung, 1963 [1961], p319-321). This represented another attempt to establish the location of the archetypes at a neurological level. At this pre-conscious level, 'penchants' could just as suitably be understood as a description of part of the functioning of instincts, for at this level there is no practical distinction between archetypes and instincts.

From all these different explanations, it is hard to define what was Jung's perception of the relationship between instincts and archetypes. But whatever the confusion about the exact relationship between the two ideas, the idea of instincts and the theoretical work of Lorenz and the ethologists became increasingly important to Jung.[116] However, as Jung made no direct reference to Lorenz's work, the degree of their influence is still being explored.[117]

One of the ethologists' theoretical observations was that each species demonstrated specific 'patterns of behaviour' and that no species could produce their 'patterns of behaviour' unless it had some basis in their biological function and heritage. The 'patterns of behaviour' would affect all subsequent attempts to learn new thoughts, feelings or behaviour (Stevens, 1989, p46).[118] This concept gave Jung another way to link his ideas on the psyche with the work of others working in more conventional biological disciplines (Humbert 1983 cited in Gordon, 1985, p293-5). The possibilities of further theoretical connections was increased with the publication of one of the most influential ethological texts, Niko Tinbergen's *The Study of Instinct* (1951), which suggested that behaviour patterns are triggered by *innate release mechanisms* (IRMs). These IRMs remain passive until they are triggered by an appropriate external stimulus—called a sign stimulus, and when the IRM is triggered the animal responds with its characteristic pattern of behaviour (Stevens, 1982, p57; Stevens and Price, 1996, p8-9). This trigger action can result in the release of considerable energy to power or impel the instinctive action and the instinctive 'buzz' from this release may be akin to the glow from action and the imperative and compulsion to act described in clinical cases where people are inflated by the 'numinous' power of an archetype.

Ethology was important to archetypal theory because it potentially provided evidence of links between instincts and common behaviour and thought patterns from beyond Jungian psychology. The interplay of the two theories raises two important questions: *What is the relationship between 'patterns of behaviour' and archetypes?* And: *What is the parallel between internal symbols and the external innate release mechanisms of instincts?*

Connected to these questions, the study of instincts revealed the important distinction between 'closed' and 'open instincts'. Some instincts operate through a fixed pattern of trigger and response, which is termed a 'closed' or 'stereotyped' instinctive pattern.[119] In contrast an 'open' instinctive pattern, is where the more developed life-form requires an element of adaptation so that the response is fixed but the trigger is left open.[120]

In 1957 Jung used this theory to wonder: 'If archetypes are similar to open instinctive patterns this may be related to the ability of archetypal ideas to affect behaviour.' Jung also suggested that archetypes had evolved their 'current highly complex configuration', and acknowledged: 'the appearance of seemingly miraculous complex behaviour may be the result of a long chain of adaptation where we only see the final hybrid pattern', but he observed that instincts were nonetheless even 'older and more conservative than the body's [current] form' (Jung, 1991 [1957], §576-577).[121]

In this late period, for all his writings on instincts, speculations on genetics and ideas on the psychoid, Jung was aware that he was still dealing with ideas that could not be pushed beyond the status of hypotheses. On the 14th June 1958, he wrote:

> It is true that I have set aside hitherto general biology. This for good reasons! We still know far too little about the human psychology to be able to establish a biological basis for our views. In order to do that, we ought to know far more about the psychology of the unconscious and what we know about consciousness cannot be connected with biological viewpoints directly. Most attempts in this direction are rather futile speculations. The real connections with biology are only in the sphere of the unconscious, i.e., in the realm of instinctive activities... I don't flatter myself on having a theory of heredity. I share the ordinary views about it. (Jung, 1976 [1951-1961], p450)

Nonetheless, while one must realise it is not possible to make a definitive distinction between archetypes and instinct because archetypes were not sufficiently defined, it is possible to include some of Jung's formulations on archetypes into a provisional presentation of Jung's understanding of the evolution of thinking. Firstly in this provisional presentation came action on the basis of 'closed' instinctive behaviour patterns, which was unconscious. Then came 'open' instinctive behaviour patterns, which could be partially conscious. In both cases, the instinct is providing an action in response to an external trigger. This process follows a range of sophistication; from unconscious fixed responses, to unconscious open responses, to semi-aware, semi-thought-through action. Jung's addition to his understanding of the theoretical consensus of his day was that instincts might not only be triggered by external IRMs, but might also be prompted by internal IRMs in the form of symbolic images. Developing this observation, it follows that archetypes can be understood as IRMs for internal developments that provide an intuitive or symbolic picture to trigger a developmental outcome.

The other avenue of his thinking was that archetypes might have a parallel internal process as the image of an instinct, or the image of a more evolved open instinct. To portray this in terms of the stages of the archetype, firstly there is the psychoid archetype that is an instinctive energy-releasing complex, where the symbol is a trigger and/or a representation. It may be an innate symbol pictogram or a dream-adapted image that is created in the unconscious and then presented to consciousness through a dream. (This close connection often causes people to confuse the archetype with its current dream image.) When the dream is told in a wider social setting it can become a living cultural symbolic image. Finally, it exhausts its psychological importance and becomes a dead cultural image.

Summary

In summarising the evolution of Jung's archetypal theory Shamdasani observed that, as Jung synthesised the *a priori* archetypes of Plato with the categories of Kant and the neo-Lamarckian learned engrams of Semon, he created for himself an 'unstable compound' (2003, p236). This instability was exacerbated as he was unable to clarify the relationship between archetypes and instincts and this has weakened the 'theoretical foundations of the theory' (Shelburne, 1988, p133). Possibly Jung was unable to do this because, as we have seen, his use of the idea of archetypes covered too many phenomena and was not sufficiently defined, having been formulated over such a long time. In any event, the uneven development of the model was to make it increasingly difficult to apply.

The 'Classes' of the Archetypes[122]

> *Just as it may be asked whether man possesses many instincts or only a few, so we must also raise the still unbroached question of whether he possesses many or few primordial forms, or archetypes, of psychic reaction.* (Jung, 1991 [1931a], §274)

As the first half of the chapter looked at Jung's confusion in evolving the theory about the archetypes, the second half of the chapter will consolidate the definition of archetypes, so that Wotan's archetypal credentials can be assessed.

Archetypes are hard to define, which is hardly surprising since their 'location' in the psyche takes place 'below' consciousness. Jung warned: 'When one carefully considers this accumulation of data, it begins to seem probable that an archetype in its quiescent, unprojected state has no exactly determinable form but is in itself an indefinite structure which can assume definite forms only in projection' (Jung, 1969 [1936/1954], §142). Maybe the question that one ultimately needs to ask is whether it is intellectually useful to label such diverse phenomena under the heading 'archetypes'?[123]

Jung argued that the archetypes were the same at their point of origin but, 'Empirically speaking, we are dealing all the time with "types", definite forms that can be named and distinguished.' However he went on to note how the types blurred so that: 'one comes to the conclusion that the basic psychic elements are infinitely varied and ever-changing, so as utterly to defy our powers of imagination. The empiricist must therefore content himself with a theoretical "as if"' (Jung, 1969 [1936/1954], §143).

Despite these reservations, Jung made some effort to draw distinctions: 'One must, for the sake of accuracy, distinguish between 'archetype' and 'archetypal ideas.' The archetype as such is a hypothetical and irrepresentable model, something like the "patterns of behaviour" in biology' (Jung, 1969 [1934/1954], §6, footnote 9). But this only goes part of the way to explaining what an archetype is. Later he clearly made the distinction between archetypes as 'personalities' and 'archetypes of transformation'.

In setting out Jung's varied classes of archetypes the reader could object that some of the formulations Jung offers are too obscure, and that in hindsight is maybe so, but for now the task of this part of the chapter will be to draw out the distinctions Jung used and attempt to resolve some of the confusion caused by his failure to make systematic use of these distinctions or explore their implications. That he did not carry through a systematic reformulation of his work may have been because of his antipathy to systems, or his awareness of the dangers of proposing theoretical structures that were too prone to dogmatic use. Alternatively it may also have been because he regarded himself as a pioneer and did not live long enough to undertake the rewriting of his life's work that he felt all but his *Answer to Job* required.

ARCHETYPES AS 'PERSONALITIES', 'AUTONOMOUS FIGURES' OR 'SOULS'[124]

Perhaps the easiest types of archetype to understand are the 'personalities' which frequently occur in people's dreams. These include 'the shadow' a personification of the inferior side of the personality, and the 'anima / animus' which represents the contrasexual part of the psyche, and the less frequently seen 'wise old man, and 'the earth mother', as embodiments of mature development (Jung, 1986 [1948], §1157; Jung, 1991 [1927/1931], §92). Jung suggested that these personalities arise because the psyche tends to present autonomous aspects of itself symbolically in dreams in an anthropomorphic form. To explain this autonomous faculty Jung drew parallels with a variety of mental illnesses that involve 'the split-off products of hysteria and schizophrenia, mediumistic "spirits," figures seen in dreams,' but, he added, 'when we go into the matter more deeply, we find that they are really archetypal formations. There are no conclusive arguments against the hypothesis that these archetypal figures are endowed with personality at the outset and are not just secondary personalisations' (Jung, 1956 [1911-12/1952], §388).

ARCHETYPAL IDEAS

In contrast to the autonomy of the archetypes that have 'personalities', Jung also identified a radically different category of archetype that he referred to as 'archetypal ideas', in which he grouped a range of phenomena.

ARCHETYPAL IDEAS AS 'SYSTEMS FOR ACTION' TRIGGERED BY 'IMAGES' OF 'SITUATIONAL MOTIFS'

This class of 'archetypal ideas' features a number of 'systems for action' that are triggered by appropriate 'situational motifs'. The most basic class of these archetypal ideas are those that relate to 'situational motifs' of threatening situations, such as woods or bends in tracks, or movements involving 'ascent and descent', and the crossing (ford or strait) (Jung, 1998 [1930-1934], p382; Jung, 1986 [1948], §1157). Jung explained rather colourfully how these processes were set down:

> Now that is an archetypal situation which has occurred innumerable times; if it is not just crocodiles, there are enemies waiting to catch you when perfectly helpless in the water. ... such places are supposed to be haunted by dragons or serpents; there are monsters in the deep waters, enemies in the woods, behind rocks, and so on. Fording a river, then, is a typical situation expressing a sort of impasse, so just that archetype is formulated when one is in any dangerous predicament. (Jung, 1989 [1934-1939], p23)

This process of acquisition by repetition seems rather Lamarckian, but the existence of image-triggers and action-response is substantiated from other sources. Stevens notes Bowlby's observation that: 'in a wide array of animal species including man... Noise, strangeness, rapid approach, isolation, and for many species darkness too—all are conditions statistically associated with an increased risk of danger' (1982, p57).[125]

In this respect, when he referred to archetypes as 'systems of readiness for action' (Jung, 1991 [1927/1931b], §53), the entity he was describing came very close to an idea of instincts, while in the part of the sentence where he defined archetypes as 'at the same time images and emotions', this includes in the description the internal IRM of the 'manifest image' and the emotional energy for the response. Another feature of archetypes to note at this point is that they paradoxically demonstrate the strong conservatism of an age-old instinctive behaviour pattern and yet, within their 'open' framework, the means for rapid response and adaptation.

Just as these types of archetypes seem to contain an awareness of the situation and its dangers, they also contain 'remnants of the functional possibilities of all preceding epochs of evolution' (Jung, 1990 [1917/1926/1943], §132). They do this, Jung explained on 3rd June 1936, 'as a system or a functional unit which contains the picture of the conflict, the danger, the risk—and also the solution of it... as a pre-existing solution of certain average conflicts. I mean certain elemental conflicts or differences, like the archetype of the crossing of the ford for example' (Jung, 1989 [1934-1939], p977).[126]

Of all the 'types' of archetypes these narrow situational and functional possibilities most closely resembled instinctive patterns of actions as they are very similar to 'closed instincts', inasmuch as a simple stimulus activates the sympathetic nervous system's flight and fight reaction to provide at least more energy, even if the response is not specified. Maybe the lack of a specified response is an indication of their relatively late evolutionary pedigree? Indeed perhaps one should ask whether these 'systems' are instincts or should they be understood as instincts being mediated through the symbolic function?

Archetypal Ideas as 'Functional Motifs'

In contrast to the circumscribed 'situational motifs', Jung described a selection of broader 'functional motifs' that were made up of more abstract representations that feature such things as 'tension and suspension between opposites, the world of darkness, the breakthrough (or invasion), the creation of fire, helpful or dangerous animals, etc.' (Jung, 1986 [1948], §1157). As the psyche moves into more abstract areas it seems to be moving from a process of action by unconscious trigger-and-response cognition, to one more akin to abstract symbolic representations. These 'functional motifs' are more abstract and thus more properly fit Jung's ideas of symbols as forms of basic ideas.

This distinction may be the key difference needed to distinguish between archetypes and instincts. It would seem that autonomy and originality of some archetypes requires some higher order cognitive activity beyond instinct's unconscious trigger and fixed response mechanism. Instinct remains relatively fixed and unconscious; but the higher archetypal symbolic function may produce a new symbolic representation related to the activity of a part-formed 'archetypal idea' and, in the most advanced stages, an autonomous personalised archetype may be activated.

ARCHETYPAL IDEAS AS 'TYPICAL MYTHOLOGEMS'

Jung thought that there were 'typical mythologems' that constituted the root of many core concepts, such as the concept of energy[127] or the ability to form abstract ideas.[128] He also counted as mythologems the mechanisms and basic forms from which language was constructed (Jung, 1969 [1934/1954], §67). Jung, according to von Franz, thought of this class of archetypes as being examples of 'a sort of Platonic form which sooner or later mankind has to posit' (1975, p126).

As an aside, if one compares this aspect of Jung's archetypal theory with Bastian's *Elementargedanken*, both ideas suggest that there are some innate concepts or ideas, but Jung's selection seem to be a little more abstract. (For the interested reader there is a small addition on Bastian in Appendix D.)

ARCHETYPAL IDEAS AS 'IMAGES' OF 'ORGANISING DOMINANTS': THE INTERNAL IRMS OF THE PSYCHE

A very different phenomena, and perhaps the most abstract form of archetypal ideas, are the 'images' of 'organising dominants'. Reviewing the following lists one seems to be dealing with images or triggers of order or transformation. Jung describes these 'organising dominants' on one occasion as 'the self, the circle, and the quaternity, i.e., the four functions or aspects of the self... or of consciousness' (Jung, 1956 [1911-12/1952]), while at another time he writes of 'mandala symbolism and the supraordinate personality (God-image, Anthropos symbolism)' (Jung, 1986 [1948], §1158).[129] Jung also described these 'organising dominants' as 'another class of archetypes which one could call the *archetypes of transformation*. They are not personalities, but are typical situations, places, ways and means, that symbolise the kind of transformation in question.... these archetypes... cannot be exhaustively interpreted, either as signs or as allegories' (Jung, 1969 [1934/1954], §80).

In this vein of his thinking some ideas seem to have an almost Platonic metaphysical reality as, for example, the properties of certain numbers, and the way that some of these numbers seem to echo certain mental processes. A commonly observed one is the power of the thrice-repeated phrase. This has long been used by rhetoricians for three-part slogans in ideology or theology, which range from the Nazis' *'Ein Volk, Ein Reich, Ein Fuehrer'* to Lenin's 'Land, Peace and Bread!' On a more esoteric level there are the occurrence of dreams featuring images using some aspect of the number four. This may include a figure having four sides, or an event having four stages, but whatever dream narrative, the quality of four often seems to indicate a process of psychological maturity and integration. Towards the end of his life Jung saw in natural numbers the most primitive element of the 'spirit' and thought that they might be the 'key impulse' underlying archetypal images' (von Franz, 1975, p126).

Thus far, with what he has written about 'images' of 'organising dominants' and numbers, he seems to be describing the very building blocks of some cognitive processes. But with what he mixed in with his references to the Self we have a very different order of psychic organ, for with Jung's ideas about the Self we have some of his most innovative and subtle observations. Indeed it can be argued that what he was describing here could be seen as two different types of psychic organs. There are the relatively simple 'organising dominants', which could be described as the psychic tools (and their symbolic image) through which the psyche facilitates balance or synthesis and then there is the Self, which is a more complex entity.

In Jung's conception, the Self can be understood as representing the totality of the psyche with the autonomy of function that totality confers, so to our confusion the Self is also an 'organising dominant', and yet it is so much more! The Self with its blend of breadth and autonomy seems to be part psychic organ, part an individuating imperative. It combines the personal ego and a psychic totality that might poetically be described as one's soul with a deeply personal process that is guiding one's destiny but is an unknowable mystery.

The combination of the subtlety and the complexity of what Jung was trying to describe with his observations about the Self suggest that in this taxonomy of psychic organs it needs a class of its own. Given that the Self is so much more enigmatic and diverse than any of the more limited developmental personalities, perhaps we do ourselves a disservice to uncritically label it just as an archetype. Possibly a way forward is to recall that the Self's mirror-image in consciousness, the ego, should not be defined as an archetype but should be regarded as a psychic organ or complex. If that is so, then maybe the Self should also be understood as a psychic organ akin to a complex? Maybe one of the tasks for Jungian psychology in the future is to ponder what this distinction may yield. Although Jung's deepest ideas on the Self are too rich to be explored here, for our purposes the psychic organs have two important qualities. They seem to have tremendous emotional resources to impel change and this change comes independently of the conscious ego.

The Symbols of 'Universal Human Experience'

Other phenomena that Jung includes as a variety of archetype are the symbols derived from the common actions of the human species (Jung, §146, 1938-1940). This distinction makes these symbols a clumsy inclusion in the category of archetypes. That said, the idea of symbols derived from universal experience is easy enough to understand as Stevens summed them up, 'the archetypal endowment with which each of us is born presupposes the natural lifecycle of our species—being mothered, exploring the environment, playing in the peer group, adolescence, being initiated, establishing a place in the social hierarchy, courting, marrying, childrearing, hunting, gathering, fighting, participating in religious rituals, assuming the social responsibilities of advanced maturity, and preparation for death' (1982, p40). These common actions ethologists have termed 'universal human experiences'. The universal occurrence of such experiences means that they are highly likely to produce commonly recurring ideas and themes so that experts in the study of myth and folk law confirm that there do seem to be a selection of common themes (Nagy, 1991, p147).

To give an example of the impact of such 'universal human experiences', one can take the connections between the parental archetype and the evolution of various conceptions of the deity (Jung, 1969 [1936/1954], §125-129). Developing this line of thought Jacoby suggests that, if the infant is fortunate enough to have a nourishing relationship with its mother, this constitutes a true, or primary archetype of wholeness which is a fertile base for a mythic historical form.[130] Thus, in the mother-infant relationship, there is the germ of the wider idea of 'a worldly paradise'. This archetype can therefore be understood to have its roots in a fundamental stage of development, and, as such, will almost inevitably occur throughout history (1985, p66). In this way, 'the propensity of religious beliefs and mythic themes—particularly those concerning life, death, and regeneration—are innately 'prepared for' in the human brain like the propensity for speech' (Stevens, 1997, p683).

THE CLASSIFICATION OF ARCHETYPES

Having looked at various types of archetype and being aware of how Jung juxtaposes the idea of archetypes and instincts, one must acknowledge that the theoretical situation was confused and unsatisfactory. From this one can ask whether his ideas can be reformulated in a more coherent fashion.

For this reformulation we will introduce the idea of 'immanent' archetypes and symbols and to explain the idea we will use the distinction between the reality of the mother-infant relationship and the symbolic idea of a 'heavenly state'. The mother-infant bond has all the innate instinctive behaviour of breast-feeding and cuddling to establish it. Archetypes and instincts of this sort can be termed innate as these mammalian behaviour patterns are genetically hard-wired into human biology. In contrast symbolic ideas, as for example the 'heavenly state', are not genetically lodged in the psyche. The seeds of ideas of heaven may have their emotional roots in an innate archetypal or instinctive situation, but there is no direct genetic connection with the instinctive aspects of the mother-child relationship. Thus ideas like paradise are not instinctive, but their cause is universal, and to all practical purposes the images they engender (such as the yearning for a lost paradise) are almost inevitable. In recognition of this latent and almost inevitable aspect these phenomena can be referred to as 'immanent' archetypes.[131] The reader should also be aware that 'immanent' archetypes also have an *imminent* quality about them in as much as the ideas could be formulated from their 'immanent' roots at any time.

There is a further distinction between archetypal ideas that are 'immanent' in the external situation and those that occur as 'manifest' archetypal symbols which are 'immanent' in the human body as bi-products of the body's organic structure (as discussed previously[132]). Both types of 'immanent' archetype seem to be built into either the human condition or the biology of the body, so that their generation is almost fated, for while they cannot be attributed to genetic inheritance, they are almost inevitable bi-products of the human condition. This distinction between innate and 'immanent' archetypes can be helpful in making a clearer definition of what is an archetype.

TOWARDS A POST-JUNGIAN CLASSIFICATION OF THE ARCHETYPES

With the clearer definition offered in this part of the chapter, it is possible to provide a clearer set of distinctions to describe Jung's perception of the range of psychic organs that includes instincts and all the different varieties of archetype. This can be seen in the table overleaf.

The Psychic Organ

The Type of Psychic Organ	The Organ's Function
The psychological 'organs' seem to have a highly genetic component as they are universal, but the impact of social factors varies considerably.	To produce the Instinctive or archetypal behaviour or idea.

Instincts
 	
For 'primitive' physical actions.
• breast feeding and Mother/Infant Bonding.
• infant swimming.
• According to the Ethologists the following activities could also be included:
  o hunting
  o pseudo-speciation
  o group-bonding
  o awareness of territory and hierarchy.
	To convey relatively fixed behaviour patterns that concern external concrete action. To convey relatively fixed behaviour patterns that concern *external concrete action.*

The Psychic Organ's Manifest Form		
The Graphic or Symbolic Representation	The Origin of the Symbol	Complexity of the Symbol
Instinct may be mediated through the symbolic function, or acted on automatically without consciousness.	Innate Biological Symbols.	Closed to Open Instincts and Simple to Complex Instinct patterns.

What is an Archetype?

Having clarified the 'types' of archetype, we will now consider the criteria that a psychic organ must fulfil to be an archetype. An archetype can either be defined in terms of its pattern of behaviour, or in terms of the characteristics of its 'manifest image'. To take a composite of various post-Jungian formulations, to qualify as an innate archetype requires three sets of criteria. The first criterion is 'universality'—that the pattern in question is found in all known cultural groups. The next is 'phylogenetic continuity' between human and other mammalian species, so that the behaviour in question can be traced backwards from human beings through primates to their earliest mammalian origins. The last criterion is 'evolutionary stability', which means that the pattern is an evolutionary asset and those who fail to continue the new pattern become extinct, so the genetic innovation becomes stable (Stevens and Price, 1996, p33).

To define archetypes in terms of their characteristic imagery Hobson suggests:

> A theme must be isolated clearly enough to recognise it as a typical phenomenon, i.e. a particular motif must occur in the imagery of different individuals and must recur in a series of dreams or fantasies of one person. Thus, regularities, which might be figures or situations, are isolated and classified together:
> - The theme must be shown to occur in many parts of the world in many ages.
> - The motif must have a similar context and functional meaning whenever it occurs.
> - The fantasy image must not have been acquired through education, tradition, language, or indirectly via religious ideas, and all motifs must be excluded which have been known and forgotten. (1973, p74)

This list can be extended from Hubback's guidelines (1989, p43):

- Archetypes occur generally, or even universally.

- Archetypes have a purpose and often integrate conflicting psychological themes.
- Their effect is very powerful and is sometimes numinous.
- Archetypes are associated with bodily, instinctive levels of experience.[133]

If one takes this composite list of qualifications, one sees that many of Jung's types of archetype do not meet all the criteria.[134] This draws attention to the wide range of phenomena to which Jung was alluding and their different origins, manners of operation and consequences. With the definitions and qualifications of an archetype established, one is now equipped to see how well Wotan meets these criteria.

A Review of the Theories of the Collective

The theory of the collective unconscious was one of the distinctive features of Jung's paradigm. It was made up of a number of ideas and was dependent on three components:

- The existence of the racial and national layers of the unconscious.
- A process that allowed inherited common characteristics to be transmitted.
- The universal influence of the archetypes.

In our examination of the collective unconscious we have found that the theory had been predicated on a Lamarckian understanding of genetic inheritance from which Jung only partially distanced himself. After the break with Lamarckian ideas, Jung's theoretical discussion was largely made up of arguments based on the cultural influences on the unconscious, although he continued to refer to the 'collective unconscious'. His retention of his original terms masked the profound shift in the focus of his argument. This has been underestimated by commentators if they have merely viewed the collective unconscious as 'something of a scandal', as Clarke observed, or have just dismissed it as 'mystically conceived', as did Wilhelm Reich (1992, p117).

From our critical analysis of the collective unconscious in chapter five, one can see that the 'cultural psyche' was more evident in Jung's thinking than has been realised. But equally importantly, once Joseph Henderson had pinpointed the entity and coined the term, 'the cultural psyche' (1991), this gives a much clearer exposition of what Jung was trying to articulate when he spoke of the collective unconscious.[135] As well as Henderson's 'cultural psyche', Jung's ideas of national psychologies and cultural complexes are potentially useful but one must free them from being used as Jung first formulated them, for although these ideas are collective and maybe unconscious, they are cultural entities and in this way may be transmitted across the generations.

If the classical collective unconscious and archetypal theory were so flawed, why did Jung not reformulate his ideas at that time? There are a number of possible reasons that may lie behind this, although it is not possible to prioritise them.

At a practical level he was very busy with patients, his wide range of interests and, more than anything else, the burden of his international duties in the IGMSP which was inextricably bound up with the struggle with 'the campaign' and concern for the future of psychotherapy and all those involved in the increasingly threatening atmosphere. On a theoretical level, perhaps he had emotionally invested heavily in the theory, and the rift with Freud may have induced him to give even higher priority to the influence of his interpretation of unconscious collective factors, as these were his distinctive ideas. It is also possible that the Romantic tradition may have inhibited Jung's scientific ability to look critically at his model. One also needs to recall that Jung was not attempting to formulate a finished theoretical paradigm and this position may have unconsciously inhibited him from critically comparing the mismatch between the neo-Lamarckian theory and his post-Lamarckian cultural observations.

If all this seems a curious position for someone of Jung's intellect to sustain, one can account for the contradiction by referring to Hall's account of Michael Polanyi's idea of 'dynamo-objective coupling'.[136] This was an idea that Polanyi developed to account for the mind-set of Freudian and Marxist theorists. He was interested in the ability of supposedly rational thinkers to argue simultaneously in a logical fashion about a piece of theory while supporting an irrational emotional position. He thought that, for many theorists, 'a system of beliefs that [are] consciously and overtly held for allegedly objective reasons are actually and covertly held because of [a] strong moral commitment' (Hall, 1986, p129-131). Polanyi suggests that this produced a self-supporting alliance between an intellectual logic-driven idea and an emotional and potentially irrational psychological position (Hall, 1986, p129). To use this idea to explain Jung's position, one can suggest that his emotional investment in his theory led him to retain it uncritically in the face of its inadequacies and the rising importance of the cultural evidence in his discussion.

7. The Effect of the Archetypes in the Political Arena

[T]he creation of symbols has counted for so much in the history of the world. People kill each other for symbols; whether they kill each other for National Socialism or Communism... it is still the same old thing. And the creation of such symbols is exceedingly important for mankind because so much depends upon finding the right or true formula for the instincts. With a suitable formula one can live decently, the majority of the instincts can be expressed. If it is an unsuitable symbol, which does not allow such an expression, it produces a neurotic condition. Then there will be a world wide upheaval. (Jung, 1998 [1930-1934], p915)[137]

This chapter looks at the impact Jung suggested archetypes could have on behaviour and emotional states and considers how this shapes war and international politics.

Let us start then by briefly considering his perception of the role of enantiodromia, with its stress on the tension of opposites and the psychic energy this conflict creates (Odajnyk, 1976, p63-64).[138] For Jung this energy represented a major source of psychological change and creativity (Jung, 1990 [1916-34], §237). The tension either creates a synthesis for something new to emerge, or, more likely, results in a pendulum relationship between opposite poles, an enantiodromia, where sooner or later one end of a continuum gives way to its opposing aspect. In Jung's writing these processes are considered basic characteristics of human activity. Odajnyk lists a number of dichotomies that occur in relation to Jung's discussion of political issues—for example, the line between consciousness and unconsciousness, or individualism and collectivism. Other dichotomies are scepticism to fanaticism; control to rebellion; security to insecurity; individual faith to collective ideology; and emotional needs as against material needs. What are missing are the more fundamental continuums of want and fulfilment around such basic needs as those of food, shelter, sex, emotional warmth and security. This lack reflects in part Jung's concern with the more rarefied problems of individuation beyond middle age, but the omission has important implications because it hints at a tendency to pass over the more basic human drives, a critique often made by Freudians of many Jungian writings (Glover, 1950).

The presence of constantly shifting balances meant that, for Jung, history was always likely to be caught in an enantiodromia of change as an imbalance created the tension that fuelled further activity by accelerating change or provoking a counter reaction. It follows from this that as one extreme was exhausted, the dynamic initiative would swing to the other extreme. The operation of this seemingly autonomous enantiodromia created an appearance of a higher will or a *deux ex machina* at work in politics, and from this one might be lead into hypothesising the influences of an archetype, as will be shown in the discussion of 'Wotan'.

ARCHETYPES IN THE POLITICAL ARENA

In politics Jung thought that archetypes had their strongest impact in social situations which exhibited acute emotion that triggered a corresponding archetypal configuration. For example, a crisis situation could activate corresponding archetypal constellations in the individual when anxieties about power and security have reached sufficient levels of primitive emotion. Jung explained that if a neurosis was identified in a large number of people, then: 'we must assume the presence of constellated archetypes, since neuroses are in most cases not just private concerns but social phenomena'. He added that these psychological forces were 'explosive, dangerous and unpredictable', so that: 'There is no lunacy people under the domination of an archetype will not fall a prey to' (Jung, 1969 [1936], §98). In this way he highlighted the interaction between the archetypal drive and the external situation. Jung suggested that because of this process in times of crisis, such as the demise of a social system, it was likely that there would be a regression to archaic modes of thought and emotion. At such times, humanity's common archetypes, if no longer bound by traditional dogmas, could provide inspiration and the core of a solution to a wide range of problems as they represent 'the age-old experiences of mankind that speak to him from his blood' (Jung, 1990 [1929], §11).[139]

At the start of this process of change the presence of an archetype may not be recognised as initially the archetype is set so deep in the unconscious that it remains an unconsciously latent symbol. As it surfaces it sheds its archaic pattern and takes on a cultural overlay as it finds expression in the political realm (Progoff, 1983, p193). Jung suggested that one of the first symptoms of archetypal influence on the political arena was the rise in psychological disruption. This, according to Jung, was 'mostly in the form of abnormal over- or under-valuations which provoke misunderstandings, quarrels, fanaticisms, and follies of every description... [In this way] there grow up modern myth-formations, i.e., fantastic rumours, suspicions, prejudices' (Jung, 1990 [1917/1926/1943], §152). Jung then explained that the most pernicious effect of these archetypal influences was 'the danger of psychic infection'. This happens by projection, but projection can only occur where there is a grain of truth in it, which makes the accusation doubly difficult to counter.

As was explained in the last chapter, because the archetypal image is such a primitive psychic organ, it retains its potential for numinous power. This draws the individual back to the unconscious and potentially more primitive forms of thought and emotion. This regressive lure of the numinous is a politically significant factor because of the compulsive energy and primitivity it can unleash. This primitivity, if it is emotive enough, may create a situation where, to paraphrase Marx, *politics becomes the opiate of the (unconsciously religious) masses.*

Jung argued that the numinous effect of the archetypes accounted for the phenomenon of charisma in political attraction. This happens as the compelling power of the archetypal complex fascinates and unconsciously influences a person's actions or ideas, irrespective of their conscious wishes (Jung, 1956 [1911-12/1952], §467). This compulsion can work on the audience or on the speaker, so that both the orator and the listeners can be seduced into believing by the sheer eloquence of the speech. Jung suggested that history showed that religious ideas were very powerful, and he classed all collective movements or '-isms' as representative of collective utopian and fundamentally religious ideas. Furthermore he warned that where projections are too strong to be withdrawn, this was probably because a religious archetype has been constellated. This situation can happen regardless of the individual's confessional position, as a secular faith can easily displace a religious one (Jung, 1969 [1936/1954], §125-129).

All these processes mean that archetypal possession imposes forms of emotion and types of thought on the 'possessed'. It means that once an archetypal situation occurs, and archetypal reaction patterns set in, the thought processes may be contaminated by negative shadow projection or run along archetypal patterns that foster political myths.

As archetypal personalities are autonomous and can be active in a person close to a psychosis, this can lead to mental states that resemble possession (Jung, 1969 [1934/1954], §82).[140]

Jung argued that such was the power of archetypal ideas that they could rapidly lead to a dangerous state of brutal megalomania as they fostered an inhuman lack of compassion or reflection. Jung explained, on the 19th October 1938, that because the archetypes had evolved before present levels of evolutionary development 'they reach down into an epoch where man could hardly be differentiated from the animal. And that entirely unconscious background of the archetypes gives them a quality that is decidedly inhuman. So anybody possessed by an archetype develops inhuman qualities' (Jung, 1989 [1934-1939], p1343).

This combination of disruption, possession, inflation and inhumanity produces a super-human personality that forms the constituent parts of the magic of the charismatic leader. Jung called such people *'mana* personalities', taking the word *mana* to represent the impression of holy power that seems to emanate from such figures. Such charismatic figures can construct round themselves a 'cult of personality' which gives form to an anthropomorphic myth so that 'A man can then take on archetypal dimensions and exercise corresponding effects; he can appear in the place of God' (Jung, 1956 [1911-12/1952], §101).

In the last chapter it was argued that Jung used the term archetype too widely. If one accepts the categories employed in that chapter, it is no longer appropriate to offer vague suggestions of archetypal influences without attempting to establish what sort of psychic organs one is referring to and whether a biological or an 'immanent' process created them. Given the emotional potential that archetypes can unleash it is important to consider which type of psychic organ is likely to affect politics because that may give some indication of the emotional polarities involved if specific archetypal configurations raise emotional levels.

Consider the following case: a political leader may have a given amount of institutional power, political capital and personal charisma, but if he were able to trigger an archetypal emotional configuration by taking on the mantle of parental power over his followers, then this archetype pushes the emotional dynamics to run in directions that enhance obedience and authority. Thus the emotional numinous affect of the archetype will raise emotions and act to increase feelings of dependence and loyalty.

Some archetypes seem to be obviously politically significant. It is also worth noting that many of these archetypes have a developmental aspect. This may account for their emotional power, which originally evolved to meet the species' survival requirements. Given this potential, a more focused understanding of archetypes in politics offers the political commentator the possibility of determining which archetype has been constellated and this may furnish insights into the emotional dynamics of the situation and the likely chain of events.

Let us now make a brief overview of those archetypes which can most readily be considered political.

The Variants of the Archetype of Paradise

The first political archetypes to be considered are the 'immanent' archetypes derived from childhood that are in some way connected to the experience of paradise. These archetypes can be forward or backward looking. The basic form of the 'immanent' archetypes is formed from the infant's experience of the relationship with its mother.

Infancy, according to Neumann, is a time when the primary relationship between mother and infant is experienced as a 'unitary reality' with no rift in creation (1972, p211).[141] Jacoby, summing up the conclusions of many child psychologists like Alice Miller and Erik Erikson, argues that for an infant in the pre-ego state, security and confidence in a satisfactory mother-infant relationship are vital for establishing confidence and maturity in later life (1985, p8). If this time was a happy experience it creates a feeling basis for the idea of paradise, which Eliade observed is near-universal in all cultures (Jacoby, 1985, p4). The feeling of the mother-infant relationship acts as the foundation of the immanent archetype of paradise. In political imagery this childhood feeling of home security may give rise to the powerful political motif of the Motherland or Fatherland.

'The Golden Age' or 'The Good Old Days'

When memories of infantile happiness take a regressive form, people look back to a golden age for which Armin Geertz and Jeppe Jensen (1991), coined the phrase 'the politics of nostalgia'[142] (McCutcheon, 2001, p13).

Mario Jacoby, who has written a lot about this area, takes a very negative view of the political role of nostalgia (1985, p4, 6). He implicitly seems to suggest that nostalgia is the illusion of the middle classes and the middle-aged. But while old securities can stifle adaptation, leading to a loss of vitality and the onset of cultural senility, leaving a culture ill-prepared to meet fresh challenges, Jacoby's criticism of nostalgia goes too far. Nostalgia can be argued to be an almost inevitable emotion and, as such, a socially 'immanent' archetype. For those in middle-age it can be just as important as young people's need for heroes. In this way nostalgia serves as a vital balance for healthy society. The historical validity of 'good times' must be acknowledged because later they can become historico-social myths that reinforce social cohesion with their echoes of the childhood 'paradise'. In this way one sees how a biological 'immanent' archetype based on the mother-child bond acts as a 'force multiplier'[143] that accelerates the effect of a socially 'immanent' archetype.

The Utopian Future

The forward-looking variant of the archetype of paradise is the hope of 'a promised land' or Utopia. A more limited edition of this basic 'immanent' archetype occurs in dreams and stories, or even political manifestos which promise a wonderland of plenty, rich in wish fulfilment, the fairy-tale image of an 'Aladdin's cave' (Costello, 2003). The idea of a paradise 'yet to be attained' can take form in any number of ideologies from the Communist 'society of artists' to the racial perfection of the National Socialist Thousand Year Reich.

The Death Wish

There is a darker vision of the future, which represents a negative image of paradise, and seems to be derived from a profound feeling of alienation. This very different 'immanent' archetype is derived from the pressures and fatigues of life and can lead to a desire for everything to be blotted out. As such the feeling is a by-product of life's tribulations.

This desire for the solace granted by complete negation, Freud referred to as the 'Nirvana principle', which he then elaborated into a component of what he came to call 'the death wish' in *The Economic Problem of Masochism* (Freud, 1924, p159).[144] Within his formulation the 'death wish' and Libido were the original drives and, from a classical Freudian conception, they would be regarded as the primary drives underlying all subsequent speculations about the structure of the psyche that might include phylogenetic remnants, archetypes and instincts.

Death is always likely to hold a fascination, as it is the inescapable hallmark of the human condition. It is part of what Joyce referred to as that which is 'grave and constant in human sufferings'.[145] In political terms, one of the most radical examples of the desire for a literal end to things was Hitler's political testament and his scorched-earth order that Germany should be reduced to a wasteland, as she was unworthy of his genius (Trevor-Roper, 1971, p195; Petrova and Watson, 1995, p36).

WAR, THE HUNTING INSTINCT AND THE ARCHETYPE OF THE 'OTHER'

In considering the place of war in our archetypal discussion I want to briefly refer to some of the more recent post-Jungian work in this area that uses anthropological, ethnological and neurological studies. Stevens and Price argue that recent neurological research substantiates Jung's intuition that the main archetypal systems could be traced to the older parts of the brain. James Olds writes about the 'cold' and the 'hot' brain. The 'cold' brain is the cortical region of the cerebral hemispheres and is involved in rational thought. The 'hot' brain is the phylogenetically much older midbrain that deals with the powerful emotions of aggression and sexual desire (Stevens, 1989, p19).[146] Following on from this MacLean demonstrated that the human brain is an evolved composite that he termed the 'triune brain' made up of an advanced cerebral cortex, an older mammalian brain and, older still, a reptilian brain (Stevens and Price, 1996, p15, p40). [147] Both of the latter still have their respective behaviour patterns hard-wired into the psyche; thus, when frightened, humans react with the older more primitive limbic system that provides instinctive reactions and the appropriate emotional response.

How does this apply to war? Neurological research suggests that there is an instinctive or archetypal bias for hunting and aggression that is a fertile base for the emotions needed in conflict and war. Can we then speak of an archetypal component of war?

In one of his more poetic essays Jung wrote: 'the deeper we descend into the [psyche]... finally we reach the naked bed-rock, and with it that prehistoric time when reindeer hunters fought for a bare and wretched existence against the elemental forces of wild nature. The men of that age were still in full possession of their animal instincts, without which life would have been impossible' (Jung, 1991 [1927/1931b], §55). So what were these 'animal instincts' so vital for survival at a time when life in the state of nature was 'nasty, brutish and short', to borrow Hobbes's famous aphorism? The answer surely is the human omnivore's instinct to hunt; and according to Lionel Tiger, hunting constitutes the 'master pattern of the human species'. This predisposition has a number of implications (Stevens, 1989, p49).[148]

Firstly, consider hunting and the hunter. To chase down and kill requires more than anything instinctive aggression, for hunting requires enough emotional drive to cope with all the dangers involved. Now, in many animals, ethologists observe that different parts of the brain are involved in aggression against animals of the same species compared with aggression against animals of other species. In animals that make this distinction, there are instinctive mechanisms to regulate conflict within the group, but such mechanisms are obviously not appropriate to hunting other species. However, humans are caught in an unfortunate situation, as they appear to lack intra-species aggressive inhibitions (Stevens, 1989, p40, 49).

This hunting master-pattern constitutes one of the prime instinctual packages of behaviour belonging to chimpanzees and men, and this biological package has not evolved beyond its raw hunter-killer package in the last 35,000 years. Humans have the same pack-hunting instincts as numberless Palaeolithic generations, as we can see by considering human history. A million years ago, Java or Peking man may have been using clubs and cutting-stones to butcher carcasses. By 70,000 years ago Neanderthal man was hunting with spears. By 35,000 years ago the Neanderthal had either been out-hunted or driven to extinction by Cro-Magnon man. The bow was invented between 12,000 and 8,000 BC, and since then human missile technology has gone on to ever-greater heights. The advent of missile weapons has been very significant in understanding aggression between humans because, as humans have no natural weapons, they have few innate instinctive inhibitors for intra-species aggression. This means, as Lorenz noted, sympathy and pity can play little role with the advent of long-range weapons. With missiles there is no face-to-face impact that might foster inhibitions. Not surprisingly, Alfred Adler argued that human 'social instincts' are over-stretched and hard-put to cope with the demands of civilisation.

The other factor that makes hunting so significant is the relationship between the hunters and the hunted. For the hunters, the chase requires enough male bonding to build teamwork in the face of the risks they will face (Stevens, 1989, p49). But this predisposition to group loyalty has many roots and other implications. Stevens and Price acknowledge Erik Erikson's 1965 observation that mankind seems to have a universal disposition to perceive humanity in terms of 'in-groups' and 'out-groups' (2000, p126[149]). Humans, like all mammals, share the territorial propensity to distinguish 'us' from 'them'. Erikson coined a term for regarding outsiders as alien and potentially inhuman as that of creating 'pseudospecies'. This happens in spite of there being 'no biological foundation for pseudospeciation, in the sense that there are no different human species. However, there is biological basis for our propensity to pseudospeciate' (Stevens, 1989, p42, 44). Stevens and Price explain that it is 'this propensity that incites us to xenophobia, racialism, militant nationalism and to war. It would have us conceive ourselves as 'chosen people' possessing a monopoly of goodness and decency and being the unique recipients of divine gifts of immortality and central position in the universe, while, at the same time, it encourages us to see the out-group as subhuman adversaries with virtually limitless capacities for treachery, hostility and evil' (2000, p132). Just as one group can be rejected, Stevens suggests that humans must have an innate predisposition for indoctrination into group ideas, as this is a vital aspect of group bonding and cohesion (2000, p107). The bonding of young males for aggressive pursuits is not so much an instinctual urge as an archetypal disposition which can be activated, trained, and exploited by more senior males in positions of authority. The male capacity for group conflict is an innate 'facility' in the sense that it is an open program which may be brought into action whenever circumstances appear to demand it—in as few, or as many men, as seems appropriate (Stevens, 1989, p52).

Having considered our instinctive pre-disposition for hunting and pseudospeciation, one can say that this array of instincts makes war a socially and biologically immanent archetype and that this instinctive hunting 'master pattern' clearly has enormous political potential.

The Self and the 'Organising Dominants'

The power of the 'organising dominants' comes in part from their developmental role at a stage in psychological development when the ego may be less influenced by such archetypal personalities as the Hero, and have a more integrated relationship with the shadow and the anima / animus that allows for more abstract organisational processes to come to the fore.

The 'organising dominants' are unusual as 'archetypal ideas' in that they can often be politically significant. This is noteworthy because these political effects are due to 'immanent' characteristics of the 'organising dominant', but this has no relation to their original purpose.

The Self

The Self as it represents the totality of the human's potential is at the core of religious motivations. The emotional systems that are derived from the Self can have political consequences and this will be dealt with in the next chapter.

The Utopia of Order

A common political organising dominant is the archetype of order that emerges in times of chaos. On 10th January 1929, Jung wrote:

> At the founding of the great religions there was to begin with a collective disorientation which everywhere constellated in the unconscious an overwhelming principle of order (the collective longing for redemption). ... it has a fascinating effect on everyone, it is 'true'—temporarily valid because it is meant *only for a particular situation.* (Jung, 1973 [1906-1950], p60)

> These structures not only express order, they also create it. That is why they generally appear in times of psychic disorientation in order to compensate a chaotic state or as formulations of numinous experiences. (Jung, 1991 [1952a], §870)

This archetype can also draw on early developmental experience and can combine with the 'immanent' archetype of paradise in its regressive or progressive form.

Dichotomy of 'the Other'

This archetype is made up of both innate archetypes and 'immanent' biological and sociological archetypes. Having so many roots, and reaching into so many aspects of the human psyche and the human condition, it is one of the most influential of psychic factors.

The Hero and the Shadow

The hero and the shadow are connected with the task of ego development. The hero is needed to establish a strong ego and break free of the Oedipal situation, and the shadow is a product of all the suppression and repression involved in the socialisation required to reach the ego ideal.

The archetype of the hero is based on the need for the adolescent to mature and is heavily influenced by the role external models play in this process. However, this is inherently dangerous as the numinous halo of the archetypal pattern may be projected onto a mundane political leader. Nor is the hero always a positive figure,[150] as the hero and the shadow can often overlap. It is often observed that criminals are failed heroes, as de Castillejo remarked: 'how fine is the line between heroism and delinquency' (1973, p45). The shadow is the archetype that has the most immediate political impact when it is projected on to other peoples or countries. As was stated in the first chapter, there is an extensive literature on the shadow and its consequences in politics, so there is little to be gained from rehearsing established arguments. However, one can note that part of the shadow is made up of the less-developed attitudes and functions of the individual, called the Inferior Function. These inferior qualities have a high degree of emotional energy in a primitive state that can overwhelm consciousness with their numinous quality (de Castillejo, 1973, p34). This is an especially dangerous combination when it is twinned with other archetypal energy systems, and the whole effect is doubly pernicious if it is operating in an area where consciousness and self-reflection are already weak.

THE MESSIAH

The last archetypal personalisation that will be mentioned is that of the Messiah, who may be cast in political or religious terms and seems to be a synthesis of the 'Wise Old Man', the 'hero' and, arguably, the Self. Of especial interest are Jung's ideas on the charismatic aspect of messianic leaders and the implications this has for understanding the psychology of dictatorships. This fascinating topic has recently featured in a number of detailed studies that look at the natural linkage between the possibility of a genetic component of the psychology of fatherhood, father figures and leaders (Lindholm, 1990; Storr, 1996; Stevens and Price, 2000). There are also links between the idea of the charismatic and Jung's idea that, if an archetypal reaction pattern were activated, it could have a powerful emotional 'numinous' effect. This figure will be discussed in the next chapter.

Phase Three:
When Theory Meets History

Whoever speaks in primordial images speaks with a thousand voices; he enthrals and overpowers, while at the same time he lifts the idea he is seeking to express out of the occasional and the transitory into the realm of the ever-enduring. He transmutes our personal destiny into the destiny of mankind, and evokes in us all those beneficent forces that ever and anon have enabled humanity to find a refuge from every peril and to outlive the longest night. (Jung, 1979 [1922], §129)

8. THE TEST CASE: WOTAN AND NAZI GERMANY.

And in Germany those National Socialists, those Swastika people, are building Wotan's fires again. Jung, 11th March 1931. (Jung, 1986 [1930]-32 p288)

The book now comes to its climax as we look at what Jung wrote about the Third Reich as the European crisis deepened and the war clouds gathered. This subject was the only pre-war issue to engage Jung in lengthy political analysis and his musing on the psychological aspects of the Third Reich is the nearest he came to applying his collective theories to understanding international politics.

The chapter will focus on his 'Wotan' essay, published in a journal the same month that Hitler invaded the Rhineland (Glover, 1950, p150). It can be seen to have had two equally important functions: one was to establish the validity of his theories of the collective, and the other was to act as a political warning. 'Wotan' and the shorter Knickerbocker interview for *Cosmopolitan* would be the vehicles for Jung to deploy his ideas in the political arena.

In examining his only test case, one can make an even finer assessment of how theoretically coherent Jung's ideas were. As we have found, when examining Jung's ideas, caution is needed, as it must be remembered that his ideas constituted an uneasy synthesis between what he explicitly stated and what he implicitly believed; also his ideas changed over time and were confused in their presentation. This means that as one is commenting on a synthesis of Jung's position, one must work with care when drawing observations and making conclusions.

In this chapter we consider how Jung applied his theories and how successful he was in attempting to provide evidence for them. Did the theories help or hinder his understanding of international politics. Did he have anything useful to contribute to an understanding of events, or did others make similar observations using more conventional perspectives and how did Jung's use of 'Wotan' fare as a prophetic essay?

THE ARCHETYPAL HOPE

In the inter-war period Jung became increasingly alarmed by a number of political developments. As he became concerned he warned that people seemed to be possessed and in danger of being overwhelmed by ideologies that were driven by archetypal themes. His concern prompted him to warn in 1927: 'Our fearsome Gods have only changed their names: they now rhyme with –ism. Or has anyone the nerve to claim that the World War or Bolshevism was an ingenious discovery?' (Jung, 1990 [1916-34], §326). Jung was most concerned by the emotional and collective power of religious psychology, which he thought drove mass movements (Jung, 1969 [1934/1954], §125). Later he suggested that 'the current "isms"' were dangerous because their roots lay in 'dangerous identifications of the subjective with the collective consciousness. Such an identity infallibly produces a mass psyche with its irresistible urge to catastrophe' (Jung, 1991 [1947/54], §426). Jung warned that the way to prevent such identification was to recognise the importance of the archetypes and the impact of the shadow and so not be caught unawares.

Jung's archetypal perspective was linked to his awareness of the devastating affects on Germany of defeat and depression (see chapter two). He suggested that times of great anxiety 'would bring up archaic material, archetypes that join forces with the individual as well as with the people... Such an outburst is always a regression into history and it always means a lowering of the level of civilization' (Jung, 1986 [1936a], §1323). He suggested that archetypal possession had a survival value as it created strength, conviction, and courage[151], but these emotional advantages were always bought at a cost of sweeping away old norms and so undermining social stability.

Despite this pessimism, Jung, in the early thirties, briefly entertained hopes that events were taking a positive turn and, for a comparatively brief time, this was a significant aspect of his theory, which might be expected as this perspective—of good emerging out of the unknown—was a direct parallel with his clinical optimism. This attitude came into play in Jung's thinking on the Third Reich with his theoretical idea that archetypes could reinvigorate European, or at least German society, by re-incorporating the virile psychological elements of pagan antiquity that had been repressed during the Christian millennium. This belief will be referred to as 'the archetypal hope'.

In 1918, in 'The Role of the Unconscious', Jung argued that in Iron Age Germany, Christianity had been artificially forced onto an immature pagan cultural base. In taking such a perspective he was continuing Nietzsche's concern about the debilitating effects of artificial morality on the unconscious 'blond beast' in European psyche.[152] Central to Jung's concern was the view that this 'lower, darker half still awaited redemption and a second spell of domestication. Until this happened, it would remain associated with the vestiges of the prehistoric age, with the collective unconscious'. He predicted that: 'As the Christian view of the world loses its authority, the more menacingly will the "blond beast" be heard prowling about in its underground prison, ready at any moment to burst out with devastating consequence' (Jung, 1991 [1918], §17).

This concern with spiritual vitality and the viability of Christianity was a long-running theme in his thinking and was one of the roots of his break with Freud who, he felt, was ignoring the therapeutic necessity of acknowledging the primitive mythic base of the psyche and the potential this held for spiritual renewal. (See chapter two.) Jung argued that the greater the distance between the cultural heights of consciousness and the unknown depths of primitive unconscious emotion, the greater the tension. This conflict contained the possibility of producing more energy and more potential for change but also more danger of violent regression. He explained after the war, that this conflict was especially marked in Germany where 'hungering for the infinite' had been betrayed by listening to a liar and psychopath who promised so much and misused both the energy and the hope (Jung, 1991 [1945], §423). He saw the lack of relation between the two contrasting levels of development as an acute case of 'disassociation... [which was] one of the signs of a psychopathic disposition' (Jung, 1991 [1946a], §476-477). [153] Jung was not alone in such a view. Erikson, writing afterwards on the 'black miracle of Nazism', advanced a similar idea about the distance in German society between the 'highest point of civilised achievement' and 'the weakest point of their collective identity' (1982, p294).

In 1923, Jung again argued his case with eloquent images: 'The Germanic tribes, when they collided only the day before yesterday with Roman Christianity, were still in the initial state of a polydemonism with polytheistic buds. There was as yet no proper priesthood and no proper ritual. Like Wotan's oaks, the gods were felled and a wholly incongruous Christianity, born of monotheism on a much higher cultural level, was grafted upon the stumps. The Germanic man is still suffering from this mutilation' (Jung, 1973 [1906-1950], p39-40). So Jung continued to focus on the threat posed by the 'blond beast' and an archetypal hope that the German's spiritual potential for good could be safely transformed.

The archetypal hope has to be understood as part of Jung's theoretical perspective. But it also has to be assessed to see what impact the theory had on Jung and how it distorted his powers of political realism and his ability to assess critically his own theory.

In the turmoil of the thirties, to see great movements in the depths of history and the psyche may not have been so dramatically strange as it appears to us now. The interwar period saw many unusual social phenomena that could have suggested the possibilities of radical change. One can get a flavour of how events were perceived from H.G. Baynes' recollection that, up to the end of 1934, one frequently met in Germany devoted and enthusiastic youths with 'an unmistakable religious feeling in those vast camps'. Hitler seemed prophetic and positive. He was 'exalted by the bright flame of revolution. There was a numinous flame, a compelling sacrament of power which had taken possession of German youth, and Hitler responded to it'. Baynes went on to add: 'after the criminal *volte-face* of June 1934, the whole movement took a sinister turn.' This was the 'Night of the Long Knives', when Hitler liquidated much of the SA leadership and many other individuals who represented a personal threat (1941, p88).

To understand the part the archetypal hope played in Jung's thinking one needs to look at Jung's pre-war attitude to Nazi Germany and the following points provide a useful overview.

- In chapter two it was argued that contrary to the opinion of many of Jung's critics in the secondary sources, Jung was not anti-Semitic, but was in conflict with the hostile Freudian 'campaign'.
- Jung's conflict with the Nazi regime had to be muted while he was engaged in institutional conflict with their polices in the IGMSP.
- There is as yet no evidence that Jung had any sympathy with Nazi ideology, party politics or foreign policy.
- Despite being a neutral, once war broke out Jung became actively involved in the Allied cause through his contacts with the Office of Strategic Services (OSS) which was the forerunner of the CIA.

When we look more closely at Jung's perception of events in Germany it seems that his theories went through a number of stages. [154] This hypothesis is provisional as there is limited documentary material. Jung was a complex thinker who could simultaneously hold contradictory ideas, so to construct a scheme of a consistent evolution in his ideas maybe an illusion. With these reservations, the phases of Jung's understanding seems to be as follows:

- *The period of hope and early warnings* began with his warnings about Germany from 1918. This was mixed with his hopes for Germanic renewal. Alongside these general views, by 1932 or May 1933, Jung was privately hostile to the Nazi leadership, but thought the Nazi revolution might still facilitate his 'archetypal hope'.
- *The period of transition* saw Jung fully engaged in political and institutional struggles with the Nazis within the IGMSP. This

period saw little overt political comment by him, although it did include Jung's statements in the misjudged end of the Weizsäcker interview. This may have been due to residual hope; the pressure of work or diplomatic expediency; the barrage of flattery; or the cumulative effect of his anger against the 'campaign'.
- *The period of open conflict.* By 1935 Jung no longer thought that the German revolution had a prospect of bringing about positive archetypal changes. On 4th October, 1935 Jung gave a series of public lectures in the Tavistock Clinic in London that was highly critical of Nazi Germany.
- *The end of hope.* It is not possible to determine at what point Jung gave up all hope of an archetypal transformation, but by 1945 Jung had abandoned thinking about history in the sort of archetypal terms he had attempted in 'Wotan'.[155]

It is Jung's thoughts in the early years that are interesting for us here. Contrary to the assertions of some commentators and the accusations of his critics[156], Jung came to see the Nazi threat remarkably early, as we will read in the next two sections. In trying to unravel Jung's thoughts it is important for the reader to be aware that in most cases Jung first expressed criticism of the Nazis in private and then gradually became more outspoken in public.

The period of hope seems best described by two post-war interviews about Jung's attitude. Although the speakers were imprecise about the exact time to which they refer, the statements fit within the spirit of the early period.

The first interview comes from Gene Nameche who talked to a number of people who knew Jung in the thirties and forties.[157] One of the more interesting interviewees was Wilhelm Bitter, the founder of the Stuttgart Institute for Psychotherapy, who was analysed and later became involved in the attempts by dissident Germans to end the war by negotiation. Bitter felt that between 1933 and 1934 there was great sympathy for the Nazis in Jung's circle. Nameche sought clarification from him and asked:

> Nameche: 'You did say here that Jung and some of his pupils became Nazis in 1934. Would you say it so strongly?'
> Bitter: '1933, yes.'
> Nameche: 'That *he* became a Nazi?'
> Bitter: 'Jung? Not a Nazi in the strict sense.'

Bitter also stated:

> It's so easy for the Freudians, and not only the Jewish, to say Jung was a Nazi, an anti-Semite... This statement is wrong. But for a short time he believed in the possibilities of Nazism, and favoured it. He spoke of Jewish psychology, but not in an anti-Semitic sense. His best pupils are Jewish—Erich Neumann, Gerhard Adler... and Jacobi are all Jewish pupils. (Noll, 1997, p274) [158]

As Bitter took pains to point out, Jung was interested primarily in the spiritual revitalization of the German peoples so that: 'He thought of rebirth, rebirth in the good sense.' This optimism can also be seen from a statement of Jung's on Nazi Germany on 13th February 1935: 'You know that there is nothing so evil that something good could not come out of it' (Jung, 1989 [1934-1939], p377). Jung's perspective is also recorded in a 1969 interview with Jolande Jacobi. She had been one of his closest disciples from the thirties and recalled: 'His idea [about the Nazi movement] was that chaos gives birth to good or to something valuable. So in the German movement he saw a chaotic (we could say) pre-condition for the birth of a new world.' Jacobi told how Jung responded to her anxiety about the Nazis, 'He answered me: 'Keep your eyes open. You can't reject the evil because the evil is the bringer of light.' Lucifer means light-bringer. He was convinced of this, you see. That shows that he didn't see and didn't understand the outer world. For him this [the Nazi movement] was an inner happening which had to be accepted as a psychological pre-condition for rebirth' (Noll, 1997, p274).[159] Later, Jung wrote: 'Every archetype contains the lowest and the highest, evil and good, and is therefore capable of producing diametrically opposite results. Hence it is impossible to make out at the start whether it will prove to be positive or negative' (Jung, 1991 [1946a], §474-475). From this one sees that Jung's theoretical perspective, which was part of his clinical attitude, as well as his political realism, cautioned him about what to say in public, but his theoretical attitude did not seem to disrupt for long or to any great degree his realist insights into the Nazi regime.

So Jung had 'hope' but that did not mean he could not see many of the dangers of the Nazi regime. It may surprise many of Jung's critics to know that from a very early date Jung demonstrated a shrewd and negative assessment of Hitler's character. In 1932 Jung was asked to comment on a newspaper photo of Hitler and in his response he wrote that it showed: 'A too intensive unconscious sphere as counterpart to a somewhat blocked conscious sphere—therefore too much distance between the conscious and unconscious. Higher up too purely intellectual, below too much like a primeval forest. A kind of pre-war Russian soul. He is thinnest at the centre of the face... so there is a split into oppositional pairs... no balance but a tendency towards obsession. The eyes express: discharge of the unconscious in fantasies he then tries to interpret' (Hayman, 1999, p310).

But if even at such an early stage Jung was unimpressed with Hitler, like many of his contemporaries, he under-estimated the Nazis' ability to survive. In 1933 he reassured James Kirsch that the Nazis would be a very transient phenomenon (Stein, 1991, p100). He later explained that he found it hard to foresee that such a civilised country could regress so far and underestimated the Nazi danger, as did Freud and Einstein (Jung, 1991 [1946a], §474; Lukacs, 1997, p253). In Germany, despite the visible aggression of the SA storm troopers on the streets and the unspoken dread of the concentration camps, many bankers, generals and members of the ruling classes thought they could pacify Hitler. Professional politicians inside Germany from all shades of the political spectrum underestimated Hitler. From the conservative politicians the most notorious case of delusion was Franz von Papen who hoped to control Hitler in government, and he was not alone in this error as the leader of the Catholic BVP, Fritz Schaffer, told von Papen he thought Hitler could work in a joint cabinet. The anarchist Erich

Mühsam welcomed Hitler's election as he hoped ministerial responsibility would show Hitler's true form (Kershaw, 1998, p392, 336). Across the political spectrum in Weimar political circles underestimation and miscalculation by Hitler's opponents cleared the way for his 'miraculous' rise. At the same time many from the intelligentsia were quick to align themselves with Hitler, the most eminent example being the academic philosopher Martin Heidegger and Carl Schmidt, the senior constitutional lawyer (Kershaw, 1998, p336, 424, 481).

Most tragically, even in the case of Jews, despite the crippling restrictions of the 1935 Nuremberg Race Laws, many Jews hoped that having been reduced to second-class citizens they would see an end to the persecutions and a return to a relatively orderly existence which would allow them to resume their livelihoods in business and industry (Redlich, 1998, p320).

Outside Germany, experienced foreign politicians were also deceived. Lloyd George, who had led Britain to victory against earlier German expansionism, thought that Hitler was the greatest European figure since Napoleon (Lukacs, 1997, p253, 248) and many believed it was possible to negotiate with Hitler either through Chamberlain's appeasement policy (Meehan, 1992), or Stalin's Molotov-Ribbentrop pact of 1939. For too many the Nazis were a transient evil that could be bought, placated, corrupted or appeased. Jung was not being self-serving when he wrote retrospectively of how different things looked in 1933 or 1934: 'there were not a few things that appear plausible and seemed to speak in favour of the regime... after the stagnation and decay of the postwar years, the refreshing wind that blew through the two countries was a tempting sign of hope' (Jung, 1991 [1945], §420).

Looking at the evolution of Jung's hostility to the Nazis, the next evidence after the photo commentary is from May 1933, and an account of a confrontation between Jung and Hitler's propaganda minister Dr. Joseph Goebbels. According to Kirsch, on a visit to Berlin Jung was invited to see Goebbels and the following conversation took place:

> *Goebbels:* You wanted to see me, Dr. Jung.
> *Jung:* No. You wanted to see me.

> *Goebbels:* No. You wanted to see me.
> Jung turned around and left Goebbels' office—and vomited! From there he came to my house for lunch where my wife had prepared an ocean fish. He ate with excellent appetite! This was the end of the courting of Jung by the Nazis. (1982, p77)

Kirsch was too optimistic however when he suggested that this was the end of the 'courting' by the Nazis. For example, Matthias Göring was presumably making a concerted effort to impress and flatter Jung in 1937 when he arranged for Jung and C.A. Meier to see a big military parade in Berlin from a place of honour 'only a few yards away' from Hitler and Mussolini, while Jung was in Berlin to give a lecture (Donn, 1988, p22; Hayman, 1999, p347; McGuire and Hull, 1980, p133).

By 1934 Jung was aware of evil in the Nazi regime, but in the period of transition he was still cautious in his response and warned: 'Go slow. Go slow. With every good there comes a corresponding evil, and with every evil a corresponding good. Don't run too fast into one unless you are prepared to encounter the other' (McGuire and Hull, 1980, p87). Jung showed his hope when he wrote to Neumann in August 1934 that 'historically Hitler is an attempt at collective individuation for the Germans' (Neumann, 1989, p279). But significantly Jung did not say that Hitler was a result of some successful collective individuation as his assessment of Hitler was already negative. By this time he was also starting to bait the Nazis to a limited degree inside the Reich, as was recounted in chapter two. This may not have been good for his negotiations within the IGMSP, but it does reflect Jung's occasional impatience and failure to keep his temper.

By 1935 Jung began to be more publicly outspoken. The following passage gives one the opportunity to see Jung expressing himself in a private seminar in his poetic style that is very different from his more politically articulate statements. On 22nd May 1935 he explained how events in Germany were due to a regression:

> This is an exceedingly dangerous time and we are confronted with a problem which has never been

known in the conscious history of man... This is not a light but a darkness; the powers of darkness are coming up... Today it is not in the light, but in the blood, so the position is entirely different; we cannot compare it with the conditions two thousand years ago.

You see, to be moved by the blood means that you are really moved by the things in the twilight zone, where things begin to become visible. And if we want to do something about that fact, I surely should not organize it, up in the light of day; inasmuch as it is a phenomenon coming up from the twilight it should be kept at bay. It should not be a big organization, it should be an *heureux paganisme*—enrich human life and not upset it is as you were to turn a river over your perfectly good fields; of course they need water, but if you turn a whole river onto them, you simply destroy them. And if you turn on that river of blood, it will be a most horrible destruction. But if you keep it in its place, and don't raise too much fuss about it, it will be quite nice. (Jung, 1989 [1934-1939], p500, my italics)

He then goes on:

If you take it [these energies] right up and make a system of it, you have actual Germany, and that is really not a good example. So this fact of the blood is a most upsetting problem, because it brings up an order of things which is really no order, and it cannot be made into a human order.

'Of course we are all thinking of the so-called *Neuheidnische Bewegung* [the neo-pagan movement], and there you see the mistake; that thing should not be organized. If anybody has a Wotan experience—and I don't doubt that there are such things—he should keep perfectly quiet and think, 'Well, this is a pleasant slip into former times...' It is all individual fantasy; those are germs, or faint possibilities, which might develop into something in the course of many centuries, but for the time being it is an individual slip... (Jung, 1989 [1934-1939], p501)

Such is the language of this passage with references to 'blood' and 'Wotan' that it is difficult to resist the impression that Jung was again being too poetic; but a more sophisticated reading suggests he was employing a symbolic metaphor to explain Nietzsche's argument that the current age was seeing an up-rush of primitive unsocialised energies. Jung's main point was that it was not good for these energies to be unleashed at a collective level where they lost any potential for an individual's re-rejuvenation. Furthermore if these energies were active at a collective level it would be all to easy for them to be exploited by the state.

A reader might reasonably challenge Jung by saying that while these might have been difficult times for those attempting to individuate, Jung had blurred the significance between what was happening in mass society and individual experience. To this wider social context, Jung made little comment, as he did not perceive this to be his job. He acknowledged it, but did not pursue it—which was his privilege. But does this mean that he suffered from political myopia that inhibited his awareness of wider issues? Jung's statements were restrained, but there is no evidence that he was politically blind to what was going on.

In October 1935, Jung began to be publicly critical of the Nazis at the Tavistock lectures. Later on the 29th of March 1946, Jung talked to E.A. Bennet who recalled: 'He said that until 1935 it had seemed possible, in Germany and Italy, that some good could come from Nazism. Germany was transformed; instead of roads crowded with people without work, all was changed and peaceful. Then he saw other things and knew it was evil' (Bennet, 1985, p13).

By 12th February 1936, Jung explained in the *Zarathustra* seminars, what his hopes had been, but that the transformative opportunity had passed. He explained that it should have been possible to 'extend' one's consciousness beyond the ego to achieve a more mature holistic breadth of vision. This meant 'a certain realization of the Self' which was his interpretation for the 'Superman'. However, Jung explained that when these would-be Supermen failed to achieve consciousness, 'it causes a sort of mental infection which draws people together in a sect, or it causes a mental epidemic such as one sees actually happening in Germany. That is the Superman on the level of non-realization; the whole people is like one man, and one man is shown as an emblem or symbol of the whole nation' (Jung, 1989 [1934-1939], p826).

If Jung had lost hope in any possibility of positive change from the Nazi revolution, he still had lingering hopes that something could happen behind it. In the *Zarathustra* seminar on 26th February 1936 he almost pleadingly expressed himself: 'but first the destruction is most visible; and since Wotan is a historical figure we cannot hope that it is a progression. I am convinced that behind it something else follows, but it won't be Wotan. It cannot be' (Jung, 1989 [1934-1939], p870). This echoed what he had written in 'Wotan': 'we are driven to conclude that Wotan must, in time, reveal not only the restless, violent, stormy side of his character, but also his ecstatic and mantic qualities—a very different aspect of his nature. If this conclusion is correct *National Socialism would not be the last word*. Things must be concealed in the background which we cannot imagine at present, but we may expect them to appear in the course of the next few years or decades' (Jung, 1991 [1936], §399, my italics).

Here he linked the destructiveness of the Nazis with a Wotanesque regression, but his by now probably faint hope was that the unconscious potential for psychological transformation could be realised once the aberration of the brutal Nazi state had been swept away. Yet even this late wistful positive note is counterbalanced by his statement that the Germans 'have an opportunity, perhaps unique in history, to look into their own hearts and to learn what those perils of the soul were from which Christianity tried to rescue mankind' (Jung, 1991 [1936], §391). For there he saw Wotan as the threat with no prospect of a positive outcome and so, after the war, he downplayed aspects of his theories of the collective and put more stress on the idea of the collective shadow. This modification also reflected his return to his primary concern which had long been the process of individuation.

In summary, Jung was privately critical of the Nazis by 1932, and between 1934 and 1935 he became more critical in public.

What does this suggest? Firstly Jung's political realism was operating reasonably effectively and, in terms of realising the Nazi threat, Jung was quicker than many. But like the rest of the civilised world he was unable to foresee the depths of the horrors that were about to be perpetrated. Secondly, Jung attempted, with mixed results, to restrain himself so as not to provoke the Nazis prematurely while he tried to limit the damage they could do to the psycho-analytic professional world.[160]

Once Jung began to lose hope, could he have become more outspoken sooner or more publicly? Probably he would have done neither because he had good reasons to keep quiet while he was locked in an institutional struggle, but it is also possible that the theory may have given him some residual hope that reduced his anxiety. In any event, looking at the overall picture one is struck by Jung's consistent realism rather than the naivety that some have accused him of.

Yet if Jung's political awareness was not at fault, did he misjudge the viability of his hypothesis, or was he encouraged to be hopeful longer than the evidence around him warranted? Stein agrees with James Kirsch's observation that Jung may have felt invigorated by this upsurge in energy and the stirring times. But where is the evidence for this? The only case that seems pertinent was the flattery of the interview with Weizsäcker where, at the end, Jung made some ill-considered statements that suggest that he was momentarily carried away. There is a good case for supporting Cohen's observation that Jung had a long-standing academic investment in his ideas about the collective and mythic renewal (1975, p105-107), and Gallard's suggestion that Jung's archetypal ideas about good coming out of evil clouded his perspective as to the viability of his theory (1994, p225). But while I would agree that both these factors might have led him to overstress this archetypal view or the viability of his arguments about Wotan, it is not possible as the evidence stands to take this argument further? So let us now consider the theory.

THE ARCHETYPAL CAUSES OF WAR IN THE PERIOD OF TRANSITION

By April 1934 Jung had become more focused in his concerns and argued that war had an archetypal cause which he linked to his growing critique of Nazi Germany. In his growing anxiety, he warned:

> It is the psyche of man that makes wars. Not his consciousness. His consciousness is afraid, but his unconscious, which contains the inherited savagery as well as the spiritual strivings of the race, says to him, 'Now it is time to make war. Now is the time to kill and destroy.' And he does it.
> The most tremendous danger that man has to face is the power of his ideas. No cosmic power on earth ever destroyed ten million men in four years. But man's psyche did it. And it can do it again... All of us are subject to mass infections. Man's infections are greater than man... He shouts and parades and pretends that he is the leader, but really he is their victim. (McGuire and Hull, 1980, p86)

In the passage he referred to 'inherited savagery', 'spiritual strivings' and 'race', which were all part of the cluster of ideas surrounding his archetypal discussions, but it was very clear who he meant when he mentioned the man who 'shouts and parades'. It is the more impressive as it pre-dated the return of German conscription introduced on March 16th 1935, and the military occupation of the Rhineland on March 7th 1936, which started Hitler's military adventures.

In 1935 Jung wondered how people were 'seized by the fascinating power of an archetype.' This he described in detail: 'One cannot resist it... your brain just counts for nothing, your sympathetic system is gripped. It is a power that fascinates people from within, it is the collective unconscious which is activated, it is an archetype which is common to them all that has come to life. And because it is an archetype, it has historical aspects and we cannot understand the events without knowing history' (Jung, 1986 [1935a], §372). This lecture showed Jung believed in the actual operation of his hypothesis of the archetypal and collective unconscious. It may also be an autobiographical reference to the Weizsäcker interview of 1933, and may suggest that he too had struggled with the seductive emotions of the times.

Jung clearly stated that an archetypal pattern was driving events, as he went on to state:

> It is German history that is being lived today... the archetypes... explode collectively. These impersonal images contain enormous dynamic power... Of course, we would not call Fascism or Hitlerism ideas. They are archetypes... Give an archetype to the people and the whole crowd moves like one man, there is no resisting it. (Jung, 1986 [1935a], §372)

As he explained earlier:

> As a rule, when the collective unconscious becomes really constellated in larger social groups, the result is a public craze, a mental epidemic that may lead to revolution or war or something of the sort. These movements are exceedingly contagious... because, when the collective unconscious is activated, you are no longer the same person. You are not only *in* the movement—you *are* it. (Jung, 1986 [1935a], §93)

The following paragraph makes equally clear that Jung saw history as being made by the laws of collective psychology and by the archetypes in the collective unconscious. He said:

> [W]hat the unconscious really contains are the great collective events of the time. In the collective unconscious of the individual, history prepares itself; and when the archetypes are activated in a number of individuals and come to the surface, we are in the midst of history, as we are at present. The archetypal image which the moment requires gets into life, and everybody is seized by it. That is what we see today... The powerful factor... which changes the surface of our known world, which makes history, is collective psy-

chology, and collective psychology moves according to laws entirely different from those of our consciousness. The archetypes are the great decisive forces, they bring about the real events, and not our personal reasoning and practical intellect. (Jung, 1986 [1935a], §371)

So if in this period Jung was going to advance an explanation of war at the archetypal level, with Wotan he would try to make the case for the existence of a specific archetype.

WOTAN OF THE WILD WOOD: THE PROBLEMATIC SEARCH FOR THE ARCHETYPE

In *Wotan*, Jung was attempting to give an archetypal explanation of Nazi Germany and a warning about the prospect of war. He wrote: 'We are always convinced that the modern world is a reasonable world, basing our opinion on economic, political, and psychological factors. But I venture the heretical suggestion that the unfathomable depths of Wotan's character explain more of National Socialism than all three reasonable factors put together. There is no doubt that each of these factors explains an important aspect of what is going on in Germany, but Wotan explains yet more' (Jung, 1991 [1936], §385). Here Jung acknowledged the place of 'economic, political, and psychological factors', but he focused on the archetypal depth below that of conventional psychology.

However, before we explore Jung's argument it is important to be clear what Jung was not doing. Jung was not thinking of Wotan as a literal deity, even though he records in 1928 that Wotan worship was still practised in the canton of Zurich (Jung, 1984 [1928-1930], p71). Indeed he described someone as 'childish' that still 'thinks of the gods as metaphysical entities existing in their own right' (Jung, 1991 [1936], §386-8). Given this perspective it is not surprising that in a seminar on February 5th 1936 he ridiculed the self-declared pagan Germans by saying 'they are in such a dream state where they naively admit their immorality and talk of foolish things like Wotan' (1934-1939, p813), and in 'Wotan' he explicitly referred to them as cranks (Jung, 1991 [1936], §389). But as we saw, this had an unforeseen consequence; for by dismissing the neo-pagan's belief in Wotan as a deity he undermined his incentive to look at their 'evidence' which impoverished his own case.

Though he did not conceive of Wotan as a literal deity, Jung believed that the occurrence of neo-pagan events connected to Wotan was a valid psychological topic for him to explore, but his position is not always easy to understand. Jung tried to make his methodology clear (Jung, 1991 [1936], §391) and suggested that one could look for evidence of an archetype at work in the world by either a study of contemporary politics or a literature review of ancient cultural mythologies. However, he did not explain why these approaches were equally valid and this was unfortunate because if he wanted to provide an alternative to the socio-political explanation he needed material evidence to clarify his theoretical position. Here it seems he was caught by his habit of concentrating on a mythic explanation and neglecting to give adequate empirical evidence or a clear argument to make his own case, which is confusing. So for anyone coming fresh to Jung and his arguments in 'Wotan', they might well ask of Jung:

- What are the social effects that are being ascribed to an archetype?
- What are the psychological effects that are being ascribed to an archetype?
- What is your evidence and why do you believe that an archetypal explanation is justified?
- If an archetype is operating, is this a racial archetype and if so is this innate to the Germans or is it a cultural complex?
- If an archetype is at work, what type of archetype is it and how is this established?

In the article Jung did not succeed in conveying a clear picture of his hypothesis or solid proof to substantiate it, so sadly these questions cannot be clearly answered. Indeed in his seventeen pages he spends the first six in a swirling play of ideas and images that is impressive as a piece of rhetoric but it is far from clear how his ideas hold together. This leaves the reader struggling to follow his thoughts. So rather than get lost in this maze I want to extract for the reader his core arguments and then we are less likely to get lost when we explore in more detail what happens in 'Wotan'.

Jung's Core Themes in Wotan

Jung sought to use Wotan to provide him with both the cause of Germany's discord and an explanation of how people were affected. If the 'Wotan' article had been written as a straightforward text it had two lines of argument. The first was about the inter-reaction of an archetype and race, as Jung explained: 'Because the behaviour of a race takes on its specific character from its underlying images we can speak of an archetype "Wotan".' (Jung, 1991 [1936], §391), which could have been better expressed as: *A race / nation has its characteristic behaviour moulded by their cultural portrayal of a specific archetype. Furthermore this portrayal may only feature some aspects of that archetype. In this way one can speak of Wotan as an archetype, as mediated through elements of Germany's history and culture.*

Parallel with this idea, though not so explicitly articulated in 'Wotan', Jung was applying his ideas on emotion and psychic energy and suggesting that there was a fundamental clash between thinking and emotion. Paul Bishop in *The Dionysian Self* (1995), draws out how important this Nietzschian idea of creative energy was for Jung as one can see from his seminars on *Thus Spoke Zarathustra* which ran from 1934 to 1939. He follows Jung's changing relationship with Nietzsche's ideas and charts the course of Jung's thought on the importance of instinctive psychic energy that has largely been bypassed in the secondary Jungian literature. Bishop explores Jung's recurring concern with the problem of the vitality of instinct and how this energy is to be acknowledged and transformed without being warped or denied. He shows the way that Jung used Nietzsche and his ideas of the Dionysian to counter his perception of Freudian intellectualisation and psychic materialism, which Jung saw as a negation of the instinctive that denied people their access to the spiritual potential for renewal in the unconscious. In this way the Dionysian element was part of the 'archetypal hope' that had a long pedigree going back to the time of his partnership with Freud.[161]

In 'Wotan', which was written at the same time as the seminars, Jung briefly illustrated how he saw the intellectual civilisation of Europe being disrupted by a rush of crude emotion that erupted in Germany, and so, in psychological terms, we can sum up Jung's position by borrowing from Bishop's chapter-heading: *Wotan [was] the Shadow* of Dionysos (1995, p298).

If Jung had just been attempting to describe the most primitive emotions of frustration and intoxicating rage, which in a more advanced form could also inspire and vivify, he would have been in a strong position. Unfortunately he went on, and impelled by his anxieties exclaimed: 'No doubt it sounds better to academic ears to interpret these things as Dionysus, but Wotan might be a more correct interpretation. He is the God of storm and frenzy, the unleasher of passions and the lust of battle' (Jung, 1991 [1936], §375). There, surely, he got carried away and the confusion spread when Jung tried to bring together archetypal theory and the collective unconscious in such dangerous times.

Now we have some insight into the confusion we can return to Jung's two lines of argument and examine them in detail.

As Jung's discussion and definition of Wotan was centred upon events in Germany, we will first look at Jung's pre-war approach to German history that provided the context for his Wotan hypothesis. We will then consider what evidence Jung supplied that some form of Wotanic outbreak had actually occurred, and the coherence of his argument that Wotan was specifically the German archetype.

Jung's Account of Primitive Germany and the Collective Unconscious

Jung had mentioned the warlike virtues of the early Germans in 'The Role of the Unconscious' (1918) where his perception was similar to Tacitus's contemporary account in *Germania*. Following Jung's line of argument, one could argue that the Germans were different, inasmuch as it took a long time for the early primitive German tribes to be assimilated into the body of Christendom; but once Rome had fallen and Europe was Roman Catholic and feudal, it is hard to see why the Germans' lack of a classical past should still have the effect Jung suggested. Another doubtful generalization by Jung was that the Germans were a uniform whole, which ignores the widespread differences in the German lands, as for example between the Romanised West of the Rhine and Prussia, where paganism survived until the thirteenth century (Christiansen, 1980, p100). This at least Jung should have credited as he reflected after the war: 'In certain parts of Europe Christianity goes back not much more than five hundred years—a mere sixteen generations. The last witch was burnt in Europe the year my grandfather was born' (Jung, 1974 [1951], §271).

There are other problems. Jung suggested that, despite the feudal period, 'the adventurous Germanic tribes with their characteristic curiosity, acquisitiveness, and recklessness', were significantly immature and undeveloped, but he did not explain why they had these characteristics. Nor did he examine the contradiction in his idea, because as he was suggesting that the late pagan Germans were the most warlike people, he did not explain why the other Germanic warrior nations that lived beyond the *pax Romana* (peoples such as the equally bellicose Anglo-Saxon English, the Odin-worshipping Norsemen or the ex-Vikings in the devoutly catholic military feudal state of Normandy) had lost their immaturity and compulsive aggression.

Even his assumption that the Germans were unduly warlike was of dubious value. Germany's reputation for military success was founded on the recent victories of the Prussians in the 1870 war with France. Nor was it quite so evident that there was a link between German rearmament and the 'pagan' Nazis; German rearmament had already started secretly with the *Reichswehr* before the Nazis (Hohne, 1979). Also, in contrast to Jung's suggestion of an implacable Germanic battle lust, the German public, according to secret SD sponsored opinion polls, showed no enthusiasm for war in 1939 (Redlich, 1998, p153). This attitude only changed after a succession of almost bloodless victories—and who is immune to cheap success?

JUNG'S ACCOUNT OF THE INFLUENCE OF PROTESTANTISM ON THE GERMAN NATIONAL PSYCHOLOGY

Jung was on firmer ground when on the 26th June 1935, in a Seminar, he noted how the Protestant tradition of loyalty to the state assisted the Nazi seizure of power and its subversion of the citizens' loyalty: 'he sells his soul without knowing it, devotes his soul to the state as if it were a god' (Jung, 1989 [1934-1939], p595). This issue of authority and church compliance has been noted by historians of the German churches' resistance (Hilberg, 1979; Barnett, 1992, p11).

In another article, Jung inconsistently suggested that this German wildness led to the rejection of Catholic order in favour of less restrained Protestantism, but he did not look at why this should have been the case in Northern Germany and not in Bavarian or Austrian lands (Jung, 1991 [1938-1940], §82). Nor did he ponder the implications for his argument that most of the roots of the Nazi movement lay in Bavaria and a disproportionate number of its fanatical members came from Catholic Bavaria and Austria (Whiting, 1999, p163).

In an extension of his critique of modern materialism Jung also argued that Germany's scientific and technological innovations and lack of a stable world order had created an unstable psychology in Germany. By implication this instability was a contributory factor in undermining Germany and leaving it vulnerable to the Nazis (Jung, 1991 [1938-1940], §83).[162]

These observations about technology may have some merit as the Nazis had both benefited from the post-Great War economic chaos and were obsessed with technology. However, in focusing on these concerns, Jung ignored the more conventional socio-historic explanations for the character of the Nazis that other commentators used. These included the 1918 defeat, the Great Depression, the loss of Danzig and her sizeable foreign empire and the nearness of the Soviet Behemoth, which more than adequately accounted for the rise of the Nazis and the drive to military expansion that predated them. These ideas he would incorporate after the war when he moved away from his original archetypal stance.

JUNG'S EVIDENCE FOR WOTAN'S POSSESSION OF GERMANY

To help prove the existence of the collective unconscious Jung needed to offer substantial evidence that the pagan practices were due to spontaneous eruptions from an Iron-Age strata of a racial unconscious or that they were archetypal images from the collective unconscious. For Jung's case to be established these examples would have to show that significant numbers of the Nazis were pagan and that their paganism was generated by spontaneous revelation rather than the product of recent historical trends and events.

The Test Case: Wotan and Nazi Germany 233

How good a case for Wotan and a German racial psyche did Jung make?

If Jung wanted to look for evidence that indicated that unconscious themes were erupting out of the racial unconscious he had a number of choices. The two options he specifically mentioned were the Indologist Professor Jacob Hauer's attempt to formulate an eclectic pagan revival with his *'German Faith Movement'*, and the *'German Christians'*, who sought to set up a Germanic Christianity free of any references to Christianity's Semitic roots. The other option was to look for evidence of spontaneous pagan influences in the lives of Nazi party members that were not aligned with either movement. As we shall see later, there was material that needed examination, but Jung's case was undermined by his failure to pursue this with the vigour he had deployed with his mythological amplifications in his other books.

In the Zarathustra Seminar on 26th February, 1936, Jung made a good general observation about many of the Nazis' hostility to the Church and their nationalist agenda, but he did not develop the theme:

> It has become a fact to the extent that the attitude of the ruling party in Germany is really against the church; they are trying to subjugate the church and to translate, as it were, the terminology of the church into a sort of pagan belief. That idea of Pagan Christianity or the German faith is of course nothing else than the nationalization of God; they then have a specific national God, Wotan for the German as Jahveh was for the Jew. That is quite inevitable. And it is understandable that in the face of such events even friends might be alarmed. One is alarmed! I have quite a number of German friends and I must say I am alarmed by the fact that they are so gripped. (Jung, 1989 [1934-1939], p868)

Of the two institutions, the obvious place for Jung to make his case would have been the *'German Faith Movement'*, as Jung knew Hauer and had read his book[163]. But though in 'Wotan' there are references to Hauer and his movement, Jung seemed more concerned with his old colleague than using this opportunity to give any evidence to substantiate his theory. [164] The same neglect can be seen in the long paragraph of background information on Hauer in the footnote in the Collected Works (p190), which was added by Jung for the convenience of the London audience in 1947.[165]

Of the little Jung says on Hauer, he argued that Hauer was caught by the emotion of the time and had attempted to 'build a bridge between the dark forces of life and the shining world of historical ideas' (Jung, 1991 [1936], §397-398). This was a logical argument, but Jung failed to establish why his own use of historical analogy and minimal evidence was sufficient proof that Wotan was an archetype, yet Hauer's eclectic efforts to found a religion were inadequate; and this lack of implicit balance was not a good base to foster confidence in his readers.

The only detailed evidence of pagan influences referred to in 'Wotan' is a footnote about a 1936 Swiss newspaper report of a SA evangelical clergyman who gave a funeral elegy with numerous explicit pagan references (Jung, §397, footnote), but Jung gave no evidence of what lay behind this man's action. The footnote is worth quoting for the heavy irony with which Jung ridicules the irrationality of the time:

> The spirit of this movement may be contrasted with a sermon preached by Dr. Langmann, an evangelical clergyman and high dignitary of the Church, at the funeral of the late Gustloff. Dr. Langmann gave the address 'in SA uniform and jackboots.' He sped the deceased on his journey to Hades, and directed him to Valhalla, to the home of Siegfried and Baldur, the heroes who 'nourish the life of the German people by the sacrifice of their blood'—like Christ among others. 'May this god send the nations of the earth *clanking on their way* through history.' 'Lord bless our struggle. Amen.' Thus the reverend gentleman ended his address, according to the *Neue Zürcher Zeitung* (1936, no. 249). As a service held to Wotan it is no doubt very edifying—and remarkably tolerant towards believers

> in Christ! Are our Churches inclined to be equally tolerant and to preach that Christ shed his blood for the salvation of mankind, like Siegfried, Baldur, and Odin among others?! One can ask unexpectedly grotesque questions these days. (Jung, 1991 [1936], footnote 15 page 190 CW10)

Aside from this piece of drama, which was buried as a footnote, there is also a vague reference to what may be a gathering of German Christians: 'Wotan... could be seen, looking rather shame-faced, in the meeting-house of a sect of simple folk in North Germany, disguised as Christ sitting on a white horse. I do not know if these people were aware of Wotan's ancient connection with the figures of Christ and Dionysus, but it is not very improbable' (Jung, 1991 [1936], §373).

Beyond the two organisations, Jung made some unrelated references to German and Nazi use of pagan practices as evidence of an archetypal up-rush from the racial layer of the collective unconscious, but these were very scattered.

Jung mentioned that there had been sheep sacrifice in the early years of the inter-war German Youth Movement, which was possibly connected with a celebration of the summer Solstice, but he is not clear whether this incident involved the Nazi *Hitler Youth* (Jung, 1991 [1936], §373, 375).[166]

In paragraph 389 of 'Wotan', Jung argued that 'Wotan hits the mark as an hypothesis', and provided the following 'datum', but beyond noting the Nazi obsession with race, his material was so sparse that it needs expanding. What Jung provided in the way of 'datum' is put in italics, and the possible sources of the material are added in plain script:

- *the devil as an international Alberich in Jewish or Masonic guise;* may refer to Hitler's anti-Semitic rhetoric; Himmler was especially concerned with the Masons.
- *the Germanic heritage, blood and soil;* was a favourite theme of Walther Darré[167] and Himmler.

- *the ride of the Valkyries,* comes from Wagner who was one of Hitler's favourite composers and the Nazi propaganda made use of such stirring Germanic themes (Köhler, 2000).
- *Jesus* as a blond and blue-eyed hero, the Greek mother of St. Paul was an example of the ideas current in the German Christians.
- *the Nordic aurora borealis as the light of civilization;* may refer to one of the mythic fantasies sponsored by Himmler that suggested that the original Germans came from the legendary northern land of Ultima Thule[168].

These are all very general allusions and offer poor evidence for Jung's case. It is regrettable that he did not discuss who originated these ideas, and because he fails to give any specific information they can only be treated as hints of a pagan outbreak. There are, however, scattered through Jung's other works and talks, some more specific examples of references to pagan activities in Germany, but these are also problematic, as will be shown in the following instances.

In the same year that he wrote 'Wotan', on the 14th October Jung lectured in London on 'Psychology and National Problems' and stated: 'Again it is Germany that gives us some notion of the underlying archetypal symbolism brought up by the eruption of the collective unconscious. Hitler's picture has been erected upon Christian altars. There are people who confess upon their tombstones that they died in peace since their eyes had beheld not the Lord, but the Führer. The onslaught on Christianity is obvious; it would not even need corroboration through a neo-pagan movement incorporating three million people' (Jung, 1986 [1936a], §1329). This is very dramatic, but as we shall see later, his estimate of the strength of the neo-pagan movement was wildly exaggerated.

In 1938 Jung talked of 'the widespread revival in the Third Reich of the cult of Wotan. Who was Wotan? God of wind.[169] Take the name *'Sturmabteilung'*—Storm Troops. Storm, you see—the wind. Just as the swastika is a revolving form making a vortex moving ever towards the left—which means in Buddhist symbolism sinister, unfavourable, directed towards the unconscious'

(McGuire and Hull, 1980, 1939, p125). This comment is dramatic, but does it bare close examination? What does 'widespread' mean and where was the evidence? The chapter will show that the Nazi authority's attitude to neo-paganism was more contradictory and erratic than Jung implied. On a small point of detail the meaning and the direction of the Swastika in Buddhist and Hindu iconography is more complex than Jung allows, as it designates male and female and positive and negative (akin to *yin* and *yang*), but there is not the implied value judgement of 'sinister and unfavourable' (Levenda, 2002, p58).

Another line of evidence Jung offered was that the frequent occurrence of irrationality, euphoria and the popularity of the *Wandervogel* (youthful hiking groups) and migrant workers were symptoms of archetypal possession. In post-Great War Germany there were two groups of people that fitted Jung's general observation, these were the ex-soldiers of the Free Corps and large numbers of the disaffected youth. Furthermore, both were crucial seedbeds of Nazism, and curiously both groups described themselves as 'wanderers out of the void' (a term Hitler also used to describe himself).

However when one looks at the historical and social evolution of these groups there is no need to account for their origin with Jung's archetypal hypothesis. Both 'orphaned' groups felt that only a great leader could provide fresh unsullied inspiration that would bring order and earn their commitment. Both groups had a yearning for community, meaning and inspiring leadership. For youth this was driven by the need for group bonding and idealism coupled with teenage rebellion against parental discipline. The war veterans sought the return of the exhilaration of battle, the brotherhood of arms and the fierce protective loyalty to their officers. One of the best expositions of this comes from an ex-storm-trooper, Ernst Jünger's celebration of his 'front experience' that attracted many readers in the wake of the war.[170] He wrote:

> The condition of the holy man, of great poets and of great love, is also granted to those of great courage... [Participation in battle] is intoxication beyond all intoxication, an unleashing that breaks all bonds. It is a

frenzy without caution and limits, comparable only to the forces of nature. There the individual is like a raging storm, the tossing sea and the roaring thunder. He has melted into everything. He rests at the dark door of death like a bullet that has reached its goal. And the purple waves dash over him. For a long time he has no awareness of transition. It is as if a wave slipped hack into the flowing sea. (Lindholm, 1993 p96)[171]

These shattering experiences were not only formative, but remained central to the lives of many veterans, because they had no prospect of prosperity to return to that might have mellowed these stark emotions (Lindholm, 1993 p97). Not only were numbers of the soldiers addicted to the adrenaline of combat, many could only conceive of their survival as miraculous. This could lead to a dangerous sense of mission, as we can see in the case of Hitler who attributed his survival to divine intervention. In 1914 Hitler just missed death after a direct hit on the regimental command post where he was a runner and, by 1937, he consciously or unconsciously had so embellished the story that he told a British journalist he had been saved by a higher voice that urged him out of the bunker (Kershaw, 1998, p92; p634 note 111).

These veterans and wanderers were a fertile source for Nazi recruitment, but one needed no hooded God in the shadows to explain them. Thus another element of Jung's evidence does not bare close examination. Indeed, taking what Jung presented so far we could concede that 'cranks' were active in Germany, but this scattering of references had conspicuously failed to provide convincing evidence of a great up-rush of pagan material from the unconscious.

If Jung failed to provide sufficient evidence, could it be that on re-examining the material one could make a better case for his hypothesis? To explore some of the mythic ideas at work in the Reich we will refer to the contemporary references in the diaries of Felix Kersten, [172] and in Hermann Rauschning's *Hitler Speaks* (1939).[173] Then, to add some scholarly depth to those contemporary sources, we will make use of Nicholas Goodrick-Clarke's seminal work on the occult roots of Nazi ideas and Michael Burleigh's recent study of the interplay of religious themes in Nazi Germany.

For this survey we will start by acknowledging that the range of neo-pagan and Germanic Romantic sources the far right could draw on as a wealth of material would invalidate the need for Jung to posit the psyche as a source of unconscious inspiration. We will then go on to look at how great a role neo-pagan ideas played in Hitler's career, as he was the epicentre of the Nazi storm. If he was not 'possessed' and the Neo-pagans wielded little influence, then Jung's hypothesis is radically undermined. We then need to repeat this exploration considering the case of Himmler, as he had tremendous power and opportunity and it might be that his SS Empire provides a better example for Jung.

The Neo-Pagan Sources of Nazi Germany

When one comes to examine the overlap of Nazi ideas with religious images one finds that the arcane elements of Nazi belief drew on an incredibly fertile range of sources that echoed Jung's interests. For their ideas on Aryans and race, both Himmler and Rosenberg drew heavily on the nineteenth century French writer Ernest Renan who had led an early school of debate on the linguistic and cultural sources of Christianity (Steigmann-Gall, 2003, p107-9). Other lines of thought that the Nazis could draw on were even more bizarre. For example, one of the significant early contributors, the self-styled Baron von Sebottendorff, had actually studied alchemy in Turkey! He later became a key member of the pre-war secret anti-Semitic Leipzig *Germanen-Orden*[174], an elite reactionary occult group. This group sponsored as its elite literary wing a Munich *Völkisch* club, *The Thule Society*, set up in 1917-18. Its members included future Nazi ideologues and politicians, Dietrich Eckart,[175] Alfred Rosenberg, Rudolf Hess and Hans Frank (Kershaw, 1998, p138). From the *Germanen-Orden* also came a proletarian political party, the *Deutsche Arbeiterpartei* under Anton Drexler. The latter group would, under Hitler, become the NSDAP (Lavenda, 2002, p74-77).[176]

Another line of influence comes from the impact of Nietzschian ideas on German religion and politics in the late nineteenth and early twentieth century. As Steven Aschheim explains, at the beginning of the twentieth century there was a proliferation of counter-religious post-Christian groups in Germany that either advocated a reworking of Christianity using Nietzschian ideas, or its rejection and replacement by some form of neo-paganism. By 1909 many of these 'free-thought' groups had amalgamated into the 'Weimar Cartel' that claimed sixty thousand members (1988, p219).[177]

There was a growing impetus for some form of muscular Germanic Christianity. Nietzschian ideas were smuggled into Protestant churches by Pastors like Albert Kalhoff (1850-1906) and theologians like Hans Gallwitz who advocated his perception of Nietzsche's masculine warrior values (Aschheim, 1988, p224, 221). Similar ideas feature strongly in populist writers like Arthur Bonus who drew heavily on the anti-Semitic Orientalist Paul de Lagarde (1827-1891) who later became a major source for the Nazi race theorist Alfred Rosenberg (Snyder, 1976, p203). These ideas received added impetus under the heady patriotism of the Great War (Aschheim, 1988, p227).

Others like the brothers August and Ernst Horneffer, editors of the Nietzsche archive in Weimar, set about at the turn of the century to form a neo-pagan Nietzschian religion with books like *Pagan Life Course* and *Religion of the Future,* under the impetus of Nietzsche's withering criticism of Christianity. Later when the Nazi movement came to power they welcomed the revolution as the fruition and climax of their neo-pagan Nietzschian perspective (Aschheim, 1988, p241-243) [178].

Given the eclectic times it was almost inevitable that the esoteric and the Nietzschian themes would run together and with an almost pantomime connection, the pagan Professor Hauer had discovered Nietzsche in a dentist's waiting room and borrowed freely from the philosopher. The Nazi party made good use of his journal and Hauer continued through the war at the university of Tübingen to advocate Aryanisation in political and scholarly forms, but Hitler, as we shall see, remained unsympathetic (Aschheim, 1988, p244-245).[179]

HITLER'S RELATION TO PAGAN IDEAS

To explore the pagan question further one must start by trying to assess what Hitler's position was. Hitler was raised as a Catholic and never left the Church, but by the time he lived in Vienna his selection of ideological *bette noires* had come to include 'Reds' and the Jesuits (Kershaw, 1998, p58). In Vienna Hitler certainly read *Legends of Gods and Heroes: The Treasures of Germanic Myth* and he hoped to take up Wagner's unfinished project from 1849 and write an opera of *Wieland the Smith* (Köhler, 2000, p90). This was emotionally important to Hitler as the latter's music transported him into a world of Germanic myth with its symphonies of emotion enthralling and inspiring his imagination (Kershaw, 1998, p40-43).

Once Hitler moved to Vienna it becomes difficult to assess the evolution of his thought due to the bohemian nature of his lifestyle and the muddying of the picture during the Nazi construction of his political myth.

Certainly there was a rich source of themes he could draw on. There was a range of pagan ideas about Armanism, Ariosophy[180] and 'rune occultism' in numerous Austrian and German nationalist publications like *Ostara*, which between 1890 and the Nazi revolution of 1933 combined the heroic and the esoteric.[181] Such publications served to compensate for economic, political and cultural insecurity, but fostered 'narcissistic, paranoid and grandiose fantasies' (Goodrick-Clarke, 1992, p203-204). At a slightly more elevated level, in the thirties, publishers like the *Eugen Diederichs Verlag* flooded the German bookshops with cheap editions of the Nordic *Edda* to foster a spiritual rebirth amongst the *Völk* (Bishop, 1995, p305, fn11).[182]

What impact this had on Hitler is more difficult to determine. On reviewing the biographical literature, in Lukacs's judgment: 'We have no evidence that—even during his formative years, in Vienna—Hitler read or took seriously the late-nineteenth century French or German racialist philosophers, such as Gobineau... or that the hysterical racist pamphleteers of the *Ostara* type had a strong or definite influence on him' (1997, p121), whereas Kershaw, reviewing the evidence that Hitler read *Ostara*, considered it likely yet far from certain, and suggests that it was by no means clear that he adopted Lanz's bizarre racial theories (1998, p50-51).

Another of Hitler's early mentors from the *Thule Society* was Dietrich Eckart. Eckart made pagan references and wrote: 'In Christ, the embodiment of all manliness, we find all that we need. And if we occasionally speak of Baldur, our words always contain some joy, some satisfaction, that our pagan ancestors were already so Christian as to have indications of Christ in this ideal figure' (Steigmann-Gall, 2003, p18).[183] Here Eckart was aware of Nazi use of pagan references, but he did not present them as revelations as a neo-pagan might and instead used the Christian argument of Christ being pre-figured by early pagan gods.

Whatever the influence of arcane ideas, some form of occult ideas did play a role in Hitler's mental world. According to Rauschning, 'Hitler was fond... of mystical talk' and read about special 'forms of perception and supernatural powers' of early man. Speculations of this sort fascinated Hitler, and he would sometimes be entirely wrapped up in them. He saw his own remarkable career as a confirmation of hidden powers. He saw himself as chosen for superhuman tasks, as the prophet of the rebirth of man in a new form. But for this progress to take place there must be a regression, as Rauschning summarised Hitler's view:

> Just as, according to the imperishable prophecies of the old Nordic peoples, the world has continually to renew itself, the old order perishing with its gods, just as the Nordic peoples took the sun's passing of the solstices as a figure of the rhythm of life, which proceeds not in a straight line of eternal progress but in a spiral, so must man now, apparently, turn back in order to attain a higher stage. (1939, p240-241)

Rauschning asked himself whether Hitler believed this. Hitler only talked in such terms to a limited circle, not to the *Alte Kämpfer*, the Party veterans from the early street-fighting days, who would have no patience with such ideas. Rauschning speculated: 'he may have believed in it all. He is capable of entertaining the most incompatible ideas in association with one another. One thing is certain—Hitler has the spirit of the prophet. He is not content to be a mere politician' (1939, p240-242).

Whatever Hitler's beliefs, he certainly used such religious themes. Michael Burleigh provides a recent reaffirmation of the influences of religious emotions in Nazi Germany. He notes the range of pseudo-religious elements in Hitler's speeches, such as his taking all the credit for the *Anschluss*, which he described as: '"a miracle of faith", for only faith could have moved these mountains.' Hitler then went on to describe his political career on 31st March 1938, as a 'pilgrimage throughout Germany' and a week later declared: 'In the beginning stood the *Volk*, was the *Volk*, and only then came the Reich... I believe that it was also God's will that from here a boy was to be sent into the Reich, allowed to mature, and elevated to become the nation's Fuhrer, thus enabling him to reintegrate his homeland into the Reich. There is a divine will, and we are its instruments.' Looking at all these statements Burleigh concludes that they were not just inflated rhetoric, but were clear evidence of Hitler's 'messianic conviction' (2000, p276-277).

From Hitler, and other Nazi propagandists, the religious element spread. Burleigh refers to an anonymous SPD report of 4th April 1937 on 'the Church struggle' as the Nazis attempted to seize ideological control of the Protestant Churches. Burleigh praises the reporter's powers of observation. The study noted the way the Nazi movement demanded everyone's moral and spiritual commitment. It rejected any suggestion that Nazism was just a secular *Weltanschauung* or that it was actually neo-pagan, but what it did produce was a fanatically intolerant 'Church-state' complete with all the trappings of religion and a belief in a holy mission to move towards the final confrontation with the demonic Bolsheviks and Jews (2000, p252, 253).[184]

So far it might seem that while Hitler's religious images may not have been products of the unconscious, they were at least genuinely held, which would give supporting evidence to Jung. But even this is doubtful. In focusing on the religious elements of Nazism, Burleigh looks at the same sort of evidence that concerned Jung, but with the advantage of more information and hindsight comes to a very different conclusion. He argues that the veneer of paganism was largely due to Hitler's cynical showmanship. Propaganda was one of the Nazis' most successful skills. Their showmanship ranged from Albert Speer's theatres of light to celebrate the modern dynamism of the Nazis, to the flaming torchlight processions that echoed the warrior pageant of Germanic myth. As Burleigh noted, this was a 'heroic and quasi-religious dimension' being exploited with a skill the Churches had lost. But for all the theatre it was not a genuine attempt by Hitler to revive pagan alternatives to Christianity (2000, p7-9) and he did not hesitate to reject Houston Stewart Chamberlain's ideas of an Aryan Christianity if it did not suit his plans (Rauschning, 1939, p213, 275, 57).[185]

In all this activity, the personal influence of neo-pagan ideas on Hitler is difficult to determine. While he was willing to draw on early role models, like Eckart's religious views, Hitler's hostility to the pagans in the Nazi state was unequivocal. In 1924 General Ludendorff and his deeply anti-clerical second wife Mathilde von Kenmitz had attempted a pagan rebirth through their Tannenberg League, but the sect proved to be so far-fetched in its paranoia that even the Nazis rejected it, and in *Mein Kampf* Hitler wrote:

> The characteristic thing about these people is that they rave about old Germanic heroism, about dim prehistory, stone axes, spear and shield, but in reality are the greatest cowards that can be imagined. For the same people who brandish scholarly imitations of old German tin swords, and wear a dressed bearskin with bull's horns over their bearded heads, preach for the present nothing but struggle with spiritual weapons, and run away as fast as they can from every Communist blackjack.[186]

Given this strength of feeling, from 1927 Hitler found it increasingly easy to dismiss this rival for leadership of the extreme right (Kershaw, 1998, p262, 269). He could then remove Ludendorff from the NSDAP and ban the Nazi Party members from the Tannenberg League[187] (Steigmann-Gall, 2003, p88).

Hitler's disdain for neo-paganism is again demonstrated by his dismissal of Himmler's efforts. According to Albert Speer, Hitler was withering in his derision of Himmler's eclectic military mysticism: 'What nonsense! Here we have at last reached an age that has left all mysticism behind, and now he wants to start that all over again... To think that I may some day be turned into an SS saint!' Hitler ridiculed Himmler's archaeological obsessions: 'Isn't it enough that the Romans were erecting great buildings when our forefathers were still living in mud huts; now Himmler is starting to dig up these villages of mud huts and enthusing over every potsherd and stone axe he finds' (Speer, 1970, p94, 95).

Hitler had no time for Wotan, as one can see from his discussion about one of the few Party leaders who took an active Neo-pagan stance—the appropriately named Baldur von Schirach, head of the Hitler Youth movement. However, many of the party leaders, like Hans Schemm, and Otto Wagner, were far from happy about the use of Hitler Youth events to stage Pagan rituals so they complained to Hitler who ridiculed this youthful paganism by saying: 'All that rubbish about the *Thing* places, the solstice festivals, the Midgard snake.' He assured them that it would not develop into a religion, to which one of his audience responded: 'I'm very glad to hear you say this... There is such a lot of nonsense talked about the cult of Wotan and the spirit of the Edda... These idiotic windbags have no idea what their spouting causes'[188] (Steigmann-Gall, 2003, p142).[189]

Hitler also had no patience with one of the foremost proponents for a rebirth of pagan ideas, Alfred Rosenberg, who wrote the Nazi polemic *Der Mythus des 20. Jahrhunderts* (1931) ('The Myth of the Twentieth Century') that many assumed was to be the Nazi 'bible'. Yet not only did the book never receive Hitler's overt support and had to be privately published, but in rare moments Rosenberg even admitted to himself that Hitler ultimately rejected his religion and 'set his face from the beginning against racial cultism'[190] (Steigmann-Gall, 2003, p93). Indeed Rosenberg took pains to assure his readers that he was not trying to resurrect a dead religion and clearly stated 'Wotan was and is dead' and that it was not the business of the party to engage in religious matters (Steigmann-Gall, 2003, p99 [191], p 93).[192] This last claim sits a little uneasily, as Rosenberg for all his anti-Christian theology retained his positive polemic of Jesus the Aryan, whom he mentioned much more frequently in his *Mythus* than Wotan[193] (Steigmann-Gall, 2003, p110).

Despite Rosenberg's disclaimers, Hitler was not receptive to these conciliatory measures and as a consolation-prize gave the hapless Rosenberg the grand title of *The Führer's Commissioner for the Supervision of the NSDAP's Instruction in Matters of Intellect and Weltanschauung* in 1940; but Hitler firmly declared: 'A new Party religion would only mean a regression to the mysticism of the Middle Ages. That is shown by the "SS-Myth" and in Rosenberg's unreadable *The Myth of the Twentieth Century*' (Lukacs, 1997, p89).[194]

Thus exposed, Rosenberg was easy prey for Martin Bormann, Hitler's private secretary, who—as Hitler became more withdrawn—was probably the single most powerful figure in the Reich (von Lang, 1981, p126). Bormann was implacably anti-Christian, but in his dealing with the pagan elements of the Nazi hierarchy, he pursued his own self-serving agenda at their expense. He would deliberately ridicule Hess's myriad esoteric interests and, following Hess's flight to Britain, took the opportunity to suppress all occult activity in the Reich (von Lang, 1981, p148, 160). Nor had he any qualms in sabotaging the 'crackpot' Rosenberg's ideological projects and successfully deterred him from writing a second volume to *The Myth of the Twentieth Century* (von Lang, 1981, p132, 170, 172). Lacking Hitler's support and repeatedly outflanked by Bormann, it is hardly surprising that Rosenberg was often mocked within the party (von Lang, 1981, p168). This open campaign of sabotage by Bormann is another indication of how little Hitler valued the pagan element.

Ultimately Hitler had little time for the Nazis' pagan ideas and so in early September 1938, he addressed a convention on German culture within the week-long Party rally:

> National Socialism is a cool and highly reasoned approach to reality based upon the greatest of scientific knowledge and its spiritual expression... we have no desire of instilling in the *Volk* a mysticism that transcends the purpose and goals of our teachings... For the National Socialist Movement is not a cult movement; rather, it is a *völkisch* and political philosophy which grew out of considerations of an exclusively racist nature. This philosophy does not advocate mystic cults, but rather aims to cultivate and lead a *Volk* determined by its blood. (Burleigh, 2000, p 253)

The anti-pagan theme would continue despite the increasing radicalisation of the Nazi state under the pressures of its genocidal war. In trying to sum up Hitler's position, our picture of him is blurred by his tendency to fit speeches to the needs of an audience and the sheer irrationality of the material. As he became more opposed to Christianity during the war years he always distinguished between his hostility to the dangers of this 'Jewish' faith and his respect for the Aryan Jesus (Steigmann-Gall, 2003, p260). But, for all his early mentors, it seems that whatever Hitler's curiosity about esoteric ideas, these ideas were only as important as they fitted his will and his purpose. Rauschning tried to define Hitler's philosophical perspective:

> Hitler is not superstitious in the ordinary sense. His interest in the horoscope and the cryptic elements in nature is connected with his conviction that man exists in some kind of magic association with the universe. The political element is for him only the foreground of a revolution which he pictures on the most stupendous scale. The study of apocryphal literature gives him the material for his doctrine. But what is of more importance than the doctrine is the will behind it. Hitler never tires of proclaiming... he has led the German people and the world is an unending movement, an unending revolution... It is the revolution of the new nobility against the masses. (1939, p248)

There is no case for a 'pagan' Hitler to support Jung's ideas. What Hitler was concerned with was his power and his gradually evolving perception of his messianic mission for the German race. To this end he was willing to make ideological diversions and tactical treaties as long as it suited his long-term ends. [195] His religious images were traceable to contemporary sources and the pagan elements provide no evidence of a Wotan archetype or a Germanic racial unconscious. So if Hitler does not provide an adequate case study for Jung's ideas, might not other elements in Nazi Germany?

THE NAZI IMPACT ON THE CHURCH AND THE GERMAN CHRISTIANS

The Nazis had the advantage that *Völkisch* and nationalist themes had been infiltrating the churches in Germany for a long time. The

Völkisch element of the Party was stronger in the Protestant North (Kershaw, 1998, p262-269). After the Great War, in the Protestant churches there was great hope for a national renewal and inner moral revitalisation. As one pastor recalled: 'it is as if the wing of a great turn of fate is fluttering above us. There was to be a new start'.[196] This hope was enhanced by the idea of heroic leadership that had been a feature of the Nationalist Right from the time of the Bismarck cult. These ideas were especially prevalent in the Protestant educated middle classes who were highly influenced by Germanic myths and had become disillusioned with Christianity following Germany's defeat (Kershaw, 1998, p180-181).

After the Nazis came to power, nationalism and Nazi propaganda created a surge in spontaneous statements as church leaders sought to testify to their political reliability. The ban on *völkisch* material in the Lutheran Church and in universities was lifted. This soon bore results and in the summer of 1933, a Tübingen theologian enquired if the church was ready 'to interpret a great turning point in German destiny as coming from the hand of God, and to take a creative part in it' (Baigent and Leigh, 1994, p226). The Land Bishop of Württemberg welcomed the new chancellor with his anti-Marxist credentials and the eminent theologian Karl Barth wrote that he did not think Hitler's appointment 'will signify the start of great new things in any direction at all'[197] (Kershaw, 1998, p432). Another example was the Bishop of Bremen, Weidemann, who in 1938 ordered two new churches to be built. One was to be named the *Horst Wessel* after the Nazi marching song about one of their early 'martyrs' and the other church was to be named after the Great War general as the 'von Hindenburg Memorial' church. Despite these impeccable themes, the party vetoed the names and attempted to eject Weidemann from the party, although this stalwart warrior continued to press for other political gestures and had inscribed in each building the inscription 'Church of Thanks, our gratitude to God for the wonderful salvation of our Volk from the abyss Jewish-materialistic Bolshevism through the deed of the Führer, built in the year of our Lord 1938, in the sixth year of the National Socialist revolution' (Bergen, 1996, p164). Such enthusiasm was not confined to Protestants. The president of the Catholic Bishops' Conference, Cardinal Betram of Breslau, sent fulsome congratulatory telegrams to Hitler on his birthdays. His 1939 message said: 'I told the children: *Heil Hitler*—this is valid for this world: Praised be Jesus Christ—that is the tie between earth and heaven' (Lukacs, 1997, p217).

Outside the established churches the swell of the Nazi revolution for a time had even more striking results. Since the twenties some Germans had struggled to produce a form of Christianity free of all references to Christianity's Judaic roots. In 1932 the German Christian Church was formally established under 'Reich Bishop' Ludwig Muller and between 1933 and 1934 the Nazi party supported the efforts of the German Christians to gain control of the Protestant Churches (Barnett, 1992, p26-p27).

German Christianity shared with the Nazi party many of the same post-Great War obsessions about religion, gender and race, but these nineteenth century ideas of race had completely supplanted historical and theological considerations of Christianity's place in the Judaeo-Christian tradition (Bergen, 1996, p3, 8, 29). For the German Christians, Jesus was to be transformed and defined as 'a hero and a warrior', as set out in the model answer dictated for a 1939 conformation examination (Bergen, 1996, p159). This echoed the early Christian missionaries who sought to convert the Saxons and in an epic poem, the *Heliand*, portrayed Christ as a noble hero killed on the Cross, as Wotan had been sacrificed to himself on *Yggdrasil*. [198] This eclectic evangelism was mirrored by the Nazis, and Doris Bergen gives a fascinating example of a Westphalian German Christians' Christmas cantata, circulated in 1940, which was called the *Heliand* and combined carols, German myth, New Testament texts and Nazi propaganda.

> The performance opened with a standard translation of John 1:1 'In beginning was the Word and the Word was with God, and the Word was God.' A narrator followed with doggerel verse on the ancient Germanic tribes:
> 'There dwelt a race in German lands,
> A strong, upright, and blue-eyed clan;
> The Germans, whose natural traits combined
> heroic spirit and gentle mind.'

> Allusions to Valhalla, dragons, blood feuds, and adultery gave way to the Advent hymn *'Oh Saviour, Rend the Heavens Wide!'* Commentary on the twilight of the gods preceded another hymn, *'A Ship Comes Sailing Onward,'* which retained the original reference to Bethlehem. The choir sang 'the people who sat in darkness have seen a great light' (Matthew 4:16), and a narrator told how 'the God from Bethlehem became protector of the Germans and awakened the deepest loyalty and love in their hearts and souls. (1996, p170)

The choir then concluded with a selection of hymns. This episode might have supported Jung's case, but the key point here is that the Nazis were not unconsciously echoing Germanic material but consciously invoking a nationalistic image.

At its height the church had half a million members (Bergen, 1996, p2) and the German Christians rally in Berlin of mid-November 1933 attracted an audience of 20,000, but such was the scandal caused by its critique of the Old Testament and 'the Rabbi Paul' as well as the calls for a more 'heroic' Jesus, that Hitler withdrew support from this increasing irritation, which was endangering his relations with the established church (Kershaw, 1998, p490). By 1935 only the most naive German Christian could be unaware of the hostility that their efforts engendered from the party hierarchy (Bergen, 1996, p164) and, according to Von Lang, by 1937 the attempt of the Nazi party to implement its own church had failed.

As a consequence of this failure, the following year Martin Bormann implemented a more explicit anti-Christian campaign against both regular Christianity and the German Christians. There then followed a complex interaction between Bormann and Hitler. When Hitler first gained power he declared the Church must accept his will or be destroyed (Rauschning, 1939, p59). But he had a very clear tactical appreciation of the need not to antagonise the Church as long as they supported him and as long as the war lasted (see also: Breitman, 1991, p72).[199] In contrast, Bormann was increasingly pro-active in his hostility and would orchestrate events to enrage Hitler's hostility to the churches, yet paradoxically he knew that while Hitler would occasionally restrain him, he could be certain that Hitler acquiesced to the long term objective of Christianity's demise (1981, p126-9).[200]

With Bormann against them the German Christians had little chance of success even though they sought to reinvigorate their Nazi credentials by fusing Christianity to Nazism and increasing their anti-Semitic stance. The German Christians continued their conscious proselytising and had some influence as, by the thirties, it was the dominant ideology in most theology departments of universities and had successfully infiltrated the military Chaplin's department. This trend gathered pace as the German Christians spread their image of Nazi warrior-pastors that rejected meek 'pietism' and by 1944 a spokesman for a German Community of Pastors was invoking the patriotic preachers of the wars against Napoleon and the combination of fighting, prayer and leadership[201] (Bergen, 1996, p8, 181, 182). Another tactic was to repackage Christian festivals and so the Christmas candles and advent wreaths were reworked into a nationalist celebration of identity and *Völk*. Yet for all their fervour, as the war progressed the German Christians met an increasingly hostile response from the party (Bergen, 1996, p20). Clearly this attempt at a conscious synthesis of Christianity and Germanic themes had no significant underlying weight in the Nazi movement.

The 'Grass Roots' Pagans

Beyond the German Christians, to the left of the National Socialist ideological spectrum was Walther Darré, a committed neo-pagan like Rosenberg, who in 1934 became Reich Minister of Agriculture and went on to be the *Obergruppenführer* of the Race and Resettlement Office (RuSHA) in charge of SS ideological and racial purity and as such was one of the four departmental heads of the SS in its initial organisational framework (Hohne, 2000, p145). He had coined the term 'blood and soil' (Schama, 1995, p82), and even advocated the pagan practice of farming couples copulating in fields to increase fertility (Lavenda, 2002, p115).[202]

In 1933 Rauschning wrote of the systematic efforts to reintroduce paganism into the German peasantry through anti-church propaganda at agricultural exhibitions about the history of the struggle of the Steding peasants against the Church in Bremen.

Germany's agricultural policy makers: 'were regularly invited to the new type of godless meetings of the National Socialists, "religious" evenings on which the new religions were paraded. There were Professors Hauer and Wirth and many others.' He writes that these invitations from Darré were part of a test process to see who belonged to the 'true élite' committed to 'the total revolution of National Socialism.' They were also pressured to leave the church. Rauschning gave an example of how quickly this paganisation could occur and described the home of a respectable acquaintance who was Darré's deputy in the Reich Labour Ministry: 'A new fireplace appeared in his ancient peasant homestead, its walls decorated with runes and heathen maxims. The crosses had disappeared to make room for other sacred symbols. Woden, the ancient huntsman, was in the place of honour. And on the hearth burnt the new, eternal flame' (1939, p64-65)

Evidently, men like Darré, Rosenberg, and Hauer did believe, but their ideas were fed by their eclectic readings in history and myth and were not derived from unconscious revelation. Likewise populist actions like the Nordic-cultists planting 'Hitler-Oaks' and 'Hitler-Lindens' in Hitler's honour in the spring of 1933 (Kershaw, 1998, p483) were all parts of a very modern cult of personality for all the leafy garlands! These are people Jung probably dismissed as 'the crude Wotan-worshipers whose faith is a mere pretence' (Jung, 1991 [1936 [, §398).

Heinrich Himmler and a Religion for the SS

We now come to Heinrich Himmler, who of all the neo-pagans in the Reich had the most power to mould German culture and society; especially once Himmler became minister of the interior in 1943 (Steigmann-Gall, 2003, p129). As the SS grew it became, as Himmler intended, a society within a society. This independence was a function of the curious nature of Hitler's almost Medieval organisation of competing fiefdoms spread between his dependent paladins (Kershaw, 1998, p536). But in Himmler's case things were different as Hitler had delegated to his 'loyal Heinrich' sufficient autonomy to pursue his own long-term agenda and Himmler was a man with his own independent religious visions. So was Himmler inspired by a collective unconscious?

In his youth Himmler had been a devout Catholic but from his father he was also steeped in mythic themes of the late Wagnerian era (Hohne, 2000, p35). Once he became an adult Himmler began to move in extreme right-wing circles where bizarre pseudo-scholarship based on Germanic mythology was endemic. In August 1923 he joined the Nazi party, and two months later read the *Nibelungenlied* and was greatly impressed by the writings of the ultra nationalist Munich newspaper editor, Rudolf Gorsleben, who had become so fascinated with the collection of ancient Norse songs, the *Edda*, that he founded The *Edda* Society in 1925. The following year Himmler read Tacitus's *Germania*, which became another core text for him (Pringle, 2006, p79, p16). [203]

Himmler's mythic interests were enhanced in 1924 when he joined the new *Artamanen* Society, an organisation of back-to-the-land romantics that had grown out of *völkisch* elements in the German youth movements. The society mixed the themes of agriculture and defence as it fed on the anxieties of the de-militarised Weimar republic about the vigorous Polish threat to the East. To counter this danger they advocated the formation of communities of 'defence farmers', *Wehrbauern*, on Germany's Eastern borders (Pringle, 2006, p39). In the society Himmler met and became a pupil of Walter Darré whose teaching on the prime link between agriculture and 'the blood', and the belief that the 'Nordic Race' were the instigators of civilisations in all the world's greatest cultures had a lasting impact on Himmler (Hohne, 2000, p45-47).[204]

The *Artamanen* Society continued the transformation of Himmler's thoughts but for a time he remained exotically eclectic and did not begin to take his own confessional leave of Christianity till 1933, at which point his hostility was directed not so much at Christianity but rather at the Church (Steigmann-Gall, 2003, p234).

To these early influences Himmler added his own readings from his 12,000-book reference library (Hohne, 2000, p151), as he became immersed in holistic medicine and read enthusiastically of Paracelsus, Hieronymus Boch and Hildegard von Bingen. As well as his fascination with all things Nordic and Germanic, his esoteric interests included belief in reincarnation, Karma and interest in The Koran (Kersten, 1956, p156, 39, 152). Evidently Himmler was creating his own mythic collective conscious to spread amongst the SS.

Later, when Himmler became well-established, he maintained a private luminary, Karl Maria Wiligut (1866-1946), a revered member of the *Artamanen* Society who claimed to be the last in a line of ancient pagan priests with an ancestral memory that enabled him to recall Germany's Aryan past and would be of invaluable help in the the mission of reconstruction (Pringle, 2006, p39).[205] He also believed himself to be a direct descendent of Thor! He was able to reassure the *Reichsführer* that one of his role models, Genghis Khan, was in fact not Asian, but descended from the survivors of Atlantis (Breitman, 1991, p42). He was an invaluable source of information as aside from his remarkable 'racial' memory he had a strong interest in mythology and in Arthur and the Grail legend (Goodrick-Clarke, 1992, p187-8). Wiligut at least might have been a good case study for Jung, especially given the Nazi sage's time spent in a mental hospital; but, again, his memories of a collective unconscious are no help to Jung as these Atlantian recollections are the products of delusion and not evidence for historic deposits.

In power, Himmler lavished time and money on pursuing his historical and mythical interests (1956, p295). He set up the SS-sponsored academic 'Society for Research and Teaching of Ancestral Heritage', the *Ahnenerbe*, which many academics, archaeologists and historians joined, eager for funding or political influence. The *Ahnenerbe's* first director was Hermann Wirth whom Himmler met early in 1934. Wirth had begun on his erratic path in the early 1920s when he became convinced that the carved wooden symbols in Frisian farmhouses were the fragments of a lost system of hieroglyphics and the first writing from a two million year-old Aryan arctic matriarchal civilisation! This vague romantic joined the party in 1925 but soon left to pursue his own idiosyncratic agenda (Pringle, 2006, p55, 58-60). The second head of the *Ahnenerbe*, a Sanskrit scholar Dr. Walther Wüst, was much more politically astute than his predecessor and successfully inducted Himmler into a Nazi reading of the Hindu *Rig Veda* as part of the research into the early Aryans (Pringle, 2006, p96). This was just one of many *Ahnenerbe* projects that Himmler commissioned, including also studies of the Finnish *Kalevala* to recover lost sources of ancient Germanic wisdom (Pringle, 2006, p43).

This rich pseudo-academic amalgam of history and myth would be unified for Himmler in his devotion to Hitler, and Kersten noted how he saw it as his sacred task to carry out Hitler's vision, for Hitler's words came down from a higher world that lesser minds could not reach (1956, p298-9). In August 1942, Kersten expressed surprise to Himmler that he could 'so frankly admit' how close the connection was between his religious conceptions and his personal destiny. In reply Himmler fetched his much used copy of the *Bhagavad-Gita* and quoted a passage which he felt embodied Hitler, 'It is decreed that whenever men lose their respect for law and truth, and the world is given over to injustice, I will be born anew. I have no desire for gain.' Himmler described Hitler in Messianic terms and declared, 'It has been ordained by the Karma of the Germanic world that he should wage war against the East and save the Germanic peoples. A figure of the greatest brilliance has become incarnate in his person.' Kersten reflected:

> Himmler uttered these words with great solemnity and effect. Now it became clear to me why Himmler had sometimes pointed to Hitler as a person whom men would regard in centuries to come with the same reverence that they had accorded to Christ. Himmler saw in him not simply a figure who had to be surrounded with the aura of religious myth because this was useful in the struggle against the Church—but rather a figure from another world of the sort that always rose up to bring help in times of crisis. It all fitted in with the legends of the Holy Grail and the story of Parsifal. (1956, p152-3)

Having created his own *Weltanschauung*, Himmler was fascinated by the power he had to reshape Germany spiritually in the future. He set about sponsoring its intellectual formulation to pass on these ideas to his men and so create a re-born Germanic society. Himmler intended to create a new knightly class, and this involved spiritual and cultural retraining. As part of their advanced education, SS officers on leaving cadet school had to submit essays on the *'Responsibility of Christianity for the Decline of the Ostrogoths and Vandals'* and *'Effects of Christianity on Ancestor Worship amongst our People'* (Hohne, 2000, p450). According to Himmler's rules all SS officers above a certain rank had to renounce Christianity and declare themselves *'Gottgläubigkeit'*[206]. Furthermore no priest was allowed at SS Christenings or deathbed services, and the local SS leader was to officiate at their weddings. [207] In 1935 Himmler went even further and commissioned Karl Wiligut and professor Karl Diebitsch, (a cultural advisor for the SS) to add to the SS infant-naming rituals and research a SS summer and winter solstice ceremony (Pringle, 2006, p80, 84). All this was to build up a new pagan ritual, but Himmler also sought to create more depth, even going to the extent of wanting to incorporate a Jesuitesque ethic into their training (Schellenberg, 1969, p13). This was not the only way he borrowed from other organisations. Himmler both admired and hated the Jesuits, and deliberately used the pattern of the Jesuit organisation for his SS Order. From another of his perceived spiritual enemies, the Masons, he mimicked the complex and esoteric badges and symbols of different levels of hierarchy (Hohne, 2000, p144, 150). Another way he tried to enhance the SS's spiritual preparation was to commission *Ahnenerbe* academics to produce a selection of the world's religious texts suitable for Germanic meditation, including Rumi, Omar Khayyam and Marcus Aurelius, and Himmler wrote the forward to this text (Levenda, 2002, p178, 181).

For Himmler, all the *Ahnenerbe* work had practical consequences in terms of indoctrination. As part of the programme of historical re-armament, archaeological presentations to supplement Nazi ideology became a regular feature of SS officer training with tours of digs, guest lectures by visiting academics, and even a SS department of archaeology where some scholars even hoped to find traces of *Yggdrasil*, the World-Ash in Westphalia or lower Saxony (Pringle, 2006, p43).

So how successful was Himmler in creating a new Germanic eclectic religion for the SS? Evidently all this had some impact as according to SS-*Hauptsturmführer* Dieter Wilsiceny[208] the SS saw themselves as a 'new form of religious sect with its own rites and customs'; while Rauschning, noting the indoctrination process especially into the higher ranks of the SS and the Hitler Youth, stated that 'thoroughly and systematically, with iron logic, the war of annihilation against Christianity was being waged' (Hohne, 2000, p1; 1939, p 64-65).[209] All this was only a beginning for Himmler, who looked forward to conducting three-month-long monastic retreats for the SS leadership class, but he realised he had to proceed with his usual methodical patience.

For example, when on the 12th September 1942 Kersten enquired of Himmler why he did not propagate his belief about reincarnation more widely amongst his SS elite, he replied that it was too soon, as 'the majority of my men aren't yet ready for the sort of religion we have been discussing. It would only confuse them' (1956, p153). This may not have been an unreasonable assumption on his part for on another occasion Himmler told of how in a half-conscious state he would commune with the spirit of Heinrich I (Hohne, 2000, p154).

War and power increased Himmler's radicalisation, but he showed no interest in the German Christians' attempts to produce a more muscular Christianity and at a private speech in Berlin stated flatly: 'We must finish with Christianity'[210] (Steigmann-Gall, 2003, p130). Himmler then went on to ponder how he could generate alternatives. According to Kersten, Himmler was very proud of his Bosnian Muslim troops and hoped that they would show an attitude of fearless fanaticism in battle that it might be possible to inculcate in Germans. Jung, although he attributed the possibility to Hitler, sensed these ideas and in 1938 speculated whether at some time in the future Hitler's 'religion' might feature 'a Moslem-like Valhalla into which worthy Germans may enter' (McGuire and Hull, 1980, p131).

In the meantime Wiligut helped Himmler plan to rebuild a huge SS Vatican around the castle at Wewelsburg, which he believed to be the world's centre, to be completed by the nineteen sixties (Goodrick-Clarke, 1992, p187-8). At the castle Himmler concentrated his reference library and was so impressed with the Arthurian romances that he had a round table installed where his twelve elect SS Leaders could gather (Hohne, 2000, p151).

Was all this successful in shaping a SS leadership consensus? It is ironic that despite all this effort, the Führer never visited

Wewelsberg, which says much about the different values of Hitler and Himmler (Hohne, 2000, p153). Some took Hitler's religious cynicism even further and were motivated solely by power, for example Eichmann declared that he and Heydrich had no patience with Himmler's paganism and those who 'behaved as though they were clad in horns and pelts' (Arendt, 1994, p69). To add to this antipathy at any hint of a pagan renewal, in 1942 Heydrich was equally hostile to the German Christians (Bergen, 1996, p54). The significance of such an a-religious stance is understood when one realises that Heydrich, at the height of his powers, was probably the second most powerful man in Germany, given his skill at manipulating Himmler. Had he lived he might well have outflanked Bormann and even become Hitler's successor (Schellenberg, 1969, p11, 12; Deschner, 1981, p10).[211] Yet this competitive officer whom Deschner described as a 'technocrat par excellence' and who was a convinced anti-Catholic was willing at his marriage on December 12th 1931 to have the service decked with pagan Germanic decorations (1981, p12, 11, 43).

Looking at other examples within the higher SS, contrasts abound. Felix Steiner, the most innovative of the SS Generals, once referred to Himmler as a 'sleazy romantic'! This outburst not surprisingly eroded the relationship between the two men (Hohne, 2000, p481). 'Realism' was a favourite concept of the SS intelligentsia (Hohne, 2000, p489), and a prime example was the arch-rationalist economist-trained SS-*Brigadefuehrer* Ohlendorf, who became a major war criminal as an *Einsatzgruppen* commander. Yet this cold-blooded rationalist remained true to his interest in theosophy[212] despite the criticism from 'Gestapo' Muller. The latter presents an interesting contrast of his own, for, as the third-ranking SS officer in the organisation of the holocaust's, he remained a devout Catholic church-goer despite his pre-1933 hostility to the Nazis! This residual allegiance to the Catholic Church was not that unusual; his close ally, Ernst Kaltenbrunner who succeeded Heydrich, also retained his Church membership (Hohne, 2000, p514, 177; Steigmann-Gall, 2003, p252). All this would suggest that Himmler's religious project was not driven by some deep underlying Wotanic fire.

Whatever the resistance from parts of his new elite to his mystic aspirations, the ever-patient Himmler was equally enthusiastic about his attempts to further the racial purification of the German stock and achieve the renewal of German culture through agrarian social engineering. Here he met with more success. For his new aristocracy he took the idea of breeding further by literally maintaining an SS 'clan book' that recorded the racial provenance of the soldiers and their approved spouses (Hohne, 2000, p153). Then, building on from those agricultural themes derived from the *Artamanen* Society, Himmler longed to establish SS pioneer settlements in the East with his vision of ancient communal meeting grounds, *Thingplatz* for new pagan and party events (Pringle, 2006, p142). Kersten recalled meeting, on the evening of 5th January 1941, a group of Himmler's colleagues whom he questioned about Himmler's ideas. Kersten was aware that within Himmler's immediate circle senior officers were willing to be open and critical of Himmler, but on this issue:

> On all sides there was agreement and confirmation, given joyfully and devoutly. Hard-headed men spoke with enthusiasm on this subject, their eyes shining, using almost the same expressions.
> I asked myself what was this extraordinary manifestation that I had encountered. Apparently I had touched on their holy of holies. Certain words had the effect of magical formulae upon them: 'Back To The Land', 'The New Farmer', 'Own Your Land as a Free Man', 'Really Getting Down To It', 'A New Ruling Class', 'A Better Future', 'Racial Breeding'—and above all the thought of 'The SS which Arranges Everything'.
> 'Yes, Doctor,' said one of these gentlemen with great seriousness, 'we know what we're fighting for without rest day or night... It will be the paradise of the Germanic race.

Kersten wondered at the source of this emotional conviction for 'this crusade against city life and the "evils of civilization"'. He thought that a number of factors were involved which included the cramped nature of urban life, 'coupled with German romanticism which regards the country as the fulfilment of all its dreams, a paradise in opposition to the city, a spring of youth in contrast to age and death. Himmler appeals to these basic feelings and shows his people the power of the SS which can realize their longings' (1956, p72-73). All this agrarian romance may have been wrapped in 'Aryan' packaging, but the listeners were modern industrial age warriors with a keen sense of self-interest to drive their post-war hopes, which were far from the ancient woods of Wotan.

Summary

So, in Nazi Germany was there any pagan material from the people's unconscious that was not part of the cultural matrix and could support Jung's speculation? In my reading on the Nazi period's phantasmagoria the only material that I could find that actually came from the unconscious is the surreal Nazi-sponsored 'World Ice Theory', *Welteislehre*, that grew out of a dream of an eccentric Austrian Engineer. In 1913 he published his *Hörbiger's Glaciale Kosmogonie* in which he explained his universal theory of creation based on a celestial conflict between fire and ice, which became very attractive to Himmler (Cornwell, 2003 p194).

Otherwise, there are scattered flickers of events that on first glance appear to match Jung's ideas. For example, one of the influences on Himmler was the anti-Semitic publicist Johann von Leers at whose home in early 1934 Himmler met Hermann Wirth. Von Leers' wife, Gesine, had been a protégé of Wiligut. She evidently believed she was a reincarnation of an ancient Germanic Priestess and hosted evenings for similarly exotic guests resplendent in Bronze Age style jewellery (Pringle, 2006, p55). This is eccentric, but it hardly warrants serious evidence for a collective unconscious.

In Himmler's life one can also find echoes of ideas akin to racial memory and alchemy, but these also derive from his library-gorged fantasies; a twilight world, where fictions walked abroad. Himmler for his part believed that Thor's hammer, *Mjollnir*, was not just some mythic detail but a garbled memory of some sophisticated 'unheard-of knowledge of electricity'[213] harnessed as a weapon by the ancient Aryans. Fired by this intuitive prospect of such a wonder weapon, Himmler commissioned scholars to amplify this surmise from historic studies and, in November 1944, he tasked scientists to develop this hunch into some form of electromagnetic weapon to cripple allied electronics (Pringle, 2006, p80, 282-4). More tragically, Himmler's court astrologer recounts the fate of an alchemist, who having failing to produce the desired gold was banished to the modern dungeons of the concentration camp (Wulff, 1973).

None of this however gives much support to Jung's hypothesis; given the circles Himmler moved in and the books he read, this belief in a racial memory is the speculation of an over-fed imagination, not an ancient German revelation from the pagan past. Himmler was a product of those he met and what he read, but this was enough to produce a very mythic *Weltanschauung*. As Kersten observed after one conversation, 'Himmler only recognizes gods and devils. His heroes are like the gods... Anything taken from his picture of his heroes was either the work of small minds, too inferior to grasp the greatness, or come from the malice of enemies' (1956, p63-64). This was not just Kersten's impression. In September 1942 the chief of the SS Head Office *Obergruppenführer* (General) Berger described Himmler as 'a man whose mind has never developed beyond the age of heroic legends and primitive myth... like a schoolboy who, sitting in front of a medieval atlas, and unaware that the world has changed in the meantime, distributes countries according to his wish dreams' (Kersten, 1956, p254).

In this part of the chapter we were looking to see whether in Nazi Germany there were enough spontaneous eruptions of ancient pagan material to provide the evidence for Jung to make his case for a collective unconscious. Given the anti-pagan sentiments of Hitler, who might be regarded as Jung's key witness, and the well-documented roots of so much of the opportunistic Germanic Kitsch, it seems the Nazi revolution fails to provide a satisfactory confirmation of Jung's hypothesis of Wotan and the collective unconscious.

But before we leave this part of the chapter there is an interesting footnote that can be made on Jung's awareness of events and how he has subsequently been criticised. We have read about

Himmler's attempts to create an SS aristocracy and evidently Jung was aware of some of this for in 1936 he said, 'The SS men are being transformed into a caste of knights ruling sixty million natives' (McGuire and Hull, 1980, p103), so one sees that Jung in writing about these 'knights' was either well-informed about Nazi aspirations or was showing remarkable insight into the fantasies of the *Reichsführer SS*. Later, on 8th February 1939, he observed further, 'In Germany they are imitating that idea of nobility too. In those schools of the *Ordensburgen*[214], the young SS boys receive an education which makes them into a new order of Knights—the Knights of the new state'. Jung then went on to say that the totalitarian attempts to create a new aristocracy would not work as these nobilities are 'made' and artificial and have not risen from people who are themselves noble (Jung, 1989 [1934-1939], p1523).

Unfortunately Jung's observation that the 'SS men are being transformed into a caste of knights' has led to others critically misinterpreting Jung, either through bias against Jung, or ignorance of the SS. For example, Professor Paul Roazen and Edward Glover, presumably knowing nothing of the context, interpreted Jung as making some sort of compliment to the Nazi elite. Indeed Roazen went so far as to exclaim, 'I have not attempted, nor could I bear to do so, a comprehensive review of all of Jung's political commentary' (1989, p319). That a professor of social and political science could make such a judgement only goes to show the degree of emotive misinterpretation or misrepresentation that has dogged Jung!

Was Wotan an Archetype Specific to the Germans?

Having looked at Jung's attempt to provide contemporary data we now look at how Jung tried to establish a theoretical argument for the existence of Wotan. Here we see that Jung's discussion and definition of Wotan became bound up with the question of whether he was unique to Germany.

Jung could use startlingly evocative images about 'the one-eyed old hunter, on the edge of the German forest'. Perhaps Jung's own eloquence carried him into making unverifiable suggestions and becoming poetically confused as he ran together many events with completely different origins and courses? We can see this chaos in the way Jung claimed that: 'Wotan hits the mark as an hypothesis' (Jung, 1991 [1936], §389), but he did not define what his hypothesis was and went on to refer to Wotan as:

- 'A god [who] has taken possession of the Germans', by which he meant an archetype.
- An 'unsurpassed personification of a fundamental quality that is particularly characteristic of the Germans', by which he meant an archetype specific to the Germans.
- 'An irrational psychic factor'.
- A list of cultural images.

In doing all this Jung suggested that Wotan represented an archetype that was the root cause of events; a metaphor to describe a symptom of possession and a political parable to describe the irrationality of the thirties. This range of phenomena requires more than one explanation and shows yet again how Jung's style of writing allowed him to run together his confusion about race, nation and culture and his varied definitions of archetypes.

When Jung tried to describe a German Wotan he declared, 'Wotan is a Germanic datum of first importance' (Jung, 1991 [1936], §385), as if it were unchallengeable that he was referring to a unique German phenomenon, but unfortunately Jung did not clarify this thought, but instead tried to distil an idea of Wotan's character and suggested that Wotan was a projection of an internal psychic state in ancient myth. Jung praised Ninck's 'magnificent portrait of the German archetype Wotan', and Ninck's reference to Wotan as, 'the berserker, the god of storm, the wanderer, the warrior... Wotan is not only a god of rage and frenzy who embodies the instinctual and emotional aspect of the unconscious. Its intuitive and inspiring side also manifests itself in him, for he understands the runes and can interpret fate' (Jung, 1991 [1936], §393). This may be obscurely interesting but to what purpose is this cumulative character-portrait of Wotan from the north European legends if Jung cannot then link these symptoms to case studies of modern individuals?

Here Jung also lost an opportunity to take his observations about fury and broaden it with other cultural examples of war-fever.[215] Even Jung's references to Viking berserkers (Jung, 1991 [1936], §386) and to the *'furor teutonicus'* (Jung, 1991 [1936], §388) are tendentious as he was conflating two cultures which, though related, were almost a thousand years apart and of which very little can be said with certainty.

Jung discussed the occurrence in some cultures of people 'running amok', the equivalent of 'going berserk' in Germanic saga. 'This is a more or less complete trance-state, often accompanied by devastating social effects... In war-dances primitives can become so excited that they may even shed blood' (Jung, 1991 [1938-1940], §29). He did not discuss if Indonesian *amok* and the Germanic berserker were more prevalent in these cultures due to racial or cultural factors. It is interesting to reflect that according to Ian Heath, the Viking berserk fury which seemed to have components of 'paranoia', 'a belief in lycanthropy' and in some cases may 'have been prompted by an epileptic attack' was a hereditary condition rather than something that could be learnt or induced by drugs (1985, p47). And just as Jung's discussion of aggression and frenzy was historically weak, he also neglected to bring in many obvious psychological factors that could have enriched the discussion. Indeed such was his reliance or obsession with mythic material that he neglected to bring in any cross-disciplinary material that could so easily have included a psychoanalytic study on the role of infantile frustration and the joy of destruction; the biological factors like the adrenaline rush of the 'fight or flight' syndrome, and an anthropological discussion of how cultures respond to these emotions.

As much as Jung tried to posit a German Wotan, his discussion of Wotan's location began to wander, like his archetypal subject. He referred to the English Wagnerphile and anti-Semitic theorist Houston Stewart Chamberlain, and wondered if Chamberlain's ideas were an indication that 'other veiled gods may be sleeping elsewhere' (Jung, 1991 [1936], §389). By this speculation he implied that Wotan was not unique to Germany, which of course altered the whole focus of the debate. Should Wotan be understood as the god / archetype of war and aggression? Yet Jung never makes this explicit.

In a different attempt to refine his portrait of the archetype, Jung gave a compendium of similar pagan gods as an overview, or amplification of a type of archetypal personification (Jung, 1991 [1936], §394). But how valid were these connections? Jung bracketed Hellenic Gods and their Roman editions along with their Germanic equivalents, and then added to this the Judeo-Christian *pneuma*. This suggestion was too crude to be a useful form of phenomenology and produced a mythological medley that spans over a thousand years and combines the separate Occidental and Levantine cultural-mythological systems (Campbell, 1982b, p30). Doubtless the motive was to link Wotan and Dionysus, but all it adds is a muddled discussion of the nature of archetypes. It also makes even more chaos of Jung's attempts to establish whether he was arguing for Wotan as an archetype specific to the Germans or as a general archetype. In a similar way in a *Zarathustra* seminar, given on 5th February 1936, he mixed Wotan's 'romantic character of the sorcerer' and 'the god of mysteries' and then suggested that the 'German mentality' 'reaches... from the Urals to Spain', which goes beyond the notion of what is generally understood to mean the Germanic race,[216] unless 'German' is going to be a synonym for Caucasians from Slavs to Hispanics (Jung, 1989 [1934-1939], p814). All this leaves the idea of a racial unconscious in tatters!

Together this gives another indication of why it is so problematic to label him as a psychologist of race or a psychologist of nations. Jung was in this position because he had not clearly identified how Wotan was an archetype, nor had he defined and made the distinction between what was archetypal and what was the cultural component of the phenomenon. In failing to establish that Wotan was an archetype specific to the Germanic people, he seriously undermined his evidence for both the existence of a racial layer to the collective unconscious and Wotan being an archetype specific to the Germanic peoples.

WOTAN AS THE IMAGE OF FURY AND POSSESSION

One might have expected that since Jung named this archetypal phenomenon 'Wotan', this archetype should fit within Jung's 'classes' of the archetypes that were discussed in chapter six. But in as far as Jung describes him, Wotan does not fit the criteria of the universal developmental archetypal personalities. Indeed, in the essay Jung was lamentably vague about explaining why Wotan was a distinct archetypal personality being caught between the idea of universal archetypes and his suggestion that Wotan was German. Wotan's status remains an anomaly, a would-be archetype that Jung tries to establish in his essay, but that afterwards falls into obscurity.

Maybe as a result of this lack of definition, Jung briefly introduced the suggestion that 'the Germanic god represents a totality on a very primitive level' (Jung, 1991 [1936], §394). This brings us back to his interest in psychic energy; his second line of argument was about the nature of Wotan and the archetypal patterns of emotional energy, which is very different from defining Wotan as an archetypal personality. The reference to 'a very primitive level' implies that an archetype can be represented by a number of evolved stages[217] and from this it follows that people's levels of consciousness can gradually change, as described in previous chapters.

Jung went on to describe this primitive state as, 'a psychological condition in which man's will was almost identical with the god's and entirely at his mercy' (Jung, 1991 [1936], §394), which suggested a very low level of consciousness. In support of his perception he recalled Bruno Goetz's *Das Reich ohne Raum* (1919)[218] which he declared to be prophetic as Goetz foresaw 'the conflict between the realm of ideas and life, between Wotan's dual nature as a god of storm and a god of secret musings' (Jung, 1991 [1936], §384). Here he was well set in his Nietzschian perspective and, with the second dichotomy between the clash of 'storm' and 'secret musings', Jung was describing the emotional and psychological processes in more detail.

Firstly, he was setting in opposition the berserk aggression of 'storm' and the intuitive possibilities of 'secret musings' that are latent in archetypal development and transformation. This echoed Jung's earlier optimism about the potential for archetypal growth and transformation within the individual.

Secondly, he was describing the invigorating experience of archetypal seizure and the characteristics of possession that included the unconscious autonomy of the complex and the ego-inflation of the 'God-all-mighty' complex that are symptoms of archetypal intoxication outlined in the previous chapter.

These symptoms go some way to giving an indication of his thinking about Wotan. However, as this attempt to provide specific ideas only identified symptoms not causes, it was not enough to justify the definition of Wotan as a distinct archetypal personalisation. Furthermore, even in his discussion of symptoms, Jung's case was weakened by his inadequate discussion of aggression in the brief mention of fury. He had tried to consolidate his argument by focusing on fury in paragraphs 386 and 388, but he then lost his way and got sucked into the German discussion and even referred to 'the German archetype Wotan' before getting mired in a cross-cultural comparison of ancient Gods that went against his previous speculation that Wotan is German (Jung, 1991 [1936], §393).

Despite the muddle, Jung struggled to capture the mood in the Reich where he saw the Germans possessed by a feeling of fury. Given this view, the main feature of Jung's thoughts on Wotan and emotion concerned the type of aggression that has become blind indiscriminate rage. Unfortunately Jung did not clarify whether Wotan was the defining source of this fury, or whether the fury was a by-product of the energy released by another unspecified archetypal possession. Jung was far from clear about this; indeed, he toyed with the idea of dispensing with the name Wotan as the cause of events and simply discussing the phenomenon of the '*furor teutonicus*', which, from his description, amounted to the idea of the potential for a seizure of fury (Jung, 1991 [1936], §388). He went on to dismiss this option because he thought it offered no cause for the outbreak of aggression, but he did not seem to be aware that all he had done was to describe what he thought was the cause of the aggression but had failed to prove that it was so.

Jung also elaborated on the compulsive element, the possession, which is a symptom of the fury. Jung speculated that: 'Perhaps we may sum up this general phenomenon as *Ergriffenheit*—a state of being seized or possessed' and he went on to suggest that it was the archetype of Wotan that had possessed the Germans (Jung, 1991 [1936], §386), but again recognition of a symptom does not establish the nature of the cause.

On this theme he made one of the few references in the essay to Hitler: 'The impressive thing about the German phenomenon is that one man, who is obviously "possessed," has infected a whole nation to such an extent that everything is set in motion and has started rolling on its course towards perdition' (Jung, 1991 [1936], §388). Jung suggested that this state of possession was what explained Hitler's success but again failed to provide proof for this idea or define how this vulnerability to possession had came about. Indeed, he then goes even further and specifically snatches the 'credit' from Hitler and states that Wotan is really the only explanation of events (Jung, 1991 [1936], §386).

Maybe this example of Jung unhesitatingly privileging Wotan as a causal hypothesis for events in Germany over Hitler's egomania and undoubted dictatorial skills demonstrates how unfocused Jung's thinking had become.

A Theory Lost in the Wild Wood

Why had Jung become so convoluted in his thinking? Crucially, he was likely to have problems establishing a clear case because he had never clearly delineated the various parts of his theory. In 'Wotan' he was trying to run together a medley of evidence about race and archetypes and this generated a chaotic circular argument. Another factor that may have contributed to his inability to theorise and present evidence clearly was his habitual use of symbolic thought in his clinical work. Symbolic thinking is vital in dream work and also can give a high tolerance of paradox, but this state of mind would be a disadvantage when he tried to theorise on history, as it numbed his ability to think critically and so prompted him to retain his unstable amalgam of ideas.

There is also the question of his style of writing. Let us take the following paragraph as an example:

> Wotan disappeared when his oaks fell and appeared again when the Christian God proved too weak to save Christendom from fratricidal slaughter. When the Holy Father at Rome could only impotently lament before God the fate of the *grex segregatus*, the one-eyed old hunter, on the edge of the German

forest, laughed and saddled Sleipnir. (Jung, 1991 [1936], §386)

Such lines may convey the uncanny force of the archetypal phenomenon but the style of writing can also seduce the incautious reader into supposing Jung was thinking literally. Jung too was at risk. With such writing he would either poetically overplay his speculations or reify Wotan as an entity; both extremes were unfortunate, as what Jung was trying to warn about was a type of mass hysteria. This confusion did not help him. It seems the irrationality of the times and the resulting anxiety had seeped into Jung's argument and his theory had become infected by the *Zeitgeist*.

There could also be personal factors why he over-extended his Wotan hypothesis. Jung had a violent temper and drew his inspiration from intuition. Could it be that he identified at some level with his mythic subject, at least enough to cloud his critical awareness as to the weakness of his presentation? He also may have had another bias as he showed a strong feeling for the land, nature and the peasant virtues, so as a Romantic maybe he was more prone to poetic personifications.[219] Could all this have led him to project this combination of characteristics onto his reading of events and to construct an archetypal explanation in the shape of Wotan? For, just as emotions can be projected on to other people, so emotions can affect the theoretical models one constructs and this in turn can lead to a tendency to reify, or even personify, psychic factors.

Jung had failed to establish evidence or make a sound theoretical case for a German Wotan archetype. With this his attempt to use Nazi Germany as a field study for his theory had failed. After the war he would continue to modify his archetypal hypothesis, as his writings made increasing links with the work of others on instincts, but with all the pre-War controversies that beset him 'Wotan' was his last attempt to establish the existence of a racial unconscious. This project had failed and with it his classical conception of a 'geological' collective unconscious dwindled from his thinking.

How Predictive Were Jung's Dreams?

Jung claimed to have predicted the future of Germany after reviewing many dreams that he thought gave an insight into the collective unconscious and the course of events. Evidently Jung regarded himself as a prophet, and from 1918 had been predicting problems developing in Germany. This he referred to in 1935[220] and 1957 when he recalled:

> [A]ll the time a myth is being played out in the unconscious, a myth that extends over centuries, a stream of archetypal ideas that goes on through the centuries through an individual. Really it is like a continuous stream, and it comes to light in the great movements, say in political or spiritual movements... If somebody were clever enough to see what is going on in the unconscious mind, he would be able to predict it. I predicted the Nazi rising in Germany through the observation of my German patients. They had dreams in which the whole thing was anticipated, and in considerable detail. And I was absolutely certain, in the years before Hitler—I could even say the year, in the year 1918—I was sure that something was threatening, something very big, and very catastrophic. [221] (McGuire and Hull, 1980, p284-285)

Admittedly Jung warned of the dangers of German aggression and expansionism, but he did not predict major details like the World War or the messianic dictator. Evidently Jung had lapses in his self-critical awareness of the interplay of dreams and wider events. In *Memories, Dreams, Reflections* Jung recounted a dream he had before the outbreak of the war when he was on the verge of a psychological crisis. The dream was of Europe awash with blood rising to the Alps, which he presented as evidence of both the prophetic potential of dreams from the collective unconscious, and also his own facility at this art (Jung, 1963 [1961], p169). Jung did not pause to consider whether the dream was not so much an occult vision of the future as the speculation of the unconscious mind that was aware of rising tensions in a Europe of naval and diplomatic confrontations. Given Jung's realist thinking about political issues, it indicates a Romantic lapse that he did not allow for such a mundane possibility. Returning to 'Wotan', it maybe that in the poetic flush of writing, Jung overestimated his predictive powers.

In 1946 he described how,

> As early as 1918, I noticed peculiar disturbances in the unconscious of my German patients which could not be ascribed to their personal psychology. Such non-personal phenomena always manifest themselves in dreams as mythological motifs... There was a disturbance of the collective unconscious in every single one of my German patients. One can explain these disorders causally, but such an explanation is apt to be unsatisfactory, as it is easier to understand archetypes by their aim rather than by their causality. The archetypes I had observed expressed primitivity, violence, and cruelty. (Jung, 1991 [1946b], §447)

> I had observed the German revolution in the test-tube of the individual... I was able to follow up quite a number of cases and to observe how the uprush of the dark forces deployed itself in the individual test-tube. I could watch these forces as they broke through the individual's moral and intellectual self-control, and as they flooded his conscious world. (Jung, 1991 [1946b], §450)

Unfortunately he gave no examples, and this lack of evidence undermines the strength of his claim to be able to tell the future from dream material. The quality of Jung's supposed insight must also be questioned as he apparently did not consider that the presence of 'primitivity, violence, and cruelty' in his patients' dreams might be due to the recent war, rather than an example of predictive intuitions!

WERE JUNG'S PREDICTIONS UNIQUE?

Jung showed some foresight about future dangers, but there is nothing inexplicable or profound in this, as others had already done the same, as he was aware when he cited other warning voices. On the 26th February 1936, when he was talking about Wotanesque upheavals, he said that Wagner and Nietzsche were 'the first... [to] realize the events of the future and to give voice to the unconscious that was about to manifest; and [Nietzsche] realized more or less that it would be a message that was not welcome' (Jung, 1989 [1934-1939], p870). These two men, like Jung, were locating their prognosis from a feeling about the *Zeitgeist*, rather than conventional political or historical analysis.

Heinrich Heine in his 1834 *Religion and Philosophy in Germany*, had prophesied the dangers of German expansionism in terms very similar to those Jung would use.[222] Heine wrote:

> Christianity—and this is its fairest merit—subdued to a certain extent the brutal warrior ardour of the Germans, but it could not entirely quench it; and when the cross, that restraining talisman, falls to pieces, then will break forth again the ferocity of the old combatants, the frantic Berserker rage whereof Northern poets have sung—the talisman has become rotten, and the day will come when it will pitifully crumble to dust. The old stone gods will then arise from the forgotten ruins and wipe from their eyes the dust of centuries, and Thor with his giant hammer will arise again, and he will shatter the Gothic cathedrals. (cited in Baynes, 1941, p63) [223]

Interestingly this passage was noted by two first generation Jungians who independently cited the same passage but offered different translations—Eleanor Bertine in 1939[224] and H.G. Baynes in 1941—although neither of them paused to wonder if this was a source for Jung's 'Wotan' essay. Were they too mesmerized by the mass and eloquence of Jung's style? Did the rush of events preclude critical questioning? Or were they not thinking critically as they were not writing an academic commentary?

As for Jung, he often listed those who had influenced him and made a number of references to Heine, but not to that text.[225] However as the style and content so strongly echoes Jung's 'Wotan' it is hard not to wonder about a connection.

A similar piece of contemporary writing was quoted by Baynes, who was given the reference by Gerhard Adler. This was from a letter by D. H. Lawrence, who never met Jung, and who ironically Jung regarded as too Freudian in his thinking (McLynn, 1996, p274). Lawrence wrote 'Letter from Germany' in 1923 about his impressions of the Black Forest as it had changed in the two previous years. In a wonderfully evocative piece of prose he caught the altered mood:

> But at night you feel strange things stirring in the darkness, strange feelings stirring out of this still unconquered Black Forest. You stiffen your backbone and you listen to the night. There is a sense of danger. It is not the people. They don't seem dangerous. Out of the very air comes a sense of danger, a queer, *bristling* feeling of uncanny danger. Something has happened. Something has happened which has not yet eventuated. The old spell of the old world has broken, and the old, bristling, savage spirit has set in...
>
> Something primitive, like loose, roving gangs of broken, scattered tribes, so they affect one. And the swarms of people somehow produce an impression of silence, of secrecy, of stealth. It is as if everything and everybody recoiled away from the old unison, as barbarians lurking in a wood recoil out of sight... Like a spring that is broken, and whirls swiftly back, so time seems to be whirling with mysterious swiftness to a sort of death. Whirling to the ghost of the old Middle Ages of Germany, then to the Roman days, then to the days of the silent forest and the dangerous, lurking barbarians... It is a fate; nobody now can alter it. It is a fate. The very blood changes. (1923, p107-110)[226]

Again Baynes presented the passage in the spirit of confirmation of an intuition, not as a possible source of Jung's idea.

Freud too had noted pagan trends in German culture but had placed a very different stress and interpretation on what he saw. In his last book, *Moses and Monotheism*, he echoed a number of features of Jung's 1918 article. He used the idea of national psychologies as he explicitly stated that the Jewish psyche had evolved into its present state in the ancient world. He also referred, like Jung, to the violent imposition of Christianity on the early Germans (Rieff, 1990, p326), and implicitly suggested that, below the common culture, the collective instinctive patterns remained unchanged. However, Freud's speculations were more limited (Rieff, 1990, p58-59):

> [A]ll those peoples who excel today in their hatred of Jews became Christians only in late historic times, often driven to it by bloody coercion. It might be said that they are all 'mis-baptized.' They have been left, under a thin veneer of Christianity, what their ancestors were, who worshipped a barbarous polytheism. They have not got over a grudge against the new religion which was imposed on them; but they have displaced the grudge on to the source from which Christianity reached them. The fact that the Gospels tell a story which is set among Jews, and in fact deals only with Jews, has made this displacement easy for them. Their hatred of Jews is at bottom a hatred of Christians, and we need not be surprised that in the German National-Socialist revolution this intimate relation between the two monotheist religions finds such a clear expression in the hostile treatment of both of them. (Freud, (1939 [1934-38]), p90-92, cited Maidenbaum, 2002, p249)

Other 'prophets' were conventional political theorists who had made similar observations but, unlike novelists or psycho-analysts, they could account for events without poetic illusions of a sudden up-rush of buried archaic factors. For them, Wotanesque ideas had a much more recent pedigree. To give two examples, the philosopher of history R.C. Collingwood noted that there had been a gradual decline of orthodox Christianity and a rise in the popularity of the neo-paganism in the late 1800s with its worship of the human will. He saw this as a fertile base for Fascism and National Socialism in the twentieth century. The Marxian philosopher Georg Lukacs also drew a link between the rise of Fascism and Nazism and the exalted 'irrationalism' of *Lebensphilosophie* (Noll, 1974, p38).

If the main purpose of 'Wotan' was to provide evidence of Jung's theories of the collective, Jung implied that dream material supported his hypothesis, but he failed to provide such dream evidence—so where is the virtue in Jung's work? Indeed one can go further and observe that since others gave similar warnings without reference to dream material, and the explanations and evidence of historians provide a more coherent account of what happened, there seems little case for Jung to claim that he was providing unique insights or new tools.

'WOTAN': THE UNHEEDED WARNING

The other role of 'Wotan' and the Knickerbocker interview was to act as a political warning about the impact of these psychological realities. Jung poetically summed up his position in the *Zarathustra Seminar* on 8th February 1939:

> Wotan, or it would be a god of war; that is the ancient idol. The state is merely the modern pretence, a shield, a make-belief, a concept. In reality, the ancient wargod holds the sacrificial knife, for it is in war that the sheep are sacrificed... so instead of human representatives or a personal divine being, we now have the dark gods of the state—in other words, the dark god of the Collective Unconscious... *the old gods are coming to life again in a time when they should have been superseded long ago, and nobody can see it.* (Jung, 1989 [1934-1939], p1517-8, my italics)

We can see from this that Jung saw the poetic use of Wotan as vital to convey the compulsive irrational power of political events to bring home the force of his warning, as he said, 'the parallel between *Wotan redivivus* and the social, political, and psychic storm that is shaking Germany might have at least the value of a parable' (Jung, 1991 [1936], para, 387). By this Jung was arguing that whatever the socio-political issues involved, the metaphor of Wotan conveyed the irrationality of the times. This may be true, but he had not made a strong case and whatever the stylistic virtue of the metaphor, this does not validate the wider theory. Furthermore, this style may have alienated some of his audience and lost him an opportunity to convey an understanding of his ideas. And regrettably this confusion continues today.[227]

'Wotan' did convey a startling picture of the irrationality of the times, but Jung's political realism was crippled by his writing style and this may have undercut the essay's ability to reach a wider audience. Equally importantly the style in which it was written did little to resolve the hostility of the 'campaign' towards Jung, and this controversy drowned out his attempts to warn of the dangers ahead.

Sadly, but not surprisingly, Jung's efforts met with little success. In 1939 H.G. Baynes wrote to Jung of a friend, Mr Ashton-Swatkin, who worked in the Foreign Office and had recently been in Berlin negotiating with Hitler. Baynes lent him a copy of 'Wotan', which he translated and had circulated in the FO, but in August 1940 Jung complained that Chamberlain had not read and heeded the warning in his Knickerbocker interview (Baynes Jansen, 2003, p272, 312). This failure continued to vex Jung, and Jung's son later told Bernstein of the frustration Jung felt that he had not been successful in communicating with the politicians and warning the democracies (Buresch-Talley, 2002, p52).

The archetypal explanation of Wotan was not Jung's only attempt to explain events in Germany for within the essay, and on other occasions, he made references to the archetype of the *Puer Aeternus* and the archetype of the Wise Old Man.

Germany, the Puer Aeternus and the Feeling Function

On 26th May 1937, the year after publishing 'Wotan', Jung made another attempt to analyse Germany in archetypal terms in the *'Zarathustra'* seminars. Again this was an exercise in psychologising and massive generalisation, but this time he was using the archetype of the *Puer Aeternus* and the role of emotion and sentimentality with his ideas about the Feeling Function.

The *Puer Aeternus* plays a role in the adolescent stage of development. This archetype can take a positive form that is a prelude to the hero, with an abundance of energy to face new horizons, or it can become immature, dependent and regressive. The functioning of the archetype is heavily involved with the level of emotional insight and maturity, which means that it is often discussed in relation to the Feeling Function.

In the seminar Jung declared, 'We could call it the archetype of the son versus the father. The psychology of the *Puer Aeternus* is exclusively masculine, it is a man's world'. Jung suggested that there was a clearly identifiable cultural division in Europe between the East, where 'the *Puer Aeternus* prevails psychologically, and west of that line the psychology of the anima' was evident in the arts and in politics. Jung argued that there was a deep clash between the dynamic, conflict-ridden psychology of the *Puer Aeternus* and the static, cold, rigid norms of the Christian world. Jung thought that, in consequence, Germany was typified by 'the qualities of adolescent psychology' and 'hopeful one-sidedness', but that at some point it would switch into the static rigidity of a new conservatism.

Jung then stated the 'whole new movement in Germany is typical of the *Puer Aeternus*. It is a mass movement, an intense movement, and nobody can see exactly what it means; there is a very mystical idea behind it'. Jung also suggested that a distinctive feature of the difference between German culture and the other Western Europeans was that in German literature the significance of women was much more limited (Jung, 1989 [1934-1939], p1107-8). In 1945 Jung repeated these ideas and added that Germany demonstrated a 'typical adolescent psychology, apparent not only in the extraordinary prevalence of homosexuality but in the absence of an anima figure in German literature' (McGuire & Hull, 1978, p154-155).

In highlighting the role youth played in Nazi Germany, Jung could have made a much more robust psychological hypothesis because the archetypal explanation was not hostage to a hypothesis of a racial collective unconscious. Instead the historical element was only tied to recent cultural traditions. Unfortunately Jung paid little more attention to developing the *Puer Aeternus* interpretation, although he did return to the issue of feelings and emotions in German culture in 1957 (McGuire & Hull, 1978, p284-285). He gave no indication of why he did not develop the idea, but perhaps this neglect was because the horrors of the Second World War were more dramatically portrayed by the style of the 'Wotan' essay, rather than the descriptions of emotional immaturity.[228]

The general significance of youth can be developed from a number of themes. The Nazi obsession with youth was noted by the diplomatic historian, Dr Brian Porter. He observed that a conspicuous feature of Nazi ideology was its infatuation with the youthful hero. This image reached its zenith with the elite SS *Hitler Youth* division, and the cult of the 'ace' that had expanded from fighter pilots and U-boat captains to include outstanding tank commanders (1984). At the time of the party's seizure of power its leaders were conspicuous youthful,[229] and as one German exile, Karl Otten, noted, 'The young truly love Hitler, in almost limitless ecstatic admiration' (Lukacs, 1997, p100).[230]

The question of feelings, masculinity and the significance of homo-eroticism in the group-bonding of elements of the Nazi movement, especially in the leadership hierarchy of the SA and in Hitler's inner circle, has recently been explored in Lothar Machtan's *The Hidden Hitler* (2001). This gives an insight into an explicit ideology in praise of 'masculine' toughness instead of 'female' weakness that was advanced by Röhm and by Hitler[231] who, whatever the debates about his sexuality, made clear in his table talk that he had little regard for women other than as decorative child bearers (Hitler, 1988). Interestingly, according to Catharine Rush Cabot's diary on June 17th 1935, Jung does make a brief allusion to this issue: 'Jung said he doubted whether Hitler was homosexual, but that friends of his who knew Hitler said that he was— or at least they strongly suspected he was' (Cabot Reid, 2001, p97). In any event, within Nazi Germany an ideology of machismo also strongly influenced Himmler, who was obsessed with the toughness and prowess of his SS troops (Kersten, 1956, p135), and tried to build an athletic persona to compensate for his poor physique and his lack of active service in the Great War (Padfield, 1990, p205).

A related remark of Jung's about emotion and gender from 1936 was a comment that 'Hitler's unconscious seems to be female' (Jung, 1986 [1936a], §334). Later in the war, on January 22nd 1941 Jung, told the diarist: 'When Mussolini first met Hitler, he thought: 'Poor beggar; there is nothing to him—just a *Signorino*.' But he never asked himself where was the *Signorina* (Anima) behind Hitler. Hitler's *Signorina*—the ambitious anima devil-woman—is not a 'human being.' A human being would have boundary lines somewhere, but Hitler's woman is without limits: she goes to the stars—reaches for the stars!' (Cabot Reid, 2001, p322).

Jung made another curious reflection on the effect of the anima when he suggested in 1928 that, 'The anima can give one very strange ideas: she can, for instance, give that peculiar quality which makes a man lead his life as a sort of adventure or quest, making the task the goal of his whole life.' He went on to suggest that Napoleon was caught by the romantic pursuit of a dream to become another Alexander the Great (Jung, 1984 [1928-1930], p57). Hitler certainly had ample delusions, but Jung gave no evidence to substantiate this archetypal speculation.

Another aspect of the relationship between aggression and emotional consciousness was mentioned in a short observation from 16th April 1936, 'The counterpart of sentimentality is as we know brutality. Wotan's inner meaning, represented by his lost eye, is *Erda*, the *Magna Mater*' (Jung, 1973 [1906-1950], p213).[232] This observation had some development; Jung wrote in a letter of 1945 on the links between sentimentality and aggression: 'It is also apparent in German sentimentality and *"Gemütlichkeit"*, which is really nothing but hardness of heart, unfeelingness, and soullessness. All those charges of soulnessness and bestiality which German propaganda levelled at the Russians apply to themselves; Goebbels' speeches are nothing but German psychology projected upon the enemy' (McGuire & Hull, 1978, p155). One can also note the sentimentality of Hitler's devotion to dogs, cream cakes and vapid pretty women.

Michael Burleigh suggests that the strongest feature of the Nazis was their endemic sentimentality, which he felt was even more significant than their fascination with technology and their ideology's apocalyptic undercurrents. He notes how many of the politicians resembled preachers with their rhetoric of passion, self-pity and self-absorption (2000, p210). In a way, these lesser features also matched well with the adolescent strain of emotion, which is often attracted to dynamic change and the power of technology, or is drawn to the self-pitying nihilism that can extend to an apocalyptic fixation.

So where did these ideas leave Jung? The *Puer Aeternus* hypothesis was much closer to other theories about the importance of patterns of child socialisation and its effects on the psyche. As a theory it offers a much simpler explanation than the mythic aspects of the Wotan hypothesis. However, in his reference to youth, sentimentality and feeling, it is conspicuous that both before and after the war Jung did not discuss family patterns and sociological factors. This is a curious omission when one considers Erikson's suggestion that paternal authoritarianism was amongst the identifiable roots of German authoritarianism. He had written: 'In Germany, this pattern had traditional antecedents. It always just happened to happen, although it was, of course not "planned"' (1982, p299). Asher summarised work by Freudian theorists that included studies of how long-term patterns of child-rearing, paternal dominance and maternal submission could lead to a high incidence in a population of either submission to authority or authoritarian personalities. Such an unconscious cultural value system could inhibit individuality and compassion that would enhance the growth of a brutalised society. The studies further observe that the Nazis often enabled the casualties of unhealthy child-rearing patterns the opportunity to release those pent-up frustrations and 'act out' by victimising other groups (1978, p269).

In summary, Jung and the Freudians have a different approach to the impact of male-female relations. The Freudian accounts were concerned with patterns of socialisation and sexuality within families, whereas Jung was concerned with more distant cultural processes in society and was not concerned with how these processes were established. Even after the War, when Jung's explanations were characterised by an interpretation of the psychopathology of recent events, he continued to look at wider historical events, of the sort that usually concern International Politics academics, and continued to ignore more intimate family dynamics. It seemed that in all these avenues of exploration Jung remains lost in a fog of archetypal questions.

REDEFINING WOTAN AS AN ARCHETYPE AND THE ROLE OF RELIGION IN WAR

If Jung failed to describe, define and give evidence for Wotan as an independent Germanic archetypal personalisation, can one offer another archetype that would account for the psychological symptoms Jung was observing? To unravel this puzzle one must return to examine what emotions were operating, for if Wotan was not sustainable as a racial archetype, then the Wotan phenomenon should be an aspect of one of the universal archetypal personalisations. Remarkably, when we examine Jung's other writings, we find that there are fragments of other ideas that allow us to piece together a different picture of the archetypal configuration that was stirring events.

To identify what archetype was operating one can refer to 'Psychology and Literature', an article that was written originally in 1930.[233] In this article Jung gave some details of his ideas about Wotan, without directly referring to Wotan, but in his discussion of the Wise Old Man in the 1933 translation by Baynes, the archetype is referred to in a positive fashion:

> Could we conceive of anyone but a German writing *Faust* or *Also sprach Zarathustra*? Both play upon something that reverberates in the German soul—a 'primordial image', as Jacob Burckhardt once called it —the figure of a physician or teacher of mankind. *The archetypal image of the wise man, the saviour or redeemer,* lies buried and dormant in man's unconscious since the dawn of culture; it is awakened whenever the times are out of joint and a human society is committed to a serious error. When people go astray they feel the need of a guide or teacher or even of the physician. (Jung, 1933 [1933], p197, my italics)

It was only in the 1950 edition of the Collected Works that the negative aspect of the archetype was added to give a rounded explanation of the potentials and dangers inherent in the archetype of the Wise Old Man. Jung defines: 'the figure of a healer or teacher of mankind, or of a wizard. It is the archetype of the Wise Old Man, the helper and redeemer, but also of the magician, deceiver, corrupter, and tempter... The seductive error is like a poison that can also act as a cure and the shadow of a saviour can turn into a fiendish destroyer' (Jung, 1986 [1930]/1950, §159).[234] This would imply that Wotan was an avatar of the Wise Old Man, at least in terms of Jung in 1950. But does this concur with Jung's thoughts in the thirties? The early edition may reflect his optimism in 1930, but by 1936 Jung praised Ninck's writing on Wotan,[235] which included negative aspects of the god, so some change in his thinking was already present (Jung, 1991 [1936], §393).[236]

If one accepts this development in his perception of Wotan, one can formulate an alternative definition of the archetype at work in Germany. One shifts from the suggestion that the archetype at the centre of events was some sort of iron age War-God of anger to a new position, where the anger is to be understood as a distortion of the religious imperative, and the inspiration, procession and religious fervour for renewal are all aspects of the developmental potential triggered by the archetype of the Wise Old Man, providing insight into the impact of religious psychology on events in Germany.

Why had Jung not clearly formalised this option? Firstly, as we have seen, he had not sufficiently differentiated his theories of the collective that would have allowed him to extract the Wotan hypothesis from its Germanic cultural complex to reveal the archetype of the Wise Old Man. Secondly, his archetypal explanation was confused by the aggression of the times and, as has been noted, Jung's psycho-analytic perspective was weak in its theoretical exploration of aggression.[237]

With these references to the Wise Old Man we come to Jung's main contribution to our understanding of the causes of war and his concern about the perversion of the religious instinct.

To go into this further we have to refer to one of the central formulations of Jung's model of the psyche. He suggested that within the psyche there is an autonomous, highly dynamic imperative to move consciousness forward, to seek wholeness and meaning. In its deepest sense this drive is a religious imperative. He called this archetype 'the Self', which can be understood as both the core and the totality of the psyche. But because this archetype is so deeply embedded in the mind it often appears very abstract and so we only become aware of it when it comes closer to consciousness in a personalisation. This usually takes the form of the Wise Old Man, which can be understood as an anthropomorphic portrayal of the Self and its wisdom.

Given Jung's understanding of the central position of the Self, this archetype and the religious instinct at its disposal is a tremendous source of numinous power. But this potential power is very dangerous if it is misdirected as these emotional energies can be used for good and evil[238]. The Self has tremendous power to create the aspiration for change, but this urge was not always wisely directed.

Jung referred to the Self's role in politics on the 19th February 1936, when he discussed the psychology of 'mental epidemics', ideologies and fanaticism:

> I explain this mental contagion through... the idea of the self, because for many thousands of years this idea seems to have been lurking behind the screen of historical events... Now, it is tangible, near. And because it is not completely detached from man, it has these peculiar effects. It is still in the unconscious, so the unconscious is activated; people nowadays are gripped by an unrest that they do not understand, so they spread their excitement. That is happening actually in Germany, and has happened in Russia: everybody is infecting everybody else with unrest, with a peculiarly vibrating unconscious—and there must be a reason for all that. It is as if something had gotten into man's unconscious and were stirring there, causing infectious excitement... the more those metaphysical convictions fade or vanish, the more the energy inves-

ted in those forms drops below the threshold of consciousness. (Jung, 1989 [1934-1939], p842)[239]

When one brings together the power of the Self with the authority and charisma of the Wise Old Man one has a combination of psychic organs which identifies many psychological variables that operate in politics. If we apply this to what was happening in Germany one could observe that the obsession with order was accelerated by the archetype of the Self as an 'ordering motif', while the authoritarian traditionalism and the charismatic power of the wise leader was fed by the more personified archetype of the Wise Old Man. Indeed, Jung used this archetype to describe General von Hindenburg, who had become the President of the Weimar Republic and represented the symbol of the Old Wise Man to the German people. This was unfortunate for whatever his undoubted skill as a general, he was not adapted to work in the political sphere (Cabot Reid, 2001, p96).

Jung's concern with religion can also be seen in his criticisms of the authoritarian State. Jung had argued that it was dangerous to let the religious dimension of psychology become decoupled from its spiritual milieu, as this left those devotional aspects of the psyche undeveloped, primitive and powerful. As modernity has seen an impoverishment of feelings and an over-estimation of the intellect, this has left unused religious aspirations of the Self naively vulnerable to totalitarian seduction. Jung believed this was all the more dangerous as rational thinkers tended to underestimate unconscious influences, and this anxiety drove much of his argument with Freud.[240] In a telling observation from 1933, Heyer noted the tendency of contemporary Germans 'to sentimentalise about and thus to falsify all that is great and powerful.' In this way they underestimate the power and dangers of the unconscious just as they forget the terrible 'Wotan attributes' of God (1933, p139). Not only was this an interesting psychological observation, but it also showed a Jungian using the Wotan image before Jung's essay.

Many observers have noted the religious dimension of motives for war.[241] Jungian psychology claims to give a unique insight into this area. The suggestion is that when the numinous energies surrounding the configuration of the Self are not used for the individuation process, they inflate passions and contaminate politics with too much emotion. This emotionality and irrationality accelerates the slide into war. As Jung was to say after the War, if peace is to have any chance, it is vital that individuals understand this process and accept their responsibility to forge their own insight and not be swept up in dogmas and ideologies. This stress on the religious dimension may only be a small diagnostic theoretical contribution, but given the role religious issues play in the terrorism and war we see spilling over the world today, we ignore such insights at our peril!

How useful had this part of Jung's theory been? With much of his theory Jung wanted to focus on the religious dimension and Michael Burleigh, in his recent extensive study of the Reich, suggests that to understand much of what happened in Nazi Germany it is vital to be aware of the religious dimension of many political events. He observed that the Great War created the sort of emotional turmoil that Emile Durkheim had identified as being a pre-requisite for religious experience. The emotional chaos of defeat with the loss of order and hope led to a proliferation of pseudo-religious ideas that spread into politics. In Germany the life-and-death struggles of the war and street violence gave way to a heroic 'adolescent morbidity' made up of 'mass sentimentality, compounded of anger, fear, resentment and self-pity' (2000, p8). There was no place for the compassion, individualism and compromise that are all vital for a healthy democracy.

In eloquent prose that matches Jung's, Michael Burleigh gives his overview of the Nazi era but without any super-ordinary archetypal hypothesis. Evidently, eloquence is not incompatible with conventional history.

> Among committed believers, a mythic world of eternal spring, heroes, demons, fire and sword—in a word, the fantasy world of the nursery—displaced reality. Or rather invaded it, with crude images of Jews, Slavs, capitalists and kulaks populating the imagination. This was children's politics for grown-ups, bored and frustrated with the prosaic tenor of post-war liberal democracy, and hence receptive to heroic gestures and

politics as a form of theatrical stunt, even at the expense of their personal freedom... Europe's demagogues were archly aware of the manipulative techniques they needed to generate mass faith, knowing about the impact of masses, flags, song, symbols and colours. These men were artist-politicians. (2000, p8-9)

SUMMARY OF THE CHAPTER

Jung failed to establish his theory, partly because of the theoretical confusion in his hypothesis and partly because he was applying bad historical analysis to an area of history fraught with emotion and obscured by myth. In this he was caught by 'the irresistible strength of bad history', if one may borrow Christiansen's comment on the inextricable interpenetration of politics and history in the Baltic (1980, p4).

The chapter suggested that the neo-pagans in the Nazi movement derived many of their ideas from *Völkisch* and Romantic roots, and this cultural influence gave Jung the evidence he mistook as proof for his archetypal hypothesis. Indeed the pagan elements in Germany appear to be due to the neo-pagan readings of ideologues and charlatans, not the result of spontaneous eruptions from a collective unconscious. Furthermore, as the Nazis were divided in their attitude to neo-paganism and religion, it is hard to argue for the existence of an up-rush from the unconscious. However, due to the success of Hitler's exploitation of religious elements, Jung's insights into the misuse of religious psychology offer a useful avenue to explore that aspect of events.

Ironically, while in 'Wotan' there is inadequate evidence of the impact of an ancient collective unconscious on the Germans, there is much evidence of the influence of Romantic culture and German literature on Jung's writing-style and philosophical terms of reference. One could argue that Jung was caught by, or was trying to apply, what Hegel termed a 'mythic time-consciousness'[242] derived from nineteenth century *Naturphilosophie*. This may have been made more acute by his taste for vagueness and the seduction of his own role as a Wise Old Man who had spent so much of his career studying the stuff of myths.

While it is tragic that Jung's warning was not heeded, nevertheless for a historical understanding of his theories 'Wotan' is significant, because it represents Jung's rejection of his private hope that archetypal pressures would ultimately lead to positive changes. Furthermore, this post-war change in perspective led him to relegate his inter-war conception of the theories of the collective and in its place advocate a looser, more holistic idea of the inter-relation of consciousness with the *Unus Mundus*. The significance of this change of attitude has been missed by some of Jung's critics. This has happened partially because Jung tended to express his hope in private, and partially because his fears and the warning that 'Wotan' represented were obscured by the controversies and misunderstandings with 'the campaign'. (These are important stories, which must await other books!)

But if Jung failed to establish a viable case study for his hypothesis and to give a warning to the politicians of his day, his insights into the role and power of the religious dimension of the irrational are of vivid concern for us in the twenty-first century. The charismatic demagogue and the religious fanatic all draw on deep psychological roots and it is too easy to underestimate their tenacity or overestimate the utility of the reasonable approach when confronted with such driven political figures. As Jung warned:

> Humanity, huddling behind the walls of its culture, believes it has escaped this experience [of frenzy], until it succeeds in letting loose another orgy of bloodshed. All well-meaning people are amazed when this happens. (Jung, 1991 [1936], §118)

We ignore this at our peril.

9. Jung on Hitler: A Case Study for Archetypal or Typology Theory?

If Jung failed to establish that Wotan was a separate archetypal personality or provide adequate evidence for pagan activity, there was one other area where he sought to use archetypal theory and that was his interpretation of Hitler.[243]

In his pre-war writings Jung focused on the archetypal elements of psychology that affected Hitler and observed that, 'mystical experience as well as identification with an archetypal figure lend almost superhuman force to the ordinary man' (Jung, 1986 [1936a], §1333). Here he was offering an account of Hitler's astonishing success as a leader and Hitler's faculties of intuition and charisma, which, as was noted previously, are gifts that may be derived from archetypal processes in the psyche.

In his attempts to provide an archetypal description of Hitler, Jung made surprisingly little reference to the suggestion that Hitler was in the grip of the archetype of Wotan. Instead he mainly described Hitler using the image of the shaman or the Messiah. These images could just be taken as metaphors. However because of Jung's use of terminology and his confusion of archetype and archetypal form, the images must be discussed as part of his theories of the collective. They represent a twilight concept between defined archetypal forms and the use of poetic metaphor; and as such could be described as 'semi-archetypal' forms.

The two images have some common features, so it is not surprising that Jung's comments partially overlap; however he did seem to be suggesting two different aspects of Hitler. The image of the shaman drew attention to Hitler's intuitive gifts; how he used them and the way others noted their uncanny quality. The image of the Messiah addresses Hitler's sense of mission and how others perceived him.

The object here is to explore Jung's process of understanding and explanation of Hitler up to the end of the war[244] and compare this with Hitler's contemporaries who also found him an enigma.[245] For example, in 1945, after his capture, Speer attempted to understand the nature of the regime, but pessimistically confessed, 'It is impossible for me to obtain a clear picture of his character, his methods and his views... his personality, to me at least, is a puzzle full of contradictions and opposites... there are contradictory answers to a great many questions. They all depend on what particular period, or what particular mood is under discussion' (Overy, 2001, p237). In his autobiography the head of the SS foreign intelligence service, Walter Schellenberg, echoed Speer's despair at the possibility of reaching an understanding of Hitler's personality (1969, p54). The idea of Hitler's changing personality was also taken up by Baldur von Shirach, the Reich Youth Leader, who thought that in retrospect Hitler could be divided into three periods: 1920 to 1934 was his 'human' period; 1935-1938 his 'superhuman' period; and 1938 to 1945 as his 'inhuman' period, which von Shirach attributed to mental illness (Overy, 2001, p108).[246] Given all these variables one has to assess whether Jung's archetypal hypothesis adds anything to the understanding of the enigma of Hitler's psyche.

Hitler's Shamanic Trances

According to Joseph Campbell , a highly respected scholar of world religions, the key feature of the Shamanic process is the state of trance through which the shaman communes with other 'worlds' (1982a, p242). Jung contrasted the energised charismatic stature of Hitler as an orator with his insignificance on other occasions. He wrote of Hitler 'as an ordinary person [who] is a shy and friendly man with artistic tastes and gifts. As a mere man he is inoffensive and modest, and has nice eyes.' Jung then contrasted this side of Hitler's personality with his inflated state as a demagogue so that, 'When the State-spirit speaks through him, he sends forth a voice of thunder and his word is so powerful that it sweeps together crowds of millions like fallen autumn leaves' (Jung, 1986 [1936a], §1326).

In the Knickerbocker interview, which took place in October 1938 just after the demise of Czechoslovakia,[247] Jung gave his most detailed pre-war assessment of Hitler. He stated, 'With Hitler, you are scared. You know you would never be able to talk to that man: *because there is nobody there*' (McGuire and Hull, 1980, p134, my italics). This he elaborated in an interview with Howard Philp in May 1939. He described Hitler as 'simply what the Germans have made him... It is the key to understanding him and also the Germans themselves. *He is like a mask, but there is nothing behind that mask*' (McGuire and Hull, 1980, p142, my italics).

These statements are matched by Kirsch's account of Jung who, after seeing Hitler, described him as looking like 'a *Popanz*—something like a "mere dummy"'. It was a great puzzle to Jung how this kind of a fool and psychopath could become the leader of the German people and could exert such a magical effect on the German nation—just such an effect as only a medicine man exerts on a primitive society' (1982, p70).

In 1934, Rauschning wrote in similar terms:

> For all those who have been unsuccessful in the battle of life National Socialism is the great worker of magic. And Hitler himself is the first of these; thus he has become the master-enchanter and the high priest of the religious mysteries of Nazidom. Hitler's henchmen make more and more play with this quality of his of supreme magician, a quality supposed to out-distance those of a great statesman. And amid the ecstasy of his speeches, or in his solitary walks in the mountains, he feels that he does possess this quality. But in the many vacant hours of lethargy he feels humiliated and weak. (1939, p 219)

Perhaps Jung's impression was valid, and if he had had the luxury of a more detailed biography of Hitler, he might have been able to provide more detail. Nonetheless, in his description one can distinguish a number of themes. There was the 'ordinary' Hitler who lacked emotional depth and whose only significant emotional attachment to anyone after his mother's death were his two dogs, Foxl in World War One and Blondi in World War Two (Kershaw, 1998, p93; Fest, 2001, p340), and arguably Albert Speer.[248] There was also the 'artistic' Hitler who was entranced with his architectural creations and would use this passion to retreat back to the self-contained security of his adolescence when he had hoped to be a painter (Sereny, 1995). This artistic aspect of Hitler's personality even affected his leadership style and, according to Speer, led him to shun systematic work patterns (Overy, 2001, p227, p232).

Another aspect of Hitler's poor level of emotional engagement was his refusal to be exposed to the violent results of his policies. This squeamishness worked in different ways. In part, the care he took to leave no 'paper trail' to connect him with the crimes he verbally authorized was a deliberate policy to protect his image, but he was equally unwilling to confront the suffering he had brought on the German army and people and look at troop trains of wounded or visit the bombed cities. As Lukacs observed, 'Within Hitler's person we may recognize an element of weakness in a man who otherwise could not be described as a coward; or, at best, a sensitive (and, in a way, feminine) element in the character of a man whose brutal ideas and brutal expressions were the very opposite of sensitive' (1997, p194).

In the Knickerbocker interview Jung also described Hitler as a 'truly mystic medicine man' with the 'dreamy eyes... of a seer'. Hitler claimed to be acting under the command of a voice, which Jung described as a man acting under a 'compulsion' (McGuire and Hull, 1980, p123-125, 137). Here one can acknowledge Jung's powers of observation. Others also noted Hitler's effect and used the shaman analogy. The perspective of Hitler as being dependent on others for emotional weight was echoed by Konrad Heiden, a journalist who closely studied Hitler for ten years before fleeing Germany in 1933. Burleigh writes of how Heiden observed that when Hitler was deprived of an audience, he seemed to be 'a windless flag hanging slackly on a pole, a human "nullity" waiting once more for the next occasion to seem a somebody' (2000, p101)[249]. As Schamm, another biographer of Hitler who had actually met him, observed, 'The man's head seemed to dominate his entire body; torso, arms, legs—all seemed to hang down from it' (Lukacs, 1997, p69).[250]

Heiden gave a vivid picture of Hitler and made many observations that matched Jung's. He referred to 'redemption' and the 'mightier logic of the subconscious' while describing Hitler as 'a pure fragment of the modern mass soul, unclouded by any personal qualities' and 'the greatest mass orator of the mass age' (2000, p101).

Others also made the shamanic comparison. Lindholm notes Rauschning's reference to Hitler when he wrote, 'the parallel with the Roman Emperors is entirely misleading. It is the shaman's drum that beats around Hitler' (1990, p201)[251]. Or to give another example, the *Widerstand*[252] poet Carl Zuckermayer wrote, 'Hitler was able to put people in a trance just like the medicine man of a savage tribe' (Jaffé, 1989, p93).[253]

To return to Jung's interview, what is interesting about his comments is that he went on to give an account of Hitler's power with a form of explanation that was subtly different from his archetypal model:

> Now, the secret of Hitler's power is not that Hitler has an unconscious more plentifully stored than yours or mine. Hitler's secret is twofold: first, that his unconscious has exceptional access to his consciousness, and second, that he allows himself to be moved by it. He is like a man who listens intently to a stream of suggestions in a whispered voice from a mysterious source and then *acts upon them*... Hitler listens and obeys. (McGuire and Hull, 1980, p127)

Here Jung focused on the unique character of Hitler's psychology as a man who attends to and acts on his unconscious. On this point Jung could have gone into more detail on Hitler's psychopathology, but unfortunately he did not develop this insight.

HITLER'S INSIGHTS INTO PEOPLE'S PSYCHOLOGY AND HIS SKILL AT MANIPULATION

During the war Jung suggested to Allen Dulles[254], the senior OSS American Intelligence officer in Switzerland, that the 'magical power' Hitler possessed was due to his appeal to the unconscious (Mauch, 1999, p110). This observation accords with the accounts of others, but it is rather superficial. Hitler had a great facility for reading people's emotions and judging whom he could influence. A more detailed picture is given by a contemporary, Otto Strasser, who wrote, 'Hitler responds to the vibration of the human heart with the delicacy of a seismograph, or perhaps of a wireless receiving set, enabling him, with a certainty with which no conscious gift could endow him, to act as a loudspeaker proclaiming the most secret desires, the least admissible instincts, the sufferings, and personal revolts of a whole nation' (Lindholm, 1993, p105[255]). However, Lukacs suggests that while Hitler had great insight into others' fears and what they were loathe to do, this facility would not tell him what they might do, and would not work if Hitler could not understand their personality or their fears (1997, p135). This was important because Hitler made great use of his intuition when he directed it at the 'recognition of cowardice and moral decay' (Redlich, 1998, p166), and became very skilled at manipulating those around him.[256] Hitler was uncharacteristically thorough in this aspect of his life and took great care of his public persona and was extremely protective of his photographic image as well as being very aware of the power of his hypnotic gaze, which he exploited (Lukacs, 1997, p69).

Speer also reflected on Hitler's ability to influence others. He identified Hitler's 'suggestive power of persuasion' and his intimidating use of his 'extraordinary' technical knowledge and memory for figures. These gifts were enhanced in the minds of his audience by 'the feelings of reverence for his historical magnitude with which most visitors approached him' and 'a very powerful general conviction of Hitler's greatness and mission' (Overy, 2001, p220).

In summary, one may say that the general description of Hitler as a shaman was not unique to Jung, and has even been used by the post-Freudian Erikson.[257] Jung identified a number of symptoms and stressed their uncanny impact, but did not give any deeper insight into the working of the symptoms or their cause.

Jung on Hitler as a Messiah

In the Knickerbocker interview, Jung briefly wrote about a German inferiority complex that was based on their missing the empire-building phase of European history and their defeat in World War One. He also suggested that these feelings would prompt their desire for a saviour, which proved Hitler's opportunity (McGuire and Hull, 1980, p130). In discussing Hitler as a messianic figure, Jung was alluding to how Hitler and others saw him, and indirectly Jung was also describing some of the features of Hitler's psyche. Strangely, in view of Jung's religious interests, he did not write much on Hitler's role as a messiah. This was maybe because H.G. Baynes dealt with the idea in some length in his book *Germany Possessed*, published in 1941, and Jung was aware of this, as at some point before November 1942 Mary Bancroft had read 'Wotan' and Baynes' book and had discussed it extensively with Jung (Bancroft, 1975, p121). After these discussions Jung may no longer have felt it necessary to develop the idea and in his writing after the war he reduced his references to the messianic aspect, and instead wrote extensively about the German inferiority complex.

Hitler's Decision-Making by Intuition and his Sense of Mission

Jung explained the way Hitler made his decisions: 'He is very much the character that is open to unconscious influences. I am told that Hitler locked himself in his room for three days and nights when his whole staff beseeched him not to leave the League of Nations. When he appeared again he said without any explanation, "Gentlemen, Germany must leave the League." This story sounds as if German politics were not made but revealed' (Jung, 1986 [1936a], §1333).

Jung's assessment is supported by a statement from Hitler who on the 14th March 1936 described how he operated in politics: 'I go with the certainty of a sleepwalker along the path laid out for me by Providence' (Kershaw, 1998, p526). Hitler also told Otto Wagener: 'I'm now and then aware that it is not *I* who is speaking, but that something speaks through me' (Lindholm, 1993, p105).²⁵⁸

One can ask two questions here. Firstly should Hitler's statement be treated as an honest indiscretion or may it reflect an element of bravura and a desire to cultivate an uncanny image? I would suggest that the frequency with which he referred to his divine mission suggests that he was genuine about this. Awesome self-belief was too central to his drive for him simply to construct stories cynically, however much he might then embellish!

This leads us on to the second question: if things were 'revealed' then what psychological process was taking place? The answer to this question is provided by Speer's recollections of the role intuition played in Hitler's life:

> He knew how to rationalize his intuitive decisions. I often had the impression that the rational basis was something he arrived at only after the intuitive decision had been made, in order to support it. When he tried to work out rationally and logically he was often incapable of coming to a final conclusion. He would try to evade rational arguments, however weighty. In his 'good days', he unquestionably had a 'nose' for coming events which was astonishing. He appeared to have an 'antenna'. (Overy, 2001, p235 p231)

From these accounts one can observe Hitler's dependency on unconscious intuition, the fear or inability to reflect on it, as well as the grandiosity that ascribes the intuition to a higher source. Hitler admitted the role intuition played for him but, looking deeper, Speer observed that Hitler's intuition required periods of peace to be formulated and 'it also needed a lot of self-assurance' to give him the energy and confidence to follow it. Hitler also needed sufficient leisure to accommodate his nocturnal lifestyle, for as Himmler's diary noted, Hitler got his best ideas between five and six in the morning (Padfield, 2001, p103). Just as he needed space, Speer also noted that adulation 'was his spiritual food, which even under circumstances involving difficult decisions, endowed him with a certain light-heartedness and lack of constraint.'

Speer felt that the pressure of the wartime workload and Hitler's increasing paranoia eroded his intuition's ability to function. As his intuition functioned less he became more dogmatic and megalomaniac. Speer eloquently described how overworked intuitives are deprived of their 'self-assurance' and are reduced to 'uncertainty and tortured indecision. They suddenly lose the inner meaning of their personality and no more arrive at their decisions through automatic functioning of their mind, but must, as it were, squeeze them out of their tortured brain. The instinct gives an early indication as to when a rest must be taken... [but] excessive willpower easily extinguishes this instinct. After that, it is difficult to diagnose one's own condition—as it is with over training in sport' (Overy, 2001, p230-231).

During his interrogation Speer was asked how much Hitler's perception of his destiny shaped his decisions. He replied:

> Out of innumerable isolated incidents, he [Hitler] had pieced together a firm conviction that his whole career, with its many unfavourable events and setbacks, was predestined by providence to take him to the goal which it had set him. In all difficult situations and decisions this belief of his served as a primary argument. The more his overworked condition caused him to lose his original gift of detaching himself in his thinking from the pressure of current events, and the more he was cornered by the course of events, the more emphasis he would place on this argument of his 'predestined fate'...
>
> If there was anything pathological in his ideas during the last few years, it was this unshakable faith in his lucky star. In my view, it must have been a case of auto-suggestion. (Overy, 2001, p235-236)

Just as Hitler felt inspired, he felt he had a mission to save Germany and believed fate was on his side. This was not cynical, as Lukacs observed: 'Many things—and witnesses—indicate that he not only wanted people to believe what he said, but that he himself believed everything that he said while he said it' (1997, p 190).[259]

HITLER'S POWER TO INSPIRE

Many witnesses record both Hitler's presence and his eloquence. Indeed, even in 1923, some of Hitler's followers had compared Hitler's life to Christ with his thirty years in obscurity and then unexpectedly three years of 'shining revelation' (Lukacs, 1997, p266).[260] A convert to Nazism declared, 'I felt as though he were addressing me personally. My heart grew light, something in my breast arose. I felt as if bit by bit something within me were being rebuilt' (Lindholm, 1993, p102-107).[261] While Kurt Ludecke, another follower of Hitler also described the effect of hearing him:

> Presently my critical faculty was swept away... I do not know how to describe the emotion that swept over me as I heard this man... the gospel he preached the sacred truth. He seemed another Luther. I forgot everything but the man. Then glancing around, I saw this magnetism was holding these thousands as one.
>
> Of course I was ripe for this experience. I was a man of thirty-two, weary of disgust and disillusionment, a wanderer seeking a course, a patriot without a channel for his patriotism, a yearner for the heroic without a hero. The intense will of the man, the passion of his sincerity seemed to flow from him into me. I experienced an exaltation that could be likened only to a religious experience.(Redlich, 1998, p52)[262]

Hans Frank described how at the 1938 Party Congress, 'above everything smiled the great magician Hitler, blessing, bewitching, touching their hearts' (Lukacs, 1997, p212). [263]

Subsequent historians have placed different interpretations on Hitler's power over others. Kershaw suggests that much of Hitler's power to convince stemmed from the brute force of his emotional self-conviction (1998, p243). Machtan argues that Hitler was able to be so charismatic because of his empathetic identification with Germany's fate. He argues that politics allowed Hitler to give vent to his pent-up emotions and accumulated prejudices through 'absolute self-identification with Germany's political destiny, which Hitler personified better than anyone else' (2001, p103). Hitler could empathize with all the defeats and humiliations experienced in his adopted fatherland since the defeat of 1918. All these traumas echoed his own chaotic life and allowed him to identify his fate with that of his sacred Germany. This unity of identity gave him a conviction and rawness of emotion that could not fail to move others. The scale of this emotion accelerated Hitler's grandiose ideas as Hitler and Germany became one. This was the psychological door through which his delusion of grandeur, or archetypal possession entered, and Hess reinforced this self-image during their internment in Landsberg prison (2001, p147).

From 1934 Rauschning begun to be seriously concerned about the effects of Hitler's intuition (1939, p213) and the successful occupation and re-militarisation of the Rhineland greatly enhanced his messianic sense of infallibility and pseudo-religious symbolism began to feature more in his speeches. With all his successful diplomatic gambles he became lost in euphoria and his own hero cult (Kershaw, 1998, p591), and to this was added a growing addiction to power and the exhilaration of destruction.

Hitler's Symptom of Megalomania

A consequence of this sense of mission was Hitler's grandiose megalomania and a lack of compassion. Jung sometimes described him as a 'more or less ordinary' human being with a 'superhuman courage or recklessness' (Jung, 1986 [1936a], §1333). This description is echoed by Rauschning in the early thirties who observed: 'What [Hitler] wants is to sit on the hill-top and pretend he is God' (1939, p155). Another observer, the founder of Germany's Panzer divisions, General Guderian, observed that Hitler 'had a special picture of the world which actually was a picture of another world. As he believed, so must the world be' (Overy, 2001 p106).

The contrast of Hitler's psychological states and appearance may also be reflected in von Shirach's description of the three stages of Hitler's psychology, with the combination of intuitive intoxication, early success and fear of imminent death driving him to an increasingly demonic stance. Thus, by the end, according to Speer: 'He deliberately attempted to let the people perish with himself... a man to whom the end of his own life meant the end of everything' (Overy, 2001, p256-7). Summing up Hitler's mental state, Speer argued that a combination of 'mental isolation' and acute over-work had eroded his intuitive skills so that 'he increasingly resorted instead to his abnormal faith in his lucky destiny, which was based on self-persuasion, relying on it as on an incontrovertible argument... The result of this was the extraordinary condition of the petrification and hardening of his character and his mind, his shutting himself off from all problems, his severity, injustice and obstinacy' (Overy, 2001, p236-237).

CRITIQUE OF JUNG'S ASSESSMENT OF HITLER

When one compares Jung's assessment of Hitler with some of the other contemporary observers, Jung did not display a higher level of insight or originality. For example, Rauschning had also written about Hitler's occult ideas and had noted how many of Hitler's themes had their roots in recent Germanic literature at the beginning of the century.

> At that time there existed a sort of hysterical romanticism in Germany and Austria. It flourished especially in Vienna and Munich. It is not the first time that the sick fancies of a whole fevered nation have found concrete shape in figures that have worked havoc for centuries thereafter. Whole peoples have broken suddenly into an inexplicable restlessness... A nation has become sick in mind; the circumstances may be investigated, but the root cause remains undiscoverable. National Socialism is the Saint Vitus's dance of the twentieth century. (1939, p249)

His observation about the origins of Hitler's ideas may seem obvious, but the point for our discussion is that if Rauschning could be aware of this in the early thirties it reflects poorly on Jung that he did not account for that possibility. Put bluntly, this astute historical observation rather undermines Jung's speculations about a historic collective unconscious as it identifies the possible origins of his mythic material in contemporary sources.

Rauschning's observations become even more damaging to Jung's hypothesis when linked to his statements on the origins of

Hitler's ideas. It was important for Hitler's image that he should appear to be original and unique. It was also important for Jung's archetypal explanation that Hitler should demonstrate originality if he was a product of the spontaneous unconscious, but in the pre-war years Rauschning noted that Hitler loved to expound to an uncritical captive audience: 'Like other self-taught men, he was unaware that the ideas that seemed to him to be mysterious inspirations were the product of the general intellectual outlook of today, of which he was constantly absorbing the germs'. He was unaware how many of his ideas derived from Nietzsche. The only predecessor Hitler was willing to acknowledge was Wagner. By noting these influences Rauschning was effectively referring to a cultural collective consciousness feeding Hitler's ideas, images and emotions, of which he was only partially aware (1939, p220, 226, 223).

Another aspect of Hitler's character that was stressed by Jung and Speer was the dictator's uncanny abilities in certain areas. They both argued that to understand Hitler one had to account for that extra dimension. In this, Jung's ideas in 'Wotan' are echoed in Speer's summary of Hitler where he speculated whether the dictator was just the product of recent history, but he concluded:

> His whole demonic figure, however, can never be explained as just a product of those events... He was one of those inexplicable historic phenomena of nature which emerge in mankind at rare intervals... He alone placed it and kept it on a path which now has found its end in a gloomy future. The nation was spellbound by him as a people had rarely been before in history. (Overy, 2001, p257)

But if both men covered similar ground, Speer provided the far more detailed psychological analysis. Even if one conceded his advantage of first-hand material, given Jung's access to sources like Givesius, it is remarkable that his analysis was so thin. Maybe this lack of depth was a consequence of Jung's rising anxiety about events. Or had Jung wearied of the topic? In any event, Jung's failure to devote attention to the role that intuition played in Hitler's psyche is surprising. Indeed it is perhaps regrettable that Jung did not confine his analysis to using his typology and define Hitler as an intuitive who used that function with great skill and force. That theoretical model gives a much better account of the psychological processes involved than a semi-archetypal label like 'shaman'. This diagnosis of Hitler could then be expanded as a psychopathic introverted intuitive with a crippled feeling function and *the devil of a shadow*! For this assessment one does not need an archetypal hypothesis or a collective unconscious.

By way of comparative material one might consider Jung's portrait of Hitler alongside that of his Freudian contemporary, Walter Langer, who was commissioned by the OSS during the war to make a psychoanalytic profile. Langer too quoted the Strasser speech[264], but interpreted Hitler's attitude along Freudian lines:

> In regarding his audience as fundamentally feminine in character, his appeal is directed at a repressed part of their personalities. In many of the German men there seems to be a strong feminine-masochistic tendency that is usually covered over by more 'virile' characteristics but which finds partial gratification in submissive behaviour, discipline, sacrifice, and so forth... [or] they try to compensate for it by going to the other extreme of courage, pugnaciousness, and determination. Most Germans are unaware of this hidden part of their personalities and would deny its existence vehemently if such an insinuation is made. Hitler, however, appeals to it directly, and he is in an excellent position to know what goes on in that region because in him this side of his personality was not only conscious but dominant throughout his earlier life.

Langer suggested these characteristics were more intense in Hitler:

> In addressing an audience in this way he need only dwell on the longings, ambitions hopes, and desires of his earlier life in order to awaken these hidden tendencies in his listeners. This he does with inordinate

> skill. In this way he is able to arouse the same attitudes and emotions in his listeners that he himself experienced earlier in life and is able to redirect them into the channels that he has found useful. Thus he is able to win them to his new view of life, which sets a premium on brutality, ruthlessness, dominance, and determination and which frowns upon all the established human qualities. (1972, p208-9)

Langer was focusing on Hitler's childhood, which Jung neglected, but in his discussion of 'virile' characteristics he complimented Jung's *Puer Aeternus* writings. Langer, like Speer, also gave a more detailed explanation than Jung of Hitler's 'ability to play upon the unconscious tendencies of the German people and to act as their spokesman that has enabled him to mobilize their energies and direct them.' But he added an important insight that Hitler was unconsciously pursuing solutions to his own psyche just as the German people were 'unconsciously fighting for what appears to them to be their own psychological integrity' (1972, p209).[265] This description amounted to a collective unconscious, or more accurately the unconscious of millions of individuals acting in unity.[266]

As a final reflection on Jung's style, it is noteworthy that one also finds references to Germanic mythic elements by those involved in Nazi Germany and by those commenting on it from afar or in hindsight.[267] These references can be attributed to the common Germanic culture of those involved, and this common language underlies how easy it is to mistake a common culture for evidence of a long-term historical collective unconscious. But this is not to devalue the utility of some of Jung's observations. Indeed, John Lukacs, a highly respected contemporary historian, repeatedly uses the image of sorcerer to describe Hitler (1997, p81, 88), and argues that there is a place for retaining the 'daemonisation' of Hitler and comparing him to the Antichrist. He even quotes a comment from Jung about Hitler's power being 'magic' (1997, p266).

The Past and Future of Jung's Theory in War and Peace

What conclusions can one draw about Jung's contribution to an understanding of International Politics and more specifically Nazi

Germany? So far we have seen how Jung demonstrated a high degree of political realism and was unusually well-informed about some events in Germany.[268] When we looked at Jung's theories of the collective we found that while they contained some useful theoretical insights and observations the overall theoretical package was flawed.

The third phase considered how successful 'Wotan' was as Jung's test case for his theories of the collective and their applicability to wider political issues. In the essay Jung failed to provide adequate proof for his theories of the collective due to its lack of theoretical clarity and evidence. Equally regrettably, his use of the archetype of the *Puer Aeternus* to explain Germany could have been developed much further. In comparison with his contemporaries, Jung's analysis of Hitler was not impressive. He made some useful observations, but others made similar statements and often did so with more detail.

Jung suggested that there was something different about Nazi Germany. There was some truth in this. Germany had the unique misfortune of being subject to Hitler's uncanny intuition and mesmerising effect. These skills were harder to anticipate and understand than the mere demagoguery displayed by Mussolini and Stalin. If contemporaries and subsequent historians agree that Hitler was different, what did Jung contribute to understanding this? If Wotan was unsustainable as an archetype, it is probably just as well that Jung made little direct effort to use Wotan to account for Hitler's character. But Jung could have made more of his other ideas. However, his references to the archetype of the shaman, Messiah / Wise Old Man and hero to explain Hitler were superficial. Unfortunately he did not use his insights into the intuitive function to explain some of Hitler's way of working and he also missed an opportunity to refer to Hitler's psychological complexes concerning power and destructiveness which surely would have been rich areas for a psychiatrist to explore.

Has Jungian theory so little to offer our understanding of political events? Jung's writing on Nazi Germany may seem like a catalogue of lost opportunities and a failure. But is this true? Taken as a whole, his work helps explain certain sorts of religious pathology when archetypes are distorted, and this perspective gives us a greater insight into how these religious archetypes can invade politics. Here Jung did offer something new to help our understanding of power-politics as his work helps us to understand the irrational and infectious possessions that led to grandiose ideas, destruction and war.

In a way this insight is fitting, because it was Jung's concern with religious collectivity that had first led him to explore the possibility of archetypes affecting international politics in Europe in the thirties. One cannot afford to ignore even this reduced intellectual harvest: what happened in the heart of European civilisation needs to be accounted for. As Goodrick-Clarke argues, it is vital to understand what happened as 'the Nazi fantasies offer important materials for a study of apocalyptic hysteria in the leadership of a modern state. With the growth of religious nationalism in the late twentieth century, an understanding of the pre-conditions for such apocalyptic remains a crucial factor in the maintenance of global security' (1992, p203-204).

There is one further benefit that can be drawn from Jung's work as psycho-analytic studies provide a good foundation for understanding complicated historical events. This asset needs to be stressed as professional historians like Lukacs have been highly critical of the psycho-analyst's and psycho-historian's weakness with empirical evidence (1997, p25). As Kershaw observed in his nearly two-thousand-page biography of Hitler, for the psycho-historians wanting material on Hitler's childhood 'the fact has to be faced that there is little to go on which is not retrospective guesswork' (1998, p11). But reading the summaries of numerous historians' interpretations of Hitler and Germany, one is confronted by a bewildering array of different, relatively narrow accounts. This is because the historians are in the business of tracking down enough references to build a definite line of argument to such questions as: *Was Hitler was rational or irrational?* Or: *Was the Holocaust a preplanned policy or did it evolve out of confusion and institutional pressures?* In contrast to such mono-causal explanations, a reader from a psycho-analytic background may be more used to ambiguity and be aware of the ways individuals can, through denial or fluctuations in emotional consciousness, exhibit a mass of contradictory wishes, fears and plans. A political leader may not have just one policy, but a changing agenda of policies, or a hierarchy of policies. Furthermore, these policies may be pursued despite the politician's fluctuating semi-conscious awareness of their own contradictions! Given all these possibilities, it is an aid to the historian to be as aware as possible of the impact of unconscious emotions.

Despite the flaws in Jung's theory it is appropriate to end with a summary of Jung's contributions to understanding international politics and war that will continue to be of use to understanding future conflicts.

1. Jungian psychology offers a way to explore the origin and effects of distorted religious emotions in politics.
2. Some of Jung's archetypal theory seems to identify unconscious features that accelerate certain emotional patterns occurring in international politics in war and peace (see chapter seven).
3. The psycho-analytic disciplines provide a strong observational basis to understanding the ambiguities and contradictions of emotions and motives.

10. Post-Jungian Archetypal Theory and International Politics

> But the mythological figures are also in themselves concoctions of the creative phantasy and still await their translation into a conceptual language, of which only the arduous beginnings exist. (Jung, 1979 [1922], §127)[269]

In the final chapter we will look to the future of Jungian theory and consider how some of Jung's observations and hypotheses could be reformulated using post-Jungian ideas to propose a revised theory of the collective. Once this is done, the resulting theoretical innovation will be illustrated with a few examples concerning the causes of war and some comparative re-examinations of events in Hitler's Germany.

When Jung explored individual psychology he suggested that thoughts, as well as the basic forms of language, were constructed on archetypal 'images and motifs that lead straight back to the primitive wonder-world' (Jung, 1969 [1934/1954], §67), but his archetypal theory was not sufficiently developed and was too fractured. Jung confused instinct, cultural commonalities, archetypal personalities and common symbols and so was unable to provide a clear understanding of themes that had different origins. Furthermore, his attempt to use the theory of the collective unconscious to explain race, politics, Nazi Germany and the descent into war with Wotan as an archetypal cause was poorly argued. War is too complex a phenomenon and too multi-causal to be explained in terms of archetypal reductionism.

But if Jung's collective theoretical model was deeply flawed, his observation about the way it sometimes appears that ideas or emotional moods create dynamics of their own in events, seems to have some utility. It can appear that ideas or emotional themes create in groups and cultures common unconscious mechanisms. There can be an uncanny way that 'the best laid plans of mice and men' go awry when a *deus ex machina* is against them. Ideas of fate are often believed and can be persuasive. In different cultures such ideas have been described in various ways from vague notions about the divine will to sophisticated political ideas of the Chinese 'mandate of heaven' (von Franz, 1994, p11). Fate even has its advocate in a modern university War Studies department where the philosopher Dr Barrie Paskins mused that there was an almost pagan way in which the ingredient of a successful general seemed to be luck (1988). Whatever the material reality, such impressions are what Jung would have referred to as 'psychic facts' and they need to be accounted for.

Whither, then, Jung's ideas about the collective unconscious? Instead of attempting to explain events using Jung's original interpretation of archetypes and the collective unconscious it might be fruitful to revise these ideas. To do this the chapter will set aside Jung's broadly applied theories of the collective and take as a starting-point the most basic components of Jung's observations on events. These observations can be summarised as follows:

- There are collective moods or ideas that sweep across groups or eras.
- The impression can be formed that behind events there is some extra-human autonomous and purposeful agent at work, in short a *deus ex machina*.

From these observations the objective is to develop a modified hypothesis using a post-Jungian critique of Jung's original hypothesis and recent theoretical innovation.

THE SECRET LIFE OF POLITICAL FORMS

The first idea to bring forward is Andrew Samuels' speculation on the possibility of there being 'political forms', that is political ideas or emotions that have an autonomous existence as the sort of political phenomena that Jung was attempting to account for. In proposing the term 'political forms' Samuels provides an added service because he gives a label to a package of observations and frees one from Jung's use of 'archetypes' with all its appropriate and inappropriate associations.

Samuels asks:

> Where do new political ideas come from? How are they carried within a culture? How do they acquire form and spread? The commonsense or obvious answers to these questions are that political ideas spread by word of mouth, by people's (subversive) reading of texts, by spawning organisations and so forth. But there might be something else that a psychological approach can flesh out—a political Zeitgeist, a political spirit of the time, a secret life of politics. (2001, p62-64)

He goes on to ponder the utility of the idea of political forms:

> The reference is to units of understanding and action within a society that combine the effects of ideology, narratives of emotional experience and eventual organisational structure. I see such forms as having a purpose or goal, and also as having a much less tangible, more hermeneutic function. We talk about such things all the time when we talk about what kind of organisation an institution or even a country is... What are we doing when we characterise organisations in this way? We are speaking a language of political forms. We have a gestaltic image of the political form: its appearance plus its character plus our evaluation of it, all held together at once. The idea is to add something psychological to a materialist version of the social...

Another feature of form is that the same elements can lead to different forms... Perhaps political forms involve psychological fields which influence their creation, existence and, above all, mutability. It is still rather a mystery how political forms come into being and change over time... But there might be a place for a kind of 'social vitalism' based on psychology. (2001, p64-66)

This is an extremely rich stream of thought and a number of aspects need to be extracted and amplified. In describing political forms as 'units of understanding and action' that blend ideology, emotion and organizational structure, one can use this multifaceted idea to explore even such vague emotional factors as dogmatism or emotional attraction. Samuels' suggestion that political forms develop an organisational structure is also a very creative observation because ideologies and the groups that are influenced by them *do* take on an organizational pattern or political momentum of their own. This corresponds to the Jungian description of the way archetypes have a *deus ex machina* influence in the unconscious; the numinous attraction of the archetypal idea can overwhelm a weak ego.

The strength of Samuels's idea is that it gives a much clearer way to comprehend what Jung sought to discuss. Samuels advocates a form of perception that tries to identify the component parts of the idea as well as the individual's relationship to the package of ideas. (*'A gestaltic image of the political form: its appearance plus its character plus our evaluation of it, all held together at once.'*) In this way he gives a higher degree of focus to a psycho-analytical understanding of social and historical events. This will be magnified later with Papadopoulos's concept of 'collective patterns of meaning'.

Thus far, Samuels' idea of political forms has both asked the question and, more importantly, set the pitch for a discussion of how depth psychologies might discuss political events. One finds oneself looking at the ephemeral half-formed state between conscious emotional values and philosophical ideas. This is a place where political forms may be too unformed and subtle to be easily examined by the rigour and logic of political philosophy. However it does not mean that they are not worth pursuing. These things are worth study as they have an impact coming from the unconscious hinterland of politics, the dream state of ideologies before they are formulated and acted out in the world of 'blood and iron'.[270]

If political forms help to define where one looks for parts of unconscious aspects of politics one must then question why these political forms appear to have a purpose or goal. Samuels speculates: 'Perhaps political forms involve psychological fields which influence their creation, existence and, above all, mutability... there might be a place for a kind of "social vitalism" based on psychology' (2001, p66). Thus he questions what is it that allows political forms their autonomy and their ability to proliferate.

One way to account for the impression of 'psychological fields', or the existence of some form of 'social vitalism' and their seeming autonomy is through Richard Dawkins' concept of *memes*. Dawkins, an Oxford geneticist, came to develop a theory of the cultural proliferation and transmission of ideas that he saw as sharing many evolutionary similarities with Neo-Darwinian insights into genetic evolution. Briefly put, he suggested that ideas, through a process of natural selection, become more successful by being more attractive because they fulfil a purpose and by being easier to copy, thus gaining an almost archetypal inevitability. They fit an environmental niche in much the same way that Konrad Lorenz noted various species independently developing parallel characteristics as they fit into comparable gaps in their respective eco-systems. These niches place specific adaptive strains on the organism so that is forced to evolve to fit this 'external' archetype (Cohen, 1975, p36).

In the context of meme theory and the evolution of ideas, one could suggest that some ideas, as part of man's response to the external world, have a near-evolutionary inevitability as they are socially or biologically 'immanent'. To take a crude example, in possibly all cultures fire will have some sort of special significance. This will be a universal realisation because fire is always dangerous and useful.

The attractiveness and the subsequent spreading of ideas may be enhanced by the human habit of imitation. Susan Blackmore suggests that the key to understanding human evolution is the ability of the species to imitate. With this skill one could replicate behaviour patterns at a faster rate than it takes to learn what the behaviour means, or copy how the pattern was discovered. She goes on to suggest that, as culture became more important, with its ability to nurture greater changes, a symbiotic relationship grew between genes and adaptive learning because there was a premium on genes that accelerated imitative ability (1999, p116). This process she calls 'memetic driving' where attractive ideas spread with increasing speed due to their being taken up and giving advantages to quick imitators.[271] The success of these imitators means that they flourish, thus spreading both the successful ideas and the genes of the successful imitators. Thus far, meme theory provides part of an answer as to how ideas are spread by their own success rather than just by conscious human volition. This gives a clue to their seeming independence.

A new twist in this memetic account of the independence and attractive transmission of ideas is supplied by Dawkins who observes: 'What we have not previously considered is that a cultural trait may have evolved in the way that it has, simply because it is advantageous to itself' (1989, p201). This gives even greater depth to the *deus ex-machina* effect. By definition successful memes are the most infectious ones. They do not have to be 'useful' or 'sensible', for successful dissemination puts a premium on 'attractive' ideas rather than 'useful' ideas because attractiveness guarantees rapid reproduction and reproduction is the key issue however irresponsible or pathological the idea is.[272] If this seems far-fetched one need only consider the problems society faces when trying to carry out policies that are useful but not attractive or cheap. This seeming profligacy is because ideas are spread very quickly, unlike adults or cultures that take years to create.

Having accepted the replicating autonomy of groups of ideas, one can use this explanation to account for the systemic aspect of the collective unconscious. It provides a way to understand how myths have a self-driving autonomy and political forms a life of their own. Thus it seems that memetic theory provides a better explanation for the phenomena of political forms in history that Jung had tried to account for by using intra-psychological archetypes and the collective unconscious. Furthermore, memetic theory gives a possible answer as to how political forms (that Jung took to be archetypes) are transmitted and inherited, without the need to lapse into Lamarckian ideas. Instead the spread of a meme can be explained by a combination of the success of 'attractive' ideas; the easy imitation of certain ideas; and the possibility that the idea may confer an evolutionary advantage. One can also note that all of these factors can operate unconsciously, and this too echoes a characteristic of the hypothetical collective unconscious.

Another aspect of the seeming autonomy of political forms is the way events and ideas cluster in a systemic fashion. This system constellates rules of its own which gives an illusion of an unconscious will, or gives the era the possibility of developing a character and being conceived of as a *Weltanschauung*. But where does this systemic aspect come from?

Jung did refer to such systemic processes but his speculations were too esoteric and the idea was not developed.[273] However he did suggest that, when it came to the generation of symbols, the systemic activity takes place through the 'matrix of the mythopoetic imagination'. Ideas on the system-building quality of the mind have been advanced by many, including Papadopoulos, who referred to the human capacity to create structures of meaning (1997, p7).[274] Blackmore notes that this systemic habit creates a momentum of its own as the reproductive and systemic strengths of groups of memetic ideas are enhanced by their forming into clusters which Speel called memeplexes (1999, p19).[275] Blackmore further suggests that a group of ideas may have a self-sustaining advantage as a combination of ideas can reinforce each other. Furthermore she suggests a general formula for certain forms of successful memeplexes:

> Take a highly emotional naturally-occurring human experience with no satisfactory explanation, provide a myth that appears to explain it, and include a powerful being or unseen force that cannot easily be tested. As optional extras include other functions such as social coercion (the Old Hag gets you when you do wrong), reduction of fear (you'll live forever in heav-

en), use the altruism trick (good people have this experience or believe this myth) or the truth trick (this explanation is The Truth).

Until recently, no one designed such memeplexes on purpose. They were designed by memetic selection. We may imagine that hundreds of thousands of myths and stories have been invented over the millennia and passed on by thousands and millions of people. The few that survived were the ones that had all the good tricks to aid their recall and propagation. Modern culture is the legacy of thousands of years of memetic evolution. (1999, p183)

Another contribution into the way ideas reinforce themselves is to use Polyani's idea of dynamo-objective coupling or moral inversion as was referred to in chapter seven. This hypothesis about memeplex propagation explains the spread and longevity of what Jung took to be universal, archetypal myths because Blackwell's formula of emotions is a common pattern that can be constellated and propagated in all cultures. This formula can be said to underlie many cultural memeplexes. Maybe it could be termed a 'master memeplex'—that is, a primary form of memeplex that accounts for culturally defining memeplexes that would include myths and today's political ideologies.[276]

If one now returns to Samuels' idea of political forms as 'units of understanding and action within a society that combine the effects of ideology, narratives of emotional experience and eventual organisational structure', one begins to see how they can be summarised as a memeplex, and with this perspective, one has a way to answer Samuels' question concerning how ideas seem to infect groups and be transmitted.

Another way to approach this area is through Renos Papadopoulos' theory of 'collective patterns of meaning'. He explains this idea through a systematic analysis of how archetypes interact.

> Archetypes... form interrelated structures... For example, the positive and negative anima interrelate with the positive and negative animus within the con-

text of close relationships. Moreover, these images also exist 'outside' the individuals and thus form what could be called a systemic network...*The notion of archetype posits a dynamic interaction between, on one hand, collective structuring principles (collective patterns of behaviour and their reciprocally related archetypal images) and, on the other hand, intra-psychic processes located within the individual in personal, family, group, and interpersonal, social contexts, i.e., the various dimensions of an individual psychosocial world.* (1996, p138, my italics)

In this passage Papadopoulos highlights how in a social situation there is an interaction between intra-psychic archetypal configurations in the individuals and the constellated social patterns. These intra-psychic and inter-psychic social patterns form a systemic interaction of which all the actors are more or less prisoners. These unconscious archetypal factors and unconscious socio-cultural factors also have an interaction that has its own dynamics ['collective structuring principles']. Such is the power of this collective structure that it is as if people find themselves in a social mini-system. An example of this would be the people in a family who may find themselves trapped in an 'archetypal destiny'. This 'destiny' is formed by 'the belief systems that the family hold, which connect with the particular constellation of archetypal images operating across time' (1996, p148).

To give more weight to the impact of memetic ideas one can note that Lacanian and post-modern theorists stress how a historically conditioned mind-set will travel the path that a social pattern sets. This observation not only brings awareness that an idea has an ancestry, but it observes that the memetic momentum of the idea propels it into the future.

The point to underline is that most of the psychological origins of systems can be understood to be located in the social realm, not in a genetically fixed unconscious. There is greater heuristic utility in taking Papadopoulos's interpretation that puts the archetypal and the social together and leaves open the implied second-order question of what lies at the roots of the social dimension.

Another virtue of the idea of the memeplex is that it provides a way to amplify the working of some of the external aspects of collective structures of meaning that are highlighted by systems theory. As a memeplex is a more complex social structure it provides a better indication of a *Zeitgeist* that spreads over time. While some may challenge such intangible ideas, others would suggest that such an exercise is perfectly permissible when considering political, religious or cultural periods (Burleigh, 2000, p11).[277] Hall provides an example of the interaction of different levels of the personal, the archetypal and the social. He notes how collective guilt that is imposed on a social group has an affect that is similar to the unearned guilt that a neurotic individual suffers. This guilt is especially pernicious as 'it also contains an innate tendency to engender reaction formation and so perpetuate a cycle of collective inflation and deflation over an extended period of time' (1987, p118). He suggests that a current example of this process in world politics is politically motivated terrorism that targets individuals who are held by the terrorist to represent their enemy groups.

Such long-term political problems are made even more intractable by processes of moral inversion. The neurotic individual rationalises his emotional position with spurious intellectual arguments or moralises his intellectual position with emotional arguments fronting as a moral position. The great danger of this is that: 'Shadow projections based on moral judgements continue to be acted out, but the moral basis of the action is denied.' Hall suggests that for this complex interaction of emotion and intellect to be unravelled society must have the maturity to reflect on, and if necessary dismantle, its collective systemic illusions (1987, p132).

In summary, the systemic explanation adds to an understanding of memetic political forms and gives a clearer explanation of political processes than Jung's more mystical 'archetypal' explanations. Thus, memetic political forms seem to give a better explanation of events which Jung was attempting to explaining with his theories of the collective.

At this point it is helpful to summarise how the idea of a memetic amalgam gives an account of many of the factors Jung took to build his theory. The memetic political forms provide:

- An account of the creation of collective social factors and common unconscious complexes and the inter-relationship between them.
- An account of how systemic relationships involve repeating patterns.
- An account of the *deus ex-machina* effect leading to the autonomy of psychic factors, their replication and their infectious qualities.

What needs to be stressed here is the implications of such 'collective structures'. What is important at the collective level is not just the influence of an archetype at the instinctual level, but also the possible interaction of a number of archetypes in a systemic interaction. Taking this collective feature deeper, it may be that the resulting feature is also an *archetypal situation*. This represents a meme or a memeplex that is 'grave and constant in the human condition'. To take as an example the social institution of marriage, this involves not only the intra-psychic relationships of the marriage partners but the social systemic network to which they are subject.

If, as Papadopoulos suggests, Jung did not fully identify the extent of the systematic element in 'intersectional systemic structuring principles' (1996, p196), then the use of memeplexes and master memeplexes allows one to explain political forms and collective structures of meaning. This gives one a heuristic tool to describe the historical and political events Jung tried to understand.

The use of memetic political forms allows a dual-track geological model to be built featuring a binary model of the unconscious. The 'classical' Jungian half of this revised model of a common human unconscious features the various types of archetypes explained in chapter six. The 'post-Jungian' part of the model is of a socio-historical construction of master-memeplexes and memeplexes that goes to make long-term political forms and collective structures of meaning. This includes such long-term features as historical epochs, *Zeitgeists* and nation states. It also includes such pan-dimensional social forms as the international system and such complex multi-dimensional phenomena as War. In this way a model has been produced akin to Waltz's three-tier model.

Level of Political Operators	Conscious Psychological Activity		Unconscious Psychological Activity
The Level of Individual Actions		Conscious individual action.	In individuals, innate archetypes and biologically 'immanent' archetypes affect activities.
The Level of Sociological / Political Influences	The Cultural Unconscious is a product of society, but it affects social norms, social institutions, groups and individuals. This activity takes place at a conscious and an unconscious level.	'Conscious' life at a social level may be understood to be represented by 'rational' political and legal action.	Originating in the social setting, socially 'immanent' archetypes affect individuals.
The Level of the International System and its Political Influences	'Conscious' activity at an international level may be undertsood to be represented by 'rational' political and legal action.		'Unconscious' activity at an international level may be understood to be represented by the pressures of strategic political forms built into the international system that are only partially understood and controlled.

MEMETIC POLITICAL FORMS AND THEIR UTILITY IN EXPLAINING INTERNATIONAL POLITICS AND WAR

Having introduced memetic political forms one can first apply them to international politics and then move on to apply them to Jung's observations on the politics of the Third Reich.

The first writer to try to understand war using Dawkins' theory of memes was Barbara Ehrenreich. If one re-visits her argument one can see how it amplifies war as a political form with many archetypal features. Ehrenreich observed that war exists independently of society's economy, culture and system of gender relations. She explains: 'War is "contagious"... spreading readily from one culture to the next. And once the famous "cycle of violence" has begun, there is, of course, no stopping it; each injury demands the counter injury known as revenge. Thus war is, in some not yet entirely defined sense, a self-replicating pattern of behaviour; possessed of a dynamism not unlike that of living things' (1977, p232).

Developing this idea further she writes:

> If war can be thought of as a meme, clearly it is a meme like religion rather than like, for example, a popular tune... it would have to be conceived as a loose assemblage of algorithms or programs (in the computer sense) for action. When living in the vicinity of a tribe that possesses large numbers of spears, it is wise to make spears of one's own. When approached by a group of men brandishing spears, it is a good idea to muster up a spear-bearing group of one's own. When attacked, fight back, or run very fast. And so forth.
>
> Considered as a self-reproducing cultural entity or meme, war appears to be far more robust than any particular religion, perhaps more robust than religion in general... In the case of war, there is very little choice... your group can fight back—or prepare to face extinction. Given its tenacity and near universality, war is surely one of the 'fittest' of memes. (1977, p233-4)

One can see the dynamic autonomy of these memeplexes in three political or psychological factors operating in war-time: the competition for resources; the momentum of arms races; and the infecting quality of hate.

The competition for resources in war acting as a meme is illustrated with brutal clarity in primitive cultures where demographic pressure bring about a systemic pressure on 'primary' peoples to be moved to war, *regardless of their conscious hopes*. An example of this homeostatic model to explain primitive warfare was given by Stevens who cited Andrew Vayda (2000, p135).[278] Vayda suggested that some primitive tribes can become victims of what we would refer to as a homeostatic form of memeplex. The tragedy of this situation is that they are unlikely to have any understanding of the homeostatic economic imperatives of which they are prisoners and that drive them to war.

Even when the political actors are more sophisticated they can still become captives of the systemic momentum of a memeplex. Dawkins termed this situation as the 'Red Queen' effect, which he explains with the example of an arms race between two equally armed power-blocks. While both sides would benefit from not squandering their capital and technology on an arms race, once one has started to increase defence expenditure they are both prisoners of an arms race. Yet this race may see neither of them benefiting from winning, but spending their all just to maintain the unstable parity (1986, p184).

The third example of the pull of the emotive psychology of war comes from Papadopoulos's work with Bosnian refugees whom he describes as being frightened that they too may be swallowed by the collective fanatical nationalism. This attraction of nationalism he felt was especially dangerous following the work of the Russian historian and anthropologist Valery Tishkov[279]. According to Papadopoulos, Tishkov found that, in times of high uncertainty and transition, ethno-nationalistic hate had a number of functions and served to provide a therapy for the ills suffered under a previous regime as well as offering seeming short-cuts to solve highly complex problems in the present (1997, p22). Staub made similar connections about the desperation of a threatened ethnic identity in his work on the psychology of genocide (1989).

All these examples display the irrational, the collective, the *deus ex machina* effect and as a side-effect, the intoxication of hate and the inflation it brings.

The Third Reich

As a final exercise one turns to the Third Reich to apply the idea of memetic political forms. To do this we return to Burleigh's re-appraisal of the religious parallels in Nazi politics to appreciate the memetic trends in Nazi ideology. In looking at Nazi society Burleigh provides all the features that Jung alluded to but without recourse to Jung's crude Wotan hypothesis. Instead, Burleigh's description has an almost systemic and memetic form.

Burleigh lists many of the features of the Nazi program that attracted followers. The Nazis offered a cure for despair and hopelessness that went beyond specific policies such as full employment or re-arming the Rhineland. The Nazis' attraction included their claim to provide a revitalised meaning for life and an account of past problems that gave Germany's suffering a heroic sense and an external enemy. They also gave assurances of control and stability. They offered group security and dynamism. They claimed to have an intuitive understanding that saw beyond the confusion of the times and gave them unique answers consolidated by their faith in their dogma and their Messiah. Burleigh writes that while Hitler was cynical about religion, he saw in his mission to the German people: 'not simply applied biology, but the expression of eternal scientific laws, revealed by God and in turn invested with sacred properties. Science and nature were re-enchanted. Clarity was compatible with mystery, religion with science, and adolescent morbidity with vitalism... This was politics as a biological mission, but conceived in a religious way' (2000, p13).

Taking these ideas further he adds Saul Friedländer's observation that Hitler amalgamated biological ideas of 'degeneration and purification' with religious themes of 'perdition and redemption' and in pursuit of this goal Hitler could harness the trappings of Wagner's mythic Germanic revival just as he could demonise the Jews to provide him with figures of implacable evil. He concludes that however much it drew on genetics and pseudoscience or the anti-Semitic baggage of parts of Christianity, its totality was more than the sum of its parts; it was 'a creative synthesis' of all these elements (2000, p14).

Although Michael Burleigh's coverage of the religious and political forms the Nazis used has been very much abridged here, it is evident how far a conventional historian can account for what Jung observed without a Wotan hypothesis. Independently he acknowledges the mythic element in Nazi Germany when he writes how Germany 'was haunted by and suffused with apocalyptic imaginings and beliefs which were self-consciously pagan and primitive... Nazism had one foot in the dark irrationalist world of Teutonic myth, where heroic doom was regarded positively, and where the stakes were all or nothing—national and racial redemption or perdition' (2000, p12).

Burleigh, and some of Jung's contemporaries, explained much of the Nazi phenomenon with lists of psychological factors that were all historically derived memes that can be accounted for without reverting to an archetypal explanation. Burleigh's contribution is to take a perspective akin to that of religious phenomenology and identify the range of political forms. Some of these were 'conventional' political forms but some are best described as religious memeplexes. Taken together these memetic political forms and religious memeplexes offer one an accessible phenomenological explanation of Germany's fate without the need to posit archetypal uprushes from the misty oak glades of ancient Germania. This is a useful service as the Nazi phenomenon continues to be a topic worthy of study, offering unrivalled opportunities to develop Jung's insights on the mutation of religious emotions. These are all skills we urgently need with the current rise of religious fundamentalism in war and politics.

Jung's ideas on unconscious irrational emotions, such as the perversion of the religious emotions leading to Messianic inflation and utopian ideologies or the shadow, are valuable tools to understand international politics and the causes of war. His attempts to account for events in terms of his theories of the collective were less successful, but his attempt to explain events opened a rich line of enquiry. In the study of conflict the idea of memetic political forms can provide a new way to understand part of the causes of war or many other political issues. This theory can give a way to look at the impact of ideas in politics and history, but it is for the scholar to choose the appropriate political form. This will remain an elusive task in the twilight world between depth psychology and political history.

Adieu to Wotan?

So where does this leave Jung's 'Wotan' essay? His suggestion that there was an archetype of Wotan at large in the German psyche was badly argued for two reasons. Firstly, Wotan was a poor fit as an archetype, and secondly Jung's limited evidence and his suggestion of scattered psychological traits as symptoms fails to provide a convincing picture of a racial unconscious which is a vital component for the existence of Wotan as a German archetype.

Yet if we want to discuss the neo-Pagan *zeitgeist* that Jung was trying to identify in 'Wotan', we can argue retrospectively that Jung misdiagnosed his subject and made a category error. What he thought was an archetype would be better described as a meme, and he made this mistake because Hitler's revolution displayed a number of memetic features that mimicked archetypes. The neo-Pagan package demonstrated a certain amount of addictive allure, and in this it demonstrated the attractive potential of the meme but it lacked the transformative potential of the archetype that is part of the developmental role that the true archetype must possess. Another difference between the meme and the archetype is that archetypes with their genetic component are part of the enduring heritage of humanity, whereas the Third Reich, for all its dreams of a thousand years, had a thankfully short but murderous 'shelf life', because it was a cultural entity and not a developmental genetic asset of humanity. Lastly, Hitler with his combination of intuition and divide-and-rule clothed in grandiose megalomania manifested the type of inhuman momentum that an archetypal regression also engenders. All these factors lured Jung into thinking Wotan was an archetype, but memes are a better model. Therefore, if we want to consider the application of Jungian psychology to the problem of war and Nazi Germany, it is better to drop the Wotan hypothesis and then disentangle the two trends Jung drew to our attention: the destructive fervour (the instinct of aggression) and the subverted religion of the Wise Old Man (archetype).

Archetypes for the Twenty-First Century?

I have suggested that if Jung's hypothesis of archetypes is to remain of value in a clinical context it must be used in a much tighter fashion and ultimately this may mean that the definition of archetypes becomes much smaller than the range of alternatives Jung posited. In other words, archetypes and instincts are probably a lot closer than Jung's early speculations allowed, and if the two are so clearly related, archetypes must have a genetic (universal) and a developmental aspect. Under this restricted understanding, archetypes can only explain so much and beyond a certain point they are a descriptive liability as one is trying to over-extend a core idea.

It follows from this that the use of the term archetype needs reformulating because a habit of confusion has grown around its use. Discussion of archetypes becomes more problematic due to the ingrained tradition of amplification using mythic material, where at most the myth may illustrate a stereotype of a historic culture's reception of part of an archetypal process. The myth is not the archetype. Unfortunately for many Jungians it is all too easy to mistake the cultural or mythical amplification for the archetype *per se*; and this is always going to be a problem as the more vague the psychic organ, the easier the confusion. If Jungian psychology is to escape from this forest of confusions, this challenge will have to be addressed.

Appendix A
The Question of Anti-Semitism in the *Zofingia* Lectures

I acknowledge Brockway's argument, *Young Carl Jung* (1996), concerning a statement by Jung in *The Zofingia Lectures*, but must beg to differ. The earliest piece of evidence for possible anti-Semitism in Jung comes in two statements in the second of five Zofingia student lectures Jung gave between 1896 and 1899. Jung was recounting the struggle of the vitalists, whom he supported, and the defeat of the 'noble Zollner' in 'his struggle against the Judaization of science and society' by 'the stubborn Wundt, the slippery Carl Ludwig, and the spiteful DuBois-Reymond'. In this struggle for vitalism, according to Jung: 'All [was] in vain—the Berlin Jew came out on top' (Jung, 1983 [1897], §108), and here, by 'the Jew' Jung meant DuBois-Reymond whom he wrongly believed to be Jewish (Brockway, 1996, p146).

Brockway regards this statement as straightforward evidence of anti-Semitism (and he might be correct that this represented Jung's view at the time), however his distress at this possibility leads him to assume that 'Jung, in his youth clearly identified the materialists as Jews, and spoke of a Jewish conspiracy as well as of the Jewish corruption of German society' (1996, p146). But this alarmist picture is not backed up by any further evidence in the lectures. To take his picture point by point, Jung only identified one person as a Jew, DuBois-Reymond, so he was not presenting a generic anti-Semitic perspective. He made no mention of a conspiracy, nor did he refer to any thing that might imply a Jewish corruption of German society. Against this it is perhaps relevant that DuBois-Reymond was a member of what has been called the 'school of Helmholtz' that advocated materialism and the core role of experimentation and scientific orthodoxy (Cocks, 1997, p7). There is here at least a link of a perception that Jews are materialists. One can also imagine why DuBois-Reymond drew the widely-read Jung's fire, as he had rejected all attempts to combine 'philosophical and metaphysical elements into the study of the brain as untenable by stating it was *'Ignoramus et ignoramibus*—we do not know and we shall never know' (Cocks, 1997, p9).

If the statement were indeed anti-Semitic, its lack of emphasis in the paper would suggest one was dealing with a very minor prejudice. In over a hundred pages this was the sole anti-Semitic reference, and it concerns only DuBois-Reymond. Evidently Jung did not like DuBois-Reymond, but of the six references to him, only paragraph 108 contains any references to his being Jewish. This suggests at the very least that the focus of Jung's antipathy was to DuBois-Reymond, not his presumed religion.

How much weight then is one to accord this early piece of juvenilia? Given that this was a student meeting in which one is looking at a very minor part of a speech on an entirely different issue, it seems both biographically and academically problematic to have much confidence in this as evidence of anti-Semitism in Jung's thought, or place any weight on this being a significant part of his ideas or prejudices. Brockway takes the statement to be both unequivocally anti-Semitic and part of an unassailable wider picture. This seems an over-reaction, as perhaps Brockway has also been influenced by the majority of second-generation Jungian writers who uncritically assume that Jung was anti-Semitic.

Appendix B
The Freudians and Collective Theory

Ironically, despite the bitter break between Freud and Jung, some of the closest kinship to Jung's theories of the collective can be found in independent parallels with some of Freud's ideas. Both Freud and Jung admired and freely quoted from Le Bon's *Psychologie des Foules* (1895) [280], and all three men were influenced by Lamarckian ideas about trans-generational ideas being inherited. Le Bon's ideas would provide a suitable theoretical basis for the early presentation of Freud's thoughts about repeated actions in archaic times being imprinted on the psyche. Freud occasionally mentioned these ponderings[281] and hinted at ideas of 'archaic remnants'[282] or 'the clichés we bear within us',[283] but he did not develop them to the extent that Jung did (1916-1917, p418; 1918, p418). Instead, this train of thought allowed Freud to develop ideas about the influence of the early 'dominant males' in the original hunting groups of mankind. In *Totem and Taboo* (1912-1913) he made uneasy use of the idea of the collective mind that would allow the persistence for millennia of a feeling of guilt, after the key event, or *Kairos*, with the murder of the 'primal father'. In his preface Freud acknowledged his debt to Jung's social psychology, but following his break with Jung he may have been deterred from following this line of argument.

However, an idea of a racial unconscious did resurface in Freud's last major work, *Moses and Monotheism* (1939 [1934-38]). Philip Rieff explains how Freud hypothesised that Moses had been murdered and that this created a defining shock or *Kairos*, that had a permanent effect on the Jews and, as such, created a Jewish psyche (1990, p53). In this way Freud again came close to hypothesising a racial unconscious stretching across generations, and was hinting at an idea akin to Jung's of an enduring national unconscious.

Totem and Taboo and those 'racial' parts of *Moses and Monotheism* in a way were exceptions in Freud's thinking. For the bulk of his later writing Freud distanced himself from the timeless unconscious memory of a primal murder, and was concerned with the past in terms of a span of two generations at any one time. He argued that mankind's experience was universal by virtue of common occurrence, rather than universal in the sense of Jung's idea of the collective in archetypal theory, which is genetically universal. In this way, for Freud, the Oedipus complex became paramount, because he stressed the consequences of early childhood experiences on adult psychology as a universal psychological experience.[284]

Following another line of thought, the possibility of a theory of a collective unconscious was also superseded by Freud's more developed theory of the life and death instincts (Allingham, 1987, p8). From a Freudian theoretical viewpoint this theoretical avenue undercut the necessity of a collective unconscious as it was set at such a fundamental level of the unconscious.

Given these theoretical trends, Freudian theories of the collective were never developed and subsequently the potential equivalents have been marginalized by the Freud-Jung split. For Freudian theory the key to socio-political events was to be found in the psychic state of the individual. The developmental outcome of the Oedipus complex would establish emotional patterns such as fear, submission, aggression and loyalty, and out of the individual's life experience and instinctive tensions would grow the emotional seeds of an infinite variety of external social events. The recognition of this inner dynamic was, for Freud, the realisation of a historical truth. Freud argued that if one were to come to understand an action, one must know its 'inner source' and the 'secret motives'[285] that drove it. For Freud, 'the secondary, outer-events and institutions were a distortion and disguise of the inner psychic states' (Rieff, 1990, p55-56). So from this perspective it was in the individual's psyche that one should account for the genesis of outer events, rather than locating the key to events in material conditions, as would a Marxist theorist.

APPENDIX C
JUNG'S PERSPECTIVE ON INTERNATIONAL POLITICS AFTER 1945

After the war Jung was pessimistic about the long-term prospects for peace and declared: 'Man's war-like instincts are ineradicable—therefore a state of perfect peace is unthinkable. Moreover, peace is uncanny because it breeds war' (Jung, 1991 [1946b], §456).

In 1945, Jung was quick to see the rapidly-forming confrontation of the Cold War alliances and the dangers that this would pose in the new nuclear age. He warned: 'already those huge continental blocs are taking shape which, from sheer love of peace and need of defence, are preparing future catastrophes. The greater the equalised masses, the more violent and calamitous their movement!' (Jung, 1986 [1945], §1367). On 31st October 1946 he wrote pessimistically about the improbability of any super-power co-operation: 'when one sees the struggle the great powers have in order to reach any kind of agreement on apparently the most reasonable measures for the well-being of the world at large, and how they fail because one or the other refuses to be talked to or cannot give way, this becomes even more impossible when certain moral questions are touched upon' (Jung, 1973 [1906-1950], p446).

James Kirsch relates how in 1947, at a dinner party, Jung was able to talk at length on political issues with Churchill, who did not respond to more mundane topics (Kirsch, 1982, p71). The following year Jung told Esther Harding it was necessary to support the Marshall Plan to keep the Russians out of Western Europe (McGuire and Hull, 1980, p177). He was also concerned in a letter on 2nd July, 1948, about how the West could negotiate with the Soviets (Jung, 1973 [1906-1950], p504). For readers today, after détente and arms negotiations, Jung's concerns seem pessimistic, but this was the Russia of Stalin, Molotov and Beria. Jung was right to ask in this letter, 'But what are you going to do with that mass mentality of the leaders, mostly downright criminals or lunatics (of the reasonable variety, particularly dangerous!)?' As Jung knew very well it was the 'violence and ruthlessness' of these leaders that had allowed them cynically to attack Poland, Finland and the three Baltic states before the war. How could the West face 'the Russian avalanche of 200 million slaves?' Jung bluntly questioned. '[H]ow will America proceed to embrace Russia without realising that the Kremlin is right below the threshold of her own consciousness?' This proved to be apt as it took a generation of negotiations on arms control for the Soviet teams to acquire the strategic finesse to allow the first breakthrough in negotiations when it came in the 'walk in the woods' which set the precedent that would lead to the SALT talks (Freedman, 1988).[286]

In September 1949 Jung again explained his psychological viewpoint on political events in a lengthy letter to Mrs D. Thompson, an American journalist who had worked as a reporter in Germany but was expelled in 1934 because of her anti-Nazi sentiments. As he had believed since 1916, Jung took it as unproblematic that 'a political situation is the manifestation of a parallel psychological problem in millions of individuals.' Jung then went on to set out a list of clashes between unconscious and conscious psychological pressures, which took the form of rivalry between highly evolved psychological and ethical positions and more primitive irrationally driven emotions and political actions. Interestingly he made a reference to 'the laws of the herd, suppression of individual responsibility and submission to the tribal chief (totalitarian ethics)' (Jung, 1973 [1906-1950], p535), which was akin to Freud's idea of the horde and the primal father (Freud, 1939, [1934-38]).

Jung related this clash between unconscious and conscious psychological pressures to twentieth century events. He cited as examples the demise of German democracy in the face of the Nazi regression and the horrors of post-civil war Stalin's Russia which swept away the embryonic democracy of the *Dumas* and the first revolution. 'In Russia, which has always been a barbarous country, the unconscious half of the conflict has reached the surface and has replaced civilised consciousness. That is what we fear might happen to ourselves too. We are afraid of this schizophrenia all the more since Germany has clearly demonstrated that even a civilised community can be seized by such a mental catastrophe as it were overnight' (Jung, 1973 [1906-1950], p535).

Jung then advised the West on how it needed to act on what it had come to understand. He suggested that the West was not immune to its own primitive unconscious tendencies which, as they are unconscious, could dangerously undermine domestic and foreign relations. He then moved on to look at Cold War relations and gave an explanation of the policy of containment.[287]

Jung suggested that the West should not pre-emptively attack Russia, but that the West should continue to pursue its policy of containment. This advice contrasted with his pre-war Knickerbocker interview (1938) where he had suggested that Hitler should be manoeuvred into attacking Russia (McGuire and Hull, 1980, p138). Thus far, Jung was arguing conventional *realpolitik*, but then he went on to explain that containment should be pursued because the Soviets were in a dangerously unsophisticated psychological state that must be contained and ultimately integrated. He suggested that by failing to recognise that the West's fear of Russia's primitiveness was a projection of her own shadow element, the West denied itself the possibility of working for its own individuation.

Here Jung was talking solely in psychological terms by suggesting that such an attack would be an exercise in attacking an aspect of another's personality—especially unpalatable because unconsciously it is reminiscent of rejected parts of one's own psyche. This suggestion was an extreme case of psychological reductionism of a complex strategic confrontation and an illegitimate shift from individual to mass psychology. It also mirrored Jung's pre-war optimistic self-deception about archetypal renewal for whole countries. In this case Jung was advocating a strategic piece of folly derived from his theories about character development. Thus, both before and after the war, his psychological perspectives influenced him into making questionable political assessments. Unlike Jung's pre-war theories of the collective, this does not need to be further discussed as Jung did not make much use of this idea.

Instead Jung moved on to discuss the question of rearmament. Here he advocated deterrence and containment, which was a radical contrast to his previous line of thinking. His argument followed a classical liberal 'realist' line by advocating a limited response to Soviet provocation. But he was well aware of the potential danger that Russia posed in this period: 'Russia is certainly on the warpath and it is only fear of those who are in the know that holds her back. Your country is already at war with Russia, [in the sense of a phoney war]. *There is no reason and no diplomacy that will effectively deal with Russia,* because there is an *elementary drive* in her (as was the case with Hitler!)' (Jung, 1973 [1906-1950], p536).

He also warned of the dangers of military advisors, which in this context seemed to refer to advisors as policy-makers rather than military training teams. Here he warned of too-confident Soviet Generals flushed with their recent conquest of Eastern Europe and the strength of Soviet conventional military strength at that time. Jung also looked forward to the question of the unification of Europe and its collective defence, which are still problems today.

In the nineteen fifties Jung still took an interest in world affairs and the moral problems they produced and was keenly aware of the threat to the democracies from Stalin's Russia. On 22nd March 1951 he argued strongly for West German rearmament, and was scathingly critical of the naivety and utopian disarmers who would destabilise Europe.

> The disarmament of Germany is... the dream of a profoundly warlike nation that consciously considers itself harmless and peace-loving. It must indeed be dreaming if one thinks one can live unarmed in an anarchic world where only guile and force count... it is time, highest time, to rearm and the more consciously he does so the better it will be for peace. The really dangerous ones are the harmless dreamers who don't know that they want to perish gloriously yet again

through their accursed playing the saviour... One can also be neutral when armed, without falling a victim to militarism. But unarmed neutrality seems to me, and probably to all non-Germans as well, the acme of failed instinct, to which I would add, from my intimate acquaintance with the German national character, German crankiness, which is something out of this world. (Jung, 1976 [1951-1961], p11)

This was Jung at his most eloquent and politically shrewd. One also notes that the letter is free of many of his own political theories. What he does stress, from a psychological angle, is the need to be conscious and that this is not compatible with moral naivety.

E.A. Bennet recalled discussing the Korean War and communism with Jung on 14th September 1950. Jung felt that communism and its stress on materialism had arisen because of the decline of the 'spiritual power of the Church' (1985, p26). Jung continued to be highly pessimistic about the possibility of peaceful co-existence with the Soviets, and Bennet recalled on 14th January 1952: 'He spoke of communists as people without ideals, with whom you could never make a treaty; the peace talks were all nonsense, to wear out the Americans. 'You can't make peace with termites, they just go on and on; that's how it is with the Russians and it's best to realise it. It is constant attrition, and there's no end to it' (1985, p34). On another occasion that year he pessimistically thought that: 'if the Russians come we shall have the "pile of wreckage" as both sides would presumably using atomic weapons' (McGuire and Hull, 1980, p217).

Unusually, running parallel to Jung's conventional Cold War understanding, was an apocalyptic interpretation of nuclear war. 'After the last World War we hoped for reason: we go on hoping. But already we are fascinated by the possibilities of atomic fission and promise ourselves a Golden Age—the surest guarantee that the abomination of desolation will grow to limitless dimensions... [Science is] working for good as well as for evil, but it depends upon man's free—i.e., conscious—decision whether the good also will be perverted into something satanic. Man's worst sin is unconsciousness' (Jung, 1969 [1945-48], §454-455). He returned to his worry about science in 1950: 'The dechristianisation of our world, the Luciferian development of science and technology, and the frightful material and moral destruction left behind by the second World War have been compared more than once with the eschatological events foretold in the New Testament' (Jung, 1974 [1951], §68).

Jung's longest commentary on the Cold War came in *The Undiscovered Self*. Jung pondered the East / West split and the consequences if the Soviets succeeded in conquering Western Europe. Interestingly he was also concerned about fellow travellers in the West undermining the West's solidarity and unity of purpose (Jung, 1991 [1957], §488-489). Maybe he recalled how France had been fatally flawed during the phoney war, and how much help the fifth column and collaborators had been to the Nazis.

In the post-Stalin era, some prospect of East / West relations became possible. Again, both sides were stock-piling nuclear weapons and Jung wrote with increasing fear of the unconscious dangers affecting politics in a nuclear world. These fears echoed his pre-Second World War fears about chemical weapons:

> It needs only an almost imperceptible disturbance of equilibrium in a few of our rulers' heads to plunge the world into blood, fire, and radioactivity. The technical means necessary for this are present on both sides. And certain conscious deliberations, uncontrolled by any inner opponent, can be put into effect all too easily, as we have seen already from the example of one 'Leader.' (Jung, 1991 [1957], §561)

> Rational argument can be conducted with some prospect of success only so long as the emotionality of a given situation does not exceed a certain critical degree. If the effective temperature rises above this level, the possibility of reason's having any effect ceases and its place is taken by slogans and chimerical wish fantasies. That is to say, a sort of collective possession results which rapidly develops into a psychic epidemic. (Jung, 1991 [1957], §489-490)

Jung made a number of astute observations about the Cold War. He recognised that in any ideological contest, the dictatorship would have immense advantages: 'It is useless to pillory the socialist dictatorship as utopian and to condemn its economic principles as unreasonable, because... the criticising West has only itself to talk to, its arguments being heard only on this side of the Iron Curtain.' He saw that the Soviets had a massive advantage in their control of a huge labour force and that the West could not afford to create a confrontation that would 'arouse latent Russian or Chinese nationalism and chauvinism by an attack which would have exactly the opposite effect to the one intended' (Jung, 1991 [1957], §517).

Having made these observations Jung considered the West's options and recommended a continuation of the policy of containment and waiting for the Soviet system to fall apart. He rejected confrontation because of their nationalism and increasingly strong armed forces as well as the threat from a fifth column in the West at a time when he did not see much prospect of dissidents surviving in recently Stalinist Russia. Jung was concerned that the West, for all its industrial strength, military technology and wealth, was not a suitable counter to the Soviet's ideological threat which ultimately was based on 'emotional forces and ideas engendered by the spirit of the times'. He felt that a better counter would be 'an equally potent faith of a different and non-materialistic kind, and that the religious attitude grounded upon it would be the only effective defence against the danger of psychic infection' (Jung, 1991 [1957], §520).[288]

His arguments had close parallels to the Catholic ideologues who contributed to the French army's counter insurgency strategy, *guerre revolutionaire*, in Algeria. They argued that there was a vital need to produce a competitive ideology to counter Marxist polemic in the West (Paret,1964; Trinquier, 1964; Menard 1967).

Jung remained pessimistic about the long-term prospects for peace. However, after World War Two his perspective had changed as he now argued that hope depended on institutions like democracy that could channel man's aggression into controllable spheres. 'True democracy is a highly psychological institution which takes account of human nature as it is and makes allowances for the necessity of conflict within its own national boundaries' (Jung, 1991 [1946b], §456).

He argued this process would be greatly enhanced if man could become aware of his own faults and work on them rather than always seeing the problem in other people. With less irrationality, fear and hostility, the conflicts that occurred would be more likely to be peacefully resolved or fought in a limited fashion. But, peace was unlikely in the long term given the inevitable psychological swings of mood and behaviour that made stability so hard to achieve. The best that could be hoped for, argued Jung, was that individuals, in resolving their own conflicts, would mature their society and help establish peace in the wider society.

Parallel to these concerns, in 1954 he returned to his 1935 concern that 'the great problem' had become over-population. In 1958 he even wondered if over-population was more of a problem than the atomic bomb. Indeed he wondered if atomic weapons might even remove some of the surplus population. This Benthamite reflection contrasted bizarrely with Jung's speculations about astrological ages (McGuire and Hull, 1980, p234, 348), and one wonders if they were a reflection of Jung's age and his increasing concerns with religion and the metaphysics of the next world to which *Memories Dreams Reflections* makes abridged reference.

As an old man he was prone to even darker and more obscure fears. In 1959 Dr Jacobi stated, 'Jung is very much afraid that a war or catastrophe will take place in 1964 because in that year, the world moves from one epoch into another. The coming of Christ coincided with the beginning of the present era, Pisces, which is now nearing its end' (Serrano, 1966, p65). One also sees other elements of his earlier thoughts occurring, for example on 14th September 1960 he spoke of the West in atheist times as vulnerable to seduction by the communist 'religion' and so 'very much in the same predicament' as the Germany of the twenties. He feared a repeat of a greater 'world-wide Wotanistic experiment. This means mental epidemics and war' (Jung, 1976 [1951-1961], p594).

This pessimism was also seen in 1960, when Jung raised a question about the psychological dimension of world leaders and ideological movements and asked: 'how many people are giving any serious consideration to problems such as these?' But then he sought to check himself, maybe remembering difficulties that his political forays had got him into in the thirties and concluded, 'But I must not talk too deeply about such matters or I shall be accused of trying to meddle in politics' (McGuire and Hull, 1980, p398).

Appendix D
Adolf Bastian and *Elementargedanken*

The German ethnologist, Adolf Bastian (1826-1905), reacted against the orthodox Environmental Determinists in Berlin. He drew on Waitz's work, which stressed the common innate heritage. He wrote of the 'psychic unity of mankind' and argued that, as all humans were similarly endowed, all cultures displayed the same basic mental principles, the *Elementargedanken*, even if local circumstances induced variations of custom and organisation called *Völksgedanken* (ethnic ideas). This distinction allowed Bastian to recognise the modifying influence of environment and diffusion (Kuper, 1988, p127-128).

According to Brockway, the idea of *Elementargedanken*, as Campbell noted, was obviously very close to Jung's idea of archetypes, but 'there is no evidence that Jung was aware of Bastian's thought during his formative years' (1996, p48). Ellenberger also comments on the parallels, but argues that Bastian's idea was more vague and lacked Jung's attempts to establish his ideas with experimental work (1970, p730). However, Bastian did attempt to substantiate his idea by cross-cultural studies. But Kuper explains (1988, p127) on the basis of these studies, according to Koepping, Bastian only felt able to identify three operational *Elementargedanken:* a 'very vague notion of "differentiation" based upon sexual complementarities, on age succession, and on the likelihood that neurotics will become prophets' (Koepping, 1983, p37).[289] Kuper notes that Koepping wrote that Bastian also considered the widespread use of projectile hunting weapons as a common desire to extend the range of one's limbs[290] (1988, p127). Bastian's reluctance to identify a vast range of universal symbols or *Elementargedanken* is surprisingly supported by a passage from von Franz, who also stressed the ambiguity of symbols. For many years, in her study of the world's fairy tales, she was intrigued by the possibility of there being common patterns and human themes, but they were not evident. Rather to her surprise she found common situations, where sometimes one response was right, and sometimes the opposite. The only general theme seemed to be that, in dreams, disaster would follow if the promptings of little animal helpers were ignored (1995, p144).

Appendix E
Key Dates For Jung During the Nazi Seizure of Power

1933

January 30th	Hitler seizes power.
January, 1934	Jung published *The State of Psychotherapy Today*, which presumably was written in 1933.
End of February	Civil liberties abolished.
End of March	Opponents flee. Reichstag surrenders control of legislature.
April 1st	Nazi boycott of Jewish shops and professionals.
April 7th	Jewish Government employees sacked.
April 22nd	Non-Aryan doctors lose right to work in health insurance.
May 10th	Books by Freud burned.
End of May	The trade unions dissolved.
June 21st	Jung was accepted as President of the GMSP[291] (General Medical Society for Psychotherapy)
June 26th	Jung gave the interview with Weizsäcker on Berlin radio.[292]
July 14th	Sterilisation law approved.

July 20th	Catholic Church signs *Concordat* to withdraw from politics.
End of July	All opposition parties dissolved.

1934

January 1934	Sovereignty of *Lander* dissolved.
End of March	First boycott of Jewish shops.
April	Aryan paragraph. Jews dismissed from civil service.
June	Most organisations 'coordinated'.
June 30th	'Night of Long Knives'
August	Death of President Hindenburg.

After the initial violence of 1933, in 1934 anti-Semitic measures and violence were restrained for foreign policy reasons. This decrease in violence led some Jews to believe the worst was over and the rate of Jewish emigration slowed. However once the Saar Plebiscite was out of the way in early 1935, restraint was no longer necessary and in April Hitler let it be known that he no longer required the limit on anti-Semitic propaganda (Kershaw, 1998, p559-560).

1   According to Shamdasani, the term *personal equation* found its way into analytical psychology when Jung borrowed it from astronomy where it referred to the accuracy and errors in each astronomer's calculations (2003, p30).
2   I will explore the issue of the Freudian 'campaign' in a forthcoming book about Jung, Freud, the Jews and Nazi Germany. I will return to Jung's attitude to the Jews in a discussion of his ideas on land and nationalism. See page 92, below.
3   Kant, I. (1990), *Kritik der reinen Vernunft*, Hamburg, p413-414.
4   Here Jung echoed ideas of Schopenhauer's *Die Welt als und Vorstellung*, Volume 1, (p56), which Jung had already quoted in 1898 in §229 of his Zofingia lectures
5   My thanks to Dr Shamdasani for clarifying this and offering the following observation: 'The passage in question comes from the revised edition of 1952. However, it is loosely translated. I would render it as: "The dangerous ones are not the great heretics and unbelievers but the much smaller thinkers, who can only rationalise and then suddenly discover how irrational all religious assertions are."' Personal communication. 13th August, 2007.
6   James Kirsch, who knew Jung, commented on Jung's loyalty to Switzerland: 'There never was a shift of his identification to this Swiss background. He always felt to be Swiss and acted as one. He identified his unconscious with the *Germanic* psyche, but never with the German psyche and its illness—the dissociation, the lack of a genuine feeling function in the German psyche' (1982, p76). To supplement this, a fuller understanding of the history of the German-Swiss's relationship to Germany is given by Pietikäinen. He explains that that the elite of the confederation had traditionally considered themselves German till the rise of Prussia and her centralised hegemony proved incompatible with Swiss individualism. Nonetheless, cultural ties and political identification with Germany continued to cause problems between the Germanic and Francophone elements in Switzerland during the Great War. He further observes: 'However, the Swiss federalist democracy was strong enough to endure this national rift, and in the inter-war years Switzerland was one of only a handful of European nations where fascism did not have any political significance' (2001, p110).
7   A rare usage by Jung of military tactics as a psychological analogy occurs in *Analytical Psychology and 'Weltanschauung*, (1928-1931b, §691).
8   *Unzeitgemasse Betrachtungen*, ('Untimely Reflections'), *Kroner Taschenausgabe*, Volume 7, p230.
9   While serving in the *Abwehr* (German Military Intelligence), Helmuth von Moltke observed on entering France on the 13th August 1940: 'French morale was simply non-existent. Aircraft did not take off when the Germans attacked, units deserted under the leadership of their officers, the troops in fortifications and tanks struck arms at the slightest hint of an attack... It is the subject that keeps recurring' (1991, p98). There he became connected with the resistance. The *Abwehr*'s leader,

Admiral Canaris, gave shelter to a number of the German resistance and his Chief of Staff, General Oster, masterminded the German resistance and plans for a *coup d'état*, until his arrest in 1943. All three men were executed after the failure of the Bomb Plot of 1944.

10   Footnote 1, p564, CW18: '[Unpublished typescript, written in English. While it apparently was intended for the New York press, no instance of its publication or quotation has been discovered. For an interview that Jung gave the *New York Times* (4th October 1936) upon leaving New York, see "The 2,000,000 Year Old Man", in *C. G. Jung Speaking*]'.

11   Donn, 1988, p98; Martin, 1991, p4; Stein, 1991, p90.

12   See Jung, 1963 [1961], p173.

13   The Knickerbocker interview was Jung's most detailed pre-war assessment of Hitler. Other material can be found in 'Psychology and National Problems' (1936). For his post-war explanations see (1945a) 'After the Catastrophe', CW10; and (1945c), 'Interview by Eugen Kolb, Geneva correspondent of *Mishmar* of Tel Aviv', CW18.

14   Cited from Kierkpatrick, I., 1964, *Mussolini*, p189, New York.

15   The original is to be found in *Inventano Beni ex Mussolini*, No. 970, in the Italian National Archive in Rome.

16   'Overall, though, Mussolini was a more rounded person than Hitler. He had a family and seemed to care for his five children. He loved sports, rode horses, drove cars, and—to Hitler's dismay—swam on public beaches and piloted airplanes. Quite different from the inhibited Hitler, Mussolini had one love affair after the other' (Redlich, 1998, p138).

17   Freud was aware of the achievements of Soviet Russia as it rebuilt itself after the Great War, and for a time shared the hopes of some about a Marxist prosperous and peaceful worker's paradise, an idea much in vogue at the time, but he saw no prospect of any advances in civilisation by the three totalitarian powers (Freud, 1939, [1934-38], p54).

18   Lady Astor was American-born, married Lord Astor, and became the first British woman Member of Parliament.

19   According to Kuper (1981, p168), Western estimates range from five to fifteen million Kulaks killed. But these estimates may be revised as more data becomes available to post-Cold War historians.

20   'The Fight with the Shadow' (1946) does not seem to be a post-holocaust rationalisation about his not speaking out more in the thirties for two reasons. Firstly, this assessment is a clearer partial repetition of a 1934 statement (McGuire and Hull, p87). Secondly Jung's position was politically pragmatic given his institutional position, as will be argued in chapter eight.

21   Jung prescribed to a nation as he would to a patient. This is dealt with in chapter four with the section on 'The Clinical Influence on Jung's Collective Theories' and in chapter three.

22   Cited from Jung, 1973 [1906-1950], p301

23   Jaffé, A. (1971), *From the Life and works of C.G. Jung*, p102-103, New York, Harper Colophon, cited in Cohen, 1975, p144.

24 Cited from Jung, 1976 [1951-1961], p503
25 From the fall of Napoleon to the outbreak of the Great War the peace in Europe had been more or less successfully contained by a system of diplomatic treaties that bound states into alliances to deter attack from other power blocks. This diplomatic system was called 'the balance of power'. Balance of power diplomacy was the traditional European policy of Britain in the nineteenth century as she tried to assemble treaty blocks of roughly equivalent military strength to prevent any party becoming so strong that they could launch a war without fear in an attempt to gain hegemony in Europe. The policy failed to preserve peace in 1914 due to its military and political inflexibility. The system's stability was vulnerable when one side feared that an enemy could become too strong and the weaker state would no longer be able to sustain the balance. The system became increasingly unstable once tensions increased and set off a chain-reaction of mobilisations and public hysteria that the diplomats could not contain.
26 It may be that the decisive episode at the end of the Cold War was the Soviets' inability to sustain the cost of the Afghanistan war and compete with Reagan's conventional and nuclear arms build up. Gaddis, J., 1999, *The United States and the End of the Cold War*, Oxford, Oxford University Press.
27 As verified by secret Nazi opinion poles carried out by the SD (*Sicherheitsdienst*: Security Service, the intelligence branch of the SS). For their opinion polls, the *Meldungen aus dem Reich*, see Kersten, 1956, p210, 212.
28 Leslie Hore Belisha (1893-1957), Secretary of State for War from 20th May, 1937, to 5th January, 1940, when he resigned.
29 See also Jung, (1991)[1946a], §459.
30 See also Jung, 1991 [1957], §576.
31 He reaffirmed this in the 1942 edition of *The Psychology of the Unconscious*, §11.
32 From *Collected papers on Analytical Psychology*, Jung, 1917, p416.
33 Half a century later psychologists and strategists were to ponder whether this type of strategy called MAD ['mutually assured destruction'] was as stable as American strategists like Herman Kahn argued.
34 From the *Visions Seminars* on 10th of May, 1933, and part of Jung's reply to Mrs. Baynes who asked Jung: 'Does it seem to you that the German revolution is an attempt to deal with these forces of the unconscious, or is it a regressive movement, a "sacrilegious backward grasp," as it appears to many on-lookers?'
35 For a brief summary of the evolution of Jung's thoughts on the collective unconscious and the archetypes see Noll, 1974, p269-272; Samuels, 1985, p24; Frey-Rohn, 1990, p90-92. The subject is dealt with in much more detail in Shamdasani, 2003.
36 Alschuler suggests that in *The Undiscovered Self* (1957) Jung argued that political mass movements were made up of numbers of individuals who suffered from a pathological split between the conscious and the

unconscious. This had come about through the need for consciousness to suppress the instincts and the irrational.

37 Jung's explanation here was not helped as he first puts the 'collective conscious' in contrast to the 'collective unconscious' and then labels both the collective conscious and the 'collective unconscious' as being in the 'collective unconscious'. In this paragraph he confusingly divided archetypes into two phenomenological categories: the instinctual and the archetypal: 'The first includes the natural impulses, the second the dominants that emerge into consciousness as universal ideas.' Jung's definition of archetypes is very varied and will be discussed in detail in chapter six. However, according to Nagy, this essay is considered by many to be the definitive statement on the unconscious, individuation and the archetypes (1991, p169).

38 '[T]he collective unconscious is always working upon you through trans-subjective facts which are probably inside as well as outside yourselves' (Jung, 1990 [1925], p131). 'Now, all that I have said here about the influence of society upon the individual is identically true of the influence of the collective unconscious upon the individual psyche' (Jung, 1934, *The Relations Between the Ego and the Unconscious*, CW 7, p.154, cited in Shelburne, 1988, p32).

39 Brockway gives another example, the eminent scientist Bernard Von Cotta, who stressed the influence of geological structure on national character in his 1853, *Blut und Boden* (1996, p42). An example from when Jung came to study medicine in Basel in 1895 was the medical school's Professor Zschokke instituted a course in comparative zoology. He taught about the 'geology of the person' and argued that the whole range of evolutionary change had left traces that were still identifiable within the human body, a theory that later taken up by Haeckel (Hayman, 1999, p30).

40 Noll argues that the German Romantic aspect of Jung's thought was missed by his Anglo-Saxon followers who lacked the contextual understanding of the Germanic cultural heritage (1974, p95, 99). In this case, Jung failed to make them aware of how he was using ideas from contemporary German scholarship (Jung, 1990 [1925], p.xviii). This was unlikely to be due to plagiarism as he was keen to quote studies of Boas. Perhaps a better way to understand the spirit of the seminars is not to confuse it with what would be good practice in a university seminar, but to recall the amateur nature of the seminars whose purpose was to explore ideas as they were relevant to Jungian analysis.

41 I am indebted to Molly Tuby for prompting me to look at the Seminar records for a reference to Miss Corrie.

42 For example, Jung, 1969 [1934/1954], §68.

43 *Psychoid*. A Jungian term to describe the indeterminate area where the body's physical, cognitive and emotional facets are not clearly distinguished. The term can also be used in the context of physics where 'mind and matter' become indistinguishable, as they are both patterns of energy.

44 Geographical Determinism is a position still held by many historians of differing national origins today. Toynbee, with his theory of challenge and response in his seven-volume *A Study of History* argued that the character of a civilisation is profoundly affected by geography and climate and cited as examples the impact of Greek geography propelling Hellenic nautical expansion and the rigors of the far North constraining the development of Eskimo culture (Brockway, 1996, p42-43).

45 *Völkisch* ideas remain hard to define. Professor Lukacs explains: 'The words "Volk" and "*völkisch*" are not identical with the English terms "folk" and "folkish"'. He quotes Bullock who, writing in the context of the Nazi period, says that Volk is: 'a difficult word to translate: it combines the idea of nationalism with those of race and anti-Semitism—to which we may add the populist idea and element' (Bullock, A. (1962), *Hitler: A Study in Tyranny*, London, p123). Lukacs adds: 'during the nineteenth century and well into the twentieth, "*Volk*" and "*völkisch*" in Germany (and Austria) were conservative terms—anti-international, anti-Marxist, anti-Jewish, anti-French, and "Christian." It might even be said that in many places in the nineteenth century "*völkisch*" could be patriotic as much as nationalistic... But after 1890 at the latest, in Austria as well as Germany, there came a change. The conservative (and occasionally patriotic) meaning and attraction of "*völkisch*" was beginning to dissipate, while, simultaneously, its radical and nationalist meaning began to grow' (1997, p107). For Mosse, *Völkisch* ideas were a collection of mystical ideas about the way a *Volk* should live in a symbolic and symbiotic relationship to a landscape and a cultural identity. These ideas implied agrarian nostalgia that stressed the spiritual virtues of farming (1964, p15).

46 Brockway argues that *Völkisch* ideas, if understood without their later political agenda, were 'a romantic doctrine of ethnicity based on the inheritance of national traits emergent from geographical and prehistoric origins'. He argues that Noll's definition of *Völkisch* ideas as a quasi-scientific doctrine made up of an ill-defined mental and emotional response to the subtle interrelation of physical geography, culture and the history is too wide (1996, p42). To reconcile this disagreement, I suggest that there might be a useful distinction to be made between Romantic polemical ideas about the influence and virtue of landscape and culture (*Völkisch* ideas) and those more academic theories about the impact of physical geography on the body and the mind (*Bodenbeschaffenheit*).

47 Another attack on Darwin came from Rudolf Virchow, the leading German anthropologist in Munich. Virchow repudiated the ideas of his ex-pupil Ernst Haeckel who had become Darwin's advocate in Germany. Like Waitz, Virchow argued that skull proportions were modified by either environment, or mental development (Kuper, 1988, p128-129; Blainey, 1988, p115). Haeckel was also influenced by *Völkisch* ideas (Brockway, 1996, p42), and by the Environmental Determinist idea that the range of evolutionary change had left traces that were still identifi-

able within the human body (Hayman, 1999, p30). He postulated a Biogenic Law and coined the much-used phrase 'ontogeny recapitulates phylogeny', which referred to the idea that the individual human embryo passes through all of the stages of evolution of the species before birth. This idea was influential on Jung throughout his career. Brockway takes up Noll's suggestion that Haeckel was highly influential as his Biogenic Law was the foundation of Jung's concept of the collective unconscious and it was from Haeckel that Jung acquired the concept of *Bodenbeschaffenheit* (Brockway, 1996, p133). As Jung explained: 'According to phylogenetic law, the psychic structure must, like the anatomical, show traces of the earlier stages of evolution it has passed through. This is in fact so in the case of the unconscious, for in dreams and mental disturbances psychic products come to the surface which show all the traits of primitive levels of development, not only in their form but also in their content and meaning, so that we might easily take them for fragments of esoteric doctrines. Mythological motifs frequently appear, but clothed in modern dress' (Jung, 1986 [1930]/1950, §152).

48   According to Blainey (1988, p115), Waitz's book, *Concerning the Unity of Mankind* (1859), was very influential (1988, p115).

49   Kuper, 1988, p129 cites Bowler, P. (1983), *The Eclipse of Darwinism*. The German Freiburg Zoologist August Weismann, who worked closely with Haeckel, developed a theory of 'germ plasm'. He suggested that hereditary material in the parents' 'germ' (reproductive) cells dictated the character of all moral and mental aspects of their offspring (Cornwell, 2003 p82).

50   Editorial Staff of Seligman [edit.] 1930 Vol. 1, p201 *The Development of Social Thought and Institutions: War and Reorientation*; p189-228; for example, see Boas, 1911, p193-195, *The Mind of Primitive Man*, New York, The Macmillan Company [reprinted 1938].

51   All this detail has been given because the modern reader needs to be aware that even a moderate and an anti-racist like Boas considered that race was a legitimate subject to study and according to William Speth: 'encouraged study of the relations between environment and culture in a general program of anthropological research' (1978, p24-25). This balance of perspectives becomes even more interesting when one places Boas's work in the context of the rise of Nazism in Europe. In 1928 in *Anthropology and Modern Life,* Boas stressed the interrelationship of nationalism, culture and race. He went on to warn of the divisive consequences of ideas of racial purity being combined with nationalism, and how such ideas could lead to conflict when exploited unscrupulously: 'The idea of the great blond Aryan, the leader of mankind, is the result of self-admiration that emotional thinkers have tried to sustain by imaginative reasoning. It has no foundation in observed fact' (Boas, 1928, p80, New York, W.W. Norton, cited from Rosenzweig, 1994, p120).

52   This movement had its origins in the 1890s and was linked to the development of the Symbolist movement in the arts, the Occult Revival,

cultural pessimism, and Nietzschian movement of *lebens-philosophie* (2002, p29).

53 The topic continued to intrigue him, as he wrote to Erich Neumann on December 22nd, 1935 (Neumann, 1989, p281).

54 Sherry suggests that Jung was deceived by the presence of many immigrant Americans of Slavonic descent (2002, p32).

55 When re-examined, Boas's findings were found not to be statistically significant (Firth, 1958, p14).

56 Barkan, E. (1992), *The Retreat of Scientific Racism. Changing Concepts of Race in Britain and the United States between the World Wars*, Cambridge.

57 Boas, 1940 [1889], p626-638, *The Aims of Ethnology*.

58 From Boas, F., 'Changes in Bodily Form of Descendants of Immigrants' (1912), in his collected essays: *Race, Language and Culture* (1940).

59 An example from Jungian literature is Stephen Gross's hasty confidence in Frantz Fanon, a contemporary Black psychiatrist who was a critic of Jung (2000, p74, p75). Fanon projected American ideas onto Europeans by assuming that European Whites shared the White American's image of the Shadow as a Negro. This is a racist assumption on Fanon's part implying the existence of a pan-Caucasian prejudice! Fortunately Jung did not make the same error (Jung, 1991 [1927-31b], §98-99).

60 Cited from: Anna Rooth, (1984), 'The Creation Myths of North American Indians'. In Murray, H. (ed.), *Myth and Myth Making*. NY, p81; Tim Moore (1973), 'The analysis of stories'. In Cunningham, A. (ed.), *The Theory of Myth. Six Studies*. London, p36; Richard Dorson (1960), 'Theories of myth and the folklorist'. In Murray, H. (ed.), *Myth and Myth Making*. NY, p80-83; Robert Eisner (1987), 'The road to Daulis—psychoanalysis , psychology and classical mythology.' NY, p80-84; G.S. Kirk (1970), 'Myth—Its meaning and functions in ancient and other cultures' Cambridge; (1984) 'On defining myths' in Dundes, A. (ed.), *Sacred Narrative. Readings in the Theory of Myth*, Berkeley.

61 A selection of revisionist assessments is included in Blackmore's account of how Margaret Meade was misled in her famous portrayal of sexual mores in the South Seas (1999, p115). While Stevens and Price re-appraise the sixties anthropologists' accounts of hunter gatherers (1996, p25; Stevens, 1989, p167).

62 In all the reading done for this book, this is one of only three examples that seem to imply a negative value judgement by Jung, but even this impression must be treated with care. This is clearly not a racist comment as it refers to iron-age German Europeans who he was reminding people were 'no better' than primitives. The other comment is from 1912 and is mentioned later, but can be found in McGuire and Hull, 1980, p36.

63 Sherry points out that Hull's translation of 'On the Role of the Unconscious', published in 1964, distorted the original 1918 article '*Ober das Unbewusste*'. He uses this detail as part of an interpretation of Jung's perspective on the Jews, which is too complex to critique here. He

writes: 'The English reads "As civilized human beings, we in Western Europe have a history reaching back perhaps 2,500 years" *(Wir haben als Kulturmenschen em Alter von etwas Funfzehnhundert [1500] Jahren).* To his original German-language readers, the "we" was a plainly marked reference to themselves as Germans and the "1500" would refer back to the time when the German tribes were converted to Christianity. In the English version, the "we" gets broadened to include Western Europeans' (Sherry, 2002, p24). However this detail does not substantially affect Jung's argument about different layers of psychological evolution, in fact it provides more detail!

64   *Participation mystique* was coined by the Sorbonne scholar Lucien Lévy-Bruhl in his influential work *'Les functions mentales dans les sociétés inferieures'* (1910) which was a scholarly study based on the reading of others' field reports (Pietikäinen, 1999, p, 151). The reader may find useful Neumann's elaboration: 'What Lévy-Bruhl called *participation mystique* and pre-logical thinking is identical with what Cassirer... called the experience of the "oneness of life" and "the predominance of feeling..." Pre-logical thinking is not to be taken as an incapacity to think logically. Primitive man is quite capable of this, but because his view of the world is determined unconsciously, it is not oriented toward the logic of conscious thinking. To the extent that modem man is unconscious, he too thinks pre-logically, outside the categories prescribed by his conscious, scientific, world views.' (Neumann, 1954, p269).

65   A similar example is found in Jung, 1991 [1930], §963-966, and at the end of his life Jung gave autobiographical examples of this feeling (Jung, 1963 [1961], p22).

66   This speculation is similar to his ideas about genetic incompatibility and schizophrenia, as expressed on 30th October, 1935 (Jung, 1989 [1934-1939], p642-643). In Jung's defence one may find it profitable to consider a comment by the Professor of Anthropology at the University of London, Raymond Firth, in his book *Human Types,* first printed in 1938. Firth stated: 'It is vulgarly said: "A half-caste has the vices of both parents and the virtues of neither." In so far as this is true—and it may occasionally be so—it is due primarily not to the fact of being of mixed-blood, but of the social environment in which the mixed-blood, grows up' (1958, p28).

67   He made similar positive comments about 'primitive' culture on 8th June, 1942 (Jung, 1973 [1906-1950], p317-318; Jung, 1990 [1930 / 1950], §150).

68   Jung's lack of precision was shown again in a letter of 10th July, 1946, where although Jung expressed himself in terms of race and colour, as would a crude racist, he was in fact criticising the Japanese for taking on Western errors (Jung, 1973 [1906-1950], p430). One can also note that in 1957 Jung still used 'Negro' as an equivalent term when talking about 'primitives', but this suggests a habitual sloppy use of words rather than any implicit or unconscious racism (McGuire and Hull,

1980, p272).
69 The exact day is not given.
70 See also Jung, 1990 [1929], §2.
71 Wilhelm Dilthey (1833-1911).
72 This exercise has some potentially practical insights, as is demonstrated in strategic literature that has to operate in an environment that places a premium on pragmatic utility. Strategic historians have noted that differences in culture may be a significant factor in political negotiations (Halberstam, 1972; Booth, 1979). It is even possible to formulate various aspects of the cultural psyche into a typology. The most extensive use of Jungian typologies in a political context has been Bernstein's Cold War assessment *Power and Politics: The Psychology of the Soviet American Partnership* (1989). This observation is supported by a more recent observation of Samuels, that different psychological types may be drawn to different political philosophies and forms of action (2001, p31).
73 The use of the term 'rooted' is important for Noll who refers to Mosse's explanation of how the idea was often used by *Völkisch* thinkers who wished to stress the living link in the natural order of the universe between a people and their ancestral homeland that was vital for their spiritual security and welfare. (Cited from Mosse, 1964, p16.) In contrast 'uprootedness' was a morally rejected state that inevitably characterised the outsider and the foreigner who could by definition never establish a 'properly functioning soul' (1974, p98).
74 A similar argument can be applied to Sherry's concern about the translation of 'host people'. He argues: '"The Jew already had the culture of the ancient world and on top of that has taken over the culture of the *nations amongst whom he dwells* [*Wirstsvolk*]" (§18, my italics). The English translation glosses over a nuance that is highly significant in the original German. *Wirtsvolk* is better translated as "host people", and had become commonplace in discussions about the relationship of Jews to the larger, national communities around them. Given this linguistic premise, there were two possible words to describe Jews. For Jung and the majority of people of the time, they would be considered as "guests". Others, influenced by the medical rhetoric of the burgeoning racial hygiene movement of the time had begun to view them as "parasites". In either case, they were "aliens" separated from their Aryan neighbours' (2002, p24). The Nazis added another layer of meaning to the word, as Gottfried Heuer explains: '*Wirt* is also a term that is used in German—as, indeed, in English--in a biological context writing about bacilli, microbes and parasites that "sit" on a host to harmfully exploit him... For a German language speaker used to the Nazi / anti-Semitic context, this aspect of *Wirt* also resonates' (Heuer, 2007). The problem for the reader is that whatever a Nazi reader may project onto the word *Wirt*, in the context in which Jung writes he may be addressing the 'otherness' of the 'guest' people, but there is no agenda about parasites and there is no pejorative implication in having two

cultures as, for Jung, *Kultur* is an asset, and the more the better as long as one does not deal inappropriately with the 'primitive' aspects of the psyche, which is what he interpreted Freud to have done.

75 Jung was not certain when he gave the interview when questioned in 1949.

76 To give a recent conflict that raised the same issues about identity and national complexes, Hobsbawm speculated about the swiftness in which Yugoslavia broke down along its ethnic fracture lines. He wondered whether: 'Perhaps the resurgence of nationalism was something already written into the genetic code of those societies. Is it possible that the national divisions continued to operate at a much deeper level that we supposed' (2000, p42). In the debate about the significance of 'race' in the Bosnian conflict, Papadopoulos relates how the initial reaction of Western journalists was to explain the conflict in term of a re-emergence of ethnic and historical violence that had been suppressed during the Tito regime. In criticism of this perspective he cites Malcolm, who suggests that this was a flawed explanation as there was never any ethnic purity in the region (1998, p460). Another interpretation is that the violence was not ignited by issues of supposed racial purity, or the distinctiveness of ethnic identity, but by fears and irrationality when a community's security or identity disappears. The importance of this has been stressed by a number of writers. Staub asserts the importance for psychological health of a culture's common features, patterns of behaviour and beliefs (1994, p xiv). He agrees with Odermatt that when part of cultural or national identity is damaged, collective anxiety increases (1988). It is the disintegration of states that unleashes the panic and savagery that leads to ethnic fragmentation (Ignatieff, 1998).

77 Written in the 'fall, 1913', Jung, 1973 [1906-1950], p30.

78 Jung, 1974 [1906-1914], 52F, 15th November, 1907.

79 For example there are lengthy commentaries in *Symbols of Transformation* and the *Vision Seminars*.

80 In his discussion of archetypes on 14th September, 1960, Jung explained: 'We are confronted with autonomous animalia gifted with a sort of consciousness and psychic life of their own, which we can observe at least partially, not only in living men but also in the historic course of many centuries. Whether we call them gods, demons or illusions they exist and function and are born anew with every generation... They are basic forms, but not the manifest, personified, or otherwise concretised images. They have a high degree of autonomy, which does not disappear when the *manifest images* change' (Jung, 1976 [1951-1961], p593, my italics).

81 Shamdasani further explains that Jung's account of his relationship with the Romantics was not straightforward (2003, p166-8), but it evidently shaped part of the mental culture of his ideas.

82 Freud, *The Complete Psychological Works*, Volume 12, page 82. Freud's choice of words was interesting as others had already used 'mythopo-

etic' in related contexts. Ellenberger writes: 'The *mythopoetic* function (a term apparently coined by [Fredrick] Myers) is a "middle region" of the subliminal self where a strange fabrication of inner romances perpetually goes on... In this conception the unconscious seems to be continually concerned with creating fictions and myths, which sometimes remain unconscious or appear only in dreams' (1970, p318). Jung was aware of Myers' work and referred to him and William James as important pioneers (Jung, 1991 [1947/54], §356, 382n). Noll also noted that the nineteenth century philologist Friedrich Max Müller referred to the pre-Christian period of European history as the 'mythopoetic age' (1997, p111). Another echo of this line of thought comes from Shamdasani whom, when reviewing the legacy of the German Romantics, refers to Gotthilf von Schubert's *The Symbolism of Dreams* (1814). Schubert, and other writers of his ilk, had written that dreams were made by the 'poet hidden in us' that spoke in metaphors using universal 'hieroglyphic image language' (2003, p109).

83 Nietzsche, *Human, All-Too Human*, translated by Zimmern and Cohn, p24-27; cited, Nagy, 1991, note 9, p193. Jung cited this passage to his students like Honegger and Spielrein when he wrote *Transformations and Symbols of the Unconscious* (1912) (Shamdasani, 2003, p117, 140).

84 Cited, Nagy, 1991, p133.

85 In another article he referred to 'reactivated archetype' or 'primordial images' as: 'the primitive, analogical mode of thinking peculiar to dreams' (Jung, 1990 [1916-34], §219). Other examples are: 'The primordial images are the most ancient and the most universal "thought-forms" of humanity. They are as much feelings as thoughts' (Jung, 1990 [1917 / 1926 / 1943], §104, ed. 1942); 'image creating mind' (Jung, 1991 [1939/1953], §781); 'numberless interconnections' and parallels with 'typical mythologems', 'myth-forming' (Jung, 1969 [1940], §259).

86 See also Jung, 1981 [1918], §27 and §34.

87 He later wrote of how 'numberless interconnections' and parallels with 'typical mythologems' appear in dreams and psychoses that cannot be accounted for by any form of prior knowledge. He concluded that one has to 'assume that we must be dealing with "autochthonous" revivals independent of all tradition, and, consequently, that "myth-forming" structural elements must be present in the unconscious psyche' (Jung, 1969 [1940], §259).

88 As a different example of the interaction of the psychoid and the symbolic function, Cohen notes the way certain bodily reactions are often portrayed in a repetitive symbolic pattern. For example, doctors dealing with advanced alcoholism often encounter (as part of the symptom of the *delirium tremens*) hallucinations of little, scurrying animals, usually insects or rodents. He concluded that: 'They are the only example I know, where one can define conditions that predictably cause an archetype to manifest itself' (1975, p71). Another biological explanation of seemingly mythic archetypal material is provided by Blackmore who gives a detailed range of physical reactions that account for the psychic

experiences of people having seemingly other-worldly near death experiences (1999, p179).
89 Hobson argues: 'The detection of analogies is arbitrary and open to special pleading, the parallels often seem to be too few to argue universality, and in many of his examples cryptomnesia and the influence of suggestion could have been important... It seems probable, too, that much of his work has been done on a highly selected biased sample of exceptional people capable of practising active imagination' (1973, p74). Furthermore this small group could have attracted a type of individual, just as alchemy and mysticism attract a limited audience, yet these cases provided Jung with much of his historical control group. Clearly there are problems with this part of Jung's work, but as Nagy concedes, while the validity of symbolic interpretation may be an artificial creation of specialist pleading, the symbolic interpretation could equally be a perfectly valid specialist skill not readily accessible to the untrained (1991, p147-148).
90 Jung candidly declared: 'I had read much mythology before this fantasy came to me, and all of this reading entered into the condensation of these figures' (Jung, 1990 [1925], p92).
91 First referred to by Jung in *Wanderlunen und Symbole der Libido* (1911). (Noll, 1996, p182.)
92 Jung, 1917, 'The Psychology of Unconscious Processes', Long, *Collected Papers on Analytical Psychology*. Cited, Noll, 1996, p270.
93 'In Freud's scientific generation (i.e., those born before 1860) virtually all biologists, including his university professors in this field, were Lamarckians to an extent, in addition to whatever other theories of evolutionary change they may have espoused' (Sulloway, 1979, p274).
94 *First law*: 'In every animal that has not reached the end of its development, the more frequent and sustained use of any organ will strengthen this organ little by little, develop it, enlarge it, and give to it a power proportionate to the duration of this use; while the constant disuse of such an organ will insensibly weaken it, deteriorate it, progressively diminish its faculties, and finally cause it to disappear.'
Second law: 'All that nature has caused individuals to gain or lose by the influence of the circumstances to which their race has been exposed for a long time, and, consequently, by the influence of a predominant use or constant disuse of an organ or part, is conserved through generation in the new individuals descending from them, provided that these acquired changes are common to the two sexes or to those which have produced these new individuals.' Lamarck (1909), *Philosophie zoologique*, 1809, Volume 1, p235.
95 'As the penchants that animals have acquired through the habits they have been forced to contract have little by little modified their internal organizations, thus rendering the exercise of [these penchants] very easy, the modifications acquired in the organization of each race are then propagated to new individuals through generation. Indeed, it is known that generation transmits to these new individuals the state of

organization of the individuals that produced them. It results from this that the same penchants already exist in the new individuals of each race even before they have the chance to exercise them, so that their actions can only be of this one kind. It is thus that the same habits and penchants are perpetuated from generation to generation in the different individuals of the same races animals, and that this order of things, in the animals that are merely sensitive, should not be expected to offer notable variations, as long as there happens to be no change in the circumstances essential to their way of life, which would be capable of forcing them little by little to change some of their actions' (Burkhardt, 1977, p170-171). Cited from Lamarck, *Histoire naturelle des animaux sans vertebras*, Paris, Volume 3, 1815-1822, p269-270; *Philosophie zoologique*, Volume 2, p326; 'Habitude', p133. 'The habit of exercising a certain organ or part of the body in order to satisfy recurrent needs causes the *sentiment intérieur*, when its power is exercised, to give to the subtle fluid it displaces a facility in directing itself. Indeed the subtle fluid is given such a facility in directing itself toward the organ or part where it has so often been employed, and where it has traced open routes for itself, that this habit is changed for the animal into a penchant that soon dominates it, and which then becomes inherent to its nature' (Burkhardt, 1977, p167). Cited from Lamarck, *Histoire naturelle des animaux sans vertebras*, Paris, Volume 3, 1815-1822, p268-269; 'Habitude', p133.

96   Lamarck was unable to define his speculations about the existence of 'subtle fluids' but he gave electricity as an example (Burkhardt, 1977, p153). Cited from Lamarck, *Philosophie zoologique*, Volume Two, p15-18.
97   Cited from Lamarck, 'Habitude', *Dictionnaire 14*, 1817, p129.
98   Lamarck wrote directly in terms of instinct: 'the name instinct has been given to this cause that makes animals respond immediately to the needs that arouse them. It has been considered like a flame that enlightens them on the actions to be executed, and it has been noticed that it never misleads them. This involves, however, neither enlightenment nor any need of it, for this cause is uniquely mechanical, and turns out to correspond perfectly, like other such causes, to the effects produced. The action it brings about is never false. The felt need excites the *sentiment intérieur*, this excited feeling includes action, and there is never any error' (Burkhardt, 1977, p170. Cited from Lamarck, *Histoire naturelle des animaux sans vertebras*, Paris, Volume 3, 1815-1822, p238-239).
99   Cited from Lamarck, 'Habitude', *Dictionnaire 14*, 1817, p129.
100 Cited from Lamarck, *Philosophie zoologique*, Volume Two, p279. He also wrote: 'the *sentiment intérieur* [can] be moved by any need whatsoever, where upon it will instantly put in action the parts that must be moved to satisfy the need. This takes place without any of those resolutions that we call acts of will being necessary' (Burkhardt, 1977, p170. Cited from Lamarck, *Histoire naturelle des animaux sans vertebras*, Paris, Volume 3, 1815-1822, p238-239).

101 Cited from Lamarck, 'Instinct', p332. See also: *Philosophie zoologique*, Volume 2, p255, 373.
102 Cited from Lamarck, *Histoire naturelle des animaux sans vertebras*, Volume 1, p17-18. See also: '*Instinct*', p334.
103 Cited from Lamarck, *Histoire naturelle des animaux sans vertebras*, Paris, Volume 3, 1815-1822, p238-239.
104 Cited from Lamarck, '*Instinct*', p338. See also: *Histoire naturelle des animaux sans vertebras*, Paris, Volume 1, p245.
105 Brome cites Jones: *Freud, Life and Work*, Volume III, p336.
106 Richard Semon, 1921, *The Mneme*, London. Jung was not alone in his reference to Semon's work. Semon's work was influential on Eugen Bleuler, whom in his 1916 *Textbook of Psychiatry* took up the idea that everything that is psychically experienced leaves 'a lasting trace, or engram' (1924, p28, London, Allen and Unwin. Cited in Shamdasani, 2003, p190).
107 Interestingly, the references to Semon and mnemes still appeared in the Collected Works published after 1971 (editorial note, CW6). In *Psychological Types* (Jung, 1981 [1921], §748), which the editors of the Collected Works acknowledge had been 'somewhat revised', Jung came to distance himself from the idea. He acknowledged that Semon's idea was inadequate and ceased any further speculations about inherited images and denied that he had previously taken a Lamarckian position. Semon's work had been undermined by Mendel's work on genetics; he had a nervous breakdown in 1912 and in 1918 committed suicide following the death of his wife (Shamdasani, 2003, p191).
108 See, Jung, 1986 [1954], §142.
109 In another essay he posited a similar process being driven by Schopenhaurian 'acts of will that were frequently repeated' (Jung, 1991 [1931a], §268).
110 He referred to a similar process to account for fantasy-ideas in myths (Jung, 1990 [1925], p136).
111 For an example of such an up-rush of ancient thought forms Jung cited the upsurge of pagan symbolism in Christianity (Jung, 1990 [1917/1926/1943], §118).
112 Adolf Portmann in his 1949 Eranos lecture on 'The Mythical in Natural Research' praised Jung's linkage of psychology and biology but warned that the question of hereditary was left too open as there was a confusion of genuine biological inheritance, custom and what for Portmann was the Lamarckian misperception that repartition of historical experience was inheritable. He went on to leave the question open which understanding of the idea of archetypes would remain dominant. (Shamdasani, 2003, p264.) Stevens suggests Jung achieved this in 1946 with a clear theoretical distinction between the unconscious and unknowable archetype-as-such (similar to Kant's *das Ding-an-sich*) and the archetypal images, ideas and behaviour that the archetype-as-such produces (1997, p680; Jung, 1969 [1938/1954], §155).

113 Sometimes this confusion was encompassed within the same text. For example, in the fourth edition of *Symbols of Transformation*, whose revision spans most of Jung's working life, having defined instinct in almost Freudian terms, he went on to reject the possibility of a spiritual instinct, but in another passage, presumably written later, he suggests that archetypes have a spiritual function, and are the means by which instincts are restrained and even overcome (Jung, 1911-12 /1956, §223-224).

114 Jung, 1963 [1961], p319-321.

115 Jung, 1991 [1947/54], §439.

116 Gordon cites Elie Humbert (1983) who suggested that by 1938 Jung had developed his ideas on instincts and made links with the work of the ethologists which allowed a valuable cross-fertilisation of ideas. Gordon, 1985, p293-5; Humbert, L. (1983), *C.G. Jung*, Paris, Editions Universitaires.

117 According to Humbert, Jung made the connection between his ideas and theirs, but the ethologists were slower to draw parallels and Lorenz had initially rejected Jung's ideas because they were assumed to be Lamarckian, but later reconsidered his rejection, as von Franz recounts: 'Konrad Lorenz assures me that he accepts Jung's theory of archetypes in principle' (von Franz, 1975, p126) and it has been for later ethologists (Eibl-Eibesfeldt, 1971; Lorenz, 1970; Wickler, 1982), neurologists and Jungians to develop Jung's initial observation that man had an animal past. In 1954, Fordham linked Jung's work to Lorenz and Tinbergen and kept this connection as a central assumption of his own work (Mizan, 1998). Samuels notes that Fordham began writing the paper 'Biological Theory and the Concept of Archetypes' in 1949, but it was published in 1957 (1985, p36). By this time he could include references to Tinbergen's IRMs (1951). More recently (1996), Stevens and Price's writings on evolutionary psychiatry have drawn many links in this area.

118 Stevens lists from Murdock (1945) and Fox (1975) a number of universal social traits: 'No human culture is known which lacked laws about the ownership, inheritance and disposal of property, procedures for settling disputes, rules governing courtship, marriage, adultery, and the adornment of women, taboos relating to food and incest, ceremonies of initiation for young men, associations of men which exclude women, gambling, athletic sports, co-operative labour, trade, the manufacture of tools and weapons, rules of etiquette prescribing forms of greeting, modes of address, use of personal names, visiting, feasting, hospitality, gift-giving, and the performance of funeral rites, status differentiation on the basis of a hierarchical social structure, superstition, belief in the supernatural, religious rituals, soul concepts, myths and legends, dancing, homicide, suicide, homosexuality, mental illness, faith healing, dream interpretation, medicine, surgery, obstetrics, and meteorology. The list could go on' (Stevens, 1982, p23). See: Murdock, G. (1945), 'The Common Denominator in Culture', in *The Science of*

Man in the World Crisis, ed. R. Linton, Columbia University Press. New York; Fox, R. (1975), *Encounter with Anthropology*, Peregrine, London.
119 For example, in response to the shadow of a hawk, the chick will seek cover or the protection of its mother (Campbell, 1982a, p31).
120 The most famous examples are Lorenz's geese, whose open instinctive identification of their mother was triggered by Lorenz, who henceforth was their 'mother'.
121 Instinctive patterns can remain latent for incalculable lengths of time. One of the most powerful demonstrations of this was provided by an ornithologist who exposed Galapagos finches to predators in California that their Galapagos ancestors would not have known for 'something approaching a million years', nonetheless they exhibited their instinctive alarm patterns (Stevens, 1982, p48). Or, to take another example, modern humans retain the genetic codes to have complete body hair as their anthropoid ancestors, and this 'obsolete' pattern can still occasionally be seen in occasional genetic accidents.
122 Jung, 1969 [1934/1954], §80.
123 Hobson, in his review of *The Archetypes of the Collective Unconscious*, questioned whether it was appropriate to refer to archetypes with names like the mother, child or trickster. He wondered whether a more distanced terminology might be more appropriate. See: Hobson, R. (1961) 'Review of *The Archetypes of the Collective Unconscious*', *Journal of Analytical Psychology*, Volume 6, No. 2, cited in Henderson, 1991b, p432. This question of terminology has dogged psycho-analysis from the first Anglo-Saxon Latinisations of 'scientific' Freud, and prompted Bion and others to call for reforms of psychoanalytic terminology. This diversity should not be underestimated as Haule concludes that: 'There are at least six partly complementary, partly contradictory, meanings of *archetype* in Jung's writings' (1999, p256). These are: 'The substantive archetype' where Jung defines them as the 'source' of a symbol; 'Archetypes as inborn images'—for example: the 'mother archetype', the 'child archetype', or the 'trickster archetype'; the archetype as the teleological component in instinct—Jung in 'Instincts and the Unconscious' (1919) gave the following parallel definitions: 'instincts are typical modes of action' (§273), and: 'archetypes are typical modes of apprehension' (§280); 'The archetype as a dynamic/structural component of the psyche', such as: ego, persona, shadow, anima or animus, and Self (Jung, 1974 [1951], p 3-35); an archetypal or 'numinous' experience, an idea that Homans stressed (1979); the archetype as a typical complex, such as 'the hero' or 'wise old man' (1999, p256-258).
124 On occasion Jung also refers to them as 'dominants' (Jung, 1956 [1911-12/1952], §611).
125 Bowlby, J., 1973, *Attachment and Loss, Volume Two, Separation: Anxiety and Anger*, London, Hogarth Press.
126 A more complex reference to a possible interaction between the environment and a near-instinctive pattern of behaviour is recorded by Stevens and Price who refer to a number of studies of people's relation

to the landscape. This research suggests that either there is what might be considered an ideal landscape for human habitation, which people are almost bound to favour, or that this predilection is innate. Kaplan (1992) found that regardless of background most people favour pictures of 'natural as opposed to man-made environments', and Balling and Falk (1982) found that of all landscapes Savannah was the most preferred, especially by young children. Such vistas provide the best range of: 'large trees, semi-open spaces, hills and valleys, streams, rivers, lakes and estuaries, and a distant view of the horizon', as well as the possibility of future exploration. Stevens and Price conclude: 'All such research findings indicate that parallels exist between what people prefer and the environmental circumstances in which humans evolved and flourished' (2000, p161). See: Balling, J. and Falk, J. (1982), 'Development of Visual Preference for Natural Environments', *Environment and Behaviour*, 14, p5-28; Kaplan, S. (1992), 'Environmental Preference in a Knowledge-seeking, Knowledge-using Organism', in *The Adapted Mind*, ed. Barkow, J, Cosmides, L. and Toby, J, New York and Oxford, OUP.
127 Jung, 1990 [1917/1926/1943], §69.
128 Jung, 1969 [1934/1954], §69.
129 In Nagy's critical review of the evidence of the universality of archetypes, she concedes that the Mandala does seem to be a universal manifest symbol (1991 p147-8).
130 Interestingly, Melanie Klein in *The Early Development of Conscience in the Child*, suggested that the universal experience of parents as dangerous objects lay behind the common mythic themes of devouring monsters (Klein, 1933, p249). This could be taken as an alternative explanation for much of the symbolic imagery that interested Jung. Alternatively, these ideas could be used as a way of accounting for the ontology of some of the Jungian archetypes. An implication of this is that the facility to phantasize about the nature of the external world is akin to the symbolic function.
131 'Immanent' is used in a sense akin to Aristotle's doctrine of categories and the nature of substances which was his counter argument to Plato's idea of forms that had a metaphysical reality. Tarnas explains that for Aristotle the 'substance' was the primary reality, but it 'is not simply a unit of matter, but is an intelligible structure or form (*eidos*) embodied in matter. Although the form is entirely immanent, and does not exist independent of its material embodiment, it is the form that gives to the substance its distinctive essence.' 'Every substance seeks to actualise what it already is potentially' (1991, p57, 58).
132 See p166, above.
133 Green gives a similar list of archetypal experiences that must include a pattern of behaviour, a charge of emotional energy and a mythological image (1986, p53).
134 For example, socially 'immanent' archetypes are unlikely to be genetically inherited.

135 In a similar way Petteri Pietikäinen in his *C.G. Jung and the Psychology of Symbolic Forms* uses Cassirer's idea of 'symbolic forms' to offer a 'commonsense' interpretation of the transmission of cultural determinants so that archetypes can be understood as cultural artefacts not biological entities (1999, p218-9).
136 Cited from Polyani, M. (1958), *Personal Knowledge: Towards a Post-critical Philosophy*, Chicago, University of Chicago Press, p227-245.
137 Jung, while discussing the power of symbols, 22nd February, 1933, in the *Visions* seminars.
138 See also: Jung, 1956 [1911-12 / 1952], §681; 1956-57, §1597-8.
139 The reader might note the characteristic expression of part of the spirit being in the 'blood', which was a figure of speech of the time.
140 Jung even suggested that this archetypal possession could have an impact on external objects and 'non-psychic parallel phenomena' (Jung, 1991 [1952a], §648). Unfortunately this thought was not well developed and the references to it were too esoteric to be easily assimilated into academic political discussion.
141 See also, Neumann, E., 1973, *The Child*, New York: G. P. Putnam's Sons.
142 Cited from Geertz, A., and Jensen, J. (1991), 'Tradition and Renewal in the History of Religions: Some Observations and Reflections' in Geertz and Jensen, eds., *Religions Tradition and Renewal*, Denmark, 1991, Aarhus University Press.
143 Here I borrow a term from the military: a 'force multiplier' is something that accelerates the impact of a basic factor.
144 See chapter one.
145 'Pity is feeling which arrests the mind in the presence whatsoever is grave and constant in human sufferings and unites it with the human sufferer. Terror is feeling which arrests the mind in the presence whatsoever is grave and constant in human sufferings and unites it with the secret cause' (Joyce, J., 1916/1970, *A Portrait of the Artist as a Young Man*, p204).
146 Cited from Olds, J., in W.R. Adey, ed., *Brain Mechanisms and the Control of Behaviour* (1974). Heinemann Education Books, London.
147 Cited from MacLean, P. (1973), *A Triune Concept of the Brain and Behaviour*, Toronto, University of Toronto Press.
148 Cited from Tiger, L. (1971), *Men in Groups*, Panther, London; Tiger. L. and Fox, R. *The Imperial Animal* (1972), Secker and Warburg, London.
149 Cited from Erikson, E. (1984) 'Reflections on Ethos and War', *The Yale Review*, Volume 73, 4. p481-6.
150 Moore and Gillette have suggested a number of pathological hero manifestations. They suggest that, if adolescents are emotional insecure, they may seek to mask the feeling of insecurity with brutality. This emotion is all the more volatile given the hormonal changes in the adolescent period, and the additional weight of peer pressure. They refer to this maladaptation as a 'shadow warrior' inflation. Another pathology is the workaholic saviour, or fanatic, ridden by an internal 'sadistic warrior' who drives himself or his juniors mercilessly. Lastly there is

the masochist who takes on impossible hero tasks (1990, p90, 92). Bernstein reflects that adolescents are often overtaken by the new mental and emotional possibilities opening up in them and so easily identify with the warrior-hero. This makes them very prone to the ideological euphoria of great aims and heroic sacrifices. In contrast, the mature adult is more aware of the limits of power and the importance of moral and ethical issues that hold life and society together, and is less easily seduced by glory (1989, p44, 45).

151 This idea about the role of archetypal regression of borderline personality disorders in messianic leaders is developed in detail in Stevens and Price's *Prophets, Cults and Madness* (2000).

152 Nietzsche refers to the 'blond beast' in: *On the Genealogy of Morals* (1967), translated Kaufmann, W. and Hollingdale, R., Random House, New York; and in *Twilight of Idols* (1968), translated by Kaufmann, W. Princeton University Press. Kaufmann makes clear in his *Nietzsche Philosopher Psychologist Anti-Christ* (1968), Princeton University Press, that the 'blond' of the barbarian refers to the animal nature of all men and is taken from the colour of lions. From this it is clear that Nietzsche intended no racial allusion (Burniston, 2003).

153 For the necessary qualifications of this general statement see: 'After the Catastrophe', para. 423ff.

154 The reader may find it useful to cross-reference these changes with a list of some of the noteworthy events and dates from 1933 and 1934, provided in Appendix E.

155 He declared on the 31st October, 1946: 'After what has happened in Germany I have lost the last vestiges of any illusions I may have had about man's capacity of improvement' (Jung, 1973 [1906-1950], p448).

156 For example, Gallard writes that 'as early as' 1936, Jung was becoming critical of Nazi Germany (1994, p225). This is rather a late estimate.

157 Cited from the Wilhelm Bitter interview, September 10th, 1970, C.G. Jung Biographical Archives, Countway Library of Medicine, JBA, 17.

158 As an additional observation on Bitter's allegation that 'Jung and some of his pupils became Nazis in 1934', it is unfortunate that he gave no evidence, so one does not know what he considered 'Nazi'. If being 'Nazi' just consisted of an interest in Germanic myth, then probably all the Jungians, including the Jewish Jungians, could have been so labelled. This is a flippant point, but it is impossible to know what people were thinking, or how consistent in their beliefs they felt they needed to be. Gustav Heyer provided a graphic example of such complex inconsistency. Heyer was the only Jungian who became a party member in 1937. According to his first wife, he joined on Jung's advice (von der Tann, 1989, p56). This may have been for tactical reasons to bolster his position in Germany in negotiations with Göring. In any event, from remarks he made during the war he seemed to have been or become a believing Nazi, as he wrote from within the Reich, in 1944, that Jung was sympathetic to Nazi ideology and that 'there also are different attitudes to political situation' (Kirsch, 2000, p126). Yet he also

protected his half-Jewish mistress and trained Max Zeller, who was Jewish, until Zeller was interned in a concentration camp in 1938 (Kirsch, 2000, p127, 125). For his part, Zeller despite all his experiences, on his arrival in England was shocked at how 'Nazi' his own ideas had become (Spiegelman, 2002, p169).

159 Cited from Jolande Jacobi, Interview, December 26, 1969, C.G. Jung Biographical Archives, Countway Library of Medicine, JBA, 53.

160 Although soon after his election Jung had managed to smuggle through the measures ensuring Jewish membership of the international part of the IGMSP, this could always be rescinded. The struggle with the Nazis in Germany and the international body would be long and drawn out. In 1936 the 'Berlin Psychoanalytic Institute' lost its independence and the 'German Institute for Psychological Research and Psychotherapy', also called the 'Göring Institute' was inaugurated in Berlin (Maidenbaum, 2002, p239).

161 We can see this in his letters, for example the letter of 11th February, 1910, where Jung tells Freud: 'At present I am sitting so precariously on the fence between the Dionysian and the Apollinian' (Jung, 1974 [1906-1914], p293).

162 This argument is supported by Speer's reflection in prison in 1947: 'the vulnerability of modern civilization, built up during centuries. We know now that we live in a building that is not immune to earthquakes if the automatism of progress leads to a further dehumanization [*Entpersonlichung*] of people, depriving them of responsibility even more. [In the] decisive years of my life I have served technology, blinded to its possibilities' (Lukacs, 1997, p 268).

163 *German Vision of God: Basic Elements of a German Faith.*

164 Jung had even noted other events elsewhere, which he did not cite, although this was perhaps because they were not romantic enough for his essay? In the *Visions* seminars on 10th May, 1933, he had observed: 'you have perhaps read in the papers that a great discussion has actually taken place in Berlin, as to whether the Germans assimilated Christianity voluntarily or by force, whether it was forced down their throats by the argument of swords and spears, or whether they took it gladly. Certain professors led the discussion, and one defended the point of view that they took the pill very gladly, and another one said quite the contrary' (Jung, 1998 [1930-1934], p972). '[I]n Berlin an exhibition of the remains of Nordic religions is actually being arranged. That indicates the same tendency to revivify the Germanic religious roots. The *"Deutsche Christen"* want to abolish the Old Testament' (Jung, 1998 [1930-1934], p973).

165 See editor's footnote 1, p 179, CW10.

166 Here Jung had not gone into the same detail as previously in the *Visions* seminars on 10th of May, 1933: 'The National Socialist movement began with very strange proceedings, the *Jugend Bewegung* ["Youth Movement"], for instance. And at the summer solstice they celebrated the feast of Odin on top of the mountains, they really sacrificed sheep-

bloody sacrifices. That was ridiculous sentimentality, but it was also a symptom, it was an attempt toward the past. Then I am told that in a house in Bremen, a huge window is decorated with the figure of a man on a cross, but the cross has equal branches, it is by no means a crucifix, and the figure is Odin' (Jung, 1998 [1930-1934], p972-3). Later on 8th February, 1939, Jung again referred to sheep sacrifice at 'the beginning of the New Paganism movement'(Jung, 1989 [1934-1939], p1516).

167 Richard-Walther Darré, SS-*Gruppenführer*, appointed Reich Agricultural Leader and Chief of the Central Office for Race and Resettlement.
168 For *Ultima Thule* see Hale, 2003, p120.
169 Thomas Mann noted the etymological possibility that *Ruach*, the hot wind / breath of God evolved into *Yahweh*, while Wotan evolved from the archaic Germanic word *'Wode'* for *'rage'* (Baigent and Leigh, 1994, p271). This is the sort of syncratic parallel much beloved by some Jungians, but unfortunately the Hebrew half of the equation did not stand up as *'Yahweh'* is a composite of initials from one of the titles of God who, in the Hebrew tradition, is too holy to be named directly.
170 See also Klaus Theweleit's lengthy study of the brutalising effects of the war and the roots of Fascism in *Male Fantasies*, Volumes 1 and 2.
171 From Jünger, E. (1960), '*Der Kampf als inneres Erlebnis*' p57, Berlin, cited from Herf, J. (1984), p74, *Reactionary Modernism: Technology, Culture and Politics in Weimar and the Third Reich*, Cambridge, Cambridge University Press.
172 One is granted unrivalled access to Himmler's thoughts and those of his inner circle from the memoirs of Felix Kersten. This Baltic physiotherapist led a curious life acting as Himmler's masseur while recording Himmler's thoughts like a patient anthropologist, yet at the same time he used his influence to save thousands of lives and prepared the way for Count Bernadotte's Red Cross mission.
173 Hermann Rauschning was a Prussian politician, who as a friend of Hitler had close contact until he fell from grace and fled in 1936 to Switzerland and then Britain. There, following the publication of anti-Nazi books he was placed on the Nazi death list (Snyder, 1998, p282). His work is included with reservations. Despite being referred to by Lindholm (1993), Redlich (1998) and Machtan (2001), Professor Kershaw argues that the book is too unreliable to be quoted in a biography of Hitler. He goes as far as to say: 'Hermann Rauschning's *Hitler Speaks*, a work now regarded to have so little authenticity that it is best to disregard it altogether' (1998, p,xiv). That may be so, but Rauschning's writing remains a valuable point of comparison with Jung as he provides a contemporary's impression and assessment of Hitler. Even if most of what Rauschning described cannot be authenticated in detail, or the quotations of Hitler verified, all the material quoted here is matched by similar references from other sources so his material has been retained.
174 *Germanen-Orden*, 'German Order'.

175 Dietrich Eckart, a poet and journalist, was one of Hitler's ideological mentors, but he also was a regular opium user (Lewis, 2003, p170).
176 When Hitler joined the German Worker's Party it was just one of seventy-three *Völkisch* groups in Germany (Kershaw, 1998, p137).
177 Cited from Kelly, A. (1981), *The Descent of Darwin: The Popularisation of Darwinism in Germany 1860-1914*, Chapel Hill, The University of North Carolina Press, p91 ff.
178 Horneffer, E. (1934). *Nietzsche als Vorbote der Gegenwart*, Düsseldorf.
179 In Jung's seminars on Nietzsche's *Zarathustra* on the 5th February 1936, he said: 'You see, the Germans are moved by that new and strange spirit which is not good, and they are on top of all fools because they say so. But to us it is interesting that I must say that I am very grateful to the Germans for their paganistic movement, at the head of which is my friend Professor Hauer who taught us the Tantric Yoga [in 1932], and who has now become a saviour of the fools' (Jung, 1989 [1934-1939], p813). Shamdasani notes that Jung remained in correspondence with Hauer until 1938, and discussed various projects, and that Hauer presented a series of lectures to the Psychological Club in 1938 (2005, p111).
180 *Armanism* and *Ariosophy* were terms Lanz von Leibenfels and Guido von List used to describe their 'Aryan-racist-occult theories' (Goodrick-Clarke, 1992, p227).
181 Opinion on this area is not uniform. According to Levenda, in Vienna, for some or all of the period between 1908 and the outbreak of war, Hitler read the pagan revivalist periodical, *Ostara*, and even called on its editor von Liebenfels in 1909 (2002, p87). Whereas Kershaw, reviewing the evidence that Hitler read *Ostara*, considered it likely but far from certain, and suggests that it was by no means clear that he adopted Lanz's bizarre racial theories (1998, p50-51).
182 Cited from Stark, G., (1981) *Entrepreneurs of Ideology: Neoconservative Publishers in Germany, 1890-1933*, Chapel Hill.
183 Cited from Dietrich Eckart (1924), page 18, *Der Bolschevismus von Moses bis Lenin: Zwiegespräche zwischen Adolph Hitler und mir*, Munich.
184 Cited from *Deutschland-Berichte der SOPADE* (7th April, 1937), p497-9.
185 To give another example, in 1928 Hitler was forced to expel Gauleiter Artur Dinter from the party as the latter's calls for National Socialism to bring about a religious reformation through the purification of German blood and race were too extreme for the party (Kershaw, 1998, p298).
186 Adolf Hitler, *Mein Kampf*, trans. Ralph Manheim (Boston, 1962), p361, cited from Steigmann-Gall, 2003, p88.
187 Albrecht Tyrell, *Führer befiehl... Selbstzeugnisse aus der 'Kampfzeit' der NSDAP* (Düsseldorf, 1969), 165-6.
188 Turner (ed.), *Memoirs of a Confidant*, p277.
189 Turner (ed.), *Memoirs of a Confidant*, p278-9.
190 Cecil, *Master Race*, p100.

191 Cited from Rosenberg, *Der Mythus des 20. Jahrhunderts: Eine Wertung der seelisch-geistigen Gestaltenkämpfe unserer Zeit* (Munich 1931), p219.
192 Cited from Rosenberg, *Der Mythus des 20. Jahrhunderts: Eine Wertung der seelisch-geistigen Gestaltenkämpfe unserer Zeit* (Munich 1931), p5-7.
193 Bishop notes similarities between Jung's references to Wotan and Rosenberg's Wotan references, but there is no evidence that Jung ever read him (1995, p262, fn33). In any event, Jung's most picturesque comments pre-date Rosenberg's book, although he did denigrate the latter's book when Mathias Göring asked for it to be reviewed.
194 Cited from Speer, A., *Erinnerungen*, B, 1988, p109. Hitler admitted that he found Rosenberg's book, published in 1930, heavy going and had only read the beginning (von Lang, 1981, p169). Both *The Myth of the Twentieth Century* and Darré's *New Nobility from Blood and Soil* were published in Munich in 1930 (Padfield, 2001, p77).
195 For example, the 1939 Molotov-Ribbentrop pact, in which the ideological arch-enemies were to divide Poland between themselves.
196 Cited from Rossler, H. (1975), '*Erinnerungen an den Kirchenkampf in Coburg*', *Jahrbuch der Coburger Landesstiftung*, p155-6.
197 Cited from Scholder, K, (1977), *Die Kirchen und das Dritte Reich*, Frankfurt am Main, p.279-80.
198 See C. Ronald Murphy, *The Saxon Saviour: the Germanic Transformation of the Gospel in the Ninth-Century Heliand* (Oxford, 1989).
199 Hitler was adept at manipulating Catholic party statesmen to reassure the Church and, in *Mein Kampf*, distanced himself from neo-pagan ideas (Lukacs, 1997, p89). Cited from Friedrich Herr, (1968), *DerGlaube des Adolf Hitler; Anatomie einer politischen Religiositat'*, p220-221.
200 Hitler confided to his circle during the war that after victory Bormann's anti-church measures would no longer be restrained (Lukacs, 1997, p91).
201 A. Körner, '*Die Arbeit der Deutschen Pfarrergemeinde. Rückblick und Ausblick*', *DCNatkirchl. Einung Informationsdienst*, 1/44 (22nd January, 1944), 3-6, EZA Berlin 1/A4/566.
202 But by 1938 as preparations for war began even Himmler dismissed his ideas as 'too theoretical' (Hohne, 2000, p295).
203 According to Rauschning, Himmler had no patience with Tacitus's picture of the Germans: 'Every bit of Tacitus, in his *Germania*, is tendentious stuff. Our teaching of German origins has depended for centuries on a falsification' (1939, p 225). A different perspective comes from Schama who noted that in 1943 an *Ahnenerbe* scholar, Dr. Rudolph Till, managed to achieve Himmler's long ambition of making a facsimile copy of the oldest surviving copy of Tacitus's *Germania*. When this 'authoritative' edition was published in 1943 Himmler wrote the forward in which he expressed the conviction that success in the future would only come to those who understood their racial ancestry. When Italy collapsed, SS troops failed in their mission to acquire the original copy for the Reich (1995, p79). Darré too was fascinated by Tacitus' account of how the German God and the Germanic tribes sprang from the very

soil of the ancient Germanic woods (1995, p82).
204 In 1924 Himmler was working as a zealous party activist and wrote a memorandum which reflected his peasant mysticism. In Himmler's fantasy the reborn peasant communities would nurture and depend 'upon character rather than knowledge' along with key virtues being integrity and strength of commitment. Hohne suggests that in this memorandum one sees the seeds of his anti-Slav and anti-Semitic obsessions. Having joined the *Ahnenerbe* he soon became one of its leaders Most of the movement were not NSDAP members although Rudolf Hoess the future commandant of Auschwitz was (2000, p45-47).
205 On joining the SS he took up the pseudonym Karl Weisthor (Goodrick-Clarke, 1992, p183).
206 *Gottgläubigkeit*, 'a believer in God'.
207 Himmler was less than successful in his imposition of marriage outside of church, or his attempts to wean SS wives from Christmas. Nor was his anti-Christian campaign overly successful. In 1938, of the General SS *(Allgemaine-SS)* 54.2% remained Evangelicals and 23.7% Catholic. Only in the armed SS where the 'believers' in the majority with 53.6% of the *Verfugunstruppe* (the armed SS which became the Waffen SS) and 69% of the *Totenkopfverbände* (concentration camp guard units). Indeed, later the SS recruiters found that the anti-church stance hurt recruitment (Hohne, 2000, p156-8). Yet at least in one unit of the Waffen-SS at Radolfzell, the numbers of church leavers rose through the war (Hohne, 2000, p450). On Himmler's orders, in 1939, instead of Christmas celebration the SS *Leibstandarte* division celebrated a 'Yule festival' (von Lang, 1981, p147). Of the 125,000 Western Europeans who joined the Waffen-SS barely a third belonged to their native country's equivalent of the Nazi party (Hohne, 2000, p459).
208 SS-*Hauptsturmführer*, Captain.
209 Lindholm notes that the higher elements of SS training contained an 'eclectic blend of mysticism and Gnostic doctrine' (1993, p114). Staub cites Segev's study *The Commanders of the Nazi Concentration Camps*, which notes the SS's perception of themselves as an Arthurian elite (1994, p130). See: Segev, Ph.D. dissertation, Boston University, University Microfilms, Ann Arbour, Michigan, 77-21, 618.
210 Bradley Smith and A.E Peterson, eds., *Heinrich Himmler: Geheimreden 1933 bis 1945* (Frankfurt a.M., 1974), 159.
211 Hohne observes that while Göring and Goebbels invested heavily in the action against the SA leadership, it was Heydrich in the background who was the key instigator pushing through the framing of Rohm for treason to overcome Hitler's indecision. It was also Heydrich who dispatched the killing groups for the 'night of the long knives' (Hohne, 2000, p97). This use of fabricated evidence to unleash slaughter became something of a trademark for Heydrich. To weaken the Soviet's military he attempted to frame the Soviet Marshal Tuckachevsky for plotting a coup, although Hohne shows that Heydrich was not the prime mover he believed himself to be. Unknown to him

Stalin was manipulating him into providing 'evidence' from outside Russia with which Stalin could unleash the purges (2000, p231). Given the ruthless style of Heydrich's two coups, it is not far-fetched to speculate that he could have used planted evidence to remove Hitler—as he once threatened to do in a drunken rage if 'the old man' began to bungle things (Hohne, 2000, p164)—and he probably had access to Himmler's ample medical evidence of Hitler's increasing infirmity (Kersten, 1956, p165).

212 Theosophy would become increasingly popular in Germany following the Nazi revolution as it appealed as a more Aryan religion (Hale, 2003, p26).

213 Cited from Himmler to Wurst, 28th May, 1940, BA NS 21/227.

214 *Ordensburgen*: the four 'Order Castles', named after the medieval fortresses of the Teutonic Knights, were set up by Hitler to act as militarised ideological finishing schools for the future party leadership (Snyder, 1976, p261-2).

215 A similar idea has been explored by Papadopoulos in his discussions of panic and the nature of unreasoned racial savagery in the Bosnian conflict. See: Papadopoulos, R. (2002), 'Terrorism and Panic', in *Negotiating Power*, ed. Hall, P., London, Champernowne Trust.

216 By which one generally refers to that branch of the Caucasian race that is derived from the barbarian migrations and includes the numerous Germanic tribes, the Anglo-Saxon peoples, and the later waves of Gothic Germans.

217 Jung later came to develop this idea in his 1952 *Answer to Job*, which charted the evolution of the consciousness of the God archetype in the Bible. Other accounts of the evolution of archetypes occur in Henderson's account of the hero and von Franz's accounts of the anima and animus.

218 Goetz, B. (1919), *Das Reich ohne Raum*, Potsdam. See the bibliography in CW10, p572.

219 This trend, at its most baroque, also led Jung into exotic hyperbole. For example: 'Germany is a land of spiritual catastrophes, where nature never makes more than a pretence of peace with world-ruling reason. The disturber of the peace is a wind that blows into Europe from Asia's vastness, sweeping in on a wide front from Thrace to the Baltic, scattering the nations before it like dry leaves, or inspiring thoughts that shake the world to its foundations. It is an elemental Dionysus breaking into the Apollonian order' (Jung, 1991 [1936], §391). In a similar interview in 1945 he stated: 'All the Nazi leaders were possessed in the truest sense of the word, and it is assuredly no accident that their propaganda minister was branded with the ancient mark of the demonised man—a clubfoot' (McGuire & Hull, 1978, p156).

220 Jung, 1986 [1935], §371.

221 Jung, 1991 [1918], §17.

222 Heine, a German Jew, took on the mantle of Goethe and championed the German contribution to soul and culture while warning of the

dangers of German and especially Prussian nationalism (Baigent and Leigh, 1994, p206).
223 Heine also wrote: 'No, memories of the old German religion have not been extinguished. They say there are greybeards in Westphalia who still know where the old images of the gods lie hidden; on their deathbeds they tell their youngest grandchild, who carries the secret... In Westphalia, the former Saxony, not everything that lies buried is dead' (Heine, H., *Concerning the History of Religion and Philosophy in Germany*, Helen. M. Mustard, 1973, p417, Selected Works, New York, cited in Biagent and Leigh, 1994, p226).
224 Bertine, 1939, p172.
225 Jung's library contained Heinrich Heine's *Sämtliche Werke*, 1899, (Jung, 1967, p32).
226 D. H. Lawrence, 'Letter from Germany', in *Phoenix*, p107-10, William Heinemann Ltd, cited, Baynes, 1941, p170.
227 To give a contemporary example of the problems connected with Jung's eloquence, Grossman formed the impression that if Jung referred to something as an archetype, this automatically conferred his approval of the entity, which in this case would connect Wotan and the Nazi movement (1999, p93). Not only does this do an injustice to Jung by ignoring his comments on 'foolish' pagans or cranks (Jung, 1991 [1936], §389), but it is inaccurate and simplistic to imply that because of Jung's sympathy with some eccentric parts of the German Romanic movement this means he was a Nazi fellow traveller. As was shown in chapter two, while Jung's concern for mass society and his scepticism about untrammelled intellectualism was in sympathy with some of the *Völkisch* ideology, he lacked the 'paternalistic intolerant spirit' that was so prevalent in the right-wing ideologues (Pietikäinen, 2001, p101, 102). But he was shaped by the Romantic movement and its influence extended across a wide spectrum of groups and opinions. At its widest, what Brockway called neo-romanticism, could be described as 'apolitical, bohemian, aesthetic, and vaguely mystical' (1996, p48). These ideas influenced a range of cultural groups from the pre-political *Wandervogel* youth groups to General Ludendorff's 1925 pagan *Tannenbergbund* and a spread of political groups that included the right wing *Stahlhelm* to the socialistic left wing of the Nazi party that was grouped around Gregor Strasser (Kershaw, 1998, p262).
228 Later, von Franz briefly mentioned the idea in the context of Nazi Germany. She suggested that it was the *pueri aeterni*, the men with weak personalities and poorly developed feeling functions, ridden by their mother complexes, who form tyrannies and police states. She recounts a conversation with a stomach specialist who had a clientele rich in Nazi 'golden pheasants', the slang name for senior Nazi party members with a talent for self-enrichment. He recalled: 'When the beautiful hero persona had fallen off, he felt as if he were confronted with a hysterical woman.' Von Franz felt that the Germans of that generation suffered from a lack of differentiation of the anima (1981, p170-171,

p229). It is interesting to note that Himmler and Ribbentrop suffered from acute stomach cramps, while Hitler suffered from stomach and other disorders.
229 Hitler was forty-four, Goebbels thirty-six, Göring forty, Hess thirty-nine and Himmler only thirty-three (Redlich, 1998, p117). Of the SA in Berlin in 1931 seventy were under thirty and in the 1930 Reichstag, sixty Nazi deputies were under forty.
230 Cited from Gunther Scholdt, *Autoren über Hitler* (1993), Bonn, p660.
231 Lindholm acknowledges the high incidence of homosexuality in the SA, but takes the observation no further (1993, p97).
232 This would seem to suggest a hypothesis that God as an archetype incorporates gender poles like the archetypes of the anima and animus, but Jung did not develop this implied idea.
233 The article first appeared in English in 1930, translated by Jolas, and then in W.S. Dell and Cary Baynes' translation of *Modern Man in Search of a Soul*, published in 1933.
234 One should observe that the changes between the 1930 and the 1950 text cannot be taken as a case of retrospective political tampering as the passage was not written with reference to Wotan or Hitler, nor was Jung presenting the fifties text as an example of prophetic power.
235 Ninck, M. (1935), *Wotan und germanischer Schicksalsglaube*, Jena. (Bibliography CW10, p578.)
236 As was mentioned previously, Jung also made what might be a negative reference to Wotan on 5th February, 1936, by using the word 'sorcerer' (Jung, 1989 [1934-1939], p813).
237 After the War he gave his interpretation of events more balance by acknowledging the causes of aggression in recent German history.
238 He also held the belief in the necessity of an optimistic attitude in clinical cases because, in any archetypal configuration, a progressive outcome was possible.
239 After the War, Jung also linked these ideas about the negative potential in the Self back to his Wotan argument when he made a reference to something akin to the 'Wotan attributes' of God in a post-war discussion of a dream in which a hunter and a witch occur. Jung suggested that the contrast between a royal couple and the negative corresponding figures of a hunter and witch represented 'a distortion of [the royal pair], veering towards an atavistic, unconscious Wotanism. The fact that it is a German fairytale makes the position particularly interesting, since *this same Wotanism was the psychological godfather of National Socialism*' (Jung, 1969 [1945-1948], §453, my italics). This quaternity of the matching light and dark aspects of human nature is a significant theme in Jungian dream interpretation about the unity of all things in the Self.
240 After World War Two Jung went on to argue that there had been 'an increasing inflation of the ego, which became more and more evident after the sixteenth century' (Jung, 1991 [1945], §431). Jung gave an explicit exposition of his argument that frustrated religious drives were a cause of the Second World War when he suggested that after Bismarck-

's German unification, 'the devil stole a march on the Germans, luring them away from their spiritual potential with the prospect of power and pride. They gave themselves up to the pursuit of technology, exchanged morality for cynicism, and dedicated their highest aspirations to the forces of destruction... [Unlike some others] the Germans are not among those who may enjoy power and possessions with impunity' (Jung. 1945a, §433). He argued that Germany had been 'taken in by that fake figure of the Superman' so that everything became 'an infernal caricature of the answer the German spirit should have given' (Jung, 1986 [1945], §1375). Jung could not have been clearer when he stated flatly that this was an 'utter perversion of this goal of spiritual development, to which all nature aspires and which is also prefigured in Christian doctrine, National Socialism destroyed man's moral autonomy and set up the nonsensical totalitarianism of the State' (Jung, 1969 [1945-1948], §453). This perspective is supported by Jaffé who noted a reference by Jung in 'The Philosophical Tree', CW13, p285, note 5, on how the 'daemonization of the ego' occurs when the ego is inflated by the numinous power of the Self that is no longer contained by religious images (1989, p93).

241 For example, Harkabi's (1981) account of religious fundamentalism and the Bar Kochba uprising in Palestine, or Anzulovic's (1999), study of Messianic themes in Modern Serbian nationalism.

242 Kelly explains that Hegel in his *Philosophy of History* suggested that one could identify different historical periods with characteristic modes of thought. The earliest thought form was 'mythic time-consciousness' which was ahistorical and tended to think in terms of great ages, the remote past or the time of first beginnings and sponsored a feeling of the natural harmony of events (1993, p151).

243 Jung's library contained a 1933 copy of *Mein Kampf* (Jung, 1967, p34).

244 In the post-war era Jung largely abandoned his use of the theories of the collective to explain political events and his references to Hitler became more concerned with accounting for Hitler and Germany's history with arguments based on recent historical trends and generalisations extended from psychopathology that were then applied to national psychology. In this way he came to give a much more conventional psychological account. It may also be indicative that by January 1943, Jung had been able to use the war years to develop his alchemical writings with the completion of *Psychology and Alchemy* (Hannah, 1976, p275) and this may have furthered his pre-war perspective on the collective unconscious and archetypes.

245 This study is only concerned with Jung's pre-war statements and it would be anachronistic to compare him with later writings like those of Erikson (1982), Redlich (1998), Stevens (2000) or the vast *corpus* of Hitler biographies and studies. This is a huge field as historians struggle to explain Hitler's complex and secretive character; indeed his character has proved so illusive that there are now books about books about Hitler! (Lukacs, 1997; Rosenbaum, 1998.) In trying to interpret

Hitler one has to distinguish between what was true and what legends he, or others, spread about him, or what was simply mistaken. One also has to assess what faculties he had in some measure, whether he exaggerated them, learned to exploit them, lost them, or (more difficult to determine) whether he was exploited by them.

246 Some of these changes were due to poor health that had begun to decline from 1938 (Lukacs, 1997, p70). By 1942 Himmler and Schellenberg had begun to be seriously concerned about the decline in Hitler's mental health (Kersten, 1956, p165; Waller, 2003), and, while Himmler was under the impression that Hitler was suffering from syphilis, more recent diagnosis points to post-encephalitis Parkinson's disease, which has, as one of its symptoms, rage attacks (Lattimer, 2001, p33). The illness as well as extensive use of stimulants by Dr Morel (Irving, 1983) may have exacerbated Hitler's rages. There is debate about the degree that these rages were real, exaggerated and exploited, or just feigned. But whatever their cause, the outbursts were also a factor in increasing the emotional atmosphere and expectation around Hitler, which he exploited. Illness and pressure of work would also account for Hitler's increasing strategic impatience, intransigence and misjudgement (Lukacs, 1997, p74). Von Shirach, was the only one of all the Nuremberg inmates who spoke of Hitler as insane (Overy, 2001, p108).

247 The Knickerbocker interview took place in October 1938, but was first published in 1939.

248 Hitler admitted to having warm feelings for Speer. Eva Braun defined Speer as Hitler's friend even in the last days of the bunker (Junge, 2002, p86, 169).

249 Cited from Heiden, K. (2000) *The Führer*, London, p90-91.

250 Cited from Schamm, P. (1971) *Hitler; The Man and Military Leader*, Chicago.

251 Cited from Rauschning, 1939, p259.

252 'Widerstand': the usual term used for the German resistance movement is *Widerstand* ('Resistance'), and refers to all the various German groups against the Nazis.

253 Cited from, Zuckermayer, C., 1966, 'Als wärs ein Stück von mi', *Lebenserinnerungen*, Frankfurt-am-Main, S. Fischer.Verlag.

254 Jung and Allen Dulles first met in 1936 at Harvard University. Allen Dulles had a long talk with Jung and recalled his 'deep anti-Nazi and anti-Fascist sentiments' (McGuire, 1982, p25). During the war they met again, as Dulles was based in Bern.

255 Cited from Bullock, A. (1962) *Hitler: A Study in Tyranny*, New York, Harper and Collins, p373.

256 This insight, coupled with a ruthless exploitation of the wishes or weaknesses of others, gave him a tremendous advantage when intimidating enemy politicians (Austrian and Yugoslav), bribing his own generals with private grants, estates and promotions, and keeping his own clique bound to him by their own venal fears and inadequacies.

257 'Hitler knew how to exploit his own hysteria. Medicine-men, too, often have this gift. On the stage of German history, Hitler sensed to what extent it was safe to let his own personality represent with hysterical abandon what was alive in every German listener and reader. Thus the role he chose reveals as much about his audience as about himself; and precisely that which to the non-German looked queerest and most morbid became the Brown Piper's most persuasive tune for German ears' (Erikson, 1982, p297). Kershaw (2000) makes the point through his biography that Hitler's hysteria could be real, induced or fake.

258 Cited from Turner, H., ed., (1985), *Hitler—Memoirs of a Confidant*, New Haven, Yale University Press, p150.

259 Hitler told the Governor-General of Poland, Hans Frank, that during his hospitalisation during the Great War he had placed his hope in Providence, and that if he recovered he would take it as a sign he should become a politician. When he regained his sight: 'I was really stunned and took it as a call from Heaven for me' (Lukacs, 1997, p 109). In a speech to industrialists on 26th June, 1944, Hitler declared: 'It seems to me as if we must endure all of the trials of the Devil and Satan and Hell until we win the final victory. Perhaps I am not a pious church goer, that I am not. But deep inside I am still a devout believer [*ein frommer Mensch*], meaning that the laws of nature that a God has created correspond to this world: whoever fights bravely and does not capitulate but recovers again and again and advances anew, will not be abandoned by the Almighty but receive the blessing of Providence in the end. And that has been the lot of all great souls [*Geister*] of this world' (Lukacs, 1997, p 109). Cited from Speer, A., *Erinnerungen*, B, 1988, p570, note 19.

260 In 1927, a future Gauleiter spoke of his belief 'in the godly grace of Hitler' to end the chaos of the *Volkisch* movement (Kershaw, 1998, p263).

261 Cited from Abel, T. (1938), *Why Hitler Came into Power: An Answer Based on the Original Life Stories of Six Hundred of his Followers*, New York, Prentice Hall, p212.

262 Lüdecke, K. (1937) *I Knew Hitler*, New York, p22.

263 Cited from Frank, H., (1953), Munich, *Im Angesicht des Galgens*, p264.

264 See p.230, above.

265 There is a comment by Rauschning that suggests that Hitler may not have been quite so unconscious: 'His natural restlessness finds expression in everything. But at the back of it there is not only *his own "haunting hysteria", as he himself so significantly calls it*. A world in full process of dissolution, and a people no less hysterical than himself could not but come under the leadership of a man of this sort' (1939, p248-9, my italics).

266 Such a mass process or contemporary collective unconscious is discussed in Appendix B.

267 As early as 1934, Rauschning recalled: 'we had the feeling that [Hitler] in his exaggeration of his own importance came dangerously near to

the limit beyond which Nietzsche passed when he announced that he was the Dionysus-God, the Anti-Christ become flesh' (1939, p223). Jung would draw such parallels in his Nietzsche seminars between 1934 and 1939. In trying to describe the last days of the Reich, Albert Speer specifically referred to the 'twilight of the Gods' to describe the mixture of numb fatalism and fear that gripped the German population (Overy, 2001, p216). The politically astute Schellenberg in his *Troza Memorandum* written, directly after the collapse of Germany, as a defensive account of his actions prior to his going into allied hands, referred to the 'German character' of too many in the Nazi state, as a partial cause of the failure of his efforts to pursue a separate peace for Germany from 1942 (Waller, 2002, p78). One also notes, from the Anglo-Saxon world, a report dispatched to the Foreign Office late in the summer of 1945, which described Hitler as one who 'can and must be plainly labelled evil, but it will be no use trying to belittle his genius or to disparage his power—he can no more be laughed off than can Satan himself' (Overy, 2001, p96).

268 For examples see Jung's understanding of the SS as the 'new Knights' in the previous chapter, and the plans of the German Resistance in 1938 for a *coup d'etat*, mentioned in chapter three.
269 Re-translated by Paul Bishop (1995, p165).
270 Otto von Bismarck.
271 George Hogenson, in his article about Jung and the new-Darwinian James Baldwin, refers to the recent research in evolutionary science about the role played by the ability to guess in accelerating the process of selection. This process, he states, is akin to the role intuition plays in some of Jung's later writings on archetypes, although it must be added that there Jung was discussing archetypes and instincts, which implicitly affects the sort of archetypes to which his remarks apply (2001, p601-2).
272 Meme theory is not unchallenged. One criticism of meme theory is that it is not always clear what constitutes a meme. Dawkins includes items that range from the catchy but ephemeral pop tune or advertising gimmick, to grander notions such as deities (Ehrenreich, 1977, p233-4). Yet, in a sense, this does not invalidate the utility of the concept as a way of explaining ideas, be they big or small. The explanation may work in either case, just with different degrees of clarity and utility. In any case, a discussion of the wider degree to which memetic theory is valid is not the concern of this book. Here its utility is as an alternative way to explore some of the phenomenon Jung defined as archetypes.
273 'When a situation occurs which corresponds to a given archetype, that archetype becomes activated and a compulsiveness appears, which, like an instinctual drive, gains its way against all reason and will, or else produces a conflict of pathological dimensions, that is to say, a neurosis' (Jung, 1969 [1936], §99). 'It is perfectly possible, psychologically, for the unconscious or an archetype to take complete possession of a man and to determine his fate down to the smallest detail. At the

same time objective, non-psychic parallel phenomena can occur which also represent the archetype. It not only seems so, it simply is so, that the archetype fulfils itself not only psychically in the individual, but objectively outside the individual' (Jung, 1991 [1952b], §648). Papadopoulos noted that Jung mentioned the interaction of individual and collective aspects of the psyche, but the social collective dimension did not feature greatly in his thoughts. 'The human psyche is both individual and collective, and... its well-being depends on the natural co-operation of these two apparently contradictory sides. Their union is essentially an irrational life process that can, at most, be described in individual cases, but can neither be brought about, nor understood, nor explained rationally'. Jung wrote about these ideas back in 1916 but, somehow, they were not published until after his death, in a later edition of that work (1997, p7). See: *The Structure of the Unconscious*, 1966, p 280. In later writings Jung suggested a reason for the failure of superficial political policies. He suggested that there was a four-way process taking place as unconscious patterns mar the political response into a partial answer. This rebounds in a reversal or a repetition of the original problem (Jung, 1991 [1957], §558). This accounted for systemic interaction, but again he did not develop the idea.

274 This cognitive habit is well attested from other schools, such as the allied observation in Lacan's dictum that 'the unconscious is structured like language'. See: Papadopoulos, 1996, 136; cited from Lacan, J. (1977), *Ecrits: A Selection*, translated by Sheridan, A., London, Tavistock. A similar observation was made by Dawkins: 'The human mind is an inveterate analogiser. We are compulsively drawn to see meaning in slight similarities between very different processes' (1986, p195).

275 Speel, H. (1995), 'Memetics: On a Conceptual Framework for Cultural Evolution', paper presented at the symposium: *Einstein Meets Magritte*, Free University of Brussels, June 1995.

276 A major factor in some conflicts is when 'national myths' are constellated round political objectives (Hobsbawm, 2000, p24). This does not affect all wars but, when myths are evoked, their emotive impact and the unchallengability of their supposed historicity easily leads to fanaticism and increases the material available to ideological propagandists. In the twentieth century examples of conflicts where religious or cultural myths have played a major role have been Ireland (Smith, 1995), Israel (Harkabi, 1983) and more recently Serbia (Anzulovic, 1999). A different type of example is provided by Stalin's successful invocation of Russian and Orthodox nationalism and the prestige of Holy Russia as the 'New Rome' to support Russia when Soviet morale was collapsing in the face of the German Barbarossa onslaught of 1941 (Erickson, 1983). In all cases the emotional temper is significantly heightened in an age of total war when a state's leaders believe they face not only defeat, but also national destruction, when they are faced with what Harkabi termed a 'terminal' situation. One of the dangers about certain sorts of myths is that they may perpetuate a tendency to see threats as

leading to annihilation, as that is part of a cultural tradition of persecution and pessimism (Papadopoulos, 1991, Anzulovic, 1999).

277 'A more recent interest [in the historical literature] has been in the effects of political religions upon ethics, although the results of abandoning values which have served humanity well for a couple of thousand years were uniformly disastrous, insofar as those who could not be remade anew, because of some ineradicable class or racial taint, were cast out and murdered. Here historians dispense with conventional historical chronologies, for moral climates have fuzzy boundaries, even though anyone who has lived through the 1960s or 1980s will no more dispute their reality than their forefathers did in 1914-18 or the 1930s' (Burleigh, 2000, p11).

278 Vayda, A. (1968), 'Hypothesis about Functions of War', in *War: The Anthroplogy of Armed Conflict and Aggression*, edited by Fried, M., Harris, M., Murphy, R., Natural History Press, New York, Garden City.

279 Tishkov, V. (1996), 'Ethnicity, Nationalism and Conflict in and After the Soviet Union', in *The Mind Aflame*, London, Sage.

280 'Our conscious acts are the outcome of an unconscious substratum created in the mind mainly by hereditary influences. This substratum consists of the innumerable common characteristics handed down from generation to generation, which constitute the genius of a race' (Le Bon, 1895, p30, cited in Freud, 1921). These ideas of Le Bon may also have provided a source of support for Jung's early ideas on archetypes.

281 Freud, 1916-1917, p418, *Introductory Lectures on Psychoanalysis*; 1918, p418, *From The History of an Infantile Neurosis*; cited Samuels, 1985, p42.

282 See: Freud, 1933, p168, and more extensively in the rediscovered essay, Freud, 1987, *A Phylogenetic Fantasy*, ed. Gubrich-Simitis, Harvard, Belknap Press.

283 15th November, 1907, Freud / Jung, 1974 [1906-1914], p98, 52F.

284 Freud's ideas have been used to suggest ways in which a frequently recurring family situation can create a cluster of people with similar complexes in a society. If such a group is big enough this can have political consequences. This idea has been used by later Freudian social theorists such as Michael Allingham who uses various psychoanalytic observations to comment on psychological patterns in social interaction. He utilises Freudian ideas concerning the impact of the Father on the young in the Oedipus complex to speculate that this emotional pattern lies at the root of authority structures in society and goes on to speculate, like Flugel, that such emotional patterns lie at the root of right-wing political thought forms (1987, p112, p125). For Erikson (1982), paternal structure of discipline and child-rearing had a significant influence on the origins of authoritarian tendencies in German history (referred to in chapter seven). Finally, it must be emphasized that in all these post-Freudian descriptions collective themes are set down in the unconscious of each generation by social transmission. This conception is more limited than Jung's perspective on the trans-generational aspect of the collective unconscious. Cited from Flugal, J., (1945),

Man, Morals and Society, London, Duckworth.
285 Freud, 1949, p18, *Moses and Monotheism*, translated by K. Jones, London, Hogarth Press.
286 SALT—Strategic Arms Limitation Talks.
287 The policy of containment was part of American foreign policy developed by George Kennan that advocated that the West should put Soviet Russia in quarantine until its potential expansionist tendencies were outgrown.
288 Jung's understanding of the psychological and moral acrobatics of some Western intellectuals anticipates Polyani's explanation, which he called 'dynamo-objective coupling', referred to in chapter ten.
289 One can note that of these *Elementargedanken*, the first two require a sense of hierarchy and differentiation, which requires a neurological faculty, while the later is founded on a sociological awareness of an externally repeating pattern, which Stevens explores in *Prophets, Cults and Madness* (2000).
290 Koepping, 1983, p57-8, *Adolf Bastian and the Psychic Unity of Mankind*.
291 McGuire and Hull, (1980, p73) and Lockot, (1985, p61) give the date as the 21st of June, but von der Tann gives the date as the 3rd of June (1989, p57).
292 McGuire and Hull, (1980, p73) and Lockot, (1985, p90) give the date as 26th of June, but von der Tann gives the date as 29th June (1989, p56).

BIBLIOGRAPHY

Adams, M. (1989), 'My Siegfried Problem—and Ours: Jungians, Freudians, Anti-Semitism, and the Psychology of Knowledge', in Maidenbaum, A. and Martin, S. (ed.), (1991), *Lingering Shadows*, London, Shambhala Publications.
Adams, M. (1996), *The Multicultural Imagination: Race, Colour and the Unconscious*, London, Routledge.
Adams, M. (2001), *The Mythological Unconscious*, London, New York, Karnac Books.
Adler, G. (1975), 'C.G. Jung in a Changing Civilization', in Volume IV, *Implications and Inspirations*, (ed.) Papadopoulos, R. (1992), *Carl Gustav Jung: Critical Assessments*, London, Routledge.
Adler, G. (1979), *Dynamics of the Self*, London, Coventure Ltd.
Allen, M. (2005), *Himmler's Secret War*, London, Robson Books.
Allingham, M. (1987), *Unconscious Contracts: A Psychoanalytical Theory of Society*, London, Routledge and Kegan Paul.
Alschuler, L. (1997), 'Jung and Politics' in Young-Eisendrath, P. & Dawson, T. (ed.) (1997), *The Cambridge Companion to Jung*, Cambridge, Cambridge University Press.
Anthony, M. (1990), *The Valkyries*, Dorset, Element Books.
Anzulovic, B. (1999), *Heavenly Serbia*, London, New York University Press.
Arendt, H. (1994), *Eichmann in Jerusalem*, New York, Penguin Books.

Aron, R. (1958), 'Biological and Psychological Roots', in Freedman. L, (ed.), *War*, (1994), Oxford, New York, Oxford University Press.

Asher, H. (1978), 'Non-Psychoanalytic Approaches to National Socialism' in Cocks, G. and Crosby, T. (ed), (1987), *Psychohistory*, New York, Vail-Ballou Press.

Atwood and Stolorow. (1977), 'Meta-psychology, Reification and Representational World of C.G. Jung', in Volume I, *Jung and His Method in Context*, (ed.) Papadopoulos, R. (1992), *Carl Gustav Jung: Critical Assessments*, London, Routledge.

Bancroft, M. 1975), 'Zurich Days', in *Memories and Perspectives*, New York, Analytical Psychology Club of New York.

Barnett, V. (1992), *For the Soul of the People: Protestant Protest Against Hitler*, Oxford, Oxford University Press.

Baynes Jansen, D. (2003), *Jung's Apprentice: A Biography of Helton Godwin Baynes*, Einbsiedeln, Daimon Verlag.

Baynes, H.G. (1941), *Germany Possessed*, London, Jonathan Cape.

Baynes, H.G. (1949), *Mythology of the Soul*, London, Methuen & Co.

Baynes, H.G. (1950), *Analytical Psychology and the English Mind*, London, Methuen & Co.

Bennet, E. (1961), *C.G. Jung*, London, Barrie and Rockliff.

Bennet, E. (1985) *Meetings with Jung*, Zurich, Daimon Verlag.

Bergen, D. (1996), *Twisted Cross: The German Christian Movement in The Third Reich*, Chapel Hill and London, The University of North Carolina Press.

Bernstein, J. (1989), *Power and Politics: The Psychology of the Soviet American Partnership*, Boston and Shaftsbury, Dorset, Shambhala.

Bernstein, J. (1989) 'Workshop on Jung and Anti-Semitism', in Maidenbaum, A. and Martin, S. (ed.), (1991), *Lingering Shadows*, London, Shambhala Publications.

Bernstein, J. (1989), *Beyond the Personal: Analytical Psychology Applied to Groups and Nations*, in Volume IV, *Implications and Inspirations*, (ed.) Papadopoulos, R. (1992), 'Carl Gustav Jung: Critical Assessments', London, Routledge.

Bertine, E. (1939), 'Concerning Nazi Dynamism', in Bertine, E. (1967), *Jung's Contribution to Our Time*, New York, G.P. Putnam's Sons.

Bettelheim, B. (1991), *Freud and Man's Soul*, London, Penguin.
Biagent, M. and Leigh, R. (1994), *Secret Germany: Claus von Stauffenberg and the Mystical Crusade against Hitler*, London, Jonathan Cape.
Bielenberg, C. (1988), *The Past is Myself*, London, Corgi Books.
Bishop, P. (1995), *The Dionysian Self*, Berlin, Walter de De Gruyter & Co.
Blackmore, S. (1999), *The Meme Machine*, Oxford, Oxford University Press.
Blainey, G. (1988), *The Great Seesaw: A View of the Western World, 1750-2000*, London, The Macmillan Press Ltd.
Bond, B. (1983), *War and Society in Europe, 1870-1945*, London, Fontana.
Bonhoeffer, D. (1965), *Letters and Papers from Prison*, 1943-1945, London, Fontana Books.
Booth, K. (1979), *Strategy and Ethnocentrism*, London, Croom Helm.
Bormann, M., (ed.) (1988), *Hitler's Table-Talk*, Oxford, Oxford University Press.
Breitman, R. (1991), *The Architect of Genocide Himmler and the Final Solution*, London, The Bodley Head.
Brockway, R. (1996), *Young Carl Jung*, Wilmette, Illinois, Chiron Publications.
Brome, V. (1980), *Jung*, London, Paladin Books.
Brome, V. (1982), *Ernest Jones: Freud's Alter Ego*, London, Caliban Books.
Bullock, A. (1969), *Hitler a Study in Tyranny*, London, Penguin Books, Ltd.
Buresch-Talley, J. (2002), 'The C.G. Jung and Allen Dulles Correspondence', in Maidenbaum, A. (2002), *Jung and the Shadow of Anti-Semitism*, Berwick, ME, Nicolas-Hays, Inc.
Burkhardt, R. (1977), *The Spirit of System: Lamarck and Evolutionary Biology*, London, Harvard University Press.
Burleigh, M. (2000), *The Third Reich: A New History*, London, Macmillan.
Cabot Reid, J. (2001), *Jung, My Mother and I*, Einsiedeln, Daimon Verlag.
Campbell, J. (1982a), *The Masks of God: Primitive Mythology*, England, Penguin Books.

Campbell, J. (1982b), *The Masks of God: Oriental Mythology*, England, Penguin Books.
Campbell, J. (1985), *Myths to Live By*, London, Paladin.
Campbell, J. (1988), *The Power of Myth*, New York, Doubleday.
Campbell, J. (1989), *This Business of the Gods*, Ontario, Canada, Windrose Films Ltd.
Campbell, J. (1990), *Transformation of Myth Through Time*, Mythology Limited.
Carell, P. (1971), *Hitler's War on Russia*, Volume 1, 'Hitler Moves East' London, Corgi Books.
Christiansen, E. (1980), *The Northern Crusades The Baltic and the Catholic Frontier 1100-1525*, London, Macmillan Press Ltd.
Christopher, E. (2000), 'Gender Issues—Animus and Anima', in Christopher, E. and Soloman, H. (ed.), *Jungian Thought in the Modern World*, London, Free Association Press.
Clarke, J. (1992), *In Search of Jung*, London, Routledge.
Clark, R. (1980), *Freud. The Man and the Cause,* London, Jonathan Cape Ltd.
Cocks, G. (1989), 'The Nazis and C.G. Jung', in Maidenbaum, A. and Martin, S. (ed.), (1991), *Lingering Shadow,* London, Shambhala Publications.
Cocks, G. (1997), *Psychotherapy in the Third Reich*, second edition, New Brunswick and London, Transaction Publishers.
Cohen, E. (1975), *C.G. Jung and the Scientific Attitude*, New York, Philosophical Library, Inc.
Coles, R. (1975), 'On Psychohistory' in Cocks, G. and Crosby, T. (ed), (1987), *Psychohistory*, New York, Vail-Ballou Press.
Copleston, F. (1963), *A History of Philosophy*, Volume VII, 'Fichte to Nietzsche', London, Search Press.
Corrie, J. (1927), *ABC of Jung's Psychology*, London, Kegan Paul.
Dawkins, R. (1986), *The Blind Watchmaker*, London, Penguin Books.
Dawkins, R. (1989), *The Selfish Gene*, Oxford, Oxford University Press.
de Castillejo, I. (1973), *Knowing Woman*, New York, Harper Colophon Books.
Deschner, G. (1981), *Heydrich The Pursuit of Total Power*, London, Orbis Publishing Ltd.

Dieckmann, H. (1989), 'C.G. Jung's Analytical Psychology and the Zeitgeist of the First Half of the Twentieth Century', in Maidenbaum, A. and Martin, S. (ed.), (1991), *Lingering Shadows*, London, Shambhala Publications.

Donn, L. (1988), *Freud and Jung*, New York, Macmillan Publishing Company.

Douglas, C. (1997), 'The Historical Context of Analytical Psychology', in Young-Eisendrath, P. and Dawson, T. (ed.) (1997), *The Cambridge Companion to Jung*, Cambridge, Cambridge University Press.

Dulles, A. (Date not printed) *Germany's Underground*, Canada, Macmillan Press.

Ehrenreich, B. (1977), *Blood Rites: Origins and History of the Passions of War*, Metropolitan Books, New York.

Eibl-Eibesfeldt, E. (1971), Love and Hate, London, Methuen and Co Ltd.

Eichman, W. (1990), 'Meeting the Dark Side in Spiritual Practice', in Zweig, C. and Abrams, J. (ed.), (1991), *Meeting the Shadow*, Los Angeles, Jeremy P.Tarcher, Inc.

Ellenberger, H. (1970), *The Discovery of the Unconscious*, London, The Penguin Press.

Ellenberger, H. (1978), 'Carl Gustav Jung; His Historical Setting', in Volume I, *Jung and His Method in Context*, (ed.) Papadopoulos, R. (1992), *Carl Gustav Jung : Critical Assessments*, London, Routledge.

Engel, W. (1989), 'Thoughts and Memories of C.G. Jung', in Maidenbaum, A. and Martin, S. (ed.), (1991), *Lingering Shadows*, London, Shambhala Publications.

Erikson, E. (1982), 'The Legend of Hitler's Childhood', in *Childhood and Society* Suffolk, Triad/Granada.

Erlenmeyer, A. Springer, A.Winkelmann, K. (1987), 'Destructiveness in the Tension between Myth and History', (in ed.) Mattoon, A. (1987), *The Archetype of Shadow in a Split World*, Einsiedeln, Switzerland, Daimon Verlag.

Fernando, S. (1988), *Race and Culture in Psychiatry*, Beckenham Kent, Croom Helm Ltd.

Fest, J. (2001), *Speer The Final Verdict*, London, Weidenfeld and Nicolson.

Fordham, M. (1963), *Contact with Jung*, London, Tavistock Publications.
Fordham, M. (1995), (ed.) Hobdell, R.) *Freud Jung and Klein—The Fenceless Field* London, Routledge.
Freud S. and Bullitt, W., (1967), *Thomas Woodrow Wilson: A Psychological Study*, Boston USA, Houghton Mifflin Company.
Freud S. (1908 [1907]), 'Writers and Day Dreaming', *The Standard Edition of the Complete Psychological Works of Sigmund Freud*, Volume IX, London, Hogarth Press.
Freud S. (1912-1913), 'Totem and Taboo', *The Standard Edition of the Complete Psychological Works of Sigmund Freud*, Volume XIII, London, Hogarth Press.
Freud S. (1920), 'Beyond the Pleasure Principle', *The Standard Edition of the Complete Psychological Works of Sigmund Freud*, Volume XVIII, London, Hogarth Press.
Freud S. (1921), 'Group Psychology and the Analysis of the Ego', *The Standard Edition of the Complete Psychological Works of Sigmund Freud*, Volume XVIII, London, Hogarth Press.
Freud S. (1924), 'The Economic Problem of Masochism', *The Standard Edition of the Complete Psychological Works of Sigmund Freud*, Volume XIX, London, Hogarth Press.
Freud S. (1930a [1929]), 'Civilisation and Its Discontents', *The Standard Edition of the Complete Psychological Works of Sigmund Freud*, Volume XXI, London, Hogarth Press.
Freud S. (1933 [1932]), 'Why War?', *The Standard Edition of the Complete Psychological Works of Sigmund Freud*, Volume XXII, London, Hogarth Press.
Freud S. (1939 [1934-38]), 'Moses and Monotheism: Three Essays', *The Standard Edition of the Complete Psychological Works of Sigmund Freud*, Volume XXIII.
Freud S. (1940 [1938]), 'An Outline of Psycho-Analysis', *The Standard Edition of the Complete Psychological Works of Sigmund Freud*, Volume XXIII, London, Hogarth Press.
Freud S. (1987), '*A Phylogenetic Fantasy*', (ed). Gubrich-Simitis, Harvard, Belknap Press.
Frey-Rohn, L. (1967), 'Evil from the Psychological Point of View', in The Curatorium of the C.G. Jung Institute, Zurich, (ed.) *Evil*, Evanston, Northwestern University Press.

Frey-Rohn, L. (1990) *From Freud to Jung*, Boston and Shaftesbury, Shambhala.
Gallard, M. (1987), 'Black Shadow—White Shadow', (in ed.) Mattoon, A. (1987), *The Archetype of Shadow in a Split World*, Einsiedeln, Switzerland, Daimon Verlag.
Gay, P. (1985), *Freud for Historians*, New York, Oxford University Press.
Gay, P. (1989) *Freud A Life for Our Time*, London, Papermac.
Giegerich, W. (1975), 'Ontogeny = Phylogeny? A Fundamental Critique of Erich Neumann's Analytical Psychology', in Volume II, *The Structure and Dynamics of the Psyche*, (ed.) Papadopoulos, R. (1992), *Carl Gustav Jung : Critical Assessments*, London, Routledge.
Giegerich, W. (1982), 'Saving the Nuclear Bomb', in Andrews, V. Bosnak, R. and Goodwin, K.(ed.), 1982, *Facing Apocalypse*, Dallas, Spring Publications.
Gisevius, H.B. (1948), *To the Bitter End* London, Alden Press.
Glover, E. (1950*), Freud or Jung*, London, Ailen and Unwin.
Goethe, J. (1987), *Faust; Part One*, Translated by David Luke, Aylesbury, Bucks, Oxford University Press.
Goggin, J. and Goggin, E. (2001), *Death of a 'Jewish Science'*, Indiana, Purdue University Press.
Goodrick-Clarke, N. (1992), *The Occult Roots of Nazism*, London, I.B. Tauris & Co, Ltd.
Goldwert, M. (1983), 'Toynbee and Jung: The Historian and Analytical Psychology—a Brief Comment', in Volume IV, *Implications and Inspirations*, (ed.) Papadopoulos, R. (1992), *Carl Gustav Jung : Critical Assessments*, London, Routledge.
Gordon, R. (1985), 'Losing and Finding: The Location of Archetypal Experience', in Volume II, *The Structure and Dynamics of the Psyche*, (ed.) Papadopoulos, R. (1992), *Carl Gustav Jung: Critical Assessments*, London, Routledge.
Gross, S. (2000), 'Racism in the Shadow of Jung—The Myth of White Supremacy', in Christopher, E. and Soloman, H. (ed.), *Jungian Thought in the Modern World*, London, Free Association Press.
Grosskurth, P. (1991), *The Secret Ring*, Reading, Massachusetts, Addison-Wesley Publishing Company, Inc.

Grossman, S. (1979), 'C.G. Jung and National Socialism', in Bishop, P. (ed.), (1999), *Jung in Contexts*, London, Routledge.
Guderian, H. (1982), *Panzer Leader*, London, Futura Publications.
Guggenbuhl-Craig, A. (1980), 'Why Psychopaths do not Rule the World', Zweig, C. and Abrams, J. (ed.), (1991) *Meeting the Shadow*, Los Angeles, Jeremy P. Tarcher, Inc.
Guggenbuhl-Craig, A. (1989) 'Reflections on Jung and Anti-Semitism', in Maidenbaum, A. and Martin, S. (ed.), (1991), *Lingering Shadows*, London, Shambhala Publications.
Guggenbuhl-Craig, A. (1989), 'Jung and Anti-Semitism', in ed. Mattoon, M. 1989, *Personal and Archetypal Dynamics in the Analytical Relationship*, Switzerland, Daimon Verlag.
Halberstam, D. (1972), *The Best and the Brightest*, New York, Random House.
Hale, C. (2003), *Himmler's Crusade The true story of the 1938 Nazi expedition into Tibet*, Great Britain, Bantam Press.
Hall, J. 1986, 'The Structure of Collective Shadows: Why they Endure', in (ed.) Mattoon, A. (1987), *The Archetype of Shadow in a Split World*, Einsiedeln, Switzerland, Daimon Verlag.
Hannah, B. (1976), *Jung His Life and Work*, New York, Putman's Sons.
Harkabi, Y. (1981), *The Bar Kochba Syndrome Risk and Realism in International Politics*, Chappaqua, New York, Rossel Books.
Harms, E. (1946), 'Carl Gustav Jung-Defender of Freud and the Jews', in Maidenbaum, A. and Martin, S. (ed.), (1991), *Lingering Shadows*, London, Shambhala Publications.
Hauke, C. (2000), *Jung and the Postmodern*, London, Routledge.
Haule, J. (1984), 'From Somnambulism to the Archetypes', in Bishop, P. (ed.), (1999), *Jung in Contexts*, London, Routledge.
Hayman, R. (1999), *A Life of Jung*, London, Bloomsbury Publishing Plc.
Heath, I. (1985), *The Vikings*, London, Osprey Publishing Ltd.
Heidiking, J. and Mauch, C. (ed.), (1996), *American Intelligence and the German Resistance to Hitler*, Colorado, Westview Press, Inc.
Henderson, J. (1975), *A Bridge Across Time*, London, Turnstone Books.
Henderson, J. (1984), *Cultural Attitudes in Psychological Perspective*, Toronto, Canada, Inner City Books.

Henderson, J. (1991a), 'The Jungian Interpretation of History and Its Educational Implications', in (ed.) Papadopoulos and Saayman, (1991), *Jung in Modern Perspective*, Bridport, Dorset, Prism Press.

Herstein, R. (1982), *When Nazi Dreams Come True*, London, Abacus.

Heyer, G. (1933), *The Organism of the Mind*, London, Kegan Paul, Trench, Trubner & Co., Ltd.

Hilberg, R. (1961), *The Destruction of the European Jews*, New York, Quadrangle Books.

Hillman, J. (1972), 'An Essay on Pan', in Rosacher, H. and Hillman, J. *Pan and the Nightmare* (1979), Dallas, Spring Publications, Inc.

Hillman, J. (1982), 'Wars, Arms, Rams, Mars: On the Love of War', in Andrews, V. Bosnak, R. and Goodwin, K. (ed.), 1982, *Facing Apocalypse*, Dallas, Spring Publications.

Hillman, J. (1985) *Anima Anatomy of a Personified Notion*, Dallas, Spring Publications Inc.

Hobsbawm, E. (2000), *The New Century*, London, Abacus Books.

Hohne, H. (1979), *Canaris*, London, Secker and Warburg.

Hohne, H. (2000), *The Order of the Death's Head The Story of Hitler's SS*, London, Penguin Books.

Holt, D. (1974), 'Jung and Marx: Alchemy, Christianity, and the Work against Nature', in Tuby, M. (ed.) (1983), *In the Wake of Jung*, Kent, Great Britain, Harvest,.

Homans, P. (1979), *Jung in Context*, Chicago, University of Chicago Press.

Howard, M. (1976), *War in European History*, O.U.P. Oxford.

Howard, M. (1983), *The Causes of War*, London, Temple Smith.

Hubback, J. (1989), 'The Changing Person and the Unchanging Archetype', in (ed.) Mattoon, M. (1989), *Personal and Archetypal Dynamics in the Analytical Relationship*, Switzerland, Daimon Verlag.

Humbert, L. (1988), 'Archetypes', in Volume II, *The Structure and Dynamics of the Psyche*, (ed.) Papadopoulos, R. (1992), *Carl Gustav Jung : Critical Assessments*, London, Routledge.

Ignatieff, M. (1998), *The Warrior's Honour—Ethnic War and the Modern Conscience* London, Chatto & Windus.

Irving, D. (1983), *The Secret Dairies of Hitler's Doctor*, London, Grafton Books.

Jacobi, J. (1951), *The Psychology of C. G. Jung*, London: Routledge & Kegan Paul.
Jacobi, J. (1958), *Freud and Jung—Meeting and Parting*, (1956), (ed), Hillman, J. Zurich, Students Association, C.G. Jung Institute.
Jacoby, M. (1985), *Longing for Paradise*, Boston Massachusetts, Sigo Press.
Jaffe, A. (1984), *The Myth of Meaning in the Work of C.G. Jung*, Zurich, Daimon Verlag.
Jaffe, A. (1989), *From the Life and Works of C.G. Jung*, Zurich, Daimon Verlag.
Jaffe, L. (1990), *Liberating the Heart; Spirituality and Jungian Psychology*, Toronto, Canada, Inner City Books.
Janaway, C. (1994), *Schopenhauer*, Oxford, Oxford University Press.
Jarret, J. (1981), 'Schopenhauer and Jung', in Bishop, P. (ed.), (1999), *Jung in Contexts* London, Routledge.
Jung, C.G. (1974)[1906-1914], *The Freud/Jung Letters*, R. Manheim & R.F.C. Hull (Trans.). London: Routledge and Kegan Paul.
Jung, C.G. (1973)[1906-1950], *C.G. Jung Letters*, Volume 1, R.F.C. Hull (Trans.). London: Routledge and Kegan Paul.
Jung, C.G. (1976)[1951-1961], *C.G. Jung Letters*, Volume 2, R.F.C. Hull (Trans.). London: Routledge and Kegan Paul.
Jung, C.G. (1983)[1896], 'The Border Zones of Exact Science', *The Zofingia Lectures*, J. van Heurck (Trans.). London: Routledge.
Jung, C.G. (1983)[1897], 'Some Thoughts on Psychology', *The Zofingia Lectures*, J. van Heurck (Trans.). London: Routledge.
Jung, C.G. (1983)[1898], 'Thoughts on the Nature and Value of Speculative Inquiry', *The Zofingia Lectures*, J. van Heurck (Trans.).London: Routledge and Kegan Paul.
Jung, C.G. (1956)[1911-12/1952], *Symbols of Transformation*, C.W., 5, R.F.C. Hull (Trans.). London: Routledge & Kegan Paul.
Jung, C.G. (1974)[1913], 'The Theory of Psychoanalysis', C.W., 4, R.F.C. Hull (Trans.). London: Routledge & Kegan Paul.
Jung, C.G. (1990)[1916-34], *The Relationship Between the Ego and the Unconscious*, C.W., 7, R.F.C. Hull (Trans.). London: Routledge.
Jung, C.G. (1990)[1917/1926/1943], 'The Psychology of the Unconscious', C.W., 7, R.F.C. Hull (Trans.). London: Routledge.
Jung, C.G. (1991)[1916/1948], 'General Aspects of Dream Psychology', C.W., 8, R.F.C. Hull (Trans.). London: Routledge.

Jung, C.G. (1991)[1918], 'The Role of the Unconscious', C.W., 10, R.F.C. Hull (Trans.). London: Routledge.
Jung, C.G. (1991)[1919], 'Instinct and the Unconscious', C.W., 8, R.F.C. Hull (Trans.). London: Routledge.
Jung, C.G. (1981)[1921], *Psychological Types*, C.W., 6, R.F.C. Hull (Trans.). London: Routledge & Kegan Paul.
Jung, C.G. (1979)[1922], 'On the Relation of Analytical Psychology to Poetry', C.W., 15, R.F.C. Hull (Trans.). London: Routledge.
Jung, C.G. (1990)[1925], *The Seminars*, Volume 3, *Analytical Psychology*, (ed.) W. McGuire, London: Routledge.
Jung, C.G. (1981)[1925], *'Marriage as a Psychological Relationship'*, C.W., 17, R.F.C. Hull (Trans.). London: Routledge & Kegan Paul.
Jung, C.G. (1991)[1927/1931a], 'The Structure of the Psyche', C.W., 8, R.F.C. Hull (Trans.). London: Routledge.
Jung, C.G. (1991)[1927-1931b], 'Mind and Earth', C.W., 10 R.F.C. Hull (Trans.). London: Routledge.
Jung, C.G. (1991)[1928], 'The Swiss Line in the European Spectrum', C.W., 10, R.F.C. Hull (Trans.). London: Routledge.
Jung, C.G. (1984)[1928-1930], *Dream Analysis Notes of the Seminar Given in 1928-30*, (ed.) C. Douglas, London: Routledge and Kegan Paul.
Jung, C.G. (1991)[1928-1931b], 'Analytical Psychology and Weltanschauung', C.W., 8, R.F.C. Hull (Trans.). London: Routledge.
Jung, C.G. (1990)[1929], 'Paracelsus', C.W., 15 R.F.C. Hull (Trans.). London: Routledge & Kegan Paul.
Jung, C.G. (1998)[1930-1934], *Visions: Notes of the Seminar Given in 1930-1934*, Volume One and Two, London: Routledge.
Jung, C.G. (1986)[1930], *Radio talk in Munich*, C.W., 18, R.F.C. Hull (Trans.). London: Routledge & Kegan Paul.
Jung, C.G. (1991)[1930], 'The Complications of American Psychology', C.W., 10, R.F.C. Hull (Trans.). London: Routledge.
Jung, C.G. (1990)[1930/1950], 'Psychology and Literature', C.W., 15, R.F.C. Hull (Trans.). London: Routledge & Kegan Paul.
Jung, C.G. (1991)[1931], 'Basic Postulates of Analytical Psychology', C.W., 8, R.F.C. Hull (Trans.). London: Routledge.
Jung, C.G. (1933)[1933], *Modern Man in Search of a Soul*, translated by W.S. Dell and H.G. Baynes, London: Kegan Paul.

Jung, C.G. (1986)[1933], Review of G.R. *Heyer's Der Organismus der Seele*, C.W., 18, R.F.C. Hull (Trans.). London: Routledge & Kegan Paul.
Jung, C.G. (1981)[1934a], 'The Development of the Personality', C.W., 17, R.F.C. Hull (Trans.). London: Routledge & Kegan Paul.
Jung, C.G. (1991)[1934a], 'Rejoinder to Dr Bally', C.W., 10, R.F.C. Hull (Trans.). London: Routledge.
Jung, C.G. (1991)[1934b], 'The State of Psychotherapy Today', C.W., 10, R.F.C. Hull (Trans.). London: Routledge.
Jung, C.G. (1989)[1934-1939], *Nietzsche's Zarathustra* Notes of the Seminar in two parts (Ed.) J. Jarrett. London: Routledge & Kegan Paul.
Jung, C.G. (1969)[1934/1954], 'Archetypes of the Collective Unconscious', C.W., 9 pt 1, R.F.C. Hull (Trans.). London: Routledge & Kegan Paul.
Jung, C.G. (1986)[1935a], *Tavistock Lectures*, C.W., 18, R.F.C. Hull (Trans.). London: Routledge & Kegan Paul.
Jung, C.G. (1937)[1936], 'The Psychology of Dictatorship', in *Living Age*, September 1936-February 1937, Volume 351, New York, The Living Age Company.
Jung, C.G. (1991)[1936], 'Wotan', C.W., 10 R.F.C. Hull (Trans.). London: Routledge.
Jung, C.G. (1986)[1936], 'Psychology and National Problems', C.W., 18, R.F.C. Hull (Trans.). London: Routledge & Kegan Paul.
Jung, C.G. (1969)[1936], 'The Concept of the Collective Unconscious', C.W., 9 pt 1, R.F.C. Hull (Trans.). London: Routledge & Kegan Paul.
Jung, C.G. (1969)[1936/1954], 'Concerning the Archetypes, with Special Reference to the Anima Concept', C.W., 9 pt 1, R.F.C. Hull (Trans.). London: Routledge & Kegan Paul.
Jung, C.G. (1991)[1937], 'Psychological Factors Determining National Behaviour', C.W., 8 R.F.C. Hull (Trans.). London: Routledge & Kegan Paul.
Jung, C.G. (1991)[1938-1940], 'Psychology and Religion', C.W., 11 R.F.C. Hull (Trans.). London: Routledge & Kegan Paul.

Jung, C.G. (1969)[1938/1954], 'Psychological Aspects of the Mother Archetype', C.W., 9 pt 1, R.F.C. Hull (Trans.). London: Routledge & Kegan Paul.
Jung, C.G. (1986)[1939], 'The Symbolic Life', C.W., 18, R.F.C. Hull (Trans.). London: Routledge & Kegan Paul.
Jung, C.G. (1991)[1939], 'The Dreamlike World of India', C.W., 10 R.F.C. Hull (Trans.). London: Routledge.
Jung, C.G. (1991)[1939/1953], 'Psychological Commentary on *The Tibetan Book of the Great Liberation*', C.W., 11 R.F.C. Hull (Trans.). London: Routledge & Kegan Paul.
Jung, C.G. (1969)[1940], 'The Psychology of the Child Archetype', C.W., 9 pt 1, R.F.C. Hull (Trans.). London: Routledge & Kegan Paul.
Jung, C.G. (1986)[1941], 'Return to the Simple Life', C.W., 18, R.F.C. Hull (Trans.). London: Routledge & Kegan Paul.
Jung, C.G. (1991)[1945], 'After the Catastrophe', C.W., 10 R.F.C. Hull (Trans.). London: Routledge.
Jung, C.G. (1986)[1945], *Marginalia on Contemporary Events*, C.W., 18, R.F.C. Hull (Trans.). London: Routledge & Kegan Paul.
Kegan Paul.
Jung, C.G. (1969)[1945-1948], 'The Phenomenology of the Spirit in Fairytales', C.W., 9 pt 1.
Jung, C.G. (1991)[1946a], Epilogue to 'Essays on Contemporary Events', C.W., 10 R.F.C. Hull (Trans.). London: Routledge.
Jung, C.G. (1991)[1946b], 'The Fight with the Shadow', C.W., 10 R.F.C. Hull (Trans.). London: Routledge.
Jung, C.G. (1946)[1919], *The Psychology of the Unconscious*, Jung, C.G. [first published in 1916, reprinted from American Edition of 1919], Translated B. Hinkle, (Trans.). London: Kegan Paul Ltd.
Jung, C.G. (1991)[1947/54], 'On the Nature of the Psyche', C.W., 8, R.F.C. Hull (Trans.). London: Routledge.
Jung, C.G. (1986)[1948], 'Depth Psychology', C.W., 18, R.F.C. Hull (Trans.). London: Routledge & Kegan Paul.
Jung, C.G. (1986)[1949], Foreword to Neumann: *The Origins and History of Consciousness*, C.W., 18, R.F.C. Hull (Trans.). London: Routledge & Kegan Paul.
Jung, C.G. (1974)[1951], *Aion* C.W., 9 pt 2.

Jung, C.G. (1991)[1952a], *Synchronicity: An Acausal Connecting Principle*, C.W., 8 R.F.C. Hull (Trans.). London: Routledge.
Jung, C.G. (1991)[1952b], *Answer to Job*, C.W., 11 R.F.C. Hull (Trans.). London: Routledge & Kegan Paul.
Jung, C.G. (1986)[1952], 'Religion and Psychology: A Reply to Martin Buber', C.W.18, R.F.C. Hull (Trans.). London: Routledge & Kegan Paul.
Jung, C.G. (1991)[1957], *TheUndiscovered Self*, C.W., 10 R.F.C. Hull (Trans.). London: Routledge.
Jung, C.G. (1986)[1961], 'The Significance of Dreams', C.W., 18, R.F.C. Hull (Trans.). London: Routledge & Kegan Paul.
Jung, C.G. (1963)[1961], *Memories, Dreams, Reflections*, R. and C. Winston (Trans.). London: Collins, Routledge and Kegan Paul.
Jung, C.G. (1964), *Man and His Symbols*, London: Aldus Books Ltd.
Jung, C.G. (1967), *C.G. Jung Bibliothek Katalog*, Kusnacht, Zurich.
Jung, E. (1957), *Animus and Anima*, Dallas, Spring Publications.
Junge, T. (2002), *Until the Final Hour*, Great Britain, Weidenfeld and Nicolson.
Kahn, H. (1978), *On Thermo-Nuclear War*, London, Greenwood Press.
Karsh, E. (1994), 'The Causes of War', in Freedman. L, (ed.), *War*, (1994), Oxford, New York, Oxford University Press.
Kaufmann, W. (1980), *Discovering the Mind: Volume Three, Freud versus Adler and Jung*, New York, McGraw-Hill Book Company.
Kelly, S. (1993), *Individuation and the Absolute*, New Jersey, Paulist Press.
Kelsey, M. (1991), 'Jung as Philosopher and Theologian', in (ed.) Papadopoulos and Saayman, (1991), *Jung in Modern Perspective*, Bridport, Dorset, Prism Press.
Kerr, J. (1993), *A Most Dangerous Method*, New York, Vintage.
Kershaw, I. (1998), *Hitler 1889-1936: Hubris*, London, Penguin Books.
Kersten, F. (1956), *The Kersten Memoirs*, London, Hutchinson.
Kirsch, J. (1982), 'Carl Gustav Jung and the Jews: The Real Story', in Maidenbaum, A. and Martin, S. (ed.), (1991), *Lingering Shadows*, London, Shambhala Publications.
Kirsch, J. (1983), 'Reconsidering Jung's So-Called Anti-Semitism', in Estelle Weinreid et al., *The Arms of the Windmill: Essays in*

Analytical Psychology in Honour of Werner H. Engel, Baltimore, John D, Lucas Pringtin Co.

Kirsch, T. (1989), 'Jung and Anti-Semitism', in (ed.) Mattoon, M. (1989), *Personal and Archetypal Dynamics in the Analytical Relationship*, Switzerland, Daimon Verlag.

Kirsch, T. (2000), *The Jungians*, London, Routledge.

Klein, M. (1933), 'The Early Development of Conscience in the Child', Volume 1, *Love, Guilt and Reparation and Other Works*, London, Hogarth Press Ltd.

Kohler, J. (2000), *Wagner's Hitler: The Prophet and His Disciple*, Great Britain, Polity Press.

Kramarz, J. (1967), *Stauffenberg*, London, Andre Deutsch Limited.

Kuper, A. (1988) *The Invention of Primitive Society*, London, Routledge.

Kuper, L. (1981), *Genocide*, Middlesex, England, Penguin Books Ltd.

Kutek, A. (2000), 'Warring Opposites', in Christopher, E. and Soloman, H. (ed.), *Jungian Thought in the Modern World* London, Free Association Press.

Lambert, K. (1988), 'Archetypes, Object-relations and Internal Objects', in Volume II, *The Structure and Dynamics of the Psyche*, (ed.) Papadopoulos, R. (1992), *Carl Gustav Jung: Critical Assessments*, London, Routledge.

Langendorf, U. 1987, 'Where there is Danger Salvation is also on the Increase', (in ed.) Mattoon, A.(1987), *The Archetype of Shadow in a Split World*, Einsiedeln, Switzerland, Daimon Verlag.

Langer, W. (1972), *The Mind of Adolf Hitler*, New York, Basic Books Inc.

Ledoux, J. (1998), *The Emotional Brain*, Great Britain, Weidenfeld & Nicolson.

Leitz, C. (2001), *Sympathy for the Devil*, Great Britain, New York University Press.

Levenda, P. (2002), *Unholy Alliance A History of Nazi Involvement with the Occult*, New York, The Continuum International Publishing Group Inc.

Levi, P. (1990), *If This is Man. The Truce*, Suffolk, Abacus Books.

Lifton, J. (1986), *The Nazi Doctors; A Study in the Psychology of Evil*, Hong Kong, Papermac.

Lifton, R. (1982), 'The Image of the 'End of the World'; A Psychohistorical View', in Andrews, V. Bosnak, R. and Goodwin, K. (ed.), 1982, *Facing Apocalypse*, Dallas, Spring Publications.

Lindholm, C. (1993), *Charisma*, Oxford UK & Cambridge USA, Blackwell.

Lockot, R. (1985), *Erinnern und Durcharbeiten Zur Geschichte der Psychoanalyse und Psychotherapie im Nationalsozialismus*, Frankfurt am Main, Fischer Taschenbuch Verlag GambH.

Lopez-Pedraza, R. (1980), 'Cultural Anxiety', in Volume IV, *Implications and Inspirations*, (ed.) Papadopoulos, R. (1992), *Carl Gustav Jung: Critical Assessments*, London, Routledge.

Lorenz, K. (1970), *On Aggression*, London, Methuen and Co.

Lucas, J. (1979), *War on the Eastern Front*, London, Jane's Publishing Company.

Lukacs, J. (1997), *The Hitler of History*, New York, Alfred A. Knopf.

Machtan, L. (2001), *The Hidden Hitler*, Oxford, Perseus Press.

Maidenbaum, A. (1989), 'Lingering Shadows: A Personal Perspective', in Maidenbaum, A. and Martin, S. (ed.), (1991), *Lingering Shadows*, London, Shambhala Publications.

Maidenbaum, A. (2002), 'The Shadow Still Lingers', in Maidenbaum, A. (2002), *Jung and the Shadow of Anti-Semitism*, Berwick, ME, Nicolas-Hays, Inc.

Masson, J. (1988), *Against Therapy*, New York, Harper Collins.

Mattoon, A. (1987), *The Archetype of Shadow in a Split World*, Einsiedeln, Switzerland, Daimon Verlag.

McCutcheon, R. (2001), 'Methods, Theories, and the Terrors of History: Closing the Eliadean Era with Some Dignity', in Rennie, B. (ed.) (2001), *Changing Religious Worlds: The Meaning and End of Mircea Eliade*, New York, State University of New York Press.

McGowan, D. (1994), *What is Wrong with Jung*, New York, Prometheus Books.

McGuire, W. and Hull, R., 1980, (ed.) *C.G. Jung Speaking; Interviews and Encounters*, London, Picador.

McGuire, W. (1982), *Bollingen An Adventure in Collecting the Past*, Surrey, Princeton University Press.

McLynn, J. (1996), *Carl Gustav Jung*, London, Transworld Publishers Ltd.

Meehan, P. (1992), *The Unnecessary War*, London, Sinclair Stevenson.
Meyerhoff, H. (1962) 'On Psychoanalysis as History', in Cocks, G. and Crosby, T. (ed), (1987), *Psychohistory*, New York, Vail-Ballou Press.
Miller, D. (1989), 'The 'stone' which is not a stone. C.G.Jung and the Postmodern Meaning of 'Meaning'', in Volume IV, *Implications and Inspirations*, (ed.) Papadopoulos, R. (1992), *Carl Gustav Jung : Critical Assessments*, London, Routledge.
Miller, P. (1983), 'What the Shadow Knows: In interview with John A. Sanford', Zweig, C. and Abrams, J. (ed.), (1991), *Meeting the Shadow*, Los Angeles, Jeremy P. Tarcher, Inc.
Moore, R. and Gillette, D. (1990), *King Warrior Magician Lover*, New York, HarperCollins.
Moore, R. and Gillette, D. (1992), *The Warrior Within*, New York, William Morrow and Company, Inc.
Morgan, H. (2000), 'Modern Western Society—The Making of Myth and Meaning', in Christopher, E. and Solomon, H. (ed.), *Jungian Thought in the Modern World*, London, Free Association Books.
Mosse, G. (1964), *The Crisis of German Ideology*, New York, Schocken.
Nagy, M. (1991), *Philosophical Issues in the Psychology of C.G. Jung*, Albany, New York, State University of New York Press.
Neumann, M. (1989), 'On the Relationship Between Erich Neumann and C.G. Jung and the Question of Anti-Semitism' in Maidenbaum, A. and Martin, S. (ed.), (1991), *Lingering Shadows*, London, Shambhala Publications.
Neumann, E. (1954), *The Origin and History of Consciousness*, New York, Panther Books.
Neumann, E. (1973), *The Great Mother*, Princeton, Princeton University Press.
Neumann, E. (1990), *Depth Psychology and a New Ethic*, Boston, Massachusetts, Shambhala.
Nicholson, N. (1973), *Alex The Life of Field Marshal Earl Alexander of Tunis*, London, Pan Books Ltd.

Nietzsche, F. (1986), *Human, All Too Human: A Book for Free Spirits*, Translated Hollingdale, R., Cambridge, Cambridge University Press.
Noll, R. (1994), *The Jung Cult*, Princeton, NJ, Princeton University Press.
Noll, R. (1997), *The Aryan Christ*, New York, McMillan,.
O'Donnell, J. (1979), *The Berlin Bunker*, Reading, Arrow Books.
Odajnyk, V. (1976), *Jung and Politics*, New York, Harper and Row.
Overy, R. (2001), *Interrogations The Nazi Elite in Allied Hands*, 1945, New York, Viking.
Padfield, P. (1984), *Doenitz; The Last Fuhrer*, London, Victor Gollancz.
Padfield, P. (1990), *Himmler*, USA, Henry Holt and Co.
Papadopoulos, R. (1991), 'Jung and the Concept of the Other', in (ed.) Papadopoulos and Saayman, (1991), *Jung in Modern Perspective*, Bridport, Dorset, Prism Press.
Papadopoulos, R. (1996), 'Archetypal Family Therapy: Developing a Jungian Approach to Family Therapy', in *Psyche and Family*, (ed.) by Dodson, L. and Gibson, T. 1996, Illinois, Chiron Publications.
Papadopoulos, R. (1998), 'Jungian Perspectives in New Contexts', in Casement, A. (ed). (1998), *Post Jungians Today*, London, Routledge.
Paret, P. (1964), *French Revolutionary Warfare. From Indochina to Algeria*, London, Pall Mall Press.
Perera, S. (1986), *The Scapegoat Complex*, Toronto, Inner City Books.
Petrova, A. and Watson, P. (1995), *The Death of Hitler*, London, Richard Cohen Books.
Pietikäinen, P. (1999), *C.G. Jung and the Psychology of Symbolic Forms*, Saarikärvi, Gummerus Oy.
Plaut, A. (1986), 'An Undivided World Includes the Shadow', in Mattoon, M. (ed). (1987) *The Archetype of Shadow in a Split World*, Minneapolis, Daimon Verlag.
Portman, A. (1946), 'Biology and the Phenomenon of the Spiritual', in *Eranos Yearbooks 1, Spirit and Nature*, (ed.) Campbell, J. (1954), Princeton, Princeton University Press.
Proctor, R. (1988), *Racial Hygiene Medicine Under the Nazis*, Massachusetts, Harvard University Press.

Progoff, I. (1981), *Jung's Psychology and Its Social Meaning*, New York, Dialogue House Library.
Rauschning, H. (1939), *Hitler Speaks*, London, Thornton Butterworth Ltd.
Rauss, E. and von Natzmer, O. (1994) *The Anvil of War*, London, Greenhill Books, London.
Redlich, F. (1998), *Hitler Diagnosis of a Destructive Prophet*, Oxford, Oxford University Press.
Rieff, P. (1987), *The Triumph of the Therapeutic*, Chicago, University of Chicago Press.
Rieff, P. (1990), *The Feeling Intellect*, Chicago, University of Chicago Press.
Ritter, G. (1972), *The Sword and the Sceptre: The Problem of Militarism in Germany*, Translated Heinz Norden, London, Allen Lane.
Roazen, P. (1989), 'Jung and Anti-Semitism', in Maidenbaum, A. and Martin, S. (ed.), (1991), *Lingering Shadows*, London, Shambhala Publications.
Roberts, J. (1985), *The Triumph of the West*, London, Book Club Associates.
Robertson, R. (1987), *C.G. Jung and the Archetypes of the Collective Unconscious*, New York, Peter Lang.
Rowland, S. (1999), *C.G. Jung and Literary Theory*, London, Macmillan Press.
Rosenbaum, R. (1998), *Explaining Hitler*, London, Macmillan,.
Rosenzweig, S. (1994), *The Historic Expedition to America Freud, Jung and Hall the King-maker*, St. Louis, Rana House.
Schama, S. (1996), *Landscape and Memory*, London, Fontana Press.
Samuels, A. (1985), *Jung and the Post Jungians*, London, Routledge and Kegan Paul.
Samuels, A. (1989), 'National Socialism, National Psychology and Analytical Psychology' in Maidenbaum, A. and Martin, S. (ed.), (1991), *Lingering Shadows*, London, Shambhala Publications.
Samuels. A, (1993), *The Political Psyche*, London, Routledge.
Samuels, A. (2001), *Politics on the Couch*, London, Profile Books Ltd.
Schellenberg, W. (1969), *Schellenberg*, London, Mayflower Paperbacks.

Schoenl, W. (1996) 'Jung, C.G. (1945) 'Letter to Mary Mellon'', in *Major Issues in the Life and Work of C.G. Jung*, Maryland, University Press of America.
Scott Peck, M. (1983), 'Healing Human Evil', in Zweig, C. and Abrams, J. (ed.), (1991) *Meeting the Shadow*, Los Angeles, Jeremy P. Tarcher, Inc.
Segal, R. (1995), 'Jung's Fascination with Gnosticism', in Segal, A. Singer, J. and Stein, M. (ed), *The Allure of Gnosticism*, Illinois, Open Court Publishing Company.
Sereny, G. (1994) *Into that Darkness*, London, Andre Deutsch Ltd.
Sereny, G. (1995), *Albert Speer: His Battle with Truth*, London, Picador.
Sereny, G. (2000), *The German Trauma*, England, Penguin Books Ltd.
Serrano, M. (1966), *C.G. Jung and Herman Hesse; A Record of Two Friendships*, London, RKP.
Shamdasani, S. (1995), 'Memories, Dreams, Omissions', in Bishop, P. (ed.) (1999), *Jung in Contexts*, London, Routledge.
Shamdasani, S. (1998), *Cult Fictions*, London, Routledge.
Shamdasani, S. (2003), *Jung and the Making of Modern Psychology: The Dream of a Science*, Cambridge, Cambridge University Press.
Shelburne, W. (1988), *Mythos and Logos in the Thought of Carl Jung*, New York, State University of New York Press.
Sherry, J. (1991), 'The Case of Jung's Alleged Anti-Semitism', in Maidenbaum, A. and Martin, S. (ed.), (1991), *Lingering Shadows*, London, Shambhala Publications.
Sherry, J. (1989/2002), 'Instead of Heat, Light', in Maidenbaum, A. (2002), *Jung and the Shadow of Anti-Semitism*, Berwick, ME, Nicolas-Hays, Inc.
Sherry, J. (2002), 'Jung, Anti-Semitism and the Weimar Years (1918-1933)', in Maidenbaum, A. (2002), *Jung and the Shadow of Anti-Semitism*, Berwick, ME, Nicolas-Hays, Inc.
Singer, P. (1983), *Hegel*, Oxford, Oxford University Press.
Slim, W. (1956), *Defeat into Victory*, London, Cassell.
Slim, W. (1970), *Unofficial History*, London, Corgi Books.
Slusser, G. (1989) 'Jung and Whitehead on Self and Divine. The Necessity of Symbol and Myth', in Volume IV, *Implications and In-*

spirations, (ed.) Papadopoulos, R. (1992), *Carl Gustav Jung : Critical Assessments*, London, Routledge.
Smith, C. (1990), *Jung's Quest for Wholeness*, New York, State University of New York Press.
Smith, M. (1995), *Fighting for Ireland? The Military Strategy of the Irish Republican Movement*, London, Routledge.
Smith, R. (1996), *The Wounded Jung*, Evanston, Illinois, Northwestern University Press.
Snyder, L. (1998), *The Encyclopaedia of the Third Reich*, Hertfordshire, Wordsworth Editions Ltd.
Speer, A. (1970), *Inside the Third Reich*, London, Weidenfeld and Nicolson.
Speicher, M. (1989) 'Jung, Anti-Semitism, and the Nazi Regime', in Maidenbaum, A. and Martin, S. (ed.), (1991), *Lingering Shadows*, London, Shambhala Publications.
Speicher, M. (1989), 'Jung and Anti-Semitism', in (ed.) Mattoon, M. (1989), *Personal and Archetypal Dynamics in the Analytical Relationship*, Switzerland, Daimon Verlag.
Spiegelman, J. (2002), 'A Personal Reflection on Jung and Anti-Semitism', in Maidenbaum, A. (2002), *Jung and the Shadow of Anti-Semitism*, Berwick, ME, Nicolas-Hays, Inc.
Staub, E. (1994), *The Roots of Evil*, New York, Cambridge University Press.
Stein, R. Jung's 'Mana Personality and the Nazi Era', in Maidenbaum, A. and Martin, S. (ed.), (1991), *Lingering Shadows*, London, Shambhala Publications.
Stepansky, P. (1976), 'The Empiricist as Rebel: Jung, Freud, and the Burdens of Discipleship', in Volume I, *Jung and His Method in Context*, (ed.) Papadopoulos, R. (1992), Carl Gustav Jung : *Critical Assessments* , London, Routledge.
Stephen, M. (2002), Introduction to *Jung and the Shadow of Anti-Semitism*, (ed.), Maidenbaum, A. (2002), Berwick, ME, Nicolas-Hays, Inc.
Stern, P. (1976), *C.G. Jung The Haunted Prophet*, New York, Delta Book/Dell Publishing.
Stevens, A. (1982), *Archetypes; A Natural History of the Self*, London, Routledge and Kegan Paul.

Stevens, A. (1989), *The Roots of War: A Jungian Perspective*, New York, Paragon House.
Stevens, A. (1990), *On Jung*, London, Penguin Books.
Stevens, A. (1995), *Private Myths*, Cambridge, Massachusetts, Harvard University Press.
Stevens, A. and Price, J. (1996), *Evolutionary Psychiatry*, London, Routledge.
Stevens, A. and Price, J. (2000), *Prophets, Cults and Madness*, London, Gerald Duckworth & Co. Ltd.
Storr, A. (1968), *Human Aggression*, Massachusetts, The Murray Printing Company.
Storr, A. (1977), *Feet of Clay*, London, Harper Collins.
Sulloway, F. (1979), *Freud Biologist of the Mind*, London, Burnett Books.
Tarnas, R. (1991), *The Passion of the Western Mind*, London, Pimlico, Random House.
Terraine, J. (1974), *The Mighty Continent*, London, Hutchinson & Co.
Terraine, J. (1989), *Business in Great Waters The U-Boat Wars 1916-1945*, London, Leo Cooper Ltd.
Trevor-Roper, H. (1971), *The Last Days of Hitler*, London, Book Club Associates.
Trinquier, R. (1964), *Modern Warfare. A French View of Counterinsurgency*, London, Pall Mall Press.
Ulanov, A. (1991), 'Scapegoating: The Double Cross', in Maidenbaum, A. and Martin, S. (ed.), (1991), *Lingering Shadows*, London, Shambhala Publications.
Ulanov, B. (1992), *Jung and the Outside World*, Wilmette, Illinois, Chiron Publications.
von Clausewitz, C. (1962), *On War*, Translated Colonel Graham, J. and Colonel Maude,E. London, Routledge and Kegan Paul.
von Franz, M.L. (1964) 'The Realization of the Shadow in Dreams', in Zweig, C. and Abrams, J. (ed.), (1991), *Meeting the Shadow*, Los Angeles, Jeremy P. Tarcher, Inc.
von Franz, M. L. (1975), *C.G. Jung; His Myth in Our Time*. London, Hodder & Stoughton.
von Franz, M.L. (1980), 'The Hypothesis of the Collective Unconscious', in Volume II, *The Structure and Dynamics of the Psyche*,

(ed.) Papadopoulos, R. (1992), *Carl Gustav Jung : Critical Assessments*, London, Routledge.
von Franz, M. L. (1981), *Puer Aeternus*, Korea, Sigo Books.
von Franz, M. L. (1986), 'The Inferior Function', (1971), from *Lectures on Jung's Typology*, Dallas, Texas, Spring Publications.
von Franz, M. L. (1992), *The Golden Ass of Apuleius*, Boston, Massachusetts, Shambhala Publications.
von Franz, M. L. (1994), 'Highlights of the Historical Dimension of Analysis', in von Franz, M.L. (1994), *Archetypal Dimensions of the Psyche*, Boston, Massachusetts, Shambhala Publications.
von Franz, M. L. (1995), *Shadow and Evil in Fairy Tales*, Boston, Massachusetts, Shambhala Publications.
von Franz, M. L. (1997), *The Archetypal Dimensions of the Psyche*, Boston, Massachusetts, Shambhala Publications.
von Klemperer, K. (1992), *German Resistance Against Hitler*, Oxford, Clarendon Press.
von Lang, J. (1981), *The Secretary—Martin Bormann: The Man Who Manipulated Hitler*, Athens, Ohio, Ohio University Press.
von Moltke, J. (1991), *Letters to Freya*, London, William Collins Sons & Co. Ltd.
Waller, J. (2002), *The Devil's Doctor*, New York, John Wiley & Sons, Inc.
Waltz, K. (1965), *Man the State and War*, New York and London, Columbia University Press.
Waltzer, M. (1984), *Just and Unjust Wars*, Great Britain, Pelican Books.
Wasserstrom, S. (1999), *Religion after Religion: Gershom Scholem, Mercia Eliade and Henry Corbin at Eranos*, New Jersey, Princeton, Princeton University Press.
Wehr, G. (1988), *Jung* A Biography, USA, Shambhala.
Whiting, C. (1999), *Heydrich*, England, Leo Cooper.
Whitmont, E. (1983), *Return of the Goddess*, London, Routledge & Kegan Paul.
Wickler, W. (1982), *The Biology of the Ten Commandments*, New York, McGraw-Hill Book Company.
Widener, A. (1979), *Gustave Le Bon The Man and his Work*, Indianapolis, Liberty Press.

Wilkeson, A. (1987), 'Psychotherapy, Counter-transference and the Nuclear Arms Race', in Porter, K. Rinzler, D. Olsen, P. (ed.), *Heal or Die*, New York, The Psycho-history Press.
Winnicot, D. (1964), 'Review of Jung's 'Memories Dreams, Reflections", in Volume I, *Jung and His Method in Context* , (ed.) Papadopoulos, R. (1992), *Carl Gustav Jung : Critical Assessments* , London, Routledge.
Wistrich, R. (1996), *Weekend in Munich; Art, Propaganda and Terror in the Third Reich*, London, Pavilion Books.
Woods, J. (1974), 'Some Considerations on Psychohistory' in Cocks, G. and Crosby, T. (ed), (1987), *Psychohistory*, New York, Vail-Ballou Press.
Wulff, W. (1973), *Zodiac and Swastika*, London, Arthur Barker Ltd.
Zabriskie, P. (1989), 'Shadows and Light: Closing Reflections on Jung and Jungian Psychology', in Maidenbaum, A. and Martin, S. (ed.), (1991), *Lingering Shadows*, London, Shambhala Publications.

JOURNALS

Allan, J. (1992), 'There is no such thing as a Liberal Dictatorship' in, *Journal of Analytical Psychology*, Volume, 37, p149-151, London, The Society of Analytical Psychology.
Aschheim, S. (1988), 'After the Death of God: Varieties of Nietzschean Religion' in: *Nietzsche Studien* 17 (1988). p 218-249. Berlin, New York, Gruyter.
Bancroft, M. (1975), 'Jung and His Circle', in *Psychological Perspectives*, p115-127, Los Angeles, C.G. Jung Institute Los Angeles.
Broyles, W. (1984), 'Why Men Love War', *Esquire*, November, 1984, p55-65.
Burri, M. (1978), 'Repression, Falsification, and Bedeviling of Germanic Mythology', in *Spring*, p88-104, Dallas, University of Texas Publications.
Cocks, G. (1979), 'C.G. Jung and German Psychotherapy', in *Spring*, p121-127, Dallas, University of Texas Publications.
Dalal. F, (1988), 'Jung: Racist', in *British Journal of Psychotherapy*, Volume 4, No. 3, p263-279.

Dräger, K. (1972), 'Psychoanalysis in Hitler's Germany', in *American Imago*, p199-214, Spring, New York, Association for Applied Psychoanalysis.

Dudley, G. (1992), 'America Its Wars and Mythologies', in *Psychological Perspectives*, No. 26, p84-101, Los Angeles, C.G. Jung Institute Los Angeles.

Gaillard, C. (2000), 'Otherness in the Present', in *Harvest International Journal for Jungian Studies*, Volume 46, No. 2, p129-151, London, Karnac Books,.

Gallard, M. (1994), 'Jung's Attitude During the Second World War in the Light of the Historical and Professional Context' in *Journal of Analytic Psychology*, (April 1994), p203-231, London, The Society of Analytical Psychology.

Greene, R. (1986), 'Aggression: A Jungian Point of View', in *Quadrant*, Vol 19/2, 1986, NY.

Giegerich, W. (1979), 'Postcript to Cocks', in *Spring*, p128-131, Dallas, University of Texas Publications.

Haymond, R. (1982), 'On Carl Gustav Jung: Psycho-social Basis of Morality During the Nazi Era', in *Journal of Psychology and Judaism*, Volume 6, No. 2, 1982, p81-111, Human Science Press.

Henderson, J. (1991b), 'C.G.Jung's Psychology: Additions and Extensions', in *Journal of Analytical Psychology*, Volume 36, p429-442, London, The Society of Analytical Psychology.

Hobson, R. (1973), 'The Archetypes of the Collective Unconscious', in Fordham (ed.) *Analytical Psychology: A Modern Science*, p66-75, Heineman, London.

Hogenson, G. (2001), 'The Baldwin effect: a neglected influence on C.G. Jung's evolutionary thinking', in *Journal of Analytical Psychology*, Volume 46, p591-611, London, *The Society of Analytical Psychology*.

James, S. (1984), 'The Pope of Theory', in 'The Return of Grand Theory' in *The Listener*, 17th May, 1984, p15-16, London, The BBC.

Jung, C.G. (1937)[1936], 'The Psychology of Dictatorship', in *Living Age*, September 1936-February 1937, Volume 351.

Kirsch, J. (1984), 'Jung's Transference on Freud', in *American Imago*, Volume 41, no.1, p63-84, Spring, New York, Association for Applied Psychoanalysis.

Kirsch, T. (1998), 'Family Matters The Descendants of Freud and Jung', in *Journal of Analytical Psychology*, Volume 43, p77-85, London, The Society of Analytical Psychology.

Lewin, N. (2006) 'When Jung met Freud: Religious Preconceptions and the Start of the Relationship', *Friends Newsletter 2006: Friends of Germanic Studies at the IGRS*, University of London, London.

Liebscher, M. (2001), *"Wotan' und "Puer Aeternus' Die zeithistorische Verstrickung von C. G. Jungs Zarathustrainterpretation'*, in 'Nietzsche-Studien', Volume 30, p329-350, Berlin.

Mizan, R., (1998), review of Stevens, A. & Price, J. 1996, 'Evolutionary Psychiatry', *Journal of Analytical Psychology*, Volume 43, p185-186, London, The Society of Analytical Psychology.

Neumann, E. (1959) 'The Significance of the Genetic Aspect for Analytical Psychology' in *Journal of Analytical Psychology*, Volume 4, p124-137, London, The Society of Analytical Psychology.

Papadopoulos, R. (1997), 'Individual Identity and Collective Narratives of Conflict', in 'Harvest *International Journal for Jungian Studies'*, Volume 43 No. 2, p7-26, London, Karnac Books.

Papadopoulos, R. (1998), 'Destructive, Atrocities and Healing Epistemological and Clinical Reflections', *Journal of Analytical Psychology*, p455-474, October, 1998, London, The Society of Analytical Psychology.

Pietikäinen, P. (2001), 'Jung in the Historical Context. German Intellectual Culture and Swiss Republicanism', in *Harvest International Journal for Jungian Studies*, Volume 47, No.1, p97-115, London, Karnac Books.

Rosen, D. (1996), 'If only Jung had had a Rabbi', in *Journal of Analytical Psychology*, Volume 41, p245-251, London, The Society of Analytical Psychology.

Shamdasani, S. (1998), 'From Geneva to Zurich: Jung and French Switzerland', *Journal of Analytical Psychology*, Volume 43, p115-126, London, The Society of Analytical Psychology, 1998.

Skinner, Q. (1984), 'After Structuralism', in 'The Return of Grand Theory', in *The Listener*, 5th April, 1984, p14-16, London, The BBC.

Slochower, H. (1981), 'Freud as Yahweh in Jung's Answer to Job', in *American Imago*, Spring, p3-39, New York, Association for Applied Psychoanalysis.
Speth, W. (1978), 'The Anthropogeographic Theory of Franz Boas', in *Anthropos*, Volume, 73, p1-31.
Stevens, A. (1997), Review of Noll, R. 1994, *The Jung Cult*, 1997, *The Aryan Christ*, in *Journal of Analytical Psychology*, Volume 42. p671-689, London, The Society of Analytical Psychology.
Von der Tann, M., (1089), 'A Jungian Perspective on the Berlin Institute; A Basis for Mourning', *The San Francisco Jung Institute Library Journal*, Volume 8, No. 4, p43-73, San Francisco, California.
Whitmont, E., (1961) 'Individual and Group', *Spring*, p58-79, New York, New York Analytical Psychology Club.

PUBLIC LECTURES AND PERSONAL COMMUNICATIONS

Battie, N. (2003), Personal communication, Birbeck College London,.
Booth, K. (1984), lecture on 'Contemporary Strategic Thought', Aberystwyth University College Wales, Department of International Politics and Strategic Studies.
Booth, K. (March 26th, 2003), Personal communication, Aberystwyth University College Wales, Department of International Politics and Strategic Studies.
Brown, M. (2002), 15th June, Lecture, 'Kant and Jung—Thinking and Feeling: A Fruitful Marriage of the Opposites', London, C.G. Jung Analytical Psychology Club.
Burniston, A. (2002-2003), Personal communications, London, C.G. Jung Analytical Psychology Club.
Cunningham, A. (2003), 'The Correspondence and Relationship Between Jung and Father Victor White', 'Guild of Pastoral Psychology', Oxford Conference.
David, J. (1999), Lecture, 'On Patriarchal Thought', Oxford, England, 'Guild of Pastoral Psychology', Millennium Conference.
Freedman, L. (1988), Lecture, 'History of Strategic Thought', King's College London, Lecture in War Studies Department.
Magilner, M. 2000, Personal communication, London.

Odermatt, M. (1988), 14-16th July lecture series on 'Aggression and Anxiety', Zurich, C.G. Jung Institute lectures.

Papadopoulos, R. (2003) Tutorial at Essex University Centre for Psychoanalytic Studies.

Paskins, B. (1988), Personal communication Cumberland Lodge, King's College London, Lecture in War Studies Department.

Porter, B. (1984), lecture on 'International Systems', Aberystwyth University College Wales, Department of International Politics and Strategic Studies.

Rowland, S. (2001), 17th March Lecture on, 'On Not Being an Analyst: Jung in the Literary Academy', Goldsmiths University.

Smith, M. (2002), Personal communication, King's College London, Lecture in War Studies Department.

Steeds, D. (1984), lecture on 'International History 1939-1960', Aberystwyth University College Wales, Department of International Politics and Strategic Studies.

Wilmer, H. (1999), 26th August, Lecture, 'On Patriarchal Thought', Oxford, England, 'Guild of Pastoral Psychology', Millennium Conference.

INDEX

Adler, G., 155, 217, 273, 376
aggression, 24–28, 45, 50, 82, 88, 93, 203–205, 218, 231, 264, 266–267, 270, 279, 282, 322, 327, 335, 368
Ahnenerbe, 254, 256, 364–365
Allan, J., 54–55, 62, 399
Allingham, M., 327, 374, 376
Alschuler, L., 29, 46–47, 106, 344, 376
anima/animus, 166, 182, 206, 277, 279, 313, 357, 366–368
anthropologist(s)/anthropology, 121–122, 130–132, 148, 203, 264, 319, 346–348, 362
anthropomorphism, 182, 200, 283
anti-Semitism, 13–14, 32–37, 51–52, 56, 121, 127, 154, 156–157, 215, 217, 235, 239–240, 251, 260, 264, 320, 324–325, 341, 346, 350, 365
Anzulovic, B., 369, 373–374, 376
archetype
  earth mother, 182
  hero, 14, 61, 174, 206–208, 277, 303, 357, 366
  hope, 212–215, 229
  immanent, 14, 188–189, 200–202, 205, 207, 317, 358
  messiah, 14, 208, 288–289, 294, 303
  shadow, 107, 133, 142, 145, 182, 199, 206–207, 212, 223, 282, 315, 357
  shaman, 288–289, 301, 303
  sun, 173–174
  theory, 13, 15, 27, 146, 162, 169, 176–178, 180, 185, 194, 230, 288, 305–306, 327
  wise old man, 182, 208, 276, 281–284, 286, 303, 322, 357
Arendt, H., 80, 258, 376
Artamanen Society, 253–254, 259
Aschheim, S., 239–240, 399
Asher, H., 280, 377

balance of power, 20, 75–76, 344
Bancroft, M., 294, 377, 399

Barnett, V., 232, 249, 377
Baynes Jansen, D., 65, 81, 276, 294, 377
Baynes, H. G., 214, 272, 276, 367–368, 377
Bennet, E., 222, 333, 377
Bergen, D., 248–251, 258, 377
Bernstein, J., 69, 74, 276, 350, 360, 377
Bertine, E., 272, 367, 377
Biagent, M., 367, 378
Bishop, P., 39, 229–230, 241, 364, 372, 378
Bismarck, O. von, 21, 248, 368, 372
Blackmore, S., 165, 310–312, 348, 352, 378
Blainey, G., 65, 121, 346–347, 378
'blond beast', 213–214, 360
Boas, F., 116, 119, 121–122, 124–126, 345, 347–348
Bodenbeschaffenheit, 120, 122–124, 126, 129, 142, 346, 347 see also: geographical determinism
Bolshevik(s), 51–52, 65, 212, 243, 248
Bond, B., 21, 90, 378
Booth, K., 22, 350, 378, 402
Bormann, M., 246, 250–251, 258, 364, 378
Breitman, R., 250, 254, 378
Brockway, R., 35, 38–39, 113, 120, 324–325, 338, 345–347, 367, 378
Brome, V., 41, 45, 172, 355, 378
Broyles, W., 27, 399
Bullitt, W., 25, 381
Bullock, A., 346, 370, 378
Buresch-Talley, J., 276, 378
Burkhardt, R., 170–172, 354, 378
Burleigh, M., 47, 239, 242–243, 246, 279, 285–286, 291, 315, 320–321, 374, 378
Burniston, A., 41, 48, 360, 402

Cabot, C. R., 60, 65, 81–82, 84, 278
Cabot Reid, J., 60, 65, 82–85, 278–279, 284, 378

'campaign' against Jung, 35–37, 43, 53, 194, 215–216, 276, 287, 342
Campbell, J., 27, 149, 154, 265, 289, 338, 357, 378–379
Carell, P., 80, 379
Christianity, 15, 30, 43, 90, 151, 173, 213–214, 223, 230–231, 233–236, 239–240, 242, 244, 248–251, 253, 256–258, 272, 274–275, 320, 349, 355, 361, 369
  Catholic, 230–232, 253, 258, 335, 341, 365
  Lutheran, 21, 46, 248
Christiansen, E., 230, 286, 379
Churchill, W., 60, 77, 80, 329
Clarke, J., 106, 131, 145–146, 153, 173, 193, 379
Cocks, G., 325, 379, 399
Cohen, E., 224, 310, 343, 352, 379
conscience, 26
conscious(ness) see also: unconscious(ness)
  collective, 41, 107–108, 212, 254, 300, 345
  national, 48
  social, 107
Corrie, J., 114–115, 345, 379
cultural
  heritage, 116, 345
  identity, 53, 346, 351
  levels, 132, 159, 165, 214
  psyche, 194, 350
  tradition, 151, 278, 374
  variations, 119–120, 144
Cunningham, A., 115, 348, 402
Czechoslovakia, 59, 81–82, 290

Dalal. F., 143, 145, 147, 399
Darré, W., 15, 235, 251–253, 362, 364
David, J., 145–146, 402
Dawkins, R., 310–311, 318–319, 372–373, 379
de Castillejo, I., 154, 207, 379
death wish, 27, 75, 202, 327

demagogue(s), 29, 42–43, 49, 90, 92, 286–287, 289, 303
Deschner, G., 258, 379
dictator/ship, 13, 24, 41, 49–50, 54, 57–65, 154, 208, 268, 270, 300, 335
  liberal, 54, 62
Donn, L., 45, 220, 343, 380
Dräger, K., 70, 400
Dudley, G., 27, 400
Dulles, A., 293, 370, 380

ego, 186–187, 201, 206–207, 222, 309, 357, 368–369
Ehrenreich, B., 318, 372, 380
Eibl-Eibesfeldt, E., 356, 380
Eichman, W., 258, 380
Ellenberger, H., 44, 67, 113, 121, 338, 352, 380
enantiodromia, 75, 87–88, 196–197
Environmental Determinism, 14, 113, 119–121, 149, 338, 346
Erikson, E., 159, 201, 205, 214, 280, 293, 359, 369, 371, 374, 380

fanaticism, 37, 43, 64, 93, 107–108, 197–198, 232, 243, 257, 283, 287, 319, 359, 373
Fest, J., 291, 380
Fordham, M., 356, 381
Freedman, L., 330, 402
Freud S., 13, 23–30, 34–39, 44–45, 58, 61, 65, 71, 75, 78, 85, 88, 93, 101–102, 105, 110–111, 121–122, 147, 153, 155–157, 161, 163, 167–170, 172, 194, 202, 213, 218, 229, 274, 284, 326–327, 330, 340, 342–343, 351, 353, 357, 361, 374–375, 381
Freudian theory/thought, 13, 25, 27, 32, 35, 42–43, 70, 102, 131, 194, 197, 202, 215, 217, 229, 273, 280, 301, 327, 342, 356, 374
Frey-Rohn, L., 344, 381–382

Gallard, M., 35, 37, 145, 224, 360, 382, 400
Geographical Determinism, 120, 122–124, 126–129, 136–137, 145, 151, 154, 157, 162, 346 see also: Bodenbeschaffenheit
Gillette, D., 359, 392
Glover, E., 197, 211, 262, 382
Goebbels, J., 219–220, 279, 365, 368
Goethe, J., 27, 366, 382
Goggin, E., 117, 382
Goggin, J., 117, 382
Goodrick-Clarke, N., 238, 241, 254, 257, 304, 363, 365, 382
Gordon, R., 178, 356, 382
Göring, H., 365, 368
Göring, M., 220, 360–361, 364
Great Depression, 232
Greene, R., 358, 400
Gross, S., 348, 382
Grossman, S., 367, 383
Guderian, H., 298, 383

Halberstam, D., 350, 383
Hale, C., 362, 366, 383
Hall, J., 101, 194–195, 315, 383
Hannah, B., 30, 44, 369, 383
Harkabi, Y., 369, 373, 383
Harms, E., 36, 147, 153, 383
Haule, J., 101, 357, 383
Hayman, R., 69–70, 218, 220, 345, 347, 383
Haymond, R., 39–40, 46, 67, 106, 400
Heath, I., 264, 383
Henderson, J., 194, 357, 366, 383–384, 400
Heydrich, R. 83–84, 258, 365–366
Heyer, G., 115–117, 123, 158, 284, 360, 384
Hilberg, R., 232, 384
Himmler, H., 15, 235–236, 239, 244–245, 252–262, 278, 295, 362, 364–366, 368, 370
historical ages, 73, 103–104, 165, 213, 369

Hitler Youth, 235, 245, 278
Hitler, A., 11–12, 15, 26, 58–60, 62, 65–66, 80–83, 85, 94, 159, 202, 211, 214–215, 218–220, 225–226, 236–252, 255, 257–258, 261, 268, 270, 276, 278–279, 286, 288–305, 320, 322, 331–332, 340–341, 343, 362–366, 368–372
Hobsbawm, E., 351, 373, 384
Hobson, R., 192, 353, 357, 400
Hogenson, G., 169–170, 372, 400
Hohne, H., 231, 251, 253, 256–259, 364–366, 384
Homans, P., 108, 168, 357, 384
Hore Belisha, L., 85, 344
Howard, M., 21, 90, 384
Hubback, J., 192, 384
Hull, R., 39, 42, 49, 55, 58–60, 69, 74–76, 81, 87, 92, 105, 128, 135–136, 150, 158–159, 220, 225, 236–237, 257, 262, 270, 277–279, 290–292, 294, 329–331, 333, 336–337, 343, 348–350, 366, 370, 375, 391
Humbert, L., 178, 356, 384

idealism, 29, 39, 74, 89–90, 93, 237
Ignatieff, M., 351, 384
imperialism, 25, 49, 86, 92, 145–146, 154
inferiority, 130, 132–133, 182, 207
  German, 21, 92, 159, 294
innate release mechanisms (IRMs), 178, 180, 183, 185, 356
International General Medical Society for Psychotherapy, (IGMSP), 38, 67, 194, 215, 220, 361
international politics, 9, 13, 19–23, 25–26, 28, 37, 73, 75, 80, 87, 95, 149, 160, 196, 211–212, 281, 302, 304–305, 317, 321
intuition, 12, 15, 70, 111, 165, 203, 269, 271, 274, 288, 293–296, 298, 300, 303, 322, 372
Irving, D., 370, 384

Jacobi, J., 117, 217, 336, 361, 385
Jacoby, M., 188, 201, 385
Jaffé, A., 61, 70, 177, 292, 343, 369, 385
Junge, T., 370, 389

Kahn, H., 344, 389
Kaiser Wilhelm II, 20–21, 159
Kaufmann, W., 25, 71, 360, 389
Kelly, S., 369, 389
Kerr, J., 33, 156, 389
Kershaw, I., 219, 238–239, 241, 244, 248, 250, 252, 291, 294, 297–298, 304, 341, 362–363, 367, 371, 389
Kersten, F., 238, 253, 255, 257, 259, 261, 278, 344, 362, 366, 370, 389
Kirsch, J., 34, 36–37, 39–41, 45, 218–220, 224, 290, 329, 342, 389–390, 400
Kirsch, T., 360–361, 390, 401
Klein, M., 27, 358, 390
Kuper, A., 120, 125–126, 338, 346–347, 390
Kuper, L., 343, 390

Lamarck, J-B., 111, 121, 129, 132, 169–172, 353–355
Lamarckian theory, 14, 110–111, 120, 126, 128, 136–138, 140, 145, 148, 151–152, 162–167, 169–170, 172–176, 180, 183, 193–194, 312, 326, 353, 355–356
Langer, W., 301–302, 390
leader(s)
  charismatic, 58, 74, 199
  messianic, 74, 105, 208, 360
  strong, 58–59, 61, 94, 105
Ledoux, J., 177, 390
Leigh, R., 367, 378
Levenda, P., 237, 256, 363, 390
Lewin, N., 35, 401
libido, 27, 202
Lifton, J., 80, 153, 390
Lindholm, C., 208, 238, 292–293, 295, 297, 362, 365, 368, 391

Lockot, R., 375, 391
Lorenz, K., 178, 204, 310, 356–357, 391
Lucas, J., 90, 391
Lukacs, J., 80, 218–219, 241, 246, 249, 275, 278, 291–293, 296–297, 302, 304, 346, 361, 364, 369–371, 391

Machtan, L., 278, 297, 362, 391
Magilner, M., 147, 402
Maidenbaum, A., 37, 274, 361, 391
manifest image, 162–167, 169, 172, 183, 192, 351
Marxism, 42, 63, 92, 130, 145–146, 154, 194, 198, 248, 275, 328, 335, 343, 346
materialism, 13, 38–39, 41–42, 45, 56, 90, 92–93, 144, 146, 157, 229, 232, 248, 325, 333
McCutcheon, R., 201, 391
McGowan, D., 168, 391
McGuire, W., 39, 42, 49, 55, 58–60, 69, 74–76, 81, 87, 92, 105, 128, 135–136, 150, 158–159, 220, 225, 236–237, 257, 262, 270, 277–279, 290–292, 294, 329–331, 333, 336–337, 343, 348–350, 366, 370, 375, 391
McLynn, J., 32, 35, 37, 57, 105, 273, 391
Meehan, P., 81, 219, 392
megalomania, 199, 296, 298, 322
meme, 311–322, 372
 -plex, 312–313, 315–316, 318–319, 321
 theory, 15, 310, 372
middle-class, 38–41, 94
Mizan, R., 356, 401
Moore, R., 359, 392
morality, 19, 21, 30, 213, 315, 369
Mosse, G., 120, 346, 350, 392
mother–infant relationship, 188, 190, 201
motif(s), 42, 156, 173–174, 192, 201, 271, 284, 306, 347
 functional, 184
 situational, 183–184
Mussolini, B., 54, 58–61, 77–78, 94, 220, 279, 303, 343
mythopoetic, 163, 167, 169, 312, 351–352

Nagy, M., 163, 168, 170, 188, 345, 352–353, 358, 392
Nationalsozialistische Deutsche Arbeiter Partei (NSDAP), 239, 244, 365
Naturphilosophie, 113, 129, 286
Neumann, E., 156–157, 201, 217, 220, 348–349, 359, 392, 401
Neumann, M., 157, 220, 348, 392
Nietzsche, F., 46, 48, 50, 164, 213, 222, 229, 239–240, 266, 272, 300, 348, 352, 360, 363, 372, 393
Noll, R., 33, 113, 115, 120, 123–125, 157, 217, 275, 344–347, 350, 352–353, 393

Odajnyk, V., 105, 196, 393
Odermatt, M., 351, 403
Oedipus complex, 101, 207, 327, 374
Office of Strategic Services (OSS), 215, 293, 301
Overy, R., 289, 291, 293, 295–296, 298–300, 370, 372, 393

Padfield, P., 279, 295, 364, 393
paganism, 11, 15, 123, 148, 151, 213, 230–236, 238, 240–247, 251–252, 254, 258–261, 265, 274, 286, 288, 307, 321, 355, 363, 367
 neo-, 26, 221, 227–228, 231, 236–237, 239–240, 242–245, 251–252, 256, 275, 286, 322, 362, 364
Papadopoulos, R., 107, 309, 312–314, 316, 319, 351, 366, 373–374, 393, 401, 403

Paret, P., 335, 393
participation mystique, 27, 134–135, 139, 349
Paskins, B., 307, 403
patterns of behaviour, 73, 178, 181, 314, 351
penchant(s), 177, 353–354
personal equation, 30, 342
Petrova, A., 203, 393
phantasmagoria, 15, 260
Pietikäinen, P., 47, 55–56, 125, 131, 342, 349, 359, 367, 393, 401
political realism, 13, 23, 31, 55, 150, 214, 218, 224, 276, 303
Porter, B., 278, 403
Portman, A., 355, 393
Price, J., 192, 203, 205, 208, 348, 356–358, 360, 397
primitive man, 122, 134–135, 139–140, 349
Proctor, R., 169, 393
Progoff, I., 67, 105, 135, 198, 394
projection(s), 33, 61, 79, 91–92, 104–105, 130, 135, 139, 142, 145–146, 181, 198–199, 207, 263, 269, 279, 315, 331, 348, 350
propaganda, 65, 83–84, 88, 219, 236, 243, 248–249, 251, 279, 341, 366, 373
Prussia, 82, 230–231, 342, 367
pseudospeciation, 190, 205

rationality, 22–23, 27, 43, 67, 73, 78, 86, 104, 113, 117, 128, 139, 165, 194, 203, 258, 284, 295, 304, 315, 317, 334, 342–343, 373
of means, 22–23
Rauschning, H., 238, 242, 244, 247, 250–252, 256, 290, 292, 298–300, 362, 364, 370–372, 394
Rauss, E., 90, 394
Redlich, F., 61, 219, 231, 293, 297, 343, 362, 368–369, 394
Rieff, P., 61, 274, 326–328, 394
Ritter, G., 21, 90, 394
Roazen, P., 262, 394

romanticism, 102, 113, 120, 123, 126, 128–129, 142, 157–158, 194, 253, 269, 271, 286, 346, 351, 367
German, 103, 163, 239, 260, 299, 345, 352, 367
Roosevelt, F. D., 58–59, 85, 94
Rosenbaum, R., 369, 394
Rosenberg, A., 239–240, 245–246, 251–252, 364
Rosenzweig, S., 121, 347, 394
Russia, 21, 46, 49, 62, 65, 80, 82, 84, 90–91, 124, 218, 279, 283, 319, 329–333, 335, 366, 373
Czarist/Tsarist, 21, 90
Soviet Union, 49–50, 64–66, 70, 74, 80, 95, 232, 330–335, 343–344, 365, 373, 375

Samuels, A., 33, 44, 62, 117–118, 130, 147, 149, 152–154, 156, 159, 308–310, 313, 344, 350, 356, 374, 394
Schama, S., 251, 364, 394
Schellenberg, W., 256, 258, 289, 370, 372, 394
Self, the, 186–187, 206, 208, 222, 283–284, 357, 368–369
sentiment intérieur, 170–172, 354
Sereny, G., 80, 291, 395
Serrano, M., 336, 395
sexual
 desire, 28, 101, 155, 203
 instinct, 101, 176
 liberty, 65
sexuality, 42, 166, 176, 280, 348
 homo-, 277, 356, 368
Shamdasani, S., 100–101, 111, 121, 131, 163, 176, 180, 342, 344, 351–352, 355, 363, 395, 401
Shelburne, W., 172, 180, 345, 395
Sherry, J., 124, 348–350, 395
Slim, W., 143, 395
Slochower, H., 159, 402
Smith, M., 373, 396, 403
Snyder, L., 240, 362, 366, 396
Soviet Union *see* Russia

INDEX 411

Speer, A., 243–245, 289, 291, 293, 295–296, 298–300, 302, 361, 364, 370–372, 396
Speth, W., 119, 121, 125, 347, 402
Spiegelman, J., 361, 396
Stalin, J., 65–66, 80, 82, 94, 219, 303, 330–332, 334–335, 336, 373 see also: Russia
Staub, E., 319, 351, 365, 396
Steeds, D., 78, 80, 403
Stein, R., 218, 224, 343, 396
Stevens, A., 30, 111, 168–169, 178, 183, 187–188, 192, 203–205, 208, 319, 348, 355–358, 360, 369, 375, 396–397, 402
Storr, A., 208, 397
Sulloway, F., 170, 353, 397
Switzerland, 9, 23, 40–41, 44, 55, 66, 123, 127–128, 149, 293, 342, 362
symbolism, 43, 90, 104, 135, 139, 148, 156, 161–169, 172–173, 176–178, 180, 182, 184–189, 191, 196, 198, 222–223, 236, 252, 256, 268, 284, 286, 298, 306, 312, 339, 346–347, 352–353, 355, 357–359

Tacitus, 230, 253, 364
Tannenberg League, 244, 367
Tarnas, R., 358, 397
Thule Society, 239, 241
totalitarianism, 13, 54, 64, 262, 284, 330, 343, 369
Trevor-Roper, H., 203, 397
Trinquier, R., 335, 397

Ultima Thule, 236, 362
unconscious(ness) *see also*: conscious(ness)
collective, 10, 13–14, 32, 40–42, 74, 87, 91, 96, 99, 100, 102–104, 107–108, 111, 113, 118, 122–124, 128–130, 132, 134–136, 138–139, 144, 146, 148–149, 151, 154, 160, 168–169, 193–194, 213,
225–226, 230, 232, 235–236, 252, 254, 260–261, 265, 269–271, 275, 277, 286, 299, 301–302, 306–307, 311–312, 327, 344–345, 347, 369, 371, 374
hostility, 34
national, 14, 327
primitive, 27, 213, 331

Valhalla, 234, 250, 257
Völk(isch), 14, 39, 113, 115, 117, 119–120, 122–128, 142, 151, 154, 157, 239, 241, 246–248, 251, 253, 286, 346, 350, 363, 367
von Clausewitz, C., 19, 397
Von der Tann, M., 360, 375, 402
von Franz, M. L., 44–45, 58, 104, 176, 185–186, 307, 339, 356, 366–367, 398
von Klemperer, K., 81, 398
von Lang, J., 250, 364–365, 398
von Moltke, J., 342, 398
von Natzmer, O., 90, 394

Waller, J., 370, 372, 398
Waltz, K., 20, 73, 78, 317, 398
War
  Cold, 19–20, 64, 72, 74, 329, 331, 333–335, 344, 350
  First World, 9, 19–20, 23, 40, 45, 48, 72, 74, 86, 89–91, 212, 270, 294
  Second World, 19, 27, 40–41, 62, 66, 72–73, 87, 90, 142, 144, 147, 278, 333–335, 368
Watson, P., 203, 393
Whiting, C., 232, 398
Wickler, W., 356, 398
Winnicot, D., 69, 399
Wotan, 9, 11, 14, 67, 86, 93, 96, 104, 109, 161, 176, 181, 193, 197, 211–212, 214, 216, 221–224, 227–230, 232–236, 245, 247, 249, 252, 258,

260–269, 271–276, 278–282,
284, 286–288, 294, 300, 303,
306, 320–322, 336, 362, 364,
367–368
Wulff, W., 261, 399

Zabriskie, P., 33–34, 399
Zarathustra Seminar(s), 222–223,
229, 233, 265, 275–276, 281, 363
Zofingia lectures, 38, 45, 47, 50, 58,
72, 324, 342